For Mary…

MARY

THE MARY TYLER MOORE STORY

Also by Herbie J Pilato

Dashing, Daring and Debonair

Glamour, Gidgets and the Girl Next Door

The Essential Elizabeth Montgomery

Twitch Upon a Star

The Bionic Book

Life Story – the Book of Life Goes On

NBC & ME: My Life as a Page in a Book

Bewitched Forever

The Kung Fu Book of Wisdom

The Kung Fu Book of Caine

The Bewitched Book

MARY

THE MARY TYLER MOORE STORY

Herbie J Pilato

Jacobs/Brown Press

Los Angeles, California

LIBRARY OF CONGRESS CATALOGING-IN-PUBLICATION DATA

Pilato, Herbie J
MARY
THE MARY TYLER MOORE STORY
Herbie J Pilato

Publisher: Matthew Brown, Jacobs/Brown Press
First edition hard cover, January 25, 2019
Hardcover ISBN 978-0-9995078-4-1
Paperback ISBN 978-0-9995078-5-8
Kindle ISBN 978-0-9995078-6-5

Library of Congress Control Number: 2018956257
Copyright ©2018 Herbie J Pilato. All rights reserved.

Cover Design: Angela Derasmo
Editorial Staff: Mark Alfred, Sondra Burrows, Andrew Johnson
and Tom Tucker

Front Cover Image - Credit: Ronald V. Borst/Hollywood Movie Posters
Back Cover Image - Credit: Ronald V. Borst/Hollywood Movie Posters

Hard cover edition manufactured in the United States of America

Jacobs/Brown Press
An imprint of Jacobs/Brown Media Group, LLC
Los Angeles, California
JacobsBrownMediaGroup.com

**"I really want to be taken seriously...*Mary Tyler Moore.*
Doesn't that sound serious?"**
– Mary Tyler Moore

TABLE OF CONTENTS

Prologue

"Mary has what we call star quality."

So said Perry Lafferty, former vice-president of programming for CBS in 1974, about the Emmy-winning actress who portrayed the ambitious, single, career-minded Mary Richards on that network's groundbreaking 1970-1977 sitcom officially and simply titled: *Mary Tyler Moore*. "She's the well-scrubbed, all-American girl that everyone likes," continued Lafferty. "It's her vulnerability that makes her particularly appealing...She's [also] beautiful and all that without being threatening."

Such words could also describe Moore's previous CBS television sitcom incarnation – Laura Petrie, the loving and devoted wife to Dick Van Dyke's Rob Petrie on *The Dick Van Dyke Show*, which originally aired from 1961 to 1966.

But despite her two most famous, near-picture-perfect depictions on-screen, Moore's real life and career were marred by tragedy and blurred by indecision. She may have played TV's top, blithe, independent woman, married or single, but her spirit, off-screen, was boxed-in. She grinned in public for years, but grimaced in private, cloaking the not-so-easy moments and the toughest of times. She worked until she was physically incapable of doing so. She lived her life to the fullest, and remained dedicated to her craft and various social, political, and charitable causes, connected to animal advocacy and the diabetes with which she struggled.

Dependent on much and many, Moore frequently sought the approval of others, be they family, peers, friends, colleagues, fans, food, wine, medicine, God, or men. The latter dominated, shaped, shifted, and manufactured her life and career, for better or worse.

Her father was a fervent academic, demanding and disparaging. She spent a lifetime trying to please him, if mostly with her art. As a child, she was sexually abused by a male neighbor. Emotionally and psychologically scarred for life, she channeled her trauma into her craft. Also as a child, she once noticed a man beat a dog on the street, thus planting the seeds of her championing and affection for animals. Once again, she turned lemons into lemonade.

Moore's first marriage was to Richard "Dick" Meeker, an older man, with whom she had a son named Richie who died young. Some macabre fate echoed these facts in her career: Her first TV marriage was to Dick Van Dyke, an older man, with whom she had a TV son named Ritchie (with a "t," played by Larry Mathews), who lives immortal in reruns with her as Laura and Van Dyke as Rob.

It was Van Dyke who saved Moore's career twice in her life; first, by endorsing her as his TV wife on *The Dick Van Dyke Show*, and later by featuring her in *Dick Van Dyke and the Other Woman*, a TV special that led to *Mary Tyler Moore*, a.k.a. *The Mary Tyler Moore Show*.

Both career moves, however, were ultimately navigated and controlled by Grant Tinker, Moore's second husband. Tinker headed an ad firm that controlled *The Dick Van Dyke Show*. Moore later partnered with Tinker to form MTM Enterprises, which hired male writers Jim Brooks and Allan Burns to create *The Mary Tyler Moore Show*. This program featured a male father figure named Lou Grant, played by Ed Asner, a seeming homage to Grant Tinker. While every character on the show, including Valerie Harper's wisecracking Rhoda Morgenstern, referred to Asner's character as "Lou," Moore's Mary Richards called him "Mr. Grant."

Beyond her TV time on the *Dick Van Dyke* and *Mary Tyler Moore* shows, both of which earned her multiple Emmy Awards, Moore never again found a weekly hit on the small screen. There was a measure of success on Broadway with *Whose Life Is It Anyway?*, which earned her a special Tony Award. The following year, she garnered an Oscar nomination and won a Golden Globe for 1980's *Ordinary People*, a feature film directed by Robert Redford. It was a movie she once referred to as "the holy grail" of her career, released three years after her legendary sitcom ended. But Moore's first Broadway play, a musical rendition of *Breakfast at Tiffany's*, was a colossal flop, as were her other motion pictures like *Change of Habit* (with Elvis Presley). Alternate TV series included two variety-show attempts (*Mary* and *The Mary Tyler Moore Hour*), two sitcoms (another *Mary* and *Annie McGuire*), and a one-hour drama (*New York News*) – all clunkers.

Most of her television failures followed Moore's divorce from Tinker, whose expertise rested mostly in the medium. Tinker was the one who insisted that her role on *The Dick Van Dyke Show* be expanded; who secured the success of *The Mary Tyler Moore Show* by surrounding his wife with an A-list group of talented individuals before and behind the camera.

Moore's feature films tanked because Tinker knew little about what makes a good motion picture. In the big-picture scheme of things, the success of *Ordinary People* seemed like a fluke – a lucky break that transpired shortly before a direly unfortunate incident occurred off-screen. She finally had a big-screen hit, but in her mid-40s, which is not only a late-in-life stage to reach movie stardom, but also too young for any parent to lose a child.

But that's exactly what happened. Shortly after the release of *Ordinary People*, in which Moore played a disheartened, distant woman named Beth Jarrett, who was dealing with the death of her son, she lost her real-life child. Richie died of an accidental self-inflicted gunshot at only 24 years old. Their relationship was never strong, and Moore never thought herself a good parent. She was career-minded and success-oriented in every way but with her maternal instincts.

In like manner, Moore was a talented performer, but she often relied on her charm and personal appeal. Her strengths as an actress were never fully realized or utilized on the big screen because Tinker knew her talent was best suited to the small screen, primarily in a sitcom. But even then Moore was outshined by veterans like Dick Van Dyke, and other stars of his legendary sitcom including Rose Marie, Morey Amsterdam, and Carl Reiner, who (like Meeker and Tinker in her personal life) was a father figure in her professional life. Later, on *The Mary Tyler Moore Show*, she was paired with even stronger talents such as Ed Asner, yet another professional father figure, as well as female supporting players Cloris Leachman, Betty White, and Valerie Harper. Harper was an outstanding newcomer, a shining star-in-the-making, a scene-stealer in every way.

But when Moore's marriage to Tinker ended, so, it seemed, did continued chances for weekly TV sitcom success. Additionally, her physical state was weakened by diabetes. She tried to drown her emotional pain in alcohol. She attempted to hide and enhance her low self-esteem with various facial plastic surgeries which ultimately did not service her health.

Moore eventually married a third time, to Dr. Robert Levine who, unlike Meeker or Tinker, was not a father figure, but instead many years younger than she; potentially a son-figure. Levine, steadfast and loyal, was not a member of the cultural elite or the entertainment industry. He was a cardiologist who was devoted to his older wife, their relationship, and her well-being. If not by Moore's side in her youth, Levine was present to help her deal with the lingering, less appealing aspects of her past that at times poisoned her experiences in any era. Theirs was a remarkable real-life love story, one that rivaled not only her union with Tinker but that of Rob and Laura Petrie's fabricated wedded bliss.

Moore found Levine just as Van Dyke eventually discovered new love with Arlene Silver, a forty-something make-up artist who became his second wife twenty-eight years after he divorced his first wife Margie Willett, and three years after Michelle Triola Marvin, his long-time lover, died of lung cancer. Adding to the irony was this: Van Dyke had initially perceived Moore as too young to play his TV spouse on *The Dick Van Dyke Show*.

Mary Richards, Moore's other famous TV role, may have made it on her own, but the actress was not so blessed. Although she did discover and cherish love early, mid-term, and relatively late in life, while morsels of success blossomed in the twilight, afternoon, and morning glories of Moore's career. Each drop of rain on her parade through life was followed by a ray of sunshine.

While much of that may sound as cheery as Mary Richards, when push came to shove, that's exactly who Moore emulated, whether she admitted it or not. As an artist, her work was never done. From heartache and pain sprouted joy and victory when she stayed in the game. For most of her life and career, she was more or less on her game. Had she been less consistently successful throughout her private and public arenas, Moore may never have had the opportunity to turn the world on with her smile. However, that grin ultimately camouflaged the frowns, fears, and tears that she somehow reconfigured for the benefit of all that fell victim to its charm.

Although she failed to recapture the weekly TV magic of Mrs. Petrie of the '60s or Ms. Richards of the '70s with any new series in the '80s or beyond, Moore never stopped trying. She fought the good fight as long as possible. Her childhood, teenage years, young adulthood, middle-age, and senior moments were littered with challenges, but she had inherited from her parents a secret weapon to battle, confront, conquer and shield herself from conflict: a unique sense of humor which she once referred to as "subdued." With TV, film, or stage performances she combined an A-type personality with A-list talent that left an indelible impression.

On-screen, Moore portrayed the perfect wife and mother on *The Dick Van Dyke Show*; the ideal, career-minded single woman on *The Mary Tyler Moore Show*; and everything else in between. Audiences continued to embrace her performances, even when she periodically portrayed unlikable characters. Despite the quality of character, or the periodic lack of a solid platform, watchers could not get enough of the actress behind the performer; the performer behind the portrayal, and sometimes the betrayal. Moore became an award-winning multi-talented entertainer who acted, sang, and danced; she showcased comedy or drama, and did it all with style and grace. As the musical theme to her iconic TV show will forever remind us, "Who can turn the world on with her smile?" The answer was and will always remain the beloved, nonfictional Mary Tyler Moore, known to that world mostly as *Mary*, the name which in turn serves as the title for this book. It's the first full-scale, in-depth, objective biography of her extensive life and career, before, during, and beyond her two most famous sitcoms – including her early and later TV and movie roles; stage performances; and her several personal appearances on talk and award shows, and at charitable galas, and other events.

MARY: THE MARY TYLER MOORE STORY mixes rare, never-before-published commentary from the performer, her family, friends, and colleagues, culled from previously printed, filmed, taped and/or recorded interviews. Intermingled are pertinent insight and remarks tallied from preceding books and periodicals, as well as websites and other online sources, along with observations gleaned from exclusive, all-new conversations with some of those who knew her best throughout the entirety of her remarkable personal and professional existence.

ACT I

Born Identities

Mary is in Los Angeles at the beach with her parents George and Marjorie Moore, and baby brother John (circa, 1945-1946). [Credit: Richard A. Lertzman Collection. All rights reserved.]

Chapter

1

The iron-willed, strong-minded, and compassionate Mary Tyler Moore hailed from a family whose history was immersed in military and rigid rules. Although she was none too pleased that her ancestors mostly made their mark in war, it's a legacy that prepared her for battles of her own – some of which she lost, in some of which she prevailed – all of which she confronted head-on. With creative differences at work or at home, the actress, the businesswoman, the philanthropist, the human being, throughout her life and career never backed away from a challenge. When conflicts arose she confronted each accordingly, whether personal, professional, emotional, psychological, or physical. She considered none as obstacles but rather par for the course, and never felt sorry for   because she hailed from that sturdy stock.

For years, Mary would speak of her alleged link to Captain John Moore, to whom she several times referred as a distant relative who stowed away to America from England, circa 1765, on an importing tea ship. But according to genealogist James Pylant, there are several "stowaway to America" stories that are commonly repeated but remain unproven. "Mary was given some incorrect information about her ancestry," Pylant said diplomatically.

The more clearly defined and documented family line involved Lieutenant Colonel Lewis Tilghman Moore, a commander of the 4th Virginia Infantry in the Confederate Army, who purchased a Gothic Revival home in Winchester, Virginia. He offered it as the headquarters for

Major General Thomas J. "Stonewall" Jackson. Jackson resided four months in that home (today known as Stonewall Jackson's Headquarters Museum). Lieutenant Colonel Moore returned there, to the practice of law after being severely wounded at Manassas in 1861. He married Mary Fanny Bragonier, the daughter of Daniel George Bragonier, a noted minister of the German Reformed Church. Fanny's mother, Mary E. (Shindler) Bragonier, whose family name was originally spelled Schindler, was the great-granddaughter of George Conrad Schindler of Wuerttemberg, Germany. He arrived in America at the Port of Philadelphia in 1752. According to historian and author A.D. Kenamond, Schindler, a Revolutionary War soldier, apparently made a copper kettle for Martha Washington that was later on display at Valley Forge.

In 1872, Lt. Col. Moore and Fanny welcomed a son, George Melville Moore. He later moved to New York, where he worked as a treasurer for an electric company, and married Anna Veronica Tyler, a native of that state. Their son, George Tyler Moore, known by his middle name (and his mother's maiden name – a family tradition), was born in 1913 in Brooklyn and, due to his father's well-paying job, attended private schools. Like his father, Tyler was later employed as a clerk by an electric company (by then alternately known as Consolidated Edison, Con Edison, or Con Ed) in New York.

In that same city, on January 24, 1936, Tyler, a Catholic, secured a marriage license with Marjorie Hackett, a Protestant who converted to Catholicism.

On December 29, 1936, in the upscale suburb of Brooklyn Heights, their daughter Mary Tyler Moore was born. Her middle name continued the family tradition of utilizing the paternal grandmother's maiden moniker. She arrived shortly before World War II began, near the end of the Depression, and nine years after television was created, when America and the world were ready to smile again. Comedian Milton Berle, who made his name in Vaudeville and later, as "Mr. Television," the star of NBC-TV's Texaco Star Theatre from 1948 to 1956, helped shape the small-screen medium which would give Mary, who would later become his friend, a career. "The day Mary Tyler Moore was born," Berle would observe, "...the world became a better place."

In many of her earliest days that followed, Mary attended St. Rose of Lima Catholic School in Brooklyn. In time, she became the eldest of three siblings, presiding over her brother John Hackett Moore (born 1944), and a sister Elizabeth Ann Moore (born 1956), who also received a Catholic education. According to The Real Mary Tyler Moore by Chris Bryars, their mother Marjorie said Mary was one of "three only children," because they were born 36 months apart. Marjorie called Mary "...a pain in the neck to raise" due to her child's fervent desire to dance and act. With no clear life or career direction of her own, Marjorie stayed home, while George, like his father before him, continued to work diligently in New York.

An average student in elementary school, Mary was shy in the classroom at St. Rose's, but let loose upon hearing the day's final school bell ring. She'd pester her cousins, who resided close by, into presenting shows in her backyard. "Even then I was frantic to become a performer," she told Bryars. By no means wealthy, her family lacked for nothing beyond currency. In a videotaped conversation that was conducted by filmmaker Carlos Ferrer, Mary related that her father had said she was born in the "impoverished nobility" of Brooklyn Heights.

When Mary was 4 years old, the Moore family relocated to larger quarters in Flushing, only to return to the Flatbush area on 491 Ocean Parkway two years later. For an interview with the Brooklyn Daily Eagle, Mary later described her neighborhood as made of homes with tree-lined front yards. "Some people had Fords or Hudsons. But everyone took the elevated train when they traveled to Manhattan to catch live shows or the latest movie and stage show at Radio City Music Hall."

The New York Times later observed, "Mary Tyler Moore may not quite rank with Pee Wee Reese, the old Dodger shortstop, as a symbol of Brooklyn," but the organizers of "Welcome Back to Brooklyn Day" eventually dubbed her Homecoming Queen. In her defense, the adult Mary sent a scathing letter to the editor, detailing a core portion of her early childhood:

> I was more than a little resentful of the suggestion in your article that I was an inappropriate choice to reign as Queen for "Welcome Back to Brooklyn Day" on June 9 [1996] (anyway, I thought I was to be King). Regardless of my worthiness, it does seem to me that "type" should play no part in this warm-spirited ceremony. One wonders what your greatest concern is – am I not funny enough? I can slip on a banana peel with the best of them.

> I was born in Brooklyn Heights in 1936, where we lived for a short time before moving to Flushing. When I was 6 we returned, this time to Ocean Parkway in Flatbush. It was in this neighborhood that I lived for the next three years, learning much about the spirit that produces laughter, fear, anger and – last and above all – tolerance.

> The Moores and one other family were the only Catholics in an Orthodox Jewish community where my grandfather owned the house that we would live in. I made my first

> Communion at St. Rose of Lima Church and took no small amount of kidding for the bride-like veil I wore on that particular Sunday.
>
> "Well, so are you married to God now?"
>
> "No, stupid. How come you can't touch money sometimes? And what's the big deal about sundown?"
>
> We never let each other forget our differences, fistfights being a regular part of our activities. I don't think I was without a bruise or scraped knees for the whole time we lived there. Nor were some of them. But I remember feeling that whatever the bullying, we also had fun. We knew we were struggling with more than childhood's fight for supremacy and territory. There were differences that could have been given indelible names but weren't. Instead, we found ourselves and we found ourselves to be friends.

It's that kind of intelligence, and well, "spunk," that was part of her appeal. That descriptive word was spoken by Ed Asner as Lou Grant to Mary Richards in "Love Is All Around," the pilot episode of *The Mary Tyler Moore Show*. But this combination of smarts, courage, and comedy played an important part throughout Mary's life, even before she began her career. She said her parents blessed her with an appreciation for humor. They made her think and feel what's funny, while Mary learned to welcome the laughter in others – though not as a class clown, which she never wanted or tried to be. Her parents may not have had money, but they both majored in English in college, and taught her how to speak correctly. "We never wanted for anything," Mary said. "We never went hungry. There weren't a lot of luxuries," but dancing lessons were arranged when Mary wanted them. Although proud of her Brooklyn influences, as were and remain many celebrities born in that historically rich and cultural place, in time she sought to leave it all behind.

That happened, in one sense, at just 3 years old, when Mary would entertain members of her immediate and extended family at home, in her living room, sometimes alongside other young relatives. She and her same-age cousin Gail would "highjack" their relatives, Mary said, "tie them to their seats," and then perform musical numbers which the two young girls had witnessed at the movies. In self-defense, Mary thought, she was sent to dancing school so that, "if they had to watch me, at least I'd be trained and it wouldn't be too painful."

At first, Mary had only danced for her dad, to win his love and approval. "If I had that wonderful, perfect, loving relationship with my father that everybody craves," she said, "I might not have had the gumption to do what I do now – to put myself on the line. I guess it's too bad we didn't have a close, loving relationship, but who's to say? Maybe not. I like what I am, I love what I do – and he formed me."

"Thank God I was not being abused in any way," she later told the *Ottawa Citizen* in addressing the reason she exited her initial household. "But I was seeking approval of some sort in many different ways."

Mary's core *love-unlike* relationship with her father in particular seemed to shape her associations with men, specifically her first two husbands; a habit from which she was unable to disengage until her mid-40s.

But now, before the first television sets could be found in every household across the country, little Mary would stay close to the radio, and improvise steps to the songs she heard. Come nightfall, she would perform a personal recital, again, just for her dad. Nevertheless, it was her maternal grandfather who was most impressed with her performance skills. One day, he watched her dance around the living room and gave an altogether untypical response. "This child," he said, "...will either end up on stage or in jail."

Mary had always desired stardom, and would settle for nothing less than complete artistic expression, beginning with a focus on one particular craft. Mary said her childhood was "relatively happy," but she was "kind of quiet, a loner."

But another time, Mary described herself as an "angry...youngster...not happy about a lot of stuff. I supposed somewhere along the way that worked itself into a self-protection mechanism: if I cut myself off at the knees first, then nobody else can. And if I can do it with humor at the same time, why, God, that's just great. And I always felt more comfortable with a stronger, taller, older, wiser mate by my side – which is basically a chicken-hearted way of going through life."

"I grew up feeling that women are wonderful, but wonderful as an adjunct to a man. And if there was a fight or a difference of opinion about something important, then I must be wrong – I must just not have it right yet." In other words, she would smooth things over, and "look at the bright side."

While mates would arrive much later in her life, Mary as a child focused "solely on dancing." From the time she was very young, Mary knew what she wanted to be. "Only then I thought it was a dancer," she later told the *New York Times*.

Another time, she told *American Television*, "Some people refer to it as indulging in my instincts and artistic bent. I call it just showing off, which is what I did from about three years of age on."

Years after, for an interview with the *Toronto Star*, Mary said her first formal dance instructor, a mentor/dance pianist, was not exactly the easiest person to please. She was frequently forced to smile, if out of fear alone. Yet, those early attempts to turn her internal frown upside down eventually worked in her favor. Her smile began as a coping mechanism and became her trademark.

Unlike her studies in dance or music, the relatively reserved young lady never received formal training in acting. Still, she craved the kind of attention actors receive, and dove into the profession head first. "Shy people who haven't had the amount of attention or love that they think they need," she said, "...go into public arenas. I think they...get something back, a validation...That gives you an awful lot. It's terrific. It doesn't supplant the original need...."

Mary developed an aggressive and courageous spirit to face a myriad of challenges, including her molestation by a male neighbor when she was six years old. She detailed this horrific incident in her best-selling memoir, *After All*. The Archers lived next door to the Moores in their apartment complex. The abuser was the father of Mary's friend, little six-year-old David Archer. The day after she was molested, Mary defiantly marched down the hall and knocked on the Archers' door. David answered, and Mary told him point-by-point just exactly what his father had done. Afterwards, she felt vindicated but "a little sick" at what she had done to David.

Such treachery, however, was magnified by the reaction of Mary's mother to the incident. By not acknowledging her daughter's abuse, Marjorie Moore pretended the molestation never transpired. And as Mary later expressed to the *Baltimore Sun*, she "never felt the same about" her mother again.

But brighter days were ahead. In 1944, Mary and the Moores left the East Coast for Los Angeles, where her father was employed by the Los Angeles Gas Company. The family made the move partially inspired by Harold Hackett, Mary's uncle on her mother's side, who became her significant connection with the entertainment industry. Hackett was a vice-president of MCA. He later became president of Official Films which produced, among other things, *Robin Hood* for television. He would make frequent visits to the Moore's Brooklyn abode, speak glowingly about sunny California, and share various West Coast celebrity stories. Excited about moving and then living in "Hollywood," or at least close to it, in Studio City, an 8-year-old Mary enrolled in the Ward Sisters Studio of Dance Arts in L.A. She knew what she wanted out of life, which was to seek stardom, even if that rattled her mother.

Unsettling to both her parents was Mary's ongoing less-than-stellar performance in mainstream education, which continued at St. Ambrose School in Los Angeles. She fantasized all day long in class, while waiting for the bell to ring, so she could make a beeline for the door. Still, any wrong turn, at any wrong moment, might result in her parents stripping her of any special privileges, and she knew it. "If I ever got into serious trouble, my dancing lessons would go," she said. When push came to shove, Mary buckled down and focused on her schoolwork and then "backed off a bit" to zero in on her dance moves.

Another pivotal moment occurred when, at just 9 years old, she discovered an unyielding love for animals. According to what she later relayed to *The Pet Press*, a free monthly magazine for Los Angeles pet lovers, it happened one day walking home from school. She saw a man beating a dog with a stick. She screamed for him to stop, but he refused. So she dropped her schoolbooks, ran, and jumped. She struck his head and shoulders, and kicked him. "That was the first time I felt passion and anger at man's inhumanity," she said. "I beat the man up as best I could."

Although Mary did not take any active role in formal animal advocacy until many years later, a compassion for animals was awakened that day, even if she felt helpless at the time. "It just hadn't occurred to me that there was anything I could do as a child going to school. But that's not always true today. There are all kinds of outreach programs [for] youngsters who can volunteer and help in many ways."

When it came to animals, Mary loved them all, even those creatures for which she had no particular feeling, such as snakes or alligators or "any of the creepy crawly fellows." She still cared, and would not tolerate inhumane treatment towards them.

The seeds of Mary's charitable and philanthropic ways, combined with her artistic aspirations and associations, continued to sprout. But her strict father remained firmly planted in distant behavior, and her more free-spirited mother continued to drink.

World-renowned forensic pathologist Dr. Michael Hunter is the chief medical examiner in one of America's largest cities. He has conducted thousands of autopsies to uncover the various reasons why people die. In the Reelz Channel *Autopsy* TV documentary about Mary's last days that aired after her death, Dr. Hunter found her challenging first days of life of "particular interest...specifically her mother's drinking."

"Drinking heavily while pregnant can result in the baby born with a condition known as Fetal Alcohol Spectrum Disorder," he said, "which is something Mary appeared to believe she had been affected by. And looking at Mary's face, there are certain features which could be consistent with F.A.S.D. It's characterized by a thin, upper lip, low nasal bridge and a flat philtrum – the area between the nose and lip."

Mary's features were uneven around the eyes and nose. She herself once attributed this to the fact that her mother was drinking while pregnant. "The condition could result in severe mental abnormalities," said Dr. Hunter. "There's no evidence that Mary grew up suffering from these. However, drinking through pregnancy can also result in babies being born with heart defects, such as ventricular septal defect – an abnormality affecting the wall dividing the left and right ventricles of the heart."

Apparently, it was Mary's emotional heart which was weakened by her childhood experiences. Her earliest days were littered with challenges, which expanded and were exacerbated throughout her life. In certain instances, however, those difficulties nevertheless led to positive results that prompted her destiny for stardom.

When Mary was 10 years old, and just 24 months after her family relocated to the West Coast, she had a serious disagreement with her mom. This caused Mary to move in with her maternal grandmother and her favorite Aunt Bertie. Bertie, a.k.a. Alberta Hackett, was the sister of Mary's mother, and another relative with powerful ties to show business. Bertie had moved with the Moores from New York to Los Angeles, where Bertie became a business manager of station KNXT. Unlike Mary's mother, Bertie supported her niece's relentless artistic ambitions, including those dance lessons.

"Aunt Bertie sent me to dancing school, paid for the lessons, gave me singing lessons, and told me I could do it," Mary later related to *USA Today*. "She encouraged me to always fight on and to get what I wanted."

In her second TV appearance with Oprah Winfrey, Mary said Mary Richards was partly modeled after her aunt. "Her name was Bertie Hackett," she joked, "[but] they used to call her Bertie *Hatchet*." Despite Bertie's brusque professional mien, Mary's aunt always encouraged her niece to follow her dreams. When Mary was failing subjects in school, Bertie told her, "You're going to be a dancer, or you're going to be an actress. Whatever it is, you're going to be good at it."

According to David Davis, editor of *Mary Magazine*, a rare periodical published from 1991 to 2008, Bertie was indeed a career woman who never married, just like Mary Richards. "She was supportive of Mary's dream to be in show business and helped Mary get a job at CBS radio in the mailroom, and to pad her resume, while her parents were less encouraging. Her dad wanted her to have a regular education, and her mother, who was having severe alcoholic issues, wanted her to be a secretary."

Bill Persky was a young writer whom Mary met on *The Dick Van Dyke Show*, where they ignited a deep friendship that would last the rest of her lifetime. He penned several episodes of *Van Dyke* with writing partner Sam Denoff. Persky said that Mary loved her Aunt Bertie "…because she was the most supportive, loving and warmest person in her life," whereas her father, for one, "…was a very cold guy."

According to Jason Bonderoff's biography on Mary, George Tyler Moore was a magna cum laude graduate of Georgetown University; an intellectual who read frequently and respected the importance of education. As time marched on, Mary could no longer deflect her poor academic drive by preeminent dancing for her dad. They had let each other down. If her grades were less than perfect, his ascent up the professional ladder did not receive high marks either. His lack of ambition baffled and disappointed her. Yet in some ways Mary knew she was the spitting image of her paternal parent. Her dark English-Irish good looks came from him and, apparently, so did her distant disposition, while she secretly prayed not to inherit his passivity.

In Mary's eyes, her father had "absolutely no career drive," and she never understood why. From her perspective, he was an enigma; not cold, "but reserved." They only later learned to openly "express affection" for one another, while her ambition was "based on a childhood need to get Daddy's approval and attention."

In one conversation with the *Los Angeles Times*, Mary said her home life was not ideal. Her mother and father were not the best of parents, but they were at their best with humor. Mary always sought their approval, which she never fully received from her father. For him, achievement was everything, while her mother tried to dull any pangs with alcohol.

"She had a father who was not free with his love," Ed Asner told the Reelz Channel. "So, she probably had to fight to try and gain his love. Her mother was an alcoholic. It was not a happy family."

Laure Redmond, Mary's personal trainer and friend, added, "There was no one paying attention to what she needed."

"I went through my periods of alienation with them as I think most teenagers do," Mary once observed of her parents, "…and, with it all, we came closer together. We understood each other, and had respect for the differences that we all possess."

Mary channeled any dysfunction into her art. Fellow performer and close confidant Bernadette Peters later said her friend had to keep rising above such challenges to enjoy life, sometimes despite her early education, overseen by strict disciplinary Catholic nuns.

Mary experienced significant measures of guilt that dated back to her first confession, and other academic and religious experiences of her faith. A supervising nun once reprimanded her for speaking out of turn while lined up with her female classmates. The strict sister switched her to the boys' line, which mortified Mary.

A few years later, Mary was playing basketball in the schoolyard. The girls were delegated to one side; the boys, to another. When she decided to play with the boys, the good sister was infuriated and scolded her never to "do that" again. "You're not allowed to play with boys," the sister explained.

Consequently, Mary was forced to stay after school. "These are little scars but you carry them with you," she remembered.

As she matured, Mary's focus reached beyond academics. Her life was outside the school – dance classes, recitals. She looked down her nose at sports, the school plays, the drama club, but later regretted doing so. Although she had an intimate circle of girlfriends at school, having close female friends was something she steered away from in adulthood, save for alliances with actresses like Beverly Sanders, Betty White, and Hope Lange. She would eventually attend Hollywood parties, charity banquets, and events, but only with one of her two later husbands by her side: Grant Tinker and Dr. Robert Levine.

But years before those two distinguished gentlemen entered her life Mary embraced early romantic pursuits, to the detriment of her artistic objectives and despite the subtle jabs of her father. She wanted to be a dancer, but she was not completely devoted to her training. "I kept falling in love," she said. "I wanted boyfriends and dates. I wasn't cut out of the ascetic life of a dancer. I failed, as everybody's been good enough to remind me."

Dancing, however, was her first love and always would be, even when one of her dates escorted her to a benchmark moment in life: her high-school junior prom in May 1953. An important night for any student, even if Mary's evening was doused by her stone-faced dad. Carl Reiner, creator and one of Mary's co-stars on *The Dick Van Dyke Show*, later recounted to ABC News the story she once told him of her prom-night blues. "I was her father figure," Reiner said, "...because her father was a non-communicative man who didn't know how to talk to her. She was 16 years old before he gave her a compliment." While she stood dressed to the nines for her prom, Mr. Moore glanced toward her and said, "Mary, you look very handsome." "And that was the only compliment he ever gave her," Reiner recalled. "Imagine? A beauty like that getting her only compliment?"

One month later, Mary began formally traveling in the right social circles, as she attended the wedding of Virginia Peyton, a 1950 Las Madrinas debutante, to John Tofflemire, son of Dr. and Mrs. Benjamin Franklin Tofflemire of Lafayette. Her date was Valentine Peyton, brother to Virginia, and son of Robert Clark Peyton and Anna Peyton. They were a prominent Beverly Hills family who built an expansive home at 910 Foothill Boulevard with a butler, chauffeur, and all the amenities. Shortly after Mary attended Virginia's and John's reception, Valentine started dating Kathleen Marie Anton, who attended Immaculate Heart High with Mary. There were no hard feelings between the two, as the future starlet had still even bigger fish to fry. As documented in Chris Bryars' biography, *The Real Mary Tyler Moore*, Mary summed up her adolescence like this:

"I lived an absolute normal childhood, except that I was the only girl on the block who never wanted to be a nurse or a teacher. All I ever wanted to be was a ballet dancer. And it's a shame because that kept me from being curious about anything else. I never really tried in high school. I just said to myself, 'Well, it doesn't matter. I won't need history or English for what I'm going to do.'"

Chapter

2

On Mary's to-do list was a professional career in show business, which began at 17 as a dancer. She then transitioned to acting, if only due to lack of opportunity. She wasn't as good a dancer as she had thought, and worked somewhat, but mostly in chorus lines. She sought to be like the grand dames of motion-picture musicals, Cyd Charisse or Moira Shearer, star of *The Red Shoes*, the 1948 feature about a ballet dancer torn between the man she loves and her prima ballerina pursuits.

Leslie Caron was also one of Mary's favorites, one with whom she identified in a relatively personal way. "Caron had all those teeth," she said, "…and I was so self-conscious about my big mouth. But there she was, adored for her big mouth, plus she was a brilliant dancer. I wanted to be just like her. And she was [in the 1951 film classic *An American in Paris*] dancing with my Gene Kelly, my idol. God, I hated her!"

Mary's love-hate ambitions were wrapped up with her fantasies. Her musical film pursuits became less feasible with each passing day; such movie productions were waning in popularity, but she gave it her best shot. While still in high school, and with reference letters from her Uncle Harold in hand, she made the rounds with talent agents. She would share with them her dance history and aspirations, but to no avail. "They wanted to help and were very nice," remembered Mary, "but they had no way of knowing whether who they were looking at had any talent."

She finally found an agent who said, "Well, go ahead and try it. We'll set up some interviews for you. But just remember this, dancers can't act, and actors can't dance. And that's the way it's meant to be."

With that utter lack of positive reinforcement, she began auditioning. One tryout was arranged immediately after high school, by a friend of her beloved

Aunt Bertie. Subsequently, the young pixie landed her first professional job – as *Happy Hotpoint*, a tiny dancing/singing elf that was superimposed over and inside Hotpoint appliances in TV commercials. "The prom was on a Monday night," she recalled, "...and I went to work on a Tuesday."

The ads began airing in 1955 during early screenings of *The Adventures of Ozzie and Harriet* (ABC, 1952-1966), TV's first non-situation comedy (decades before NBC's *Seinfeld*, one of Mary's favorite shows, helped to coin that term in 1989). She appeared in 39 "Hot" spots for a total of five days' work, spread throughout the year, earning approximately $6,000 for popping out of ovens, doing acrobatics, leaping around, and saying things like, "Hi, Harriet [Nelson]...aren't you glad you're using Hotpoint appliances?"

Five months prior to her Hotpoint hiring, and after a mild opportunity to date David Nelson, son of Ozzie and Harriet, she met 27-year-old Richard Carleton Meeker, an Ocean-Spray cranberry products salesman, ten years her senior. Though older than Nelson, Meeker was the perfect "boy next store" match to her "girl next door" image. Within six weeks of their pending nuptials in 1955, they moved into a house next door to her parents and, on July 3, 1956, she gave birth to their only son, Richie. Years later, she explained to Barbara Walters why she married so young:

"I don't want to denigrate my parents, because they're wonderful people and through the years, I've come to know them much better, and like them a lot. But I was going through a stage of about 16, 17, 18, where I didn't like them very much, and I really wanted to be independent...and didn't want to be told what to do. And there was this young man to who I was obviously very attracted and...fell in love, I think, as much as you can fall in love at that age. It's hard to tell the difference."

"My parents thought that children should be born already 18, married and living in a neighboring town," Mary revealed to *USA Today*.

Mary's mother Marjorie had introduced her to Meeker, after meeting him in the neighborhood in early 1955. Marjorie liked Richard almost instantaneously, and wanted him to meet Mary, who consented. The duo soon began dating, then became engaged, and finally married. Mary said she wed Richard from a desire to assert independence from her parents. "I foolishly thought that the only option for me was to marry," Mary recalled. "I'm a part-foolish person. Always will be. Anyway, that's what girls did if they didn't go to college, isn't it? I wanted my own apartment; I wanted to be independent of my folks; I wanted to put myself in a situation where no one could tell me what to do."

Like any young and healthy human being, Mary was also interested in sex. Due to her strict Catholic upbringing, premarital sex was not an option she considered. But her marriage to Meeker remedied the dilemma.

"Marriage was the natural progression for all healthy people who didn't become nuns," she asserted. "But at the time I certainly believed that I was in love and was going to have a perfect little marriage."

She once told the *New York Times*, "Getting married was the only way I could get out of the house legally, since I didn't want to go to college." And as she later documented in her second memoir, *Growing Up Again: Life, Loves and Oh, Yeah – Diabetes*, Mary played out the happy housewife role in real life, just as she danced as Happy Hotpoint in TV commercials. "I put meals on the table, cooed and rocked, cleaned and chatted with other moms in the park. I was cared for and I was the best mom I knew how to be."

Upon wedding Meeker, Mary had described herself as "a very good Catholic girl" and a virgin. When dating there were all sorts of restrictions placed on young Catholics or, as she termed it, "too many sexual taboos." Her marriage to Meeker may have ended her formal alignment with the Catholic Church, but her spiritual life was not over. "I still pray," she said. But when the time came to leave this world, she did not call for a priest to administer last rites. And she did not agree with the Church on birth control, divorce, or abortion. "If I had a choice," she had affirmed, "…I would choose not to be raised Catholic."

But she was a good Catholic wife, and expectant she soon became. Birth control had been one of Mary's points of contention with the Church. In seeking the freedom to use it, "Naturally," Mary said, "I immediately became pregnant" – with Richie, a development which contributed to the end of her TV tenure as Happy Hotpoint. With each passing week, it became more challenging to conceal her condition while wearing the relatively revealing elf costume. The ads kept her "very busy and very happy for many, many months," but after a time, she heard, "We're going to get another Happy Hotpoint girl, so, goodbye, and good luck to you."

According to author Marc Shapiro, around this time, Mary began work on her first official movie. *Once Upon a Horse* was a 1958 comedy Western which featured the up-and-coming comedy team of Dan Rowan and Dick Martin. Her role was listed as a "dance hall girl," while Rowan and Martin would one decade later headline *Laugh-In*, one of TV's most innovative variety/sketch shows, pre-dating *Saturday Night Live* by seven years.

Also around this time, Mary also started taking anonymous modeling jobs for the covers of several low-budget, exotic LPs produced around 1958 or 1959. They were for the Tops or Gilmar record labels, featuring artists like Miguel Lopez, Raoul Martinez, Miguelito Valdez, and Lew Raymond. According to entertainment historian Randy Skretvedt, host of the popular Los Angeles radio show, *Forward to the Past*, "Tops was a label whose output was usually sold in drug stores for about $1.99 per album, while Miguelito Valdez was a famous Cuban singer and popularized the song

'Babalu' before Desi Arnaz did. And 'Lew Raymond' may have been a pseudonym for a group of studio musicians."

While posing for these now-obscure album covers, she spent a year or two as a chorus dancer on television musical variety shows like *The Eddie Fisher Show* and *The George Gobel Show*, after which her career started to expand. She knew that dancing on variety series was not going to lead to starring roles in movie musicals; the genre itself was dying. But she instructed herself, "...think about something else."

That "something else" was acting, which she had never formally studied, other than in tandem with her dance training or her performances in small shows. "I never went to the Actors Studio route," she once remembered. "I'm not an actress who can create a character. I play me. I was scared if I tampered with it, I might ruin it." She had always identified with stars of the 1930s like Ruby Keeler, Ginger Rogers, Fred Astaire, and Mitzi Gaynor. "To me, a Brooklyn girl," she said, "...show business meant singing and dancing. The sun rose and set on that Golden Girl dancing her way to stardom."

While her time on the big screen was yet to come, Mary had finally landed her first speaking role on television – as a relatively romantic interest for George Burns. That episode of *The George Burns Show*, titled "The Landlord's Daughter," aired March 10, 1959. This segment finds George in the midst of an ethical issue when Mr. Knox, his landlord, portrayed by Douglas Dumbrille, offers him a five-year lease in return for discouraging his daughter Linda, as played by Mary, from pursuing a career in the entertainment industry.

It all sounded very true to Mary's life – and work.

"Truth be told," she later wrote in *Growing Up Again*, "...work was my main focus, before, during and after" she gave birth to Richie. "If I had to do it over again," she said, "I wouldn't have pursued a career if I had a little boy to take care of."

But Mary did pursue that career, diligently and diversely. Working wife and mother Mary continued to find dancing gigs in the chorus lines of TV variety programs, acting jobs on shows like *Schlitz Playhouse* and *Steve Canyon* (another unaccredited performance), and personal appearances on game shows such as *To Tell the Truth*, all circa 1959. She performed in *Truth* with actress Joyce Bulifant, the future featured semi-regular on *The Mary Tyler Moore Show*. Bulifant would play Marie Slaughter, wife to Gavin MacLeod's newsroom writer Murray. On *Truth*, they surfaced side-by-side, posing as the wife of actor James MacArthur, the son of thespian legend Helen Hayes. MacArthur was later known for playing Dano, as in "Book 'em, Dano," on TV's original *Hawaii Five-O*.

Bulifant would later divorce MacArthur, and marry three more times: Actor Edward Mallory; *I Love Lucy/Bewitched* director director/producer William Asher (whose third wife was twitch-star Elizabeth Montgomery); and actor Roger Perry, to whom Bulifant remained married until his death in 2018. She wrote about it all, in her memoir, *My Four Hollywood Husbands*, published in 2017. As to the *Truth* of 1959, Bulifant was not sure "if the panel guessed correctly or not" between her and Mary as the legitimate wife of MacArthur. "But afterwards," she recalled, "Mary was very warm and sweet, just as she would be on *The Mary Tyler Moore Show.*"

Then billed as only "Mary Moore," Mary soon learned that producer David Heilweil was seeking an actress for a new show he was developing for Dick Powell's Four Star Productions. But she was uncertain of what the part required, other than attractive legs and hands and sexy vocal cords.

The same year her moment of *Truth* aired, Mary won her first recurring role as Sam, the sultry-voiced telephone operator and receptionist to David Janssen on his TV crime-drama *Richard Diamond, Private Detective.* It debuted on CBS in 1957; its fourth and final season was on NBC in 1960. Mary's part was an uncredited performance; viewers could hear only her tantalizing tones, and just see her shapely legs, but never her face, all adding mystique. Publicity for the show played up her clandestine participation for 13 episodes, when Mary asked for a raise, and was promptly replaced by Roxanne Brooks.

Actress Karen Sharpe had worked with Mary in the episode "Echo of Laughter," which debuted May 17, 1959. Here, Richard Diamond learns that his friend, a television personality, is having serious marital issues with his wife, who may in fact be attempting to murder him.

Sharpe, a.k.a., Karen Kramer, would later marry director Stanley Kramer (*Guess Who's Coming To Dinner?*), and retire from acting. But throughout '50s and '60s television, she was one of the medium's most respected performers. From 1957 to 1961, during which she made her *Diamond* appearance, Sharpe was married to her first husband, actor Chester Marshall, a good friend of Janssen. The Marshalls would double date with Janssen and his then-wife Ellie Graham, who Sharpe described as "a really great chef. We used to go to their house for dinner all the time."

When working on any television or film set, Sharpe did not socialize much, and kept to herself. "I was kind of a loner," she explained. Between the camera rolls on *Diamond*, she sat between Janssen and Mary, which gave the two actresses a chance to get better acquainted. Sharpe recalled Mary as "…very social, very friendly with everyone, and very easy to get along with and cooperative. I liked her a lot. And she had that *voice*," which was as lilting and cheery in conversation as heard off-camera on *Diamond*.

Either way, Mary made her mark of distinction as Sam. It resulted in later guest spots on shows like John Cassavetes' NBC detective romp *Johnny Staccato*. In her episode, "The Mask of Jason," which aired February 19, 1960, Mary portrayed a beauty-pageant contestant who hired Staccato to protect her from a menacing man who turned out to be her husband.

When Mary exited the *Richard Diamond* series, she said, "...casting directors starting using me because they thought it would be a coup to show the real 'Sam's' face." She would go on to make more than sixty TV appearances over the next several years, some starting at $85.00 per day, including an episode of NBC's western called *Overland Trail*. Described as a cross between *Tales of Wells Fargo* and *Laredo*, *Overland* aired for just one season, from 1960 to 1961, and featured William Bendix (*The Life of Riley*) as Frederick Kelly, a salty Overland Stage superintendent, and Doug McClure (*The Virginian*, *Checkmate*) in his first starring role as Flip Flippen, Kelly's more reckless young sidekick. This daring duo set out to protect the stagecoach from thieves, vigilantes, Native Americans, and general threats while navigating the West from Missouri, across the Rockies, and on to California. The chemistry was solid between Bendix and McClure, especially when trouble was afoot.

Although short-lived, *Overland* was a solid show that boasted an impressive guest cast that included Harry Guardino, Denver Pyle (*The Andy Griffith Show*; *The Doris Day Show*), Werner Klemperer (*Hogan's Heroes*), Mercedes McCambridge (*Bewitched*), John Carradine (father to David Carradine of *Kung Fu*), and others.

Mary's episode of *Overland*, "All the O'Mara's Horses," screened March 13, 1960. Here, she played Joan Ransom, a horse-savvy cowgirl, in a story about Kelly's thwarted efforts to establish a stagecoach line from Carson City to Payload. This transpired once he learned his archrival, The O'Mara (Sean McClory), named himself the town's cagey mayor, sheriff, and supervisor, and hired a band of outlaws as deputies. Mary's dialogue as Joan opposite McClure's Flip is the episode's bright spot:

> **Flip:** "I was just tellin' your father that you're real good on a horse. Not many women can handle them like you do."
>
> **Joan:** "Oh, it's not hard – not if you know the tricks."
>
> **Flip:** "Oh? Is there something I can learn?"
> **Joan:** "I think so. First you have to distract their attention. Hey, look!"
>
> [Flip turns. Joan pushes him to the ground.]

19

Joan: "Then you put them in their place..."

[She places her boot firmly in the middle of Flip's chest.]

Joan: "Then you keep them there. Otherwise they think they're dealing with a fan-talker who's more interested in good looks than good sense...and when they've learned their first lesson you tell them to go on into the house and drink their coffee."

Flip: "And since when do horses drink coffee?"

Joan: "Since when have we been talking about horses?"

This segment of *Trail* also happened to feature Karen Sharpe. Although they did not share any dialogue, and only appeared together briefly in a group scene, Mary still made an impression. "Mary had a very distinct kind of way of delivering a line," remembered Sharpe. "Before I saw her, I heard her," while Sharpe was studying her *Overland* lines. Upon hearing Mary, she glanced up from her script to see who was talking, and thought, "What an interesting cadence in the timber of her voice."

Although they would later share a stronger link Mary and Sharpe would not work together again, moving forward individually with TV guest performances. Sharpe would appear in other Westerns like *Bonanza* and *Laramie*, and in sitcoms like *I Dream of Jeannie*. Mary would surface in projects like "One Blonde Too Many," the pilot for NBC's one-season sitcom *The Tab Hunter Show*, in which the former teen idol played a bachelor cartoonist.

Airing September 18, 1960, the "Blonde" segment was directed by Norman Tokar, known for his work on *Leave It to Beaver* and feature films such as Walt Disney's *The Happiest Millionaire* (1967). Besides Hunter, it featured regular cast members Richard Erdman, Jerome Cohen, and Reta Shaw. Mary's performance in "One Blonde" was a highlight on the *Hunter* series, though her character was credited as merely "Brunette," amidst a bevy of women with platinum-colored locks. In an interesting turn of events, this episode somewhat foreshadowed her turn as Laura Petrie in the *Dick Van Dyke Show* segment, "My Blonde-Haired Brunette." In this October 10, 1961 episode, Laura dyed her hair blonde, thinking it would be more pleasing to Rob.

Mary made other pre-*Van Dyke* guest appearances on shows like *Bourbon Street Beat*, a short-lived private detective series which aired on ABC from 1959-1960 and featured, among others, Richard Long (*The Big Valley*) and Andrew Duggan (the original father on *The Waltons* TV-movie pilot, *The*

Homecoming). *Bourbon* would also feature a guest spot by Van Williams, before his fame as TV's *Green Hornet* (ABC, 1966-1967), and his performance opposite Mary in a *Van Dyke* Army-based flashback episode. In "No Rice at My Wedding," from October 1965, Williams plays a handsome soldier who competes with a very jealous Rob for Laura's affection.

Bourbon Street Beat was one of many similar young and hip detective series that were produced by Warner Bros., along with *77 Sunset Strip* and *Surfside Six*, both of which featured Mary in featured guest shots. Her *Strip* performance was particularly provocative. In "The Fix," airing April 8, 1960, she portrayed Laura Chandler, a wealthy heiress engaged to a boorish boxer who is murdered. She's dressed to the nines throughout the episode and, at one point, is grabbed and gagged.

Mary also performed on TV's *Riverboat*; *Wanted: Dead or Alive*; *Steve Canyon*; *Hawaiian Eye* (as different characters in four episodes); *Thriller*; and *Lock Up*. She made her significant big-screen debut in the feature film *X-15*. Released in 1961, this film became somewhat of an enigma. A dramatic aviation production narrated by an uncredited James Stewart, the film is a fictionalized account of the X-15 NASA research rocket aircraft program and the test pilots who guided it during the Cold War, as well as the associated NASA community that supported the program. Mary portrayed Pamela Stewart, the wife of one of the three pilots. *Variety* called her performance "competent" and said the production was a "good little film," "surprisingly appealing" with "the most original and tingling shots" being "the gleaming, kaleidoscope views of the rocket, mirrored in escort cockpits as it hisses higher and higher into the blue."

Along with Mary, the movie starred David McLean, Charles Bronson, Kenneth Tobey, Patricia Owens, and James Gregory. It marked the directorial debut of Richard Donner, who later helmed hit features like 1976's *The Omen* and *Superman: The Movie* in 1978. *X-15* received little fanfare, but Mary proved unruffled by any lack of accolades for the film, and retained what became her famous optimism. "My agents are being very kind to me," she said. "If I am getting any other offers, they're not telling me and I'm glad. I'd hate to think I was missing anything."

Actor Stanley Livingston, best known as Chip Douglas, the middle on-screen son to Fred MacMurray on the long-running CBS family comedy, *My Three Sons* (1960-1972), also portrayed a son in *X-15*. He was Mike Brandon, the on-screen offspring to Bronson and Owens. Before that, he made a few guest spots on *The Adventures of Ozzie and Harriett*, which featured Mary in those *Happy Hotpoint* commercials. Livingston recalled: "Charles Bronson's career was really the catalyst for getting the movie made," as it premiered just prior to the release of his breakout film, *The*

Magnificent Seven. "In those days, anytime you'd appear in a feature film, it was considered more prestigious than doing television."

At this time, TV stars were TV stars, and movie stars were movie stars. The twain never met, once a career was established in either arena. Today, the performance line between the two behemoths is blurred. Livingston, just 10 years old when making *X-15*, interacted mostly with Bronson and Owens on-screen, and did not share any scenes with Mary. But he later talked about a conversation with her that took place one day during lunch. Aware of Livingston's role on *Sons*, Mary wondered if he ever got nervous acting on camera.

"Naw," he replied nonchalantly. "Why? Are you?"

"Yes," she responded. "I'm *always* nervous before doing a scene."

At which point, the tiny Livingston offered the future big star some acting advice. "If you have a prop or something in your hand…something you can hold or look at during a scene…it helps not to make you so nervous." That was a suggestion the young actor learned from Fred MacMurray who, as Livingston recalled, "…was always fiddling with his pipe…some 'business' to do, instead of just standing [or sitting] there saying his lines. I don't know how I became the beneficiary of that wisdom, but I was. It was just a little trick I learned from him, and one which I used myself on *X-15*…with a watch, and then I passed on that advice to Mary. Although I don't know if she ever used it in any scene for *X-15*."

My Three Sons and *The Mary Tyler Moore Show* overlapped for *Son's* final two years, but Livingston had not seen Mary since their *X-15* days. Decades after, they reconnected behind the scenes at one of the TV Land Award ceremonies. Upon noticing her across a crowded room of classic television legends, Livingston approached Mary. She remembered him from *X-15* and they went on to chat about the movie. "Yeah, it was kind of a big deal for me," she told him. "It was my first feature, and I was just getting started. It was exciting to be there." Mary seemed happy and "looked great," Livingston asserted, which comforted him because, like many, he had been startled by news of her less-than flattering plastic surgeries post-1983. But by the time they reconnected at the TV Land Awards, circa 2002, that issue seemed to have been corrected. "Whichever doctor had just worked on her," Livingston assessed, "…did a really wonderful job. She was beautiful."

Chapter

3

"Beautiful" is most likely what the creative team behind *The Dick Van Dyke Show* thought when they first saw Mary in their search for Laura Petrie.

In 1960, Carl Reiner partnered with Danny Thomas and his *Make Room for Daddy/The Danny Thomas Show*-runner Sheldon Leonard to produce *The Dick Van Dyke Show*, which Reiner created. The sitcom was partially based on Reiner's career as a writer for Sid Caesar's TV variety series *Your Show of Shows*, which aired on NBC from 1950 to 1954, and which first brought him prominence. Here's how it went down:

After *Show of Shows* transmuted into *Caesar's Hour*, which left the air in 1957, Reiner cast himself in the lead of a sitcom pilot he wrote. Called *Head of the Family*, it was filmed with a single camera, without an audience. Drawing from his behind-the-screen experiences while raising a family in New Rochelle, New York, Reiner played Rob Petrie, a writer for the fictional *Alan Sturdy Show*. *Head* also starred Barbara Britton as Rob's wife Laura Petrie; Morty Gunty and Sylvia Miles as Buddy Sorrell and Sally Rogers, Rob's co-writers on the *Sturdy Show*; Jake Wakefield as Sturdy; and Gary Morgan as little Ritchie Petrie, Rob and Laura's son. Before filming the pilot, Reiner penned 12 additional episodes, and brought the concept to CBS, who rejected it. But Leonard recognized the sitcom's potential, and suggested Reiner bow out as the lead, to be replaced by Dick Van Dyke, who had a hit on Broadway with *Bye Bye Birdie*.

Head of the Family thus evolved into *The Dick Van Dyke Show*, which was filmed with an audience in the more traditional three-camera format. Rose Marie and Morey Amsterdam replaced Miles and Gunty. Morgan was gone, and Larry Mathews stepped in as the new Ritchie; Richard Deacon joined the cast as Mel Cooley, producer of the variety-show-within-the-show starring the renamed Alan Brady, played by Reiner.

Reiner held great hopes for *Van Dyke* from the onset, while the creative team hit a snag: Who will play the new Laura Petrie opposite Van Dyke's version of Rob Petrie?

How Mary Tyler Moore answered that call is the stuff of legend.

She had previously auditioned to replace Sherry Jackson in the role of Thomas' on-screen daughter in *The Danny Thomas Show*, co-produced by Leonard. Thomas and Leonard liked her reading, but opted not to cast her as *Danny's* daughter because she didn't look the part, specifically due to the size of her nose. It was too small, felt to be an improper match for Thomas' significantly larger sniffer. But Leonard, Reiner, and Thomas, the series partners, remembered a certain young brunette when casting the new Laura Petrie. They wondered, "Who was the kid we liked so much last year, the one with the three names and the funny nose?" The answer was profoundly Mary Tyler Moore.

But as Mary later noted, she almost did not go on the audition. When her agent informed her about the potential gig, she said, "I'm tired. I've had too many disappointments all week." To which he replied, "Get in your car and go over there!"

Mary recalled her audition for Reiner as one of the most terrifying experiences of her life. She had a crush on him from *Your Show of Shows* and thought she read her lines terribly. "I was so nervous when I went to read for him," she recalled in *The Dick Van Dyke Show*, by Ginny Weissman and Coyne Steven Sanders. "I did not realize I was going to actually be reading for him and almost blew it because of my awe for him as a performer."

In that same publication, Reiner related, "She walked into the office, sat down, and she read the first three lines of the pilot script. That's all it took; three lines. And I heard the sound. She said *hello* like a real person."

Reiner knew Mary was perfect for the part. He placed his hand on her head, "like the claw in that machine that picks out candy in the arcades," he later told *ABC News*, and steered her down the hall to Sheldon Leonard's office. Their search for Laura was over. "I immediately fell in love with Mary the moment I met her," Reiner said. "The first time she walked in the office I lit up."

Coupled with her beauty, charm, and wit, was an energetic comedic potential and, as Karen Sharpe had assessed, "that voice." Mary couldn't lose. "I heard that sound in her voice," Reiner said. "That *ping*."

As it turned out, Sharpe had also auditioned for the role of Laura, when she was submitted by her agent Norman Brokaw, then president of the

William Morris Agency. The Morris company represented her for approximately 15 years, along with other young performers like Clint Eastwood, then the star of TV's *Rawhide* western series, on which Sharpe made many guest appearances. But when it came to the *Van Dyke Show* audition, Sharpe said, "They didn't choose me, they chose Mary, even though I was better known at the time. I thought, 'That crazy voice is going to get her the job!' And it did! She said 'Oh, Rob!' like no one else. She made it great. I was never envious of anyone else's success. I was always happy for everybody, and I was really happy for Mary. I had a lot of respect for her, and I saw just how talented she was from the very beginning."

With keen insight into the early days of the movie and television industry, Sharpe painted a detailed backdrop of what it was like for young actors at the time, specifically the pre-famous Mary Tyler Moore: "She had aspirations like all of us. She wanted to make a dent in the industry…to be able to work…and become a star…which is what we were all trying to do. It starts with wanting to have the fame and the lifestyle we all read about in the movie magazines. In those beginning days, if you weren't from Los Angeles or part of the business, you thought it was so glamorous…that it was so great to be a part of it all. That's the way they made it look in all of those movie magazines. Then when you actually get into it, you think, 'Ok, what's this really about?' Well, it's about hard work….and the performance…and wanting to be the best you can be because of other people that you're working with."

Sharpe, the "loner" who focused on knowing her lines and not socializing on-set, was mostly caught up in the work. "When you're an actor," she said, "…it's just words on a piece of paper. That's all it is…and it's what you bring to [those words] that makes that character…that role…come alive. You have to bring [some unique aspect of yourself] to it. It's not written for you. There are very few directors who know how to direct you anyway. They don't take the time to direct you, particularly in television. They have too much on their plate, and say, 'Let's just get the shot.' So, you stand here, and it's usually the first take, when you really don't know anybody that you're working with…that's the take they print."

Actors have to do their homework before even stepping foot on any set, "…in order for you not to get mowed down," she intoned. The work is hard, if only in meeting the morning call, which can be as early as 4 AM for a 6 AM shoot. In the early days of television, Sharpe recalled, actresses "used to dress up to go to work. We all did. We just didn't go sloppy in our jeans and t-shirts with no make-up. We dressed nice to meet our morning call or make-up call. We never knew who was going to do our make-up or if we were going to have to do it ourselves. So, we always came prepared. That's just the ethic we had."

On many occasions, performers like Sharpe and Mary had to furnish their own clothes, whether they were a featured star or a supporting player in a TV show or film. Sharpe had two wardrobes – one that she wore every day, and another that she would utilize if called upon to replace an actress expediently, sometimes overnight. If that happened, she would have to be on the set the very next day, receiving the script if just a mere 5 or 6 hours before the shoot began. "So, you had to be on your game," she admitted, "…to survive it," much less win it, "…and so you didn't embarrass yourself."

Unlike Mary, Sharpe appeared in a number of live television productions, including anthology shows like *Hallmark Hall of Fame* and *Playhouse 90*. She was part of a stock company of actors. This allowed her to portray leading roles that she would otherwise not have had the chance to play. "It was a really good company for me to be able to do that," Sharpe said. "It was like doing theatre, live, for just one performance. It was exciting. I wouldn't attempt it for anything today. But it was very brave work."

Although Mary was never that courageous, by choice or otherwise, she had many distinguishing qualities besides her unmistakable voice. "Her work was filled with personality which made her identifiable and unique," Sharpe said. "She was more than just a good actor."

"We have those people today," Sharpe continued, "…and they're great. We'll see them in a part and say, 'Oh, yes…but I vaguely remember him or her.' Mary was never the kind of performer or person that you wouldn't remember because she was too outstanding as a personality. We had other personalities like that…the *John Waynes* and the *Lana Turners*…and the *Elizabeth Taylors*." Such actors or actor-types were the personalities moviegoers in particular expected to see when selecting a certain film to watch at a theatre. "We didn't go to see the move, per se," Sharpe clarified, "…but we went to see Lana Turner in the movie. We knew a John Wayne movie was going to be about a hero, and that John Wayne was going to be that hero. And we were seeing a *'John Wayne movie'*…not a movie that just had John Wayne in it."

According to Sharpe, Mary held that same sort of appeal, whether for TV or the big screen. When she and her legendary directing husband Stanley Kramer saw Mary in *Ordinary People*, they "thought she was brilliant."

Even though Mary's performance in *People* was acclaimed by moviegoers and critics alike, and despite the fact that she played a character much different from Laura Petrie or Mary Richards, the actress herself was still the main attraction. "When you would see a movie or a TV show that she was in," Sharpe said, "…you were seeing a *'Mary Tyler Moore* movie'…or a *'Mary Tyler Moore* TV show.' You weren't seeing a show or a movie that happened to have Mary Tyler Moore in it as the star. When you watched *The Loretta Young Show* you knew who she was…that kind of person she always played…which was more like her in real life. Whereas [an actor like] Marlon Brando was more of a personality but not really…he kind of melded into all the characters he played…but [those characters were] not who he was. Humphrey Bogart was always Humphrey Bogart…just like John Wayne was always John Wayne. You knew who you were seeing. And if you liked them you went to see their movies."

"We got away from that," she said, but not when it came to Mary who, "…had the identification of being in a '*Mary Tyler Moore* movie'…or a '*Mary Tyler Moore* TV show'…and that's the greatest compliment I think I could ever give anyone…because I didn't have that. But Mary did."

Sharpe described herself as "a working actress who was very lucky," but in viewing any of her performances on the big screen or small, she would not describe them as a "*Karen Sharpe* movie" or a "*Karen Sharpe* TV show." "You didn't go see a '*Carolyn Jones* movie' either," she said. "Carolyn Jones would be in the movie, and she was very good, but it wouldn't be defined as a '*Carolyn Jones* movie.'"

But there was something about Mary that was different. "Anything she did you would want to see or watch because she stood out," Sharpe said. "She absolutely stood out."

Mary did indeed draw attention, despite early rumblings that she may have been too inexperienced for the part of Laura Petrie. She was only 22 years old, but claimed to be 23 when she learned that Van Dyke, then 35, thought she was too young to play his wife. Richard Meeker, her husband in real life, was one decade older than her. But Van Dyke, like Meeker and everyone else, quickly caved to Mary's appeal.

Both Van Dyke and Mary admitted on more than one occasion that had neither been married, a sizzling romance between the two might have ensued during their five-year run on the *Van Dyke Show*. "I thought she was one of the most beautiful women I had ever met," he once said. "I immediately fell in love with her. We would flirt and have lots of laughs together. We never argued. We would eat lunch together and talk."

The chemistry between Mary and Van Dyke was evident from the beginning. Within just a few months, they would ad lib scenes. "We got to where we could read each other's minds," Van Dyke later recalled. "It was like doing improv."

"We had a crush on each other," Van Dyke later told *Closer* magazine. Although Carl Reiner said it was more serious than that. "They both really cared for each other, and if they weren't married to other people, they would have made a couple."

But Mary, with an unassuming manner, had said, "Dick was not in love with me. He just thought I was a nifty dame."

Van Dyke, like many more to come, had been enticed by Mary's charms. She went on to win her first Emmy for playing Laura, the optimum wife, mother, and home engineer who managed with panache Rob's behind-the-scenes hectic life and, to some extent, his career. Mary later recalled in a conversation with National Public Radio:

"Laura was going to be a wife…a television wife and that really had its classical parameters and dimensions that were established and hardly ever varied. If the wife was the star of the show, she was the funny one. But all the television wives were kind of obedient."

While Mary ensured that Laura would be far from submissive to Rob, there was some early talk of calling the show *Double Trouble*, in reference to the back-and-forth from Rob's place of employment to his home life. But since *Make Room for Daddy* was frequently referred to as *The Danny Thomas Show*, which ultimately became the title, the same reasoning was applied to *Double Trouble*; it became *The Dick Van Dyke Show*.

The pilot for *The Dick Van Dyke Show* was filmed on January 20, 1961, the same day as President John F. Kennedy's inauguration. JFK's subsequent Inauguration Ball was directed by *Bewitched* producer/director William Asher, who was also married to Elizabeth Montgomery, that show's star. This was one of a number of eerie life and career overlaps between Mary and Montgomery.

Rehearsals began for the *Bewitched* pilot on November 22, 1963, the day President Kennedy was assassinated. Montgomery's Samantha was married to Dick York's Darrin, and together they in many ways became a supernatural version of Mary and Dick Van Dyke's Laura and Rob Petrie – although Samantha and Darrin actually slept in the same bed, as opposed to Laura and Rob's twin-bedded marriage. Despite separate sleeping arrangements, the Petries somehow begat their little son Ritchie played by Larry Mathews.

In the *Van Dyke* episode, "Turtles, Ties and Toreadors," which aired December 4, 1963, Ritchie brings home a turtle with a portrait of the Petrie family painted on its back. "Oh, look! We look just like the Kennedy family," was to be one of Laura's lines. But when JFK was murdered just days before the episode's airing, this dialogue had to be altered. Through it all, Laura and Rob were being compared to Kennedy and his First Lady Jacqueline Kennedy, at least with regard to appearance.

Although the first season of *The Dick Van Dyke Show*, as with any new series, lacked the polished look, feel, and sound of its later years (for example, Rob referred to Laura as "Laurie"), its initial 30 episodes were sprinkled with gems in which Mary shone, namely, the aforementioned segment, "My Blonde-Haired Brunette" (October 10, 1961). Here, she delivered a breakout performance. It showcased her comedic chops like never before on the series, as when in a pivotal scene she cried as a half-brunette/half-blonde Laura seeking to please Rob, who she believed will find her more appealing as a blonde. But according to Bill Persky, "Mary didn't really cry...she tried *not* to cry. That's how she cried." He explained: "One day, she told Carl, 'I don't know how to cry. And he said, 'Well, then don't cry.' And that's when she went on to develop that stuttering [style] of 'about to cry,' which carried her through [many] comedic scenes."

In a later interview with *Entertainment Weekly*, Mary addressed the impact this episode had on her career: "I got to cry for the first time. That opened everybody's eyes up to the fact that I could do funny stuff."

Beyond Mary Richards' later laughter-to-tears presentation in the October 25, 1975 "Chuckles Bites the Dust" episode of *The Mary Tyler Moore Show* (which became one of Mary's favorite scenes in the entirety of that series), Persky disclosed, "In no comedy moment has Mary full out cried. But she had her own [way] of crying, which we used to call sups-sups" [the phonic-sound that her crying style mimicked].

Another grand Mary episode from *Van Dyke's* initial season is "Empress Carlotta's Necklace," which premiered December 12, 1961. In this venture, Rob innocently gifts Laura with a dreadful-looking discount necklace that he believes will bring a smile to her face for their anniversary. To save his feelings, she bites her teeth as if to stop from crying. Well, not really, but she feels like it. All the while, Rob anxiously awaits a visit from his parents so he can show off the gaudy glittery wraparound piece, which he purchased from Mel Cooley's cousin. The jewelry salesman, Maxwell Cooley, is played by Gavin MacLeod, Mary's future office sidekick on *The Mary Tyler Moore Show*.

MacLeod was scheduled to do another episode, "Romance, Roses and Rye Bread," which aired October 28, 1964, in the show's fourth year. This time, he was to play office-deli-deliverer Bert Monker, who expressed his secret crush on Sally by putting clandestine notes in the middle of her sandwiches. MacLeod was hired for the part – and even showed up for a lengthy three-day Labor Day weekend rehearsal. But, as he said, "I got sick, and went to the hospital." To help ease what was a minor illness, cast members sent books and other gifts to his room, but none of that completely dulled his professional anguish, "...crying to myself because I was missing playing that wonderful character." It was a role that was eventually went to Sid Melton, a regular from *The Danny Thomas Show* who, MacLeod admitted, "got through it beautifully."

Despite not playing Bert Monker, MacLeod won over *Van Dyke's* cast, crew, and viewers with his priceless interpretation of "Carlotta's" jewelry salesman Maxwell Cooley, who sold each item in his collection for a skimpy $29.95. MacLeod was "...in actor's heaven doing that episode." He described director Carl Reiner as "one of my heroes. I just think he's one of the most wonderful human beings that God ever created," while he remembered Mary's "up" personality, as well. "She was always so happy and joyful, just like Laura Petrie," although he added with a wink, "...after Rob gave Laura that necklace...it's a wonder their marriage continued."

Off-screen, her real-life union to Richard Meeker was failing, not due to their age difference, but simply because they had grown apart.

In mid-January of 1961, *Van Dyke Show* producer Sheldon Leonard invited advertising executive Grant Tinker to view a run-through of the sitcom's pilot episode. That day, Tinker met and was immediately smitten by Mary. Though she fought it, the feelings were mutual. But she was married, and Tinker was not a home-wrecker. He was all class and sophistication.

However, as associate producer Ron Jacobs noted in Weissman and Sanders' book *The Dick Van Dyke Show*, Mary left an after-show party, and Tinker followed. "We all laughed," Jacobs recalled. "We all said, 'Grant must have run into Mary.' It was meant as a joke but then we looked down the street and into traffic. Mary had stopped suddenly and Grant had ploughed right into the back of her car."

Thankfully, no one was hurt, at least physically. But Richard Meeker became distraught when Mary and Tinker later started dating, beginning with taking in a Broadway production of a show titled *Mary, Mary*, and later dancing at New York's hip Peppermint Lounge. "I woke up the next morning," Mary once told *TV Guide*, "...and...I was in love."

In place of Meeker's mild charms, Tinker was more debonair in Mary's eyes. He was a 1949 graduate of Dartmouth University who pursued a publishing career in New York, where he eventually worked in management training for NBC radio operations. In 1952, he joined Radio Free Europe, which broadcast news of the Free World to a then-censored Eastern Europe. After that, Tinker partnered with game-show host Allen Ludden to ignite the successful, long-running TV game show *College Bowl*. In 1954, he was hired by the McCann Erickson Advertising Agency as the director of programming for television. At this time, ad agencies were much more intrinsically involved with developing shows. Upon leaving that position, Tinker was named vice president of television programming for Benton & Bowles, which is when he met Mary, who at first wasn't all that impressed.

In her first memoir, Mary said she felt constrained "to be nice" to Tinker. This feeling of obligation was why she "disliked him so much" at first sight. In some manner, it was similar to how she felt towards her academic-minded dad. Mary said she "hated" Tinker "for being so educated and wearing such perfect neckties."

Upon once journeying to New York to promote the *Van Dyke Show*, Mary was stunned when Tinker invited her to dinner. She graciously accepted, and sought to dazzle him on their first night out, even if she planned to reject him the next time around. But that was not how it turned out. She described him as "tender, exacting, bright, witty and somewhat of a father figure."

In a video interview archived by the Television Academy years later, Tinker recalled his version of how they met. "Out of that meeting came a relationship that grew," he said. His first reaction to her was "…what anyone's would be. That she was dynamite. And what was great about her was that she wasn't 'actressy,' minus any airs. She was a real person, off-stage and off-camera and I just fell in love with her. I can't say I was hit by a hammer when I was introduced to her. But she made an immediate impression on me which grew over time. And luckily, I on her, and ultimately we were married."

By the close of *Van Dyke's* debut season, on June 1, 1962, Mary had divorced Meeker, then a CBS sales representative, and wed Tinker. In a magazine interview, *Van Dyke* regular Richard Deacon talked about how Mary changed after she married Tinker. "I watched her start out as a rather, uh, superior little girl, protecting herself against the rest of us who were more experienced, thinking of us all as hostile, so that she would say, 'Good morning, Deac,' and I didn't believe it. And then I saw her gradually acquire confidence and begin to come out and be more open, not only as an actress, but as a person."

Tinker was by then employed by NBC, where he helped to develop shows such as *Dr. Kildare*, starring Richard Chamberlain, Mary's future Broadway co-star of *Breakfast at Tiffany's*; and *The Man from U.N.C.L.E.*, featuring Robert Vaughn, who had guest-starred on the *Van Dyke Show*, which now registered as one of the Top 15 TV series on the air.

If only Mary's first marriage had been as successful. In a conversation with the *New York Times*, Mary said she and Meeker "didn't grow together. I obviously didn't know what I wanted when I was 17. I'm sad if I made my husband unhappy by leaving, but life is too short not to live it fully."

But she never regretted those years with Meeker. "I can't," she said. "I have Richie," with whom she then claimed to have a "very, very" close relationship.

In retrospect, Mary blamed herself for the collapse of the marriage. Years later she told Barbara Walters, "I thought that it was right, and that it was going to work. And it did. It worked for six years...and then it didn't. And I always hate to hear people say, 'Well, and you know...our marriage failed,' because I think even if a marriage worked for four years, five years...if you're happy during that time, that's not a time of failure. That's a time of growth and satisfaction and having given and taken from one another. And that's good."

On September 30, 1962, the *Van Dyke* sitcom commenced its second season. In his phone interview with Mary for the *Akron Beacon Journal*, reporter Jack Major said she sounded "...less like sultry Sam [her *Richard Diamond* character], and more like the young housewife who might be living next door." Mary acknowledged how her TV and real-life offspring shared the same first name, if with a slightly different spelling. The *reel* Ritchie, played by Larry Mathews, spelled his name with a "t" in the middle, and Mary claimed she "had nothing to do with the choice of names." Mary would often read her scripts aloud when at home, which occasionally confused her son.

"Mommy," Richie, without the "t," would wonder, "...why did you call me?"

In the midst of it all, Mathews, with only one "t" in his last name, had befriended the *real* Richie, who was two years his junior. "I knew Richie. We got along great. There were no issues between us. We were buds. We ran around the set and played, and had a good time. But he was sent to boarding schools a lot. He wasn't around his parents that much, meaning Mary and Tinker, even though the latter wasn't his biological father. They were both very busy in their careers, and he had some issues with 'attention,' which he craved from others, but didn't receive from Mary," Mathews remembered.

Mary later confirmed as much, revealing she felt more like a mother to Mathews than to Richie, born when she was just 18, one year into her first marriage. By the time Richie was 3, she was working consistently on television and, when he turned 6, his parents divorced. Six months later, she married Grant Tinker with his four children from a previous marriage. Both adults had bustling schedules and little time for parenting. Mary demanded much from Richie, and later accepted responsibility for his alienation. There was no question that she had let him down. When he needed her the most, she was busier and even more self-concerned than she had been when he was as she defined him "an impressionable infant."

Mary would eventually lose that child, tragically, when Richie became an adult; when she would experience the unthinkable hardship that no parent should endure. But for the moment, and in many ways, Mary was little more than a child herself. She was married and pregnant before turning 19; she modeled for those obscure Latin music album covers; danced in those TV commercials as a tiny imp; and landed small roles as a vixen or the girl next door. She may have never won the role of Danny Thomas' young daughter because her nose was too small, but she eventually become Dick Van Dyke's

TV wife, and matured right before our eyes, even though she was first thought too young to play Laura.

But nearly twenty years later, in 1980, director Robert Redford would deem her perfect for the part of the cold-hearted Beth Jarrett, whose son attempts suicide in the feature film *Ordinary People*. That's when Mary delivered another breakout performance which earned her accolades. The Oscar nomination came for a movie released shortly before Richie, at just 24, accidentally killed himself with a sawed-off shotgun. Other tragedies echoed the film's depiction of loss. Mary had lost her younger sister Elizabeth in 1978, at age 21, from a drug overdose. Then came 1986, and the death of Mary's brother John, a recovering alcoholic who lost his battle with kidney cancer at age 47. This followed John's attempted suicide to alleviate the pain, with Mary by his side, assisting in the process.

The trauma of having an alcoholic mother, a demanding and distant father, and her childhood sexual abuse were just a few of the complexities and ambiguities that infiltrated Mary's life.

Chapter

4

Mary's frustration with motherhood was not her only issue while making *The Dick Van Dyke Show*. In his *The Official Dick Van Dyke Show Book*, Vince Waldron addresses her grievance surrounding the episode, "Never Bathe on Saturday" (March 31, 1965). It's a segment that became one of the sitcom's most popular. But it was also one of the show's most notorious adventures during its development. Even legendary TV producer Norman Lear called the episode "one of the funniest things" he had ever seen.

The plot is rife with physical humor: While on their honeymoon, Laura manages to get her toe stuck in a hotel bathtub faucet, and Rob struggles to get past the locked bathroom door to rescue her. Actor/writer Bill Idelson, who had played Sally Rogers' boyfriend Herman Glimsher, was this time cast as a bellman. As he recalled to Waldron, Mary walked out in the middle of the episode's rehearsal. "She didn't want to do the show because she said the camera was never on her."

It was now Carl Reiner's turn to become frustrated. In fact, the only time he lost his temper on *The Dick Van Dyke Show* was during "Never Bathe on Saturday." But according to Mary, Reiner had only himself to blame. Before filming for "Saturday" began, he had frequently promised her that an upcoming episode would focus on Laura. Although Confucius may have once said, "Lose expectation; gain everything," Mary must have never encountered that spiritual advice. She had nothing but high expectations of the episode – until she read the script, in which Laura spends most of her time in the tub, virtually unseen.

That meant Mary would be off-camera for a good portion of the episode. All the other characters were talking about Laura, but Mary lacked any on-screen scenes. This soured her perception of any comedy in the situation.

But as the ever-diplomatic Dick Van Dyke related to Waldron, the teleplay wasn't the only culprit for her sour mood; it was Mary's choice for a healthier lifestyle. She was trying to quit smoking the same week she learned about the "Saturday" script. Van Dyke had never seen her complain about anything before, and blamed her un-sweet disposition on nicotine withdrawal. "I watched her get a little paler each day, and the circles under her eyes got a little deeper," he said. "The poor girl was beside herself. She was a nervous wreck. Everything upset her."

Mary admitted, "I was snapping and snarling at everyone all week," including Reiner. The two ended up not speaking for days, she said, "which was rather impudent of a little twenty-something-year-old novice comedian."

But they eventually made up, and Mary retained her high hopes for the future. "Someday," she said, "I'd like to be a big star."

Rose Marie, another player in the *Van Dyke* fold, was having none of these excuses. Marie and Mary barely spoke on the set. "I was jealous," Marie once told *Mary Magazine* editor David Davis. "She was younger than I was, prettier and had a better figure. All the guys had crushes on her, including Dick."

From his then-child's perspective, Larry Mathews never noticed disagreements between the actors playing his parents. "Rose and I later had candid conversations about it," he said. "She was an accomplished star, and felt that Mary was the new girl on the block, and the last to be hired. And Rose wanted a bigger presence on the show, which was really about Rob and Laura. So, she struggled with that a little bit." He remembered Marie approaching Reiner, who told her, "Rose…if you can't accept the fact that Mary is the star of the show, then you need to leave, and that's the way it is." Reiner reiterated that statement over 50 years later in Marie's acclaimed feature documentary, *Wait for Your Laugh*, in which he referred to Mary's graceful legs, initially resplendent on *Richard Diamond*, and utilized to their full extent on *Van Dyke*. Mathews continued, "Rose came to grips with it all, and things lightened up between she and Mary in the later years of the series."

Conversely, Mary's relationship with Ann Morgan Guilbert, the only other female regular on the *Van Dyke* series, was never hostile. They would hang out on the set and play board games such as Perquackey. "I really liked Ann a lot," Mary said. "We were the Scrabble champions. We'd always try to get the cast and crew to join us."

Guilbert would find sitcom fame again in the 1990s on *The Nanny*, where she played Fran Drescher's Grandma Yetta Rosenberg. On both

Nanny and *Van Dyke*, Guilbert had supporting but revered roles. Off-screen, she played another significant role; that of a wife and mother, twice married.

While appearing on *Van Dyke*, Guilbert was wed to writer/producer George Eckstein, who worked on TV drama series like *The Untouchables* and *The Fugitive*, which starred David Janssen, Mary's leading man from her first show, *Richard Diamond: Private Detective*. Eckstein had also been good friends with Jerry Paris, who had suggested Guilbert for the role of his TV wife on *Van Dyke*. With Eckstein she had two daughters, Hallie and Nora. One year after *Van Dyke* ended, Guilbert and Eckstein divorced. In 1967 she married character actor Guy Raymond, who had guest-starred on *Van Dyke* (in "A Farewell to Writing," September 22, 1965).

During the first season of *The Dick Van Dyke Show*, Guilbert was pregnant with Hallie, who would follow in her mother's acting footsteps, later appearing on Disney shows like *Lizzie McGuire*. Nora, the older of the two, also became an actress, and later a manager for young actors. In 1979, Nora co-founded with Diane Hill the Harden Young Actors Space, a performance-arts academy for young, working, and aspiring actors in Los Angeles.

In her youth, Nora was a frequent visitor to the *Van Dyke* set, where she and Larry Mathews would play together on the structural foundation under the studio-audience bleachers. "We'd climb on them like monkey bars," she recalled. "And we would sneak over to the *Make Room for Daddy* set, too."

It was on the *Van Dyke Show* premises that Eckstein had observed her mother's interaction with Mary. "They got along great," she said. "But they didn't have much of a relationship outside of the show, except for every once in a while they'd go shopping on their lunch hour. Mary was usually taking a dance class, or she would have somebody come to the set and do ballet with her. So, she and my Mom didn't socialize too much other than once and a while when there was a party."

According to Eckstein, "Everyone thinks my mother was in every episode of *The Dick Van Dyke Show*." But in actuality, Guilbert only appeared in 61 of the 158 segments. "My mother felt like she didn't have much to do. But over time she realized that she was an iconic part of the show and came to appreciate that."

Some of Guilbert's most memorable episodes featured key scenes with Mary and others, including: "Too Many Stars" (October 10, 1963), in which Guilbert's Millie performs an hilarious self-composed love song; "The Ballad of the Betty Lou" (November 27, 1963), in which Laura and Millie bond while Rob and Jerry are allegedly lost at sea; "Your Home Sweet Home Is My Home" (March 17, 1965), based on a true story, where the Petries and the Helpers quarrel over the purchase of two new homes (one of which has a rock in the basement); and "Long Night's Journey into Day" (May 11, 1966), when Laura and Millie bond once again when they spend a spooky night alone in the Petrie home.

"Long Night's Journey" was "probably my mother's biggest episode," said Nora Eckstein. So much that George Eckstein convinced his wife to take out a full-page ad in *Variety* promoting the segment. But news coverage of a NASA Gemini mission postponed the episode's airing. "It was such a disappointment for my mother," Nora recalled. "The ad featured such a cute picture of Mary and my mother with a little quiz about them."

In light of Mary's good working relationship with Guilbert, her conflict with Rose Marie, and the show's solid reviews, *Van Dyke* was lucky to survive its first season. "Frankly," Mary disclosed at one point, "…our show didn't do well at all with the ratings last season. We feel many people who watched us during the summer were watching us for the first time." She was hopeful to pull viewers away from competition like NBC's *The Perry Como Show*.

Van Dyke aired at 9:30 PM, midway and opposite *Como*, and ABC's adventure show *Hawaiian Eye*. *Van Dyke's* faltering first-season ratings were due to the poor lead-in from *Checkmate*, a drama starring Sebastian Cabot (later of *Family Affair*). Later, everyone was excited about the new sitcom, *The Beverly Hillbillies*, scheduled as *Van Dyke's* lead-in the following semester. Said Mary, "If *Hillbillies* does as well as expected we should do a lot better than last year. Our show was renewed only through the generosity of our sponsors, Proctor & Gamble, who had faith in us. We won't be doing anything different this season. We felt we had a good show last year."

The Dick Van Dyke Show shot on a five-day schedule, with the first reading taking place on Wednesday morning, followed by camera blocking on Thursday and Friday, and further rehearsal on Monday and Tuesday, with the show going before the live audience on Tuesday night. The audience reaction may well have been tweaked for balance with a laugh track. This was standard procedure of the day, sweetened or otherwise augmented in some cases, but according to *Van Dyke Show* historian Vince Waldron, Carl Reiner "prided himself on using actual audience laughter on his finished cut as much as humanly possible.

"Even as early as his one-camera pilot for *Head of the Family*, Carl insisted that the laugh track be a legitimate recording of an invited audience actually watching the finished film of his show. In later years, he bragged about loaning out tapes of laughter that was captured on his show to other producers to use as sweetener on their shows. Anecdotally, he also cited the frequent appearance of his friend (and later *DVDS* guest star) Barbara Bain as an audience member at his show, and what a great laugher she was.

According to Carl, you could easily pick out Barbara Bain's laughter on any number of episodes of his show to this day."

In either case, as Mary once explained while working on the *Van Dyke Show*, "If I blow a line, "the director will explain it to the audience. Sometimes, I'll fluff two or three times. Then, when I get it correct, the audience will applaud. The home viewers wouldn't know what the applause is all about, so the sound track has to be altered."

Such was the case with "Hustling the Hustler" (October 24, 1962), which featured guest Phil Leeds as Blackie Sorrell, pool-shark brother of Amsterdam's Buddy. In one sequence Van Dyke as Rob is supposed to make a difficult pool shot, coordinated by the crew off-stage. But with every attempt, he missed. In the aired version, the audience roars after the shot. "That scene wasn't supposed to evoke so much laughter," Mary explained, "...so again, the sound track was altered. Besides, it has been proven the home audience doesn't laugh as loud as the live audience, so we subtract laughter rather than add it."

Her tech savvy and industry knowledge was increasing. Working on *Van Dyke* helped her, as journalist Jack Major put it, "...immeasurably as an actress," with regard to more work, even on the big screen. But she also was realistic. "Right now," she acknowledged, "...a company would probably lose money if they starred me in a picture. I'm just not that well-known. Another thing...it's very difficult to get a part in movies in Hollywood. The companies are filming so many of their pictures in other locations."

The previous summer Van Dyke, the actor, reprised his Albert F. Peterson Broadway lead character for the big-screen adaptation of *Bye Bye Birdie*. It was one of the few movies completed on a California studio lot, and Van Dyke's first following a few TV appearances beyond *Van Dyke*, the TV show. Although Mary was none too pleased with the term "housewife," on screen or off, when it came to portraying Laura, Joanne Stang of the *New York Times* wrote, "Miss Moore has made housewifery a highly palatable pastime...She is neither drudge nor harpy and while pert, not 'cute' enough to make one gag."

Mary ignited a new fashion statement with her signature slim-fitting tight slacks and flat footwear. While other wives of the small screen wore billowing dresses and pearls, Mary's Laura adorned the Capri pants in the family. Doing so at first "caused a stir at the network," she said, but when the *Van Dyke Show* became a hit, her leggings were no longer an issue. "Wearing pants is what I do in real life," she told *Variety*. "It's what my friends do in real life and that's being a realistic wife who wears pants and does not care how she looks...I wanted to portray a housewife wearing clothing that *I* wore in my kitchen. The sponsors became worried that women might see it as being too avant-garde."

Carl Reiner came to her defense: "Women today are not wearing full-skirted frocks with high heels as they vacuum the rug."

A compromise was struck: Laura would wear slacks in one scene for each episode. Mary recalled, "We went along with that for half a season, then we gave them the raspberry and did what we wanted to do."

Females across America joined Laura Petrie in tossing their housedresses and putting on trim trousers. According to *Time* magazine, Mary "could beat the pants off any dozen TV actresses" with her talent, and not just her wardrobe. Joanne Stang of the *New York Times* chimed in: "The ladies are grateful to find one of the sorority portrayed with ginger, and they sense – quite accurately – that anyone who seems so nice must really be so."

Although Mary was now a contender in the television actress category of any competition, she still was not fully confident of her abilities. One week before receiving her first Emmy for Best Actress in a Television Comedy Series in 1962, for Laura Petrie, she gave props to the competition: the actress who played Granny on *The Beverly Hillbillies*. "I'd bet on Irene Ryan," she said.

In turn, Ryan felt Mary was "a lead-pipe cinch to win," as she told journalist Jack Major in a tone he described as "three parts resignation with one part bitterness." Ryan thought her show was shunned by the industry. "The *Hillbillies* may be number one in the ratings," Major wrote, "…but Hollywood gives it about as much respect as Northern liberals give Alabama governor George Wallace."

An award or accolade is always a plus for any actor, singer, dancer, writer, director, or producer, but it does not automatically seal that artist's success. Critics argued that Mary had not yet proven herself beyond portraying Laura. She might as well be playing herself. Major suggested comparisons which seemed significantly eerie: Not only did Mary and Laura each have a similar-aged son with the same name, but "they" were married to behind-the-scenes show-business people. Laura's husband Rob was a TV comedy writer; Mary's new husband Grant Tinker would soon upgrade his behind-the-scenes TV status to Vice President for NBC.

Before any of that transpired, Tinker championed Mary on *The Dick Van Dyke Show*, which he essentially single-handedly saved from being cancelled after its first low-rated season. Tinker wanted to ensure that Mary would have a starring vehicle. Through this, the *Van Dyke* series became a success by proxy.

But as author Marc Shapiro suggests in his book *You're Gonna Make It After All*, the *Van Dyke Show*'s rescue from "ratings oblivion depends on which story you believed." Apparently, Proctor & Gamble was so enamored with the sitcom they threatened to remove any and all of their advertising from CBS's daytime schedule if the network did not retain the series. Other versions of the story were reported by the *New York Post* and additional media outlets. These accounts said that Reiner and Leonard had pleaded with Proctor & Gamble not to cancel the series. At that point, the ad firm allegedly consented to fund half the show while Kent Cigarettes would cover the remaining amount.

In the midst of all the negotiations, Tinker was tinkering for Mary. He loved her and believed in her. He wanted her to be a star as much as she wanted it. Proctor & Gamble in the end invested in the series, while CBS scheduled the show to follow their monster hit *The Beverly Hillbillies*. Unsurprisingly, the *Van Dyke Show* ratings soared for its remaining four years on the air.

By *Van Dyke's* fourth season, Mary had branched out from playing Laura Petrie, with guest appearances on variety programs like *The Andy Williams Show* and *The Danny Kaye Show*. Such programs provided platforms for dance, her first love. She never claimed to have much singing talent, but she had that "spunk" – and she knew how to use it. For example, the actress stuck to her guns during a dispute with producers of *The Ed Sullivan Show*, the granddaddy of all variety shows, on which she was scheduled to perform. She accepted an invitation from *Sullivan*'s camp on condition that she could pre-record the vocals for the song she planned to perform with her dance number. But upon arrival in New York to do the show, she was told that guests were not allowed to pre-record musical numbers.

In response, she returned to California without the not-insignificant *Sullivan* credit, and began planning more appearances on the *Kaye* and *Williams* programs. "But first we have to work out a sponsor conflict," she said. This was a fairly common occurrence in the early days of television, when sponsors controlled shows and often dictated content.

She still hoped for movie stardom, especially in Doris-Day-like comedies, even though her biggest fear remained "…being forever typed as Laura Petrie." It was an issue that hearkened back to her days as Sam on *Richard Diamond*, which by now was in syndication. Mary received residuals of just $15.00 per episode per airing for this series, on which she was heard and not seen. "Which goes to show not every performer gets rich from residuals," she joked.

By this time too, *Diamond* sometimes bore the title *Call Mr. D*. This reflected the practice of changing show titles for syndication, as when ABC's future *Happy Days* became *Happy Days Again* in first-year syndication, and when *Laverne & Shirley* later morphed into *Laverne & Shirley & Company* (both of which were created by *Van Dyke* writer Garry Marshall, while many *Days* episodes were helmed by *Van Dyke* actor and director Jerry Paris).

Before meeting Mary himself, critic Jack Major envisioned her as "Snow White, with jet black hair and a fair complexion," and was startled when she joined him for lunch one afternoon with her naturally brown hair and skin with freckles. Her voice was different, too. It lacked that "whiny quality" that he often heard from Laura. That morning, she had been house-hunting in Beverly Hills and was happy for the lunch break. "We're getting an addition to our family," she told Major. "My husband's 13-year-old son is coming to live with us." That was a reference to one of Tinker's four children from a previous marriage.

Mary and the *Van Dyke* cast never felt stifled creatively, a development she attributed to series creator Carl Reiner. "He's a genius," Mary said. "Carl comes up with a lot of unlikely comedy ideas, but he always makes them funny. I trust him so much that if he were to have me get a divorce on the show and run off with a traveling salesman, I'd say, 'Great idea!' because I know somehow he'd make it amusing."

Van Dyke proved to be one of TV's first sitcoms for grown-ups and, as author Ronald L. Smith remarks in his book *Sweethearts of '60s TV*, kids were watching too. If young girls perceived themselves as one day becoming housewives, Laura Petrie was the one they idolized. She was pretty, had personality, a dancer's elegance, and she fixed her hair like Jackie Kennedy (perfectly matched to Van Dyke's dashing JFK-like design). Young boys envied Larry Mathews' little Ritchie, who got to have weekly hugs with his TV mommy, while their teenage counterparts dreamt about being married to the only small-screen housewife with unabashed sex appeal.

Donna Reed never wore Capri slacks on *her* sitcom. Barbara Billingsley's June Cleaver vacuumed with style, in pearls, on *Leave it to Beaver*. Elizabeth Montgomery on *Bewitched* charmed viewers as Samantha Stephens with her magical wiggling nose. But it was Mary's Laura Petrie who became the closest thing '60s television had to a realistic wife and mother.

According to Michael Hill of *The Baltimore Evening Sun*, unlike Cleaver, Reed, or Jane Wyatt's Margaret Anderson on *Father Knows Best*, "Laura was more of a whole human being…She wasn't just there to react, to support her husband. She had her problems, and they were dealt with in the context of the show."

Mary sought to present Laura as "a woman who had her own points of view and who would fight with her husband – a good fight, if necessary. She wasn't a 'yes' wife, nor did she focus everything on him. But that's about as liberated as Laura Petrie was. I think she truly believed that her only choice was to be a wife and mother and couldn't combine that with a career."

Laura worked outside the household only three times on the series, in the episodes "To Tell or Not To Tell" (November 14, 1961); "My Part-Time Wife" (February 26, 1964); and "See Rob Write; Write, Rob, Write" (December 8, 1965). In "Tell," issues arise when Mel requests that Laura dance on *The Alan Brady Show*. In "Wife," Laura steps in to help Rob at the office when Sally is away. And in "Write," Rob and Laura battle over who is the better author of a children's story.

In each case, Laura ultimately concedes to Rob in some way, and remains content with her position as a home engineer. The only time she Laura appears overtly in control is in the episode, "It May Look Like a Walnut" (February 6, 1963). But most of this segment is played out as a dream sequence or like an episode of *The Twilight Zone*, to which it playfully refers. Rob envisions Earth conquered by walnut-eating aliens from the planet Twilo, headed by Danny Thomas who supervises other-worldly editions of Buddy, Sally, Mel, and Laura. The aliens, besides loving walnuts, have another set of eyes on the back of their head, allowing them "20/20/20/20 vision."

In the scene-stealing moment of the entire episode, an assertive Laura glides effortlessly from the Petrie's home entryway closet on a mound of walnuts. But it's not really Laura who appears fearless and self-assured; it's the Alien-Laura – in Rob's nightmare.

Such an episode is a direct juxtaposition to "The Curious Thing About Women" (January 10, 1962), in which Rob becomes annoyed with Laura frequently opening and reading his mail. Ultimately finding humor in the situation, Rob is inspired to write a sketch for *The Alan Brady Show*. In the skit, Alan plays a husband whose wife's curiosity gets the best of her when she opens a mysterious package that contains a self-inflating raft. Rob eventually gets the last laugh, ordering the same kind of raft to be delivered to the Petrie home. But Laura is furious and embarrassed when her curiosity is mocked on Brady's nationwide TV show. She's mortified at her depiction as a "pathological snoopy-nose."

A more public embarrassment takes place in the episode "Coast to Coast Big Mouth" (September 15, 1965). Laura appears on a TV game show and inadvertently reveals to millions of viewers that in reality, Alan Brady is bald.

While Rob frequently is made to look foolish in mostly every episode of *The Dick Van Dyke Show* – let's face it, it *is* a half-hour sitcom played for laughs – he's still the presiding figure in the Petrie household. Rob and Laura are not presented as equals.

But despite such constraints of the era, as Ronald L. Smith wrote, Laura was legitimate and emotional, not "sitcom silly. She was sitcom conservative but impish, which certainly could have described her Happy Hotpoint commercial character from just a few years before. She was a content housewife and mom but she can purr, 'I'm a woman,' as she sauntered into the bedroom (which she does in the show's pilot episode). Laura left no doubt that she and Rob were having fun in the sack, even if they have to push those long-distance twin beds together to make it happen for five hit seasons."

Carl Reiner himself later dished to *TV Guide* about the Petries' sex life, describing them as "…two people who really liked each other." Interviewed for the same article, Mary agreed: "We brought romance to comedy, and yes, Rob and Laura had sex!"

Chapter

5

Mary eventually admitted that she and fellow *Dick Van Dyke* colleagues had a nickname for their leading man: "Penis Von Lesbian." But that was a remark uttered during a humorous, if somewhat off-color and now politically incorrect talk-show appearance with David Letterman – who had worked on one of her failed weekly post-*Mary Tyler Moore* TV variety-show ventures. Although no real-life romantic interchange between Mary and Dick ever transpired, they eventually acknowledged an innocent mutual attraction on the job as Laura and Rob. While neither acted on the instinct, it was there nonetheless, as both discussed on talk shows with Rachael Ray and Larry King.

Van Dyke often praised Mary's abilities as a comedic actress. He credited her with turning crying into an art form. Examples were *Van Dyke's* "My Blonde-Haired Brunette" episode, or when Laura got her toe stuck in a hotel bathtub faucet in that uncomfortable-for-Mary segment, "Never Bathe on Saturday." During one interview, Van Dyke called Mary "one of the few who could maintain her femininity and be funny at the same time. You have to go as far back as Carole Lombard or Myrna Loy to find someone who could play it that well and still be tremendously appealing as a woman."

Mary kept hidden her troubled personal life behind the *Van Dyke* scenes. She eventually confessed in *After All* that, while playing Laura, she drank heavily, and smoked three packs of cigarettes a day. They weren't even Kents, though the sponsor regularly distributed free cartons of its product to the cast and crew. Mary did not like Kents; she took her share of free cartons and traded them at a local store for the brand she preferred.

Throughout her tenure as Laura, she was excited about her career, but felt empty at home. She may have been happily married to Grant Tinker, but her son Richie began having trouble in school and spending more time with his maternal grandmother than his mother, just as Mary had ended up with her grandmother and Aunt Bertie. Mary was the perfect wife and mom on-screen, but it was quite a different scene away from the camera. Her pratfalls and wedded TV bliss on *Van Dyke* paled in comparison to her many worries and wobbles in reality.

"There is no question about it," she wrote in *After All*. By the time Richie was 5 years old, Mary had already disappointed him. When he needed her the most, she was busier and even more self-involved.

Mary eventually felt a similar emptiness with the handsome, witty, educated, and older Tinker, to whom she referred in retrospect as "a power seat." That's not a misnomer. Tinker had swiftly moved up in the executive ranks. When he met Mary, Tinker was an executive for Benton & Bowles, the advertising agency that represented *Van Dyke's* sponsor. Then he became a vice president for NBC and, post-*Van Dyke*, her business partner in the massively successful MTM Enterprises. After that, Tinker returned to NBC and forged ahead to the network's top, when it was owned by GE.

Forget that Mary's father once worked for the electric company, and that Tinker was now heading General Electric. That far-reaching irony was nothing in view of Mary's brazened acknowledgement in her memoir that Tinker's attraction for her lay in the insecure, career-obsessed young actress's "daddy fixation." With stars in her young eyes, as Mary noted in *After All*, she envisioned her and Tinker as "television's golden couple," which they eventually became, with an expanded blended family.

Tinker was pleased to have Mary's son in his life, and Richie was relatively open to melding into a new family. But as she pointed out in her book, Tinker was a taskmaster. He expected as much from his and her offspring, as he demanded from himself. He left little wiggle room for failure. Unfortunately, Richie almost always fell short of those expectations. While he adored Tinker and saw him as a fair and compassionate parent, Mary wished she herself had displayed that type of kindness to her only son, the way Laura cared for and counseled Ritchie on *Van Dyke*.

"Mary was always wonderful to me," said Larry Mathews of working with her on *Van Dyke*. Renewed for a never-produced sixth season, it most likely would have gone to color. "But Carl Reiner wanted to keep it in black-and-white, and we stopped filming because Dick went on to do movies. *That's* why we left the air. We were renewed. No question about it. [It's just that] in between seasons, Dick did movies like *Mary Poppins* and *Chitty Chitty Bang Bang* and Disney made him a big offer do more films. So he decided to do movies full time, and didn't have the time to do the TV series full time. We were all sad when the show ended, because we wanted to continue doing it, and because we all had such a great time. But everyone respected Dick's wishes, because he was *the man*!"

That is indeed one way of looking at it. But according to what Grant Tinker told Rick Lertzman, author of *The Star Makers*, an upcoming new book on the advertising agency, there was another reason. Apparently, *The Dick Van Dyke Show* ended because of Mary. She was the one who was not interested in continuing with the series, and wanted to focus on film. Van Dyke was all set to stay with the show, while simultaneously making movies. And it was Tinker all along who was responsible for ensuring Mary's place as a centerpiece of *The Dick Van Dyke Show.*

"Mary, like a lot of actresses and actors in Hollywood, was helped by other people," Lertzman said. And one of those people was Tinker, then working for Benton & Bowles which was founded by William Benton and Chester Bowles in 1929. The company later merged with D'Arcy-MacManus Masius in 1985 to form D'Arcy Masius Benton & Bowles, which later merged with Leo Burnett Worldwide to form BCOM3 which was subsequently obtained by Publicis Media, marking the demise of the Benton & Bowles brand.

But in the 1960s, the era of *The Dick Van Dyke Show*, Benton & Bowles was a leading agency which, like many other ad firms, was headed by *Mad Men*-type executives like Tinker. When Tinker fell head-over-heels for Mary, some eyes rolled, and a few tables turned in her favor. "Mary was talented, and had accomplished a lot by the time she was hired for *The Dick Van Dyke Show*," said Lertzman. "But Grant took her to an entirely different level. He had been an executive at NBC, and then one of the leaders at Benton & Bowles, which focused on sitcoms. Grant had sat in on the filming of sitcoms like *The Danny Thomas Show*, and *The Andy Griffith Show*. So he had a real understanding of television and what worked on television, and what worked for Benton & Bowles, which represented major brands like Palmolive. So, the agency carried a lot of weight."

Tinker's rallying for Mary began mostly after *Van Dyke's* first season when, one day, he accompanied Carl Reiner, Danny Thomas, and Sheldon Leonard to Cincinnati, where Proctor & Gamble's headquarters were located. "They were there to fight to keep *The Dick Van Dyke Show* on the air," Lertzman said. And they had some solid ammunition. Following its less-than-stellar performance in the regular first season, *The Dick Van Dyke Show* had proven itself in summer rerun ratings. It was ultimately renewed for its second season, partially because of Tinker's support. By then, Mary had divorced Richard Meeker and married Tinker, whose main focus was now ensuring his wife's success by demanding she receive increased screen time on *Van Dyke*.

According to Lertzman, Tinker was "one of the ivy league fair-haired boys at Benton & Bowles whose relationship with Mary was definitely romantic from his point of view. But on Mary's part, it was a combination of romance and business. She was attracted by the power of Grant Tinker. And what very few people realize is that a television series never really succeeds without the advertising person who stands behind it, especially in the days of *The Dick Van Dyke Show*." Ad men like Tinker shaped a show and "basically helped it reach the audience that they were attempting to reach. As a result, scripts would be changed. References would be changed; even characters could be changed based on the feedback acquired by and instituted by advertising agencies."

Tinker and network executives such as CBS's Jim Aubrey relied heavily on a *Q-quotient*, a measurement of the familiarity and appeal of a brand, celebrity, company, or entertainment product (like a television show). The system was primarily utilized by advertising, marketing, media, and public-relations companies The higher the *Q Score*, the more highly regarded the item or individual is, among those who are aware of the subject. "And Mary's Q-quotient was high," said Lertzman, "and Grant had a bias because he was in love with her. So, he used her Q-quotient with Carl Reiner, Danny Thomas, and Sheldon Leonard to force an enlargement of her role on *The Dick Van Dyke Show*."

Van Dyke's Rob Petrie was the main focus of the series, with Mary just as an accoutrement. "But Grant really wanted the show to focus more on Mary's comedic skills," said Lertzman, "...much to the chagrin of Rose Marie who resented Mary. They did not have a very close but a very bitter relationship. When Rose was hired for the show with Morey Amsterdam, she envisioned herself, and not Mary, as playing second lead to Dick Van Dyke. That's how her name was billed in the opening credits [while Mary's name would appear last]. Because of her years in the business, Rosie felt that the show's producers would rely on her as the female comedic centerpiece."

When Tinker came aboard with his Q-score statistics, Lertzman said, "...he made it very clear that it was Mary was who was attracting viewers. A lot of housewives loved what Mary was wearing. And of course Dick remained the centerpiece but the *home* aspect of the show was pushed more because of Mary." According to Lertzman, "It May Look Like a Walnut" was based on an idea generated by Tinker. "Grant believed it was Mary who would make *The Dick Van Dyke Show* more successful," and Tinker was proven correct.

The Dick Van Dyke Show initially began airing in an early-evening Tuesday time slot in October 1961, and only moved to its more familiar later Wednesday-night perch in the middle of its first season, on January 7,

1962. "For the record," Vince Waldron said, "the move to the more prominent time slot had little to no effect on the ratings, which would not begin to catch on in any significant way until the series was programmed following *The Beverly Hillbillies* at the start of Season Two, when it rode the country show's enormous popularity right into the Nielsen Top Ten."

According to Rick Lertzman, "Grant Tinker was a mastermind at audience research, reading ratings, and Q-quotients. He screened a lot of the episodes for customer response groups."

As *The Dick Van Dyke Show* entered its fifth season, Tinker was convinced he could make Mary an even bigger star. He set his sights on film and on Broadway, which he believed would enhance her acting ability. "So, Grant kind of pushed her out of *The Dick Van Dyke Show* when their contracts were up," Lertzman said. "Dick was on the border. He would have stayed with the show. Rose Marie had just gone through the death of her husband, and wanted to keep on working, and the rest of the cast would have stayed with the show. But Grant saw that Mary could be a major star and wanted to make sure that happened." It was just too bad that "making that happen" required Mary to exit her role as Laura Petrie.

Tinker, like Joe Hamilton, Carol Burnett's husband, business partner, and her TV show's producer and director, was "an innovator," Lertzman said. "People like them understood the advertising process, and how the advertising industry controls television, which is why *Roseanne* is now dead [following Twitter attacks by that show's star on Valerie Jarrett, Chelsea Clinton, and George Soros]. She's poison to advertisers and she'll never get back on commercial television."

In contrast to Roseanne Barr's vulgarity, Mary proved alluring to home viewers. According to Bill Persky, the fate of *The Dick Van Dyke Show* had always rested in the hands of Carl Reiner. "I don't know about any of those other facts. I do know that Carl Reiner did not want to do another year, and did not want to repeat [story-wise] what they had already accomplished. I don't know if there was a specific renewal but I know that they would have renewed it, and Carl probably said *no* before they said anything. And that he did not want to continue with the show, and Dick did not want to continue with the show, and Mary did not want to continue with the show." But ultimately, "…it was really Carl's decision to end the series."

Either way, Mary was seen as Laura Petrie for the last time in the first-run CBS screening of "The Final Chapter," the *Van Dyke Show's* closing episode, which aired June 1, 1966. The plot was apropos: After five years, Rob finally completes his first book, which Laura reads and discovers is the story of their life. Alan Brady later purchases the rights and adapts the book as a new TV show in which he will star. The recursive storyline curls back towards Reiner's original *Head of the Family* concept.

For Mary, it was important to portray Laura as truthfully as possible. No matter what was going on in her personal life, if she played the role honestly in the moment, she was safe. And that didn't mean Mary wasn't willing to take chances, but rather, she was "right on the mark." If she didn't receive an anticipated laugh, she felt it was probably due to the audience paying too much attention to the character and her relationship with the other characters; it was "meant to be that way."

Mary called the *Van Dyke* years a "college of comedy...a real baptismal [sic] by fire." Her co-stars and co-workers made it easy, especially Reiner, "the professor" who allowed her creative growth and freedom according to her capabilities. The show provided "a protected environment," in which she grew, observed, and became "the recipient of Dick Van Dyke's generosity." Corroborating Rick Lertzman's assessment, Mary said Van Dyke "was never threatened by me or anybody, and therefore allowed me to have my moments. It was a great experience."

Another time, decades after her tenure as Laura ended, she said, "We all agreed it would be best to move on and take advantage of the wonderful success that we were enjoying. But we didn't want to. It was a family, as true, real and palpable as a blood relationship."

In the spring of 1966, Mary appeared on *The David Susskind Show* to address the *Van Dyke* transition, as well as her relocation with Grant Tinker to New York, which she did not initially embrace. "I just hate it," she told Susskind who, surprised by her words, in turn wondered if she was "looking for controversy?"

This was typical Susskind; he sought ratings through notoriety. Mary's appearance with him was reminiscent of the *Van Dyke* episode, "Ray Murdock's X-Ray" (January 23, 1963). In that episode, Rob is placed on the spot by an infamously incendiary talk-show host. Rob's worst fears come true as he fidgets and eventually blurts out something embarrassing.

But that *Van Dyke* segment was exaggerated comedy; Mary's appearance on *Susskind* was all too real. She initially seemed uncomfortable, unready for his typical verbal assaults. At first she carefully measured her words, but came back swinging, never losing control.

Mary addressed her relocation: "Well, I have my own ready-made controversy at home. We just moved in or rather attempted to move in to a lovely apartment that I thought would be a lovely apartment. Turns out that the housekeeper who had been on salary for three months while we were in California and whose total job it was just to see that things were dusted, and the painters got in, *vanished* the night before we arrived, having done absolutely nothing. Then all through the last three days painters and moving men have been bringing me cartons and saying, 'Where should we put this?' And I don't have a place to tell them to put it. It's been really frightening. I went to sit down on a stool today and the seat broke off and I ended up sitting on a steel rod and oh, well...I feel like I've been starring in another situation comedy though, the way things have been happening."

At this point Susskind interrupted her, referring to a *Newsweek* magazine article. In it she reportedly had no regrets about leaving *Van Dyke* because she grew weary of playing "goodie-goodie" Laura – or as Susskind phrased it, "...ordering milkshakes in public and now you can have straight scotch."

"Oh, goodness," she recoiled. "Now, you see? It probably took me two and a half hours to say that and they [encapsulated] it down to a point where I sounded really horribly shocking and dismal and kind of bitter about life. I assure you I'm not and...that I miss every one of the people on the *Van Dyke Show* desperately. They became my good friends, my only friends, really."

She defined herself as "somewhere in between" the sweet Laura and "a wild, mad swinger." Even though Laura Petrie was created by Carl Reiner, the character's attitude was very often her own. With every part she played, Mary tried to insert as much of herself and her own reactions as possible, "simply because it's easier to sustain a character week after week after week if you do it that way."

Susskind suggested she was playing an idealized edition of the American wife. He maintained that there was no such woman in real life. "Most of them are wretched nags," he said provocatively. Mary agreed that she had portrayed an idealized wife on *Van Dyke*. But, she retorted, "Some of us having the nagging personality come to the fore more often than others. But Laura Petrie broke down and cried and she used ploys to get her way and she was nasty and short-tempered and she was also sweet and soft and she was many things."

That was a fair description of many of us. Nobody is really perfect, except maybe Susskind in his own mind. He then said, "I think [Laura's] sort of a strained idealization of the American woman...but had no connection with reality. I mean, the woman that's talking all the time in the restaurant. I claim that you can walk into an average restaurant and if you have observed life enough, American female-male relationships, you can look in the restaurant and tell who's married and who's single...where the woman is just yakking like crazy and the man has a hurt, bored expression and he's chopping his food, they're real married. And where she's listening...wide-eyed and attentive. They're engaged or she hopes to get married, and that whole posture changes. They're both selling matrimony."

When Susskind finished this rant, Mary finally had her chance to speak: "I think very often when a husband and wife reach that point it's because they don't have anything to talk about really, except the surface conversation about well, what happened with the kids today and there can only be so many variations on that theme and what happened at the office. I think a wife needs to have – and oh gosh, I'll probably get in trouble saying this, but I really do think more wives should investigate the possibilities of working, because I agree with Betty Friedan and her point of view in her book, *The Feminine Mystique*, that women are or should be human beings first, women second, wives and mothers third. It should fall in that order and that if there's enough thought and effort put into this attempt it will not hurt the family, it will not hurt the work that they can function very nicely together. I'm proving it."

The challenging interview continued during this pertinently transient period of her life. With her smile in place, no matter how much Susskind tried to make her snarl, Mary subtly addressed her father's academic demand and literary influence. It foreshadowed her role as Mary Richards in the Women's Liberation Movement, and covered topics alluding to her past, present, and future:

> **Susskind**: How could a woman be wed to two forces in life? In other words, you're only half-married if you're in show business because that demands so much of your ego, so much of an investment of your energy.
>
> **Mary**: I don't think so. I think I could waste an awful lot more energy, sitting at home, having nothing to do other than just talk with the girls about what gossip they've heard or just chase after the kids instead of spending time with my son because I know we don't have as much time as most parents and children have. I make good use of that time. I don't waste it. I don't nag him. I punish him if he deserves it or I give him a good lecture, but I don't just sort of spill it. You know, I use it.
>
> **Susskind**: Don't you think working mothers, whatever their jobs, sort of short- change their children, emotionally or even just physically they're not there enough of the time? They're not together. They're not relating, you know?
>
> **Mary**: Sometimes that happens but I don't let it happen that way. I refuse to travel without my son. I refuse to be separated from my husband and I'm very blessed. I'm very lucky in that I've been able to work out a career and still hold to this belief that I must stay with my husband, I must be with my child because they happen to be more important to me than my career. It's not a sacrifice.

Susskind: What made you break the bonds of living in Hollywood, of being in television to make the big move to New York City and to the Broadway stage?

Mary: My husband was offered a position with a company. He had been working in California, a better position which would involve our moving to New York, and we discussed it at some length because both of us are sort of dyed-in-the-wool Californians. We love the backyard life and the sort of barbequing all weekend long and running around barefoot and we're not sophisticated New Yorkers by nature, so we resisted it and finally decided that we should make the sacrifice for him. It's important and it's something he wanted to do so we decided to come to New York and coincidentally, Mr. Merrick, David Merrick's office got in touch with me and asked me if I would be interested in doing his play. It worked out beautifully! I got very lucky!

Susskind: You're going to love it here. We have polluted air.

Mary: [Laughs]

Susskind: Hopelessly snarled traffic.

Mary: Yes, we have that in California, too.

Susskind: Potential race riots in our ghettos, there's a lot to look forward to. There's something happening here all the time.

Mary: We have all of that in California. I guess it's just a matter of feeling strange. I know. I just miss the good old, snarled freeways because I knew them very well [laughs]. And I'll miss being able to drive. I'll miss the privacy of being able to get into my car, dressed in leotards with just a coat thrown over my shoulders and go to a ballet class and not have to worry that people are looking at me in my strange outfits, you know. You can't do that in New York. You sort of make entrances, wherever you go.

Susskind: You miss television, now that you're off it so much, not having that thing to look forward to, the show...the new script.

Mary: I miss the consistency of that life. It uh, was uh, a very *secure* feeling for me. I, I enjoyed knowing that I would go to that same studio every day with those same, wonderfully entertaining, good, dear friends and do a show for which I would get a lot of applause at the end and I do miss that. But I'm, I'm so looking forward to the other venture that I, uh, I don't have to sit and mope about it. Do you know what I'm saying?

Susskind: You are a television star and your husband is one of the key executives in the television business. What do you think of television, honestly? Do you watch it a lot? Do you think it's good?

Mary: Yes, I do! I think particularly for what it is for the *amount* of hours that it gives you for enjoyment, either in education or of pure entertainment, it's *remarkably* good.

Susskind: What do you watch?

Mary: People never knock books, do they?

Susskind: Yes, they do.

Mary: Not really. Not on the mass, the scale that they do television and they never really criticize magazinesand their articles. They never really criticize theater, at least, not in the West. They don't.

Susskind: I'd like to just stop and knock books, right here. I think anybody, any book list that sits with *Valley of the Dolls* on top of the list is a sick, silly, stupid book list.

Mary: Well, there are a few book readers who may or may not agree with you.

Susskind: What do you watch, Mary? What shows?

Mary: Uh [laughs], I don't know. I'm not sure.

Susskind: That's interesting. You must have favorites?

Mary: No, I really don't. I like, well, I watch things like *Peyton Place*. I think the production values on that show are *fantastic*. [The studio audience applauds.] It's like watching little, miniature movies. [She turns to the

55

audience.] Are you laughing at me or with me? [The audience applauds once more.] I think it's awfully good.

Susskind: You have a morbid, sexual curiosity.

Mary: [Laughs]

Susskind: We now are going to sell some very useful, happiness producing products to you. Will you come back with us, in a moment?

[Fade to commercial.]

ACT II

Change of Habits

In 1969, Mary appeared in the feature film *Change of Habit*, released by Universal Studios. [Credit: Ronald V. Borst/Hollywood Movie Posters]

Chapter

6

By September of 1966, just four weeks after completing the film *Thoroughly Modern Millie*, Mary – with Grant Tinker by her side – was firmly planted in New York in preparation for her newest role, this time on Broadway. While Richie attended the private Trinity School in Manhattan, she starred opposite Richard Chamberlain (hot off of TV's *Dr. Kildare*) in *Breakfast at Tiffany's*, a musical rendition of 1961's big-screen romantic comedy hit starring Audrey Hepburn and George Peppard. The film was based on the 1950 novella by Truman Capote. Mary played prostitute Holly Golightly, and Chamberlain was writer Jeff Claypool.

But Tinker lacked the savvy for stage and motion pictures that he had for TV. Rick Lertzman wrote, "Television relies on advertising. Film relies on the audience, and no advertiser can ever predict the audience reaction for film. So, those things were out of Grant's wheelhouse and strengths." Mary's talent was more suited for the intimacy of television, as opposed to stage and film. "There are certain comedic actresses that were great…they could cross over. Lucille Ball was a film star before she became a television star. So, on screen she crackled. Marilyn Monroe, on screen, carried it. You were drawn to her. But Mary didn't have the kind of talent that would draw her to you on a film. She was just an actor. She didn't have what she had on the small screen. When she did plays like *Breakfast at Tiffany's*, she wasn't Audrey Hepburn. She couldn't play Holly Golightly. She didn't have that kind of range and that kind of talent. When she did movies like *What's So Bad About Feeling Good?* [1968] she couldn't carry the film. She just couldn't play against George Peppard. She was savaged by the critics. And it was a big comedown for her."

In his book, *Not Since Carrie: Forty Years of Broadway Musical Flops*, Ken Mandelbaum explored in-depth the core issues of Mary's stage version of *Breakfast at Tiffany's*. Among other things, the character of Chamberlain's Claypool was the theatrical incarnation of Truman Capote, the man who created him:

> Capote set his book in the forties and made it a flashback narrated by an unnamed writer, obviously Capote himself, who is fascinated by his eccentric neighbor Holly Golightly but who has no romantic relationship with her. In the movie version, reset to the present, writer Paul falls in love with Holly, the attraction complicated by a newly invented affair between Paul and a rich, married older woman. The film was also given a happy ending in which flighty Holly leaves the country forever. The film, if far less moving than the novel, represented a capable job of turning a plotless mood piece into a conventional sixties romantic comedy.

> Originally, Merrick had asked Capote to adapt his own novella for the musical stage, but Capote, who had already adapted one of his own stories into the book for the musical flop "House of Flowers," declined. Joshua Logan was asked to direct, and Nunnally Johnson wrote a book for the show, which was rejected. When Burrows agreed to write a new book and to direct, the project became a reality. It's worth noting, however, that Merrill had already written most of his score – to Johnson's book – before Burrows was hired.

Mary's *Breakfast* was produced by David Merrick (*Hello, Dolly!*), directed by Joseph Anthony and Abe Burrows, and featured a book by Edward Albee, with music and lyrics by Bob Merrill. The musical also starred Sally Kellerman, after her benchmark role in the second *Star Trek* pilot ("Where No Man Has Gone Before," NBC, September 22, 1966), and six years before playing Hot Lips in the big-screen *M*A*S*H*. But *Breakfast* became an indigestible, notorious flop that closed after preview performances before it officially opened. In reviews of pre-performances in Philadelphia and Boston, critics annihilated the play, little knowing that Mary was singing with bronchial pneumonia. The production began tryouts in Philadelphia on October 10, 1966 as *Holly Golightly*. It moved to the Shubert Theatre in Boston on November 7, 1966, but reverted back to its source title, *Breakfast at Tiffany's*, before the Broadway previews began at New York's Majestic Theatre, where it closed December 12, 1966.

In her book, *A Fine Romance: Hollywood/Broadway: The Mayhem. The Magic, The Musicals*, Darcie Denkert explained how choreographer/director Bob Fosse and producer Robert Fryer were the original team hired to bring *Breakfast* to Broadway. Fosse had suggested his wife Gwen Verdon for the role of Holly. But he had second thoughts about putting Verdon through a psychologically challenging "audition," and he and Fryer opted out of the production. At this point David Merrick opted in, and cast Mary.

Mary was anxiety-ridden from the onset. She didn't think her song-and-dance abilities would be sufficient for the Broadway stage, no matter how much effort she invested in preparation. That meant working with an established voice coach, who in turn placed her in touch with a Broadway musical actor who was overwhelmed himself with the task at hand. "I couldn't believe that Mary Tyler Moore was coming to me for advice," he said.

Mary should have been more cautious about the production from the onset, and she knew it. "I was nervous about the show," she said, "…but it was a healthy kind of nervousness. I should have been more nervous when I signed, because there wasn't even a second act. But it looked like it had to the greatest hit in Broadway history…David Merrick, Abe Burrows directing, [famed choreographer] Michael Kidd for dances, Bob Merrill's songs, good story, even the Mark Hellinger Theatre [where *My Fair Lady* had premiered]. Everything just spelled success. But apparently it was a doomed project even before I went into it."

Referring to her illness during the brief run, Mary said, "Oh, I wish they could have seen it when my throat was all right. I didn't want it to be bad."

Come *Holly Golightly's* opening night in Philadelphia, Mary was in such a panic that a doctor was called in. She could hardly talk, registered a fever of 103 degrees, and was diagnosed with a bronchial infection which she later described to the press as "pneumonia." Concerned friends reached out to help as much as they could. Julie Andrews sent a box of lozenges made especially for singers. When the production switched venues to Boston and its title to *Breakfast at Tiffany's* (even after new posters and *Playbills* were printed with the alternate title, *Holly Golightly*), illnesses came as thick as the bad reviews. Chamberlain developed a cold while *The Boston Globe* gave *Tiffany's* the deep freeze with a near-sub-zero rating, calling it "a straightforward musical flop." That's when Merrick kicked his damage control into high gear, and brought in Albee to redo the libretto which Burrows and his partner, Nunnally Johnson, had ignited. The behind-the-scenes plot fluxes and changing of the guard continued when Burrows quit. In stepped director Joseph Anthony. The switch took place because Burrows had issues with Albee: "His ideas called for what was practically a whole new show, and I didn't want to direct it."

In *Not Since Carrie*, Mandelbaum explains:

> It was clear that drastic measures were called for: Burrows, known as the ace play doctor of his time, seemed unable to fix his own show, so Merrick took the surprising step of asking Edward Albee – whose only experience with musicals was as coauthor of the libretto for a forgotten 1961 off-Broadway musical adaptation of Melville's 'Bartleby the Scrivener' – to write a new book. Merrick and Albee wanted Burrows to stay on as director, but Burrows walked out when he read Albee's words to Kevin Kelly in the Boston Globe near the end of the tryout: 'All those awful jokes will be thrown out, and I hope to substitute some genuine wit. The characters, from Holly down, will be redefined, and she won't have any of those borscht-circuit lovers she's saddled with now.'

> Joseph Anthony took over the direction, Larry Kert and others joined the cast, while other performers were dropped, the score was substantially revised to fit Albee's script, and the show, now called *Breakfast at Tiffany's*, limped into New York. In spite of disastrous reports from the road, nothing could stop people from buying tickets for what they still believed to be a sure thing, and the advance sale continued to build.

While someone even as cynical as Capote initially remained relatively upbeat – "It will run fourteen months on Broadway. A successful, but not distinguished musical" – harsh reality continued to set in. The reviews in Philadelphia and Boston may have been dreadful, but in New York they were hideous. *The New York Times* labeled it "one of the most colossal disasters of the contemporary musical stage."

Mary was mortified in the midst of it all, as rumors ran rampant of potential actresses who might take over her role. She told the *New York Post*, "I've got to clear my name. We were a month in Boston. It seemed like fourteen. You can imagine how I felt having to go on every night when I read that Tammy Grimes or Diahann Carroll would replace me. Tammy was never in Boston waiting to take over as reported. And Miss Carroll was the original choice for the part. In Philadelphia, they made Holly very tough. The critics rapped us for that, so in Boston we made her sweet and they rapped us for that. David Merrick has been wonderful to me. With those reviews, I'm sure other producers would have replaced me."

She rolled with the punches. Tinker, her rock and shield, was astounded by his wife's true grit. "She lived that play day and night," he related to the *Post*. "She worked till midnight and, when she came home, she worked some more. It made things all the worse when it bombed." Eventually, nothing worked, and Capote let loose with his frustrations. After viewing the show in Boston he told *Women's Wear Daily*, "I don't like the score or the leading lady."

Advance ticket sales far exceeded those of *Cabaret*, *The Apple Tree*, and *I Do! I Do!*, the other live-stage musicals of 1966. But no matter how hard Mary, Chamberlain, Merrick, or anybody else tried, even the final performance of *Breakfast at Tiffany's* was a complete failure. *Good Housekeeping* reported: "The audience was alternately bored and shocked. Some walked out in mid-act. Others left at intermission. Hecklers shouted derision at the stage. The actors and musicians carried on gamely to the final curtain, and Mary tried to withhold her tears until she reached the privacy of her dressing room. She came out smiling though, and turned up at a cast party at Sardi's."

"I am feeling all the emotions you can imagine I must be feeling," she told a reporter at the party. "All I can say now is that I want to be with my friends and share in some warm good-byes."

On another occasion she said, "As painful as it was," performing in *Breakfast* "was exciting. The TV series we did with three cameras and an audience was lively. Pictures to me, mean long, long hours, no spontaneity, and no social or family life. Broadway meant live audiences and something special. It was a challenge, and I'm not at all sorry I did it."

"Stardom in movies would be nice," she said, "...but this idea of seeing your name up in lights on a movie marquee doesn't thrill me. If you're a musical performer, as I want to be, your name is supposed to be up in lights on a Broadway marquee, not on a movie theatre. I've had my share of the other kind of fame, from TV, and it's nice. It's nice to be able to walk into a store and open a charge account without any questions asked, and it's wonderful to go into a restaurant without a reservation and be recognized by the captain and be given a good table. That kind of fame is nice, but it isn't thrilling. Broadway is a very special kind of plum...I've seen some shows come to Broadway that were not so great, but the stars pulled them through. And I've felt maybe it was my fault that my show didn't survive in spite of it."

Whoever was ultimately responsible, Merrick took the bull by the horns. He posted closing notices two weeks prior to the scheduled December 26th premiere. According to *Playbill Magazine*, he called a press conference and made an unprecedented full disclosure:

"Rather than subject the drama critics and the theatre-going public – who invested over one million dollars in advance sales – to an excruciatingly boring evening, I have decided to close ['out of consideration for the audience']. Since the idea of adapting *Breakfast at Tiffany's* for the musical stage was mine in the first place, the closing is entirely my fault and should not be attributed to the three top writers [Burrows, Nunnally Johnson, and Edward Albee] who had a go at it."

The announcement "made Merrick a hero," Mandelbaum observed. "Never before had a producer admitted at this stage that his show was a disaster and stated that he did not wish to cheat his customers. No show had ever been stopped prior to its Broadway opening with an advance sale as large as that secured by *Tiffany's*. The show cost $500,000, but thanks to sell-out business in both road engagements, it would up losing $425,000, thus making it a bomb that actually returned a portion of its investment."

"Just as remarkable," Mandelbaum continued, was that "the *New York Times* actually ran a semi-review, written by second-stringer Dan Sullivan, the day after the final preview. Sullivan wrote, 'The preview audience left the Majestic immeasurably depressed…Both [Mary and Chamberlain] were troupers, but neither was ready for a Broadway musical.'"

Decades later, during an interview with the *Los Angeles Times*, Chamberlain offered his assessment as to why *Tiffany's* tumbled: "It was first-class, very expensive and nothing worked." After playwright Albee (*Who's Afraid of Virginia Woolf?*) was hired to rewrite the book, Chamberlain added, "We got a new director…I think I began to get shoved a little bit aside. It became a very dark musical [version of] *Virginia Woolf* and the audience hated it. David Merrick closed the show with an enormous pre-sale. He returned all the money. It just broke my heart when it closed."

Bill Persky claimed that Mary was blamed for the Broadway bombing because she hailed from TV. "At that time, if you came from television, you didn't deserve to be on Broadway." While the same may have been said for Chamberlain, Persky had seen *Breakfast* in New Haven, before it arrived on Broadway. He thought "…Mary was brilliant," but "…the show was not. But by the time it got to Broadway she was the one who took the blame for it, even after people like Edward Albee tried to fix it. There was no fixing it. It closed the date after it opened."

On the Message Board at www.BroadwayWorld.com, Roland Von Berlin summarized his thoughts on the matter in mid-December of 2016, the 50th anniversary of the play. He had seen it in Philadelphia, when it was titled *Holly Golightly*:

> The show has the reputation of being the worst flop of all
> time simply because it was so prominent, so anticipated,

and then was shut down when still in previews. But it actually wasn't that bad. The problem was that its spirit and style didn't suit the Capote original at all: it had been turned into a conventional musical comedy with a dark side, when it needed to be as unusual and flavorsome as a Sondheim-Prince kind of show.

In other words, the same creative team might have come up with a perfectly acceptable piece using completely different material. Instead, they chose this all but untranslatable story without thinking how best to musicalize it on its own terms. Further, neither of the two leads had anything substantial to play, and the support was all over the place. I remember a party scene in which the chorus guys glared at each other and sang about "dirty old men" as if Bob Merrick were a child who had just discovered a naughty term and was using it to shock the grownups. In the same scene, Holly and Mag Wildwood sang a duet called "The Home for Wayward Girls" that had nothing to do with the action.

The whole evening was like that – snippets of things that never cohered. It wasn't boring. It was a show that you could enjoy even though you knew it was terrible.

Following the dim and detrimental Broadway lights of the *Holly Golightly/Breakfast at Tiffany's* debacle, Mary at least had something to look forward to. 1967's *Thoroughly Modern Millie* was the first in a string of feature films in which she appeared, through an exclusive contract with Universal Pictures. But according to Bill Persky, this period was considered "…the end of her career." When Mary first approached the studio, he recalled, "…they gave her anything she wanted. She had the right of approval of the scripts she did. But her dream always was to be on Broadway. So, in order for her to do Broadway, she was released from her original contract with Universal, and gave up all creative control, and the studio then put her in any movie of their choice, and not hers. But then her Broadway debut was a disaster. She went back to Hollywood where Universal cast her in a bunch of low-grade movies, and her career was still going straight down hill."

Still, there were a few shining moments throughout *Thoroughly Modern Millie*. It was produced by Ross Hunter, and directed by George Roy Hill. Mary portrayed Miss Dorothy Brown, a naïve girl significantly less colorful and three-dimensional than Laura Petrie, let alone the characters played by her fellow female stars.

Due to her popularity in films like *The Sound of Music* and *Mary Poppins* (the latter co-starring Dick Van Dyke), Julie Andrews took the lead as Millie Dillmount; Carol Channing was Muzzy Van Hossmere; Beatrice Lillie was Mrs. Meers. The leading men were John Gavin as Trevor Graydon, and James Fox as Jimmy Smith. The film received solid support from a list of pro players including Herbie Faye (a guest star from *The Dick Van Dyke Show*).

Millie is about Andrews' Dillmount, a "thoroughly modern girl" from Kansas in 1922. She seeks to be a stenographer and then a rich man's bride. Following a complete makeover, she encounters Mary's Brown at the Priscilla Hotel, which is operated by Meers (Lillie). Millie takes a shine to salesman Smith, but keeps her eye on the many prizes and fortunes of the wealthy Graydon. The situation is soon marred when it is learned that the Hotel Priscilla is really a front for a white slavery ring. Dorothy is definitely not in Kansas anymore, especially when the racket intends to make her their newest employee.

In his book *The Hollywood Musical*, Clive Hirschhorn calls *Millie* "The best musical of 1967...an original, written by Richard Morris with new Sammy Cahn-Jimmy Van Heusen tunes and handful of favorites, it was an irresistible mixture of brashness, charm and nostalgia put together with expertise. It cast an affectionate backward glance at the shimmering twenties, evoking its fads, and its eccentricities, as well as the Golden Days of silent screen entertainment."

Hirschhorn hailed *Millie* as "Ross Hunter's lavishly mounted Technicolor production," but added, "Hill's direction lost its grip on the melodramatic proceedings that helped bring the film to its climax." Still, he wrote "it was, for most of the time spot-on, deliciously lampooning a much-lampooned era with a freshness and sparkle."

Per the website *TV Tropes,* "The film thrives on meta-humor, most notably the 'break' halfway through in which literally nothing happens for a few minutes. It's an odd combination of 1920s comedy and 1960s sensibilities, swerving between parody and straight-up comedy."

In his review of the 2002 Broadway musical that it inspired, *Variety's* Charles Isherwood called the original *Millie* movie "bloated...a post *Mary Poppins* Julie Andrews vehicle that goes to desperate lengths to capitalize on just about every Broadway success of the time, beginning with Andrews' similar flapper-era stage hit, *The Boyfriend*, it's about as guilty as guilty pleasures get. Where else can you see Mary Poppins singing in Hebrew? Carol Channing shot out of a cannon? Beatrice Lillie speaking fake Chinese? Or indeed, Beatrice Lillie at all? I ask you! The movie is framed as a tongue-in-cheek spoof of silent pictures...with a Keystone Kops chase finale and the somewhat haphazard insertion of title cards."

Mary was neither disappointed nor uncomfortable with interpreting a character very different from her TV image. According to Channing, Mary was up to the challenge of playing Brown, during which her professional drive and vision for the future remained in high gear: "Mary was never what you would call a shy girl. She knew what she wanted and went after it. She told us about wanting her own production company and exactly how she envisioned the MTM logo…with a kitty meowing, instead of a lion roaring [as with MGM]…long before it actually came into fruition. She was very excited about the film and her role, as were all of us. She took her part very seriously. Some may have seen this as standoffish, and she may have appeared aloof at times, but she was just very focused on her work and doing a good job. I admired her for that."

Although Mary's self-esteem was not always evident throughout her life and career, she held her own amidst the Hollywood royalty that filtered through the *Millie* set – Lillie, Andrews, and Channing. The latter two won Golden Globe awards for their leading and supporting roles in the film.

Channing, long known for her professional courtesy and cordial manner, said that she and her film veteran co-stars "were never the kind to make anyone feel intimidated," whether that was Mary during *Millie*, or otherwise. "We were interested in helping everyone do their best."

An example: Andrews once visited the *Millie* set on a rare day off to read opposite Channing for close-ups. "Usually," Channing said, "a stand-in reads the lines to you when the camera can't see the actor you're supposed to be working with. But Julie knew that a performance would be better when they edited the final product together if you were getting the same feedback from the same actor that is in the scene with you."

"Julie was the reason I won the Golden Globe," she added. "And she was so certain I would win the Academy Award."

Unfortunately, that never transpired. But Andrews was "just as supportive of Mary and her efforts" on *Millie*, which television and variety show archivist Tom Wilson described as "a Julie Andrews movie." "George Hill," he said, "was catering to Julie more than he was to Mary," whose character "was kind of a secondary role that didn't do much for her. At the time, Mary went to all of the premieres and she was very supportive of it. But as the years went on, she went through a period of where she didn't really want to talk about it. And then, as more years passed, she was proud that she was in it. In later interviews, she acted like it was fun to be a part of it. She had to come to terms with the fact the movie amassed a following and a life of its own, and she started to see things more objectively.

"But while making the movie, it was a big disappointment that it didn't help her career in films, which is what she was focused on at that point. She was excited to be in the movie, but when it was released, I think she felt,

'Oh, dear…that may not have been the best thing for me to do.' But it was her first film in her contract with Universal, and the studio thought it would be a good idea to have her [perform as] a real innocent character…to do something completely different from what she had been doing. I think she was also attracted to the fact that it was a musical in which she could actually do some dancing, which was something she didn't often have a chance to do [on the big screen]."

Mary's overtly innocent performance was most likely suggested by Ross Hunter. "I think early in the process," Wilson said, "he had her watch a few movies with Lillian Gish," an actress with a similar method of portraying innocence on the screen.

Chapter

7

One year after *Thoroughly Modern Millie*, Mary made a more diffused impact with two new movie comedies: *What's So Bad About Feeling Good?* and *Don't Just Stand There!*

Good co-starred George Peppard, TV's future *Banacek* and *A-Team* star (and the big-screen's *Breakfast at Tiffany's* original male lead). *Stand* co-starred Robert Wagner (from TV's pre-*Hart-to-Hart* hit *It Takes a Thief*). Both films hoped to ride provocative titles to big box offices, but neither did spectacularly well or excited critics, despite top-line supporting casts.

Good, directed by George Seaton (*Miracle on 34th Street*, 1947; *Airport*, 1970), featured stalwarts like Dom DeLuise, John McMartin, Charles Lane, and Thelma Ritter, along with young, bright newcomers Susan St. James and Don Stroud. Spirited and perky as ever, Mary shines as Liz opposite Peppard's Pete. The peppy premise involves a virus that makes people feel happy. Advocating the bug's good effects, Liz tells Pete something that Laura Petrie would have never told Rob: "The world's a hopeless, stinking mess."

The website www.VideoBeat.com, which reviews films of the '50s and '60s, expresses *Good* this way:

> By 1968 the psychedelic drug LSD had made enough headlines and been used by enough people that it started making its way into mainstream "grown up" films. Here it takes the form of a highly contagious virus that quickly spreads across New York City making the normal irritable and rude locals extremely happy, polite and filled with euphoria. In other words, by NYC standards, they have become "sick."

The film opens in a communal East Village, beatnik-hippie pad where former "straights" have dropped out of the mainstream to paint, wear disheveled clothes, grow beards and be free from the phoniness of the modern world.

Beatnik dropouts Pete and Liz catch the virus, get sick, and begin dressing well and spreading good will to all. Some people are immune to the virus but they catch a "contact high" and also become sick. The immediate decline in alcohol, cigarette, and tranquilizer sales alarms the city's officials, and fearing a collapse of the city's financial structure, the mayor enlists the support of the Federal government.

Lots of great shots of New York City and a wild scene in a psychedelic Greenwich Village club called "The Cesspool" that features rock and roll group, Scurvy Maggot and The Four Worms!

New York Times film critic Vincent Canby called *Good* "a comedy for the old at heart of all ages. By picturing the things it lampoons in a soft focus, the movie ultimately sentimentalizes them." Other critics of the day were similarly unimpressed, with one noting, "As the hippies who find happiness in middle class morality, Mr. Peppard and Miss Moore are blandly attractive." Film historian and archivist Robert S. Ray, also a board member for the Classic TV Preservation Society nonprofit organization, distributed his *Good* thoughts:

George Seaton's 1968 comedy, *What's So Bad About Feeling Good?* is typical example of how the old establishment types in Hollywood were desperately trying to remain, in that overused word of the day, relevant, in an era when the generation gap was at its widest. Times were changing so rapidly that what was hip and "with it" one year was hopelessly behind the times the next. And the old guard in charge of movie development in the era before the Scorsese-Coppola-Spielberg generation changed everything was clueless as to what it all meant.

In this case, Mary's character, along with George Peppard's, is more '50s era beatniks than late '60s hippies, as written by veteran director Seaton and Robert Pirosh. And when they are "infected" with the feel-good virus, they find that happiness means instantly becoming

69

the conformist establishment types they were rebelling against. The message seemed to be that if the younger generation started acting like their parents, everyone would be happier and the world would be just fine – not a message the under-30 crowd was ready to embrace as the Vietnam War raged on. As a result, this youth-oriented comedy failed to find an audience among any generation.

For all that, Mary gives a bright winning performance once she's "infected" and sheds her glum, depressing hippie persona ("The world's a hopeless, stinking mess!") which doesn't suit her at all. After she morphs into an optimist, she's adorable, even if the script doesn't give her any help. She gets one, all too brief moment to show her dexterity with physical comedy when she tries to keep a rambunctious toucan (the carrier of the virus) from being confiscated by posing as a pregnant woman.

In short, as with most of her films at Universal, she makes the material seem better than it is.

As innovative and hip as *What's So Bad About Feeling Good?* tried to be, *Don't Just Stand There!*, directed by Ron Winston and written by Charles Williams, was a little more daring. Mary was cast as Martine Randall, a Jacqueline Susann-type sex novelist who hires Wagner's Lawrence Colby, a young writer, to complete her latest work when she decides to stop writing. Romance ensues.

In his commentary from 2008, posted on www.TCM.com, the website for the heralded Turner Classic Movie channel, reader Cam Mitchell called *Stand There* "…just a hoot of a movie!...This is a fun romp – quick paced with great, glib dialog. It's one of those movies where you just know that the people filming it had fun the whole time. I don't know why most of today's movies seem to dawdle and languish and stammer about. Many lark comedies of the 1960s had a quick tempo, with crisp editing and even a bit of action: A chase here, a pursuit there, a fight or two – interspersed with snappy dialog. It is a style which began with *Bringing Up Baby* [the 1938 feature film starring Cary Grant and Kathryn Hepburn] and disappeared with the 1970s."

Mary Magazine editor David Davis took his stand on *There*:

This was a silly movie that Mary was not very fond of, and only made to fulfill her Universal contract. She had a ten-picture deal, but ended up only making five pictures, including one for television [1969's *Run a Crooked Mile*].

> She enjoyed working with Robert Wagner, but other than
> that it was an uneventful shoot and the movie came and
> went with very little fanfare. The movie had its moments,
> but it's very dated and doesn't hold up, although I did
> enjoy seeing it on the big screen [in 2017].

The above-referenced *Run a Crooked Mile*, which debuted on CBS November 18, 1969, is a made-for-TV thriller in which Mary starred with Louis Jourdan. He played Richard Stuart, an ordinary schoolteacher who, while on holiday, is a witness to a murder in a private secluded mansion. When he reports the crime, no evidence of any murder can be found, only a key on the floor. Upon further investigation, he is knocked unconscious. He wakes up in a hospital room (after an apparent polo accident). He is shocked to discover that two years have elapsed. During this time he's supposedly been unhappily married to the beautiful Elizabeth Sutton, played by Mary, and living a wealthy and extravagant life in Europe under the name Tony Sutton. Not only this, he has become involved in a plot to disrupt the entire European economy.

Acclaimed for its original premise, stylish photography (by Arthur Grant), and use of exotic locations, the film has developed somewhat of a cult following, despite not being aired in ages and unreleased on DVD. This was Mary's fifth and final movie for Universal. She was contracted for five more, but was released from her contract so she and Tinker could form MTM Enterprises and produce their own television shows.

Before that took place, however, a feature-film detour called *Change of Habit*, in which Mary would play a nun, opposite Elvis Presley as a doctor, slightly altered that course in 1969.

Habit's premise seemed to be at least partially foreshadowed during a portion of Mary's youth. A nun who taught Mary at Immaculate Heart High School in Los Angeles had once noticed how disinterested she was in extramural activities. Mary, the sister said, "...seemed to be filled with energy every day of the week, every week of the school year." Although a good student academically, Mary did not exactly stand out from the crowd. From an artistic standpoint, her teachers and fellow classmates knew of her interest in the arts, particularly dance. Whenever she was assigned an English theme to write, her topic was dance or related to some form of art. The sister assessed, "Those were the same assignments that brought her best grades, too."

Mary, like several of her classmates at Immaculate Heart, had at one point considered entering a convent. She was raised a Catholic, and educated in parochial schools. She was "just like any other girl" who was "impressed" by the religious lives that nuns presented. "Of course," she said, "the sisters always encouraged us to search ourselves to see if we had a vocation. It was serious consideration because I have always had a great deal of faith and love of God. I don't think it was an unusual situation…Every Catholic girl, at least once in her lifetime, thinks about being a nun. It's a very self-sacrificing role, one which is greatly appealing and…there's tremendous satisfaction of knowing that your life is dedicated to helping people." She knew "deep down" that the religious life was not for her. "I had to be on stage," she said. "I also needed someone to love me, and for me to love."

All of these aspects combined years later when Mary entered the fictional sisterhood in *Change of Habit*, which, besides Presley, also featured her future sitcom leading man, Ed Asner. In the process, *Habit* allowed Mary the chance to play what has become one of her more well-known, pre-*Ordinary People* feature-film characters, if for all the wrong reasons. As part of her amended motion-picture contract with Universal Studios, the movie proved most interesting, if not the most sophisticated.

In *Habit*, she portrayed Sister Michelle Gallagher in tandem with Presley as Dr. John Carpenter, who is initially unaware of her religious affiliation. "I'm a member of the order of the Sisters of Mary," she professes as Sister Michelle. During a press interview for the film in 1969, Mary expressed a measure of discomfort in playing the role, if further confirming her regard for Catholic sisterhood. "I was taught by nuns all my life," she said. "And it really did make me feel funny because they were always the subject or the object of my respect and awe…They were mysterious ladies, not so much anymore these days as they're dressing pretty much the way everybody does. But…I did find myself holding…the rosary that was draped on the belt, and moving my head in a stiff manner, not snapping it around as I normally do. It did indeed make me feel very strange."

According to Alan Hanson of www.elvis-history-blog.com, Mary had viewed her on-screen teaming with Elvis as "strange casting." "Professionally," Hanson documented, "…Presley had established an on-screen persona as an aggressive lothario forever in pursuit of his sexy leading ladies," which was in direct opposition to Mary's "prevailing image" presented on the *Van Dyke Show*. *Change of Habit*, Hanson continued, "…would prove to be a momentary juncture in two careers headed for greater heights – Presley on the Las Vegas stage and Moore on the award-winning TV show bearing her name."

Mary ventured into *Habit* due to her contract with Universal. "Presley wound up in the film," observed Hanson, "…because the deal with NBC to produce his acclaimed 1968 TV special gave Universal the rights to make one Presley movie. Apparently, with all of his previous films, Elvis had no script approval. He simply showed up on the Universal lot to fulfill his obligation on March 5, 1969, just nine days after he appeared in Las Vegas to publicize his return to live performances there in the coming summer."

Much later, Mary claimed working with Presley "...was wonderful. He was so fit and determined to do well." By this time, Presley had been performing two-dimensional roles in light-hearted movies like 1964's *Viva Las Vegas*. With *Habit*, the rock-n-roll-icon-turned-movie star sought to kick a habit of his own by playing what he felt was a more textured role in a more somber film. "[He] really wanted to express himself as an actor," Mary disclosed, "...and he chose this script. And it sounds silly, and as a matter of fact, it kind of was. But the intention was that it be a serious story about a nun who was working in [a hospital in] the ghetto, and who was therefore not wearing a habit, but regular street clothes" – a development that contributed to Dr. Carpenter, a surgeon, remaining oblivious to Sister Michelle's true identity.

Presley as Carpenter occasionally played the guitar and hummed "...a little ditty here and there," Mary mused, as he and Sister Michelle focused on helping various ailing patients. It's during these movie moments when, as the actress explained, "Elvis, the doctor...the musical singing surgeon," developed "a kind of crush on" Sister Michelle, the nun, who looks like "a regular girl," and she somewhat on him.

At the film's climax, Sister Michelle is seen at Mass with Dr. Carpenter playing his guitar, and both ultimately praying for guidance as to which life she will choose: the continued religious life, or will she "leave the Church" to be Carpenter's romantic lover? As the camera switched back and forth between images of Jesus and Elvis, the audience was left to wonder which selection Michelle made. "And you never did find out," Mary observed at one point.

In their revealing book, *Change of Habit*, Pål Granlund and David English offer much minutia about the film, which features supporting performances by Jane Elliott and Barbara McNair. Mary enjoyed Presley's music beyond his regular rock 'n' roll standards, but not his feature films. "I was an Elvis fan before I ever met him," she said, "...but probably later than most girls were. I began to like the way he sang when he began to put more feeling into his songs. I thought anybody who had been the center of all that insanity for so long would have some of it rub off on him. Most of my preconceived notions were not borne out. For instance, I was very surprised at how awfully good he is as an actor."

The closest Mary had come to meeting Presley prior to *Habit* was a comedic parody of his star persona. In a classic episode of *The Dick Van Dyke Show* titled "The Twizzle" (February 28, 1962), Jerry Lanning plays a singing/dancing Randy Twizzle, an Elvis knock-off who appears on *The Alan Brady Show* and creates a national dance craze called – what else? –

"The Twizzle." The joke gave props to Chubby Checker and his "The Twist" song-and-dance for good measure. Furthermore, "The Twizzle" segment can also be seen as a knock-off of *Bye Bye Birdie*, whose stage and film editions that featured Dick Van Dyke.

Recalling Elvis in *After All*, Mary said old-swivel-hips copped to having a crush on her since the *Van Dyke* series, "…literally kicking at the dirt below him" during his confession. Even though she was 32 years old, and he was 34, Mary said Presley had a tendency to refer to her as "*ma'am* out of respect."

Despite any of that, *Habit* helmer William Graham noticed diametrically opposing personalities between his two lead performers while making the movie. Mary wondered what she was doing in an Elvis Presley film. Graham remembered her as somewhat "…on the prissy side," but accepted that manner because she was portraying a nun. "I would expect her to be a little bit reserved."

Other members of the cast, including Elliot and McNair, viewed Mary's behavior as aloof. "I socialized with Mary and Barbara and Elvis," Elliot recalled. "I sort of moved between the two camps…She didn't get involved. She didn't socialize."

McNair did not converse with Mary "because she really was kind of standoffish. She wasn't easy to get to know." At lunchtime, "…everybody would eat together," McNair said, except Mary, who would remain in her dressing room.

For her part, Mary saw things differently. During an interview in Universal City, while filming *Change of Habit*, she said things like: "You fool around on the set, and you chat and you joke and you play records, and whatever. And yeah, the three of us, Elvis and Barbara and I had a great time together. We had a couple of nights of shooting…at 7 o'clock in the evening and wind up at 5 in the morning, and that's insanity time…And the only thing that kept us going was the camaraderie on the set."

Maybe Mary was "standoffish" because she was unhappy about working on the movie. Or maybe she just didn't feel well? *Something* was amiss. Her strict dietary selections, for one, were the result of diabetes. That's why she brought her own lunch to the set and many times had just an apple. She was self-conscious about her appearance on screen because the diabetes caused her skin to prematurely wrinkle. That's when Russell Metty, the film's director of photography, came to the rescue. He helped to film Mary in a way that gave her appearance "a kind of heavenly glow," Graham wrote.

The technique, known as "soft focus," is a common tool. According to television and film historian Robert S. Ray, Hollywood techs have applied from the beginning "for all actresses over a certain age, from the days of Gloria Swanson's heyday to the present." It's a protective film trick that's been used for Angela Lansbury on TV's *Murder, She Wrote* (CBS, 1983-1995), Doris Day on *The Doris Day Show* (CBS, 1968-1974), in several of Day's films and, as Ray said, even for a few of Mary's co-stars:

"The approach seemed especially popular in the '50s and '60s as color became more commonly used than black-and-white, especially in films that utilized hot studio lighting as in the Doris Day comedies. Although *The Sound of Music* [1965] is not a comedy, but a musical with serious overtones, its star Julie Andrews goes soft-focus in her close-up when she dances with [co-star] Christopher Plummer. And the most notorious example of soft-focus photography was its overuse in [the 1974 movie] *Mame* whenever the camera came within fifty feet of the sixty-something Lucille Ball."

Similarly, fans of the original *Star Trek* TV series will recall that the soft-focus effect served as a sort of visual clue. If a guest-starring actress shimmered under a soft focus upon her introduction, she was likely to be Captain Kirk's next conquest.

According to Alan Hanson, as www.Elvis-history.blog.com as well as on www.Neatorama.com, Pål Granlund's *Change of Habit* literary companion, and Bill Bram's incorporated interviews, Mary's fellow actors may have wanted her to be more transparent and interactive on the set, but her professional demeanor was never in question. Assistant director Walt Gilmore called her "lovely to work with…cooperative…a real nice person," who "always knew her lines, never complained [or] demanded anything – and she could have."

Graham observed: "She's a wonderful actor and…person, and she did a fine job in the movie." Elliot called performing with Mary an educational experience. "Making a movie is an extremely arduous, slow process…When you do a movie, if you're lucky you do three pages a day. Which means the preponderance of the day is spent not sweating and not working, and Mary found a way to keep her energy up, to maintain herself through the hours of sitting around…She took really good care of herself in order to preserve herself for the work. I learned a lot about that [and]…maintaining a constant level [of physical, psychological and emotional health] through a day's work."

Mary praised co-star Presley's professionalism and personality. "It's not just that he always knew his lines; that's true of any real pro. It's the way he probes the character. [He's] a lot more fun that I'd have guessed…he'd be a fine comedian…I've never worked with a more gentlemanly, kinder man." In *After All*, she said working with the King of Rock 'n' Roll was nothing but pleasant. "He was in peak form during that time, careful about what he ate and exercising as if he enjoyed it. He was a thorough professional: always prepared."

Assistant cameraman Frank Thackery recalled, "She didn't know what to think of Elvis. She liked him, but she…[kept her] distance. She wasn't snobby…she just stayed to herself."

For Elliot, acting with Mary was more challenging than with Elvis because they did not share the same way of working, and lacked a common ground. Presley "felt more … comfortable" around her and McNair, declared Elliot, who felt that Mary did not like or understand the singer. "Elvis was not comfortable with her because of her inaccessibility. [He] was a good ole boy. He thought the funniest thing in the world was to light a firecracker, and throw it into a dressing room and slam the door…That was so not Mary's style. I was in my early 20s and Barbara was a good ole girl, so we all could relate on that level and he felt…accepted. He did not feel safe with Mary."

In the midst of *Habit*, Mary was uncomfortable with a few sequences in the movie, one of which came to be known as the "rage reduction" scene. Here, Presley's Dr. Carpenter attempts a dubious procedure to treat a young, autistic girl. When rehearsing the scene, Mary and Elvis were allegedly disturbed by what they witnessed. When the cameras began to roll, the child, an inexperienced actor, became visibly flustered. Mary was not pleased, even with the child's accompanying physician close-by to monitor the situation. "She felt he was abusing the child," McNair recalled. "She didn't want to shoot the scene. She didn't want the doctor to do what he had to do to get that child to have the reaction that was necessary."

According to Cynnie Troup, the film's assistant script supervisor, Mary interrupted the scene, and said, "I will not permit this anymore. This child is hysterical. We will do this no more." After that, Troup explained, "Everybody stopped and walked away…[and]…we went on to something else. A few weeks later, they finished the scene…It was awful, but Mary Tyler Moore was the best."

Fortunately, much-needed comic relief arrived when filming the movie's football-game scene at Magnolia Park in North Hollywood. Troup had overheard an assistant director speaking with someone about whether or not a Mary would need a stand-in. "She just has to run a little bit," it was said. "She can do it. We do not need a stunt-double." At first, Mary was not fully aware of the proceedings, and wondered, "Is that the game where the ball [has a] real funny shape…?" That's how little informed she was about football. In the end, a blond double in a brunette wig was utilized for wide-frame shots where Mary's character Sister Michelle is running.

Mary and Presley had reportedly kept their distance from one another, but there was some babble of an affair between the two, even though both were married with children. Elvis had then been wed to Priscilla Ann Beaulieu Presley for two years, and their daughter Lisa Marie was a year old. Mary was by then wed to Grant Tinker for seven years, and her son Richie was 12. "Of course," Alan Hansen suggested, "...other existing connections don't necessarily keep people from making new connections." But in published interviews from 1969, Mary called Elvis "charming" and "gorgeous." In 2014, for an interview with *TV Guide*, even Elliot was asked if Presley ever flirted with her. To which she responded, "He made a pass at everybody!"

Then there was the *Habit* scene in which Presley tackled Mary on the football field. According to actor Robert De Anda, she and Elvis shared a flirty moment off-screen while horizontal on the green. He was tickling her, and she told him to "cut it out!" Elvis may have been interested in her, but the feeling was not mutual. At the movie's wrap party, make-up artist Jim McCoy said Presley attempted to "...put the make on Mary but she wouldn't go for it."

Whatever transpired behind its scenes, *Change of Habit* became the final film for Presley, making Mary his last female movie co-star. "I have slept with every one of my leading ladies...except one," he said. To which she later joked, "I don't want to bust anyone's bubble, but I know who that 'one' was...and what was I thinking?!"

The critics were wondering the same thing about her choice of roles. According to one reviewer, "Nuns and their habits have changed and if the religions they portray seem a bit too with it, enough to raise the hackles of their reactionary parish priest, Mr. Presley can't be faulted for remarking confusedly, 'I get a feeling there's a message here.' But it's only a slight and not terribly impressive one."

"Bad" film buffs Harry and Michael Medved skewered Mary's Doris Day-like role of the ultimate "attractive virgin," and wondered about a film where only attempted rape – and Elvis Presley – can alter a nun's sacred habits. Reviews like that kicked *Habit* to the curb. Mary won their "Golden Turkey Award" for "The Ecclesiastical Award for the Worst Performance by an Actor or Actress as a Clergyman or Nun." She responded that she was "thrilled" with the accolade, which she accepted in good fun and sportsmanship.

Justin Chang of the *Los Angeles Times* once wrote in retrospect, "So gale-force dominant was Moore in the world of television that her big-screen performances were relatively few and far between. She tap-danced winningly in an elevator with Julie Andrews in *Thoroughly Modern Millie*...and donned a nun's wimple to star opposite Elvis Presley in the ill-fated *Change of Habit*."

Despite Mary's valiant efforts to try something new, most of her post-*Van Dyke Show* movies were still considered bland "good girl" showcases, particularly *Habit*. She once admitted that her films were "so bad" programmers were "afraid to show them on late night Icelandic TV." And though she did not return to the big screen until *Ordinary People* in 1980, some eleven years later, she went back to the small screen with something very special.

Chapter

8

By the late 1960s, Mary's career was in a downward spiral, and her personal life was not exactly on the upswing. She and Grant Tinker hoped to have a child, but she suffered a miscarriage and was devastated. The doctors delivered more bad news: At just 33 years old Mary was diagnosed with diabetes, which meant daily insulin injections. According to Treva Silverman on the Reelz Channel, "She kind of didn't believe it and rebelled against it, she said, because the next day she just ate everything – pies, cakes, everything," thinking, "*To hell with you.*"

"We see Mary's reaction kind of going against medical advice," said psychologist Dr. Linda Papadopoulos, "and eating donuts and…sweets. And I think this was a manifestation of not only her anger at this happening, but the kind of sense of injustice. And also probably the realization that, '*Maybe I can't control things as much as I thought I could, and if that's the case, if I can't control things then I'm going to enjoy the donut.*' "

Adding to the mix were Mary's apparently complex issues with food and body image in general. "Some people say I err on the side of being too thin," she once said. "But I'm afraid that if I once overeat, I won't be able to stop."

All the while, too, she struggled with alcoholism, which did nothing for her digestion, or her diabetes, and which she continued to hide since her TV time with Dick Van Dyke, who later admitted to his own drinking issues.

Marc Shapiro said Mary's alcoholism "was one of those best-kept Hollywood secrets, which means everybody knew Mary was drinking. A lot of people had their speculations to what degree. Some said she was just a social drinker. Some thought of her as a full-blown alcoholic. She hid it very well."

"I think she kept a lot to herself," said Susan Kellerman, Mary's future co-star in the Broadway hit, *Whose Life Is It Anyway?* "Sometimes, if people drink they don't want everybody to know about it, so they do it alone."

Professionally, this period was not much better for Dick Van Dyke. Like Mary, he also made a few career-stalling films (such as 1969's *The Comic*, directed by Carl Reiner).

One sad moment led to another for both performers. But for Mary, being stricken with Type 1 Diabetes, aka Juvenile Diabetes, proved especially devastating. As she later wrote in *After All*, "Juvenile? Diabetes?! What?! I'm not that childish! And I'm not that special!" Such self-talk unleashed what she called her "stunning insecurity in slightly loopy ways." There she was, an Emmy-winner and *TV Guide* cover girl many times over, "a darling of the critics," and she required a major disease as she put it, "to make me feel complete."

Around this time, Mary started to see an analyst in Los Angeles for approximately one year, which she later recalled as "the most boring year" of her life. She went into analysis because she was afraid. She thought, "If I'm not going to be an actress, what or who am I? I wasn't a hostess, a gardener, a great cook or a full-time mother. But he never said anything. Luckily, the TV show came along and I didn't have to worry about it."

Mary needed a dose of good medicine in the form of laughter and a job. The TV show she was referring to actually began with a TV special. That same year, she reteamed with Van Dyke for what became a pivotal one-time CBS variety hour. *Dick Van Dyke and the Other Woman* was written by *Dick Van Dyke Show* veterans Sam Denoff and Bill Persky, who had worked on annual specials for the performer since his original series folded. In 1969, Persky approached Denoff and said, "It's been five years since we did *The Dick Van Dyke Show*. Why don't we do a reunion with Mary and Dick? She could really use the exposure."

Denoff agreed. They went on to script *Dick Van Dyke and the Other Woman*, which Persky said Van Dyke "...very generously turned over to Mary, and made it all about her, to show her off." "We did that special," Van Dyke said, "and I had her sing and dance. She did everything and, *bang*! Right after that, she got *The Mary Tyler Moore Show*. She still credits [that special] with getting her started. You know, and *man* – she took off!"

According to David Van Deusen, "*Dick Van Dyke and the Other Woman* was clearly the spark that initiated CBS's interest in giving Mary a chance on her own sitcom, and my sense is that she had Dick to thank for that. And the genuine, natural chemistry that occurred between Dick and Mary on this special reminded us again of her talents and abilities…comedy, singing, dancing, and more. Much of the appeal to fans was being able to see Rob and Laura together again, as it evoked fond memories of their interplay on *The Dick Van Dyke Show*. But the material for the special was also top notch, with sketches and musical production numbers that were written by Bill Persky and Sam Denoff."

Persky said *Dick Van Dyke and the Other Woman* was "one of my most favorite things that I ever did. I loved it. There were pieces [skits] in there that were just wonderful. Dick and Mary did one final scene as a bride and a groom on a wedding cake. And they had been placed in a refrigerator on their 50th Anniversary. But that was their relationship…in the fridge."

The objective of the special, Persky observed "…was to show her off as a dancer. And I've always been a repressed choreographer, so I said, 'Why don't we do something where they were on crutches…in a ski lodge?' So, there was an entire dance number were everybody was on crutches, and it was fantastic."

Another skit involved Mary portraying an Emmy Award statue, and Van Dyke playing an Academy Award, or "Oscar." The supposedly superior Oscar mocked its poor-relation Emmy. "It played so well on the special," remembered Persky, "…that CBS used it to open the actual telecast of the Emmy Awards that year."

The high ratings and critical acclaim for *Dick Van Dyke and the Other Woman* screamed to have the favorite acting couple of '60s TV back where they belonged on a weekly basis. Within a two-year period *Other Woman* indeed gave birth to *The Mary Tyler Moore Show*, and subsequently *The New Dick Van Dyke Show* (CBS, 1971-1974), a fairly standard husband-and-wife sitcom by Carl Reiner with a contemporary twist. This series didn't make it past the third season, partially because it was deemed too dated, and specifically because Reiner had a creative dispute over the contents and context of an episode titled, "The Pregnancy" (November 4, 1974).

The birth of *The Mary Tyler Moore Show*, however, was shaped from an entirely different ball of wax. According to Rick Lertzman, the sitcom became part of Grant Tinker's masterful vision to refocus Mary's career, beginning with *Dick Van Dyke and the Other Woman*. "Grant pushed with

Dick Van Dyke to do *Dick Van Dyke and the Other Woman* special because he had a plan to remount Mary for television."

A short time later, when Mary and Tinker formed MTM Enterprises to house *The Mary Tyler Moore Show*, Lertzman said, "Grant wanted the best and the brightest cutting edge talent, in front of and behind the scenes. He wanted her show it to be hipper than *The Dick Van Dyke Show*…and to take her out of the mode of Laura Petrie."

They didn't want Mary's character to come across as sweet but old-fashioned, like the character of Doris Martin, as played by Doris Day on *The Doris Day Show*. "I mentioned that to Grant," said Lertzman, "and he kind of laughed. But he really did kind of take the concept of *The Doris Day Show* to another level. And ironically, Rose Marie was the side-kick on that show. And Rose loved Doris," whereas she had not been all that keen on Mary during their *Dick Van Dyke Show* years.

Mary may not have what it required to widen her success from the small screen to the big, but as Lertzman said, "Doris Day had the chops to be an incredible star in film and on television, where her show lasted five years. But she didn't have Grant Tinker. She had [husband] Marty Melcher, who knew zilch about how to run a TV show."

It's not an idle comparison. Apparently, several elements of *The Mary Tyler Moore Show* were "taken from *The Doris Day Show* and used by Grant," according to Lertzman. For example, Mary Richards as a single woman moving to Minneapolis echoed the widowed Doris Martin's relocation to San Francisco in the second season of *The Doris Day Show*. The series initially showcased Martin living on a farm. Joining her there was her father portrayed by Denver Pyle, who, in reality, was only a few years older than Day. Her two TV children, played by Philip Brown and Todd Starke, stayed with the show for the next two years. But by the show's fifth season, it was as if all three of those characters never existed, as they were cut from the show.

Tinker wanted *The Mary Tyler Moore Show* to be "cutting edge," said Lertzman. "He didn't want [*Doris Day-Show*-like] writers who were kind of in the past." So Tinker hired Allan Burns and Jim Brooks, the latter of whom was writing groundbreaking scripts for *Room 222*. "And the same thing happened when Grant later hired Ed. Weinberger," Lertzman said. "All these great talents were writing more cutting-edge material, and a lot of them were at Paramount Studios," which cultivated that kind of talent under the guidance of director-turned-studio head Robert Evans. "Universal Studios was still stuck in the '60s," Lertzman opined, whereas Paramount's television unit was more contemporary and looking to the future.

In shaping *The Mary Tyler Moore Show*, and MTM Enterprises, Tinker did not initially envision a powerhouse that would eventually cultivate spin-offs such as *Rhoda* and *Phyllis*, or generate other series like *The Bob Newhart Show*. "That was his intent as an independent producer," Lertzman said, "but at first his focus was getting his wife back on television and as a centerpiece of a show." By that time, Dick Van Dyke was on his way back to television with his second sitcom, which co-starred Hope Lange. "But without Grant Tinker and Mary Tyler Moore, *The New Dick Van Dyke Show* just didn't fly. It did okay in the ratings, but Carl Reiner wanted out of the show. Dick made it difficult in the beginning, because they were shooting it in Arizona, where he moved because his wife wanted to leave Hollywood behind."

The New Dick Van Dyke Show, however, did not have the same benefits that Grant Tinker brought to Mary. For one, "Hope Lange's Q-quotient was awful," said Lertzman. "She had done *The Ghost and Mrs. Muir* but she was not real strong." Other actors on the *New* show were capable, including Marty Brill and future *Fried Green Tomatoes* author/screenwriter Fannie Flagg who, Lertzman said, "was essentially the Sally Rogers role of the new show. But none of them had the research done by Grant Tinker, who was big on analytics."

Tinker had utilized such research in casting *The Mary Tyler Moore Show*. "They just did not simply cast actors," Lertzman observed, "…they researched and tested the Q-quotient of those actors. Hiring Ed Asner was not just a fluke. Grant really looked for a unique character actor. He had seen Ed play a villain in a John Wayne film [*Eldorado*, 1966], and Ed just popped out at him. Grant saw something in him…as a kind a gruff boss. He had researched character actors and had looked for uniqueness in casting. He tested everyone and was really careful about who he selected from the actors to the directors to the producers. If you notice, almost everyone associated with *The Mary Tyler Moore Show* went on to successful careers…either from creating *The Bob Newhart Show*…or *Taxi*…or those like Jim Brooks created and *The Simpsons*. Elements of Grant's people are all over the business, and have had an effect on television for years."

Tinker had learned such analytics from his days at Benton & Bowles which, Lertzman said, "…was brilliant at studying American tastes, and what attracts people to commercial TV shows. Grant was always looking for certain elements to attract certain products and a certain age. And for *The Mary Tyler Moore Show*, he targeted the 25 to 50 age group."

The Mary Tyler Moore Show arrived with a different, if similar concept from *Doris Day*, and became a force never before seen on television. It was in early 1970 that Mary and Tinker formed MTM Enterprises, which brought to TV a unique voice and wit. Their work arrived on September 19th with *Mary Tyler Moore*, the sitcom's official title. As Carol Channing had explained, MTM Enterprises formed its logo from Mary's initials. Also featured was a kitten named Mimsy. It was a visual jab at MGM's long-established Leo-the-Lion logo. But according to Lertzman, Mary had considered calling the company *GAT*, reflecting the initials of Grant Almerin Tinker.

In his interview on TLC's *Behind the Fame* TV special about MTM's *Mary Tyler Moore* and *Bob Newhart* shows, Ed Asner described his journey into that universe as "a seven-year-trip through the land of Oz." On *The Oprah Winfrey Show's* later *MTMS* reunion he expanded on that thought, likening the experience to "seven years of the Yellow Brick Road." He called Lou Grant the Cowardly Lion, Gavin MacLeod's Murray Slaughter the Tin Man, who "needed the oil," leaving Ted Knight as Ted Baxter to represent the Scarecrow, "the brainless one." But the center was Mary, of course, as Dorothy, to complete the journey which Asner summed up in one word: "wonderful."

Bob Newhart once referred to MTM Enterprises, which housed both *The Bob Newhart Show* (CBS, 1972-1978) and *Newhart* (CBS, 1982-1990), as "a magical place that doesn't exist anymore," and wasn't sure "if it exists anywhere else." "There was such a freedom there," he said, where "creativity was so encouraged. And of course MTM was Mary Tyler Moore. It was her husband, Grant Tinker, Mary, and Arthur Price. They built this studio, and I was lucky enough to be part of it. They took a chance on me."

Newhart described himself as first and foremost a stand-up comedian who was able to translate his persona into a weekly TV sitcom. There had been other stand-ups who starred in weekly programs "...like Danny Thomas, Jack Benny, and George Burns," he said, "...but their shows were pretty much radio shows that transported to television. My background was totally stand-up."

MTM Enterprises, in turn, was initially uncertain of Newhart's acting ability. "But they took the chance," he said, "and that decision came right from the top...that came from Mary. She loved people. She loved actors and she loved taking chances."

"In missing Mary," he added, "I also miss that magical place that existed in the '70s and the '80s."

When *The Bob Newhart Show* celebrated its 100th episode, "Still Crazy After All These Years" (October 16, 1976), both Mary and Grant Tinker showed up for the festivities. And that appearance meant a great deal to the actor-comedian. That gesture, Newhart said, defined "family." In his eyes, Mary and Tinker were displaying "they cared about you and you were part of the family and they want to celebrate along with you."

According to Newhart, Mary and MTM Enterprises were one and the same, and there would never be another sitcom like *The Mary Tyler Moore Show*. "It was such a breakthrough show," he said. Mary Richards "was on her own…her own persona. She wasn't an appendage of her husband." Even with a series like *I Love Lucy*, which Mary once named as the best situation comedy in history, Lucille Ball's Lucy Ricardo would somehow corral her husband Ricky, played by real-life spouse Desi Arnaz "…into some kind of problem," Newhart said, "and then she'd kind of come to him at the end and say, 'I'm sorry.' And he would say, 'Oh, that's all right, Lucy.' And that was the end of the [episode]."

On the other end of the spectrum, Newhart said, was Mary Richards, "a very independent woman." But this wasn't how the character was originally envisioned. In the pilot, Mary R. had just ended a romantic relationship and was moving to Minneapolis "to start a whole new life," Newhart said.

Jim Romanovich is the current host for the *Radio Retropolis* podcasts celebrating pop culture, and executive producer of several television programs including the official *I Love Lucy 50th Anniversary* special and the critically acclaimed *Behind the Fame* specials, both for TLC. He said, "*The Mary Tyler Moore Show* was the blueprint for the 'smart-comedy' format that was copied by *M*A*S*H*, *Cheers*, *Seinfeld*, and *Friends*. That all started with Mary herself who wanted to inject a connection with the evolving television audience of the 1970s particularly with women asserting their independence, their careers and their equal rights. Her Mary Richards is a 30-year-old single woman asserting her own direction with no apologies."

Mary certainly beat several odds with the *Mary Tyler Moore* show, created by Jim Brooks and Allan Burns, who were hand-picked and hired by Grant Tinker. In archival footage for the Television Academy, Tinker intoned, "I didn't have a model…wanted to go into business for myself and have something to do with Mary's show…Jim and Allan were the keys…they created the show for Mary."

Said Burns on TLC's special about *Mary Tyler Moore*, Tinker "chose two guys who were relatively new at that time. Not that we were kids. I was in my early thirties and so was Jim." Tinker's selection of him and Brooks, Burns added, was a "kind of offbeat idea instead of hedging his bets."

Brooks had written for CBS News in New York, and was a writer and producer for documentaries. A veteran of classic TV before embarking on *Mary Tyler Moore*, Burns had created and penned episodes of *The Munsters*; contributed scripts to *The Smothers Brothers Show*; and served as an editor for *Get Smart*. Together, Burns and Brooks had collaborated on television's highly regarded school-based series, *Room 222* (ABC, 1969-1974), which was the medium's first half-hour dramedy.

"The ideas we came up with were just awful, the first ones were just terrible," said Burns of his and Brooks' initial concepts for the *Mary Tyler Moore* series. "Then we decided we wanted to do a show about divorce. It had never been done. If you can believe that, that in 1970 no show had ever been done where the lead character was divorced. Mary and Grant loved the idea…a woman of thirty, which Mary was at the time, out there on her own…how backwards were we to think that a woman of thirty couldn't be thirty and be single without being divorced. Well, we went over to tell the idea to CBS and they had a corporate heart attack. They said, 'My God they'll think she's divorced Dick Van Dyke.'" The comedian himself later recalled, "During the run of our show, there were a lot of people who really believed Mary and I were married in real life. I'd check into hotels with my wife, and people would say, 'Yeah, right.' "

It was an unexamined national assumption: If Rob and Laura were married on *The Dick Van Dyke Show* that meant Dick and Mary were, too. If Mary was going to do another show, one that didn't include Van Dyke, then her character simply could not be a divorcée.

According to Burns, the network's negative reaction on the West Coast to Mary's new TV character being divorced paled in comparison to the CBS suits of New York. "They really hated it. They claimed that there were four things the American audiences would not accept. One was Jewish leads, the other was leads from New York, and the other [was] leads with moustaches, and the other was leads who were divorced. Now, we're sitting in a room full of New York Jews with moustaches and I'm sure all of them had been divorced at least once, so they were saying that you put [characters representing themselves] on television and nobody would accept them."

After their meeting with the East Coast CBS brass, Burns said he and Brooks left knowing they had "bombed pretty badly. So, the minute we were out of the room, CBS, apparently, Mike Dan, turned to Arthur Price, Mary's manager [who] was nominally running the MTM company while Grant was still at 20th Century Fox, and said get rid of these guys; they're going to kill you."

Tinker, however, reminded CBS of their agreement to give him and Mary total control of creating, casting, and producing. The network had forfeited all rights in order to sign Mary. Powerless to enforce the network's objections, Dan and his staff had to sit back and accept Brooks and Burns in first position. This conflict would escalate, while Tinker maintained that only in an atmosphere free from network interference could his team develop and hone their vision.

In the end, the *Mary Tyler Moore* series became about Mary Richards, a single career woman who produces the local television news for the fictional WJM-TV station snuggled in the chill-ridden Minneapolis, Minnesota. "Mary was real and we wanted to keep that reality," Burns explained on the TLC special. "We thought…let's leave her single and she'll have had a long relationship, an affair, really, with an intern who was going through medical school and then a resident who couldn't get married. And that's when he's finished. He has decided…why rush things. She [then] decided this wasn't going to work."

ACT III

The Prime of Ms. Mary Richards

Mary received many accolades over the years, including multiple Emmys for playing Laura Petrie on *The Dick Van Dyke Show* and Mary Richards on *The Mary Tyler Moore Show*, which forever benchmarked her career. In this publicity photo from 1974, she holds the Emmys she received for Best Lead Actress in a Comedy Series and Actress of the Year in a Series, both for *The Mary Tyler Moore Show*. [Credit: Ronald V. Borst/Hollywood Movie Posters]

Chapter

9

According to Allan Burns, the idea of Mary Richards leaving her hometown of Rosenburg, Minnesota for a new life in Minneapolis was based on Jim Brooks' experiences at CBS News in New York. A newsroom, Burns believed, would be the ideal setting for Richards' employment. As with *The Dick Van Dyke Show*, splitting the setting between Mary's home and workplace on *The Mary Tyler Moore Show* "would be…wonderful," Burns said. "We want[ed] to be able to go back and forth between."

Brooks' former real-life newsroom was peppered with people who served as the inspiration for the fabricated workplace setting of the WJM-TV newsroom. Mary Richards' supporting characters were: Mary's crusty but adorable boss Lou Grant, played by Ed Asner; Ted Knight's silver-haired, if not silver-tongued, egomaniacal news anchor Ted Baxter; Betty White's man-hungry, Suzie-homewrecker Sue Ann Nivens; Gavin MacLeod's amiable news writer Murray Slaughter; and, for a time John Amos' TV weatherman Gordy Howard. The latter character exited, supposedly landing a job as a New York talk-show host. This ruse came about when Amos was hired then later fired by Norman Lear for *Good Times*.

At home, Mary Richards interacted with Cloris Leachman's flighty apartment-building landlord Phyllis Lindstrom; Valerie Harper's Bronx-born Rhoda Morgenstern, "Mare's" best friend. Georgia Engel joined the show in 1972 as Georgette Franklin, Ted Baxter's girlfriend-turned-fiancée-turned-wife.

In the center of this remarkable pool of talent was Mary. Journalist Kathleen Neumeyer once observed in *Los Angeles Magazine*, "Although it's Mary's name in the title, many of the plots highlight other members of the superb company and only peripherally involve Mary, who is at her best reacting to others. Her classically pretty, girl-next-door features can stretch into a silly-putty, Dresden-doll version of Joe E. Brown when she wants them to. Unlike some comics, she can get laughs without losing her dignity – a clown who can be funny without making a fool of herself."

"I would love to be able to be a buffoon like Carol Burnett," Mary told the *New York Times* in 1974. "But I'm not that way. I'm more constrained."

Around the same time, she told *Newsweek*, "My forte is not being funny, but reacting in a funny way to those around me. Women's lib would kill me for saying this, but 95 percent of the women who have had to carry the load on their own shows have not succeeded. So we decided to make me a straight woman." In the same article, Jim Brooks opined, "If Mary was in a French movie and you didn't speak French, you'd laugh at her."

While Mary Richards attempted to make it on her own, the TV times were a-changin' when it came to the way sitcoms were produced and presented. Just as the *MTM Show* debuted, CBS had purged itself, some said, too early and too quickly, of all its rural-geared comedies. These included hits like *Petticoat Junction*, *The Beverly Hillbillies*, *Green Acres*, and *Mayberry, R.F.D.* (the sequel to *The Andy Griffith Show*). Even the aforementioned *Doris Day Show* relocated its initially farm-based female lead Doris Martin to San Francisco, where she worked. In the post "kill-everything-country" edict from CBS, Martin now resided atop an Italian restaurant, run by eccentric (if relatively stereotypical) Italian characters played by Kaye Ballard and Bernie Kopell (who, post-*TMTMS*, would co-star with Gavin MacLeod on *The Love Boat*).

Competing networks soon joined the programming extermination and removed other light-hearted comedies and fantasy series to boot. Soon-to-be-gone were ABC's *Bewitched*, and NBC's replica *I Dream of Jeannie*, each replaced and/or thrown against shows like Norman Lear's culture-shifting *All in the Family*, which begat its own "realistic comedy" list of hit spin-offs such as *The Jeffersons* and *Maude*, which spawned *Good Times*. For some reason, the broadcast network bigwigs didn't feel that there was room for shows of every format to survive. Former CBS executive-turned-Screen Gems icon Harry Ackerman believed "the networks were too hasty" in making such drastic alternations in programming.

For example, in its final season from 1971 to 1972, Ackerman's *Bewitched* sitcom was holding its own against *All in the Family* on Saturday nights, after it had switched from Thursdays and then

Wednesdays. But a new era of sitcoms was in the making, and that's all that mattered. By now shows like *M*A*S*H* had long replaced the likes of *The Munsters*. The trailblazing Mary Richards was paving the way for the independent spirit, while the free spirit of Samantha on *Bewitched* lost her powers for the last time; the hypnotic horizontal hold she had long possessed since 1964 was broken. "The gimmicky had lost its appeal," as one Gannett News editorial suggested.

But MTM Enterprises was gaining momentum by expansion into more down-to-Earth formats. Besides its core *Moore* show, the company eventually corralled a stable of CBS spin-offs like *Rhoda* (1974-1978), *Phyllis* (1975-1977), and *Lou Grant* (1977-1982), as well as stand-alone, non-spin-offs such as *The Bob Newhart Show* (CBS, 1972-1978), *Hill Street Blues* (NBC, 1981-1987), *St. Elsewhere* (NBC, 1982-1988), and other shows on various networks. Although she did not receive a direct sequel series based on her Sue Ann Nivens character, Betty White eventually headed an MTM Enterprises half-hour called *The Betty White Show*, which ran for just one season on CBS (1977-1978), and which co-starred Georgia Engel. The only other *Moore* regular actor and/or character who did not receive an MTM/CBS series, one way or another, was Gavin MacLeod. But MacLeod did set sail into high ratings as Captain Stubing of *The Love Boat*, a series which enjoyed a lengthy first run via ABC from 1977 to 1986 at 9:00 PM, Saturday nights, where its numbers far surpassed those attained by *The Mary Tyler Moore Show* for the prior seven years.

MacLeod's continued success and long life (age 87 as of 2018) remains a testament to his generous and modest heart. This contributed to his winning the part of Murray on *Mary*, and the somewhat indirect role he played off-screen in helping a few of his fellow *Moore* cast members. When auditioning for the series, MacLeod had just returned from Yugoslavia, where he had filmed *Kelly's Heroes*, the 1970 feature starring Clint Eastwood, Telly Savalas, Carroll O'Connor, and Mary's future *Ordinary People* co-star Donald Sutherland. MacLeod was a member of the *Words and Music* theatre group that was performing the musical *Carousel*, in which he played Jigger. While in rehearsal, he received a call from his agent who said, "Mary Tyler Moore is doing a pilot and they want to see you."

"Oh, I love her," he replied. ("I mean, who didn't?" he added in retrospect.)

"Great," his agent returned. "I'll have them send you the scripts," as in plural.

There were two scripts. One was the pilot which featured the Rhoda character. The other involved Rhoda's mother, Ida Morgenstern, who was eventually played by Nancy Walker (best known as Rosie the waitress in the familiar Bounty paper-towel TV commercials). MacLeod read the first teleplay and thought it was "terrific." However, *Moore* creators Jim Brooks and Allan Burns envisioned MacLeod as Lou Grant, which didn't feel right for the actor. He also did not believe he was a proper fit to play anchorman Ted Baxter.

That's when the role of Murray caught his attention. "I thought I could do something with that character," MacLeod recalled. "I loved his flippant ways, his little humor." So, after he auditioned for Lou, and just before he exited the audition, MacLeod turned to Brooks and Burns and said, "I wouldn't believe myself as Mary's boss," no matter how much he loved the writing, especially Grant's famed "spunk" speech. "I mean, come on," MacLeod maintained today. "That's a gorgeous line. You can ride your entire career on that!"

No matter. He simply did not want to fill Lou's shoes, and continued to make his case to Brooks and Burns. "I've enjoyed this experience so much, meeting you young people and all," he said. "But you know what? I really like the part of Murray."

At which point, a bemused Brooks asked, "You like Murray? He's a supporting character."

"I don't care," MacLeod replied.

"Well, do you want to read for the part?"

"Sure," MacLeod returned.

Casting director Ethel Winant had "always wanted Gavin MacLeod to play Murray…because they had only seen him do heavies; they wanted him to read for Lou Grant. I thought maybe Murray was the hardest part to cast on the show. Each part was so specific in its attitude and he was sort of the catalyst and he had to be more adaptable. He had to create his own place in that configuration of characters. And [MacLeod] read for Murray and there was no question he was going to play Murray."

MacLeod auditioned for the part, "got some good laughs," he said, and exited Brooks and Burns' office once more. In the hallway he noticed another actor, balding like him, pacing back and forth. That actor was Ed Asner, whom MacLeod would frequently encounter at other auditions, along with Ted Knight. As MacLeod relayed to *Los Angeles Magazine* in 1976, those three Mary amigos would often audition for the same roles.

In any case, when MacLeod returned to rehearsals for *Carousel*, his agent stopped by and told him, "They want you to be in the *Mary Tyler Moore* pilot."

MacLeod wondered, "Do you know for which part?"

"I believe for a character named 'Murray.' Does that sound right?"

"It sure does," MacLeod replied.

Meanwhile, Ed Asner was questioning whether or not he should have auditioned for Lou Grant. "I was afraid of comedy at the time," he said on the TLC special. When he read for the part, originally, he did so "'intelligently,' but not 'funny.'"

On that same special, Burns said Asner's audition was not up to par. "So we thought...*next.*" Ten minutes later, an assistant to Burns and Brooks notified them that Asner had returned. "Oh, good God!" Burns wailed, "Why?!" But he and Brooks were polite when Asner burst into their office for the second time and said, "I was terrible...and you guys just sat there and let me be terrible. Give me some direction. Tell me what you really want in this character."

"I must have been possessed," Asner said of his second go-round. "And I read crazily, as they somewhat wished. And they laughed their asses off. Then I came back a week or two later to read with Mary, and I tried to remember what I had done because it was so crazy."

Mary remembered what happened next with a different perspective. After she and Asner read together, she turned to Burns and company, and said, "Well, I guess we keep looking, huh?" At which point, the team response was, according to Burns, "Are you kidding? He was wonderful. You were great together. Weren't you aware of how good it was? We could feel like the hairs going on the back of our necks."

Ethel Winant, also in the room, turned to Mary and said, "Take my word for it, Mary. This guy is terrific and there's real magic...great chemistry between the two of you."

To which Mary replied, "Well, OK. If you think so."

The role of Ted Baxter, meanwhile, had originally called for a young actor in his mid-thirties who could be a potential romantic interest for Mary Richards. Those up for the part included Robert Dornan, who later became a congressman, and John Aniston, Jennifer Aniston's father. The latter, Burns said, "was very good...but still wasn't quite the comedy we were looking for."

TMTMS producer David Davis had seen Knight performing in a play titled, *You Know I Can't Hear You When the Water's Running.* "There is this guy in it who's the lead who is just hysterical," said Davis. "Ted was just wonderful," added Winant. His career had not gone well those last few years before he was cast as Baxter. "He came in...he got in a blazer. He put the emblem on the blazer of the station. I mean, he really worked at it."

Knight was "a bit older than what we wanted," Burns said, "and we didn't cast him right away. It would have been our horrible mistake" not to consider him strongly, though.

Mary, Burns, Brooks, Winant and company were impressed with Knight's dedication to the audition and so, as Burns said, "we cast him."

With regard to Cloris Leachman's casting, Winant said, "It had never occurred to me that anyone else should play Phyllis."

That left only one main character to be cast for the *Mary Tyler Moore* pilot: Rhoda, a role for which Winant "auditioned everybody in the world," including Brenda Vaccaro, whom Winant had envisioned for the part but was unavailable.

Winant was becoming increasingly nervous. It was getting close to the wire, and she was attending a great deal of theatre in the form of "off-Sunset plays."

Then one night, she saw a production on Melrose Avenue in a small theatre. "It was in a small production called *American Nightmare*," Valerie Harper recalled on TLC. "It was a send-up of a British staged reading, and I played Eva Braun...and Vida Fontanne...extreme characters."

Winant exited the *Nightmare* performance after the first act and called the theatre the next day. No one had any idea where or who Harper was. "And I went crazy," Winant said. "And I drove my poor secretary crazy. We called every guild in New York. We couldn't find her. She just didn't exist. And I was so depressed because it was bad enough not having cast the part, but then to have found somebody that you thought could play the part and have lost her."

Harper was eventually tracked down. She credited "the wonderful, legendary Ethel Winant, who has cast so many people in so many shows...she's responsible for so many careers. Ethel Winant, thank you for casting me [as] Rhoda. She didn't know where I was but she tracked me down."

When Harper was brought in to finally audition for the part, Burns recalled she brought along many props, which he deemed "a no-no, but it worked for her" and the audition became "another one of those spine-tingling" moments.

"I think they were quite taken aback that someone had gone through all this trouble," Harper said. "I worked my best Bronx accent and read and then they said, 'We're going to have you back.' And I came back about a week later and there Mary was. I was her fan anyway, 'cause I'd seen her on *Dick Van Dyke* on all those years. She was warm, sweet and unassuming."

"She read with Mary and there was no just no question," said Winant. "We signed her. It was a miracle that it happened."

In a later interview with entertainment journalist David Martindale, Harper said:

"It really was down to the wire when they hired me…When they called me, I thought, 'I'll never get it.' I'm brunet with a small nose and so is Mary. I figured they'll get some short, chubby blond to be a contrast. That's how much I know."

But there was still the issue of who would play Rhoda's neurotic mother Ida Morgenstern. Gavin MacLeod recalled that Maureen Stapleton was in the running. Contrary to popular belief and similar last names notwithstanding, Maureen was not the sister of Jean Stapleton, the female lead of Norman Lear's groundbreaking, yet-to-air half-hour comedy.

That's when MacLeod suggested Nancy Walker, who Burns and Brooks knew nothing about. As it happened, Walker was in New York directing *Fallen Angels*, a play by Noel Coward. "She's one of the great comedy talents of all time," MacLeod told the *Moore* creative duo.

Ida Morgenstern was presented in one of the two early, preparatory scripts MacLeod was given to read through at his audition, but the character did not make an actual appearance on *Mary Tyler Moore* until the episode, "Support Your Local Mother," which aired October 24, 1970. MacLeod was happily surprised to see Walker in the part. A short time later, he found himself at the first table reading for the pilot, surrounded by Mary, Asner, Harper, Knight, Leachman, Brooks, Burns, and producers David Davis and Lorenzo Music. Due to the latter's last surname, MacLeod assumed Lorenzo was the show's musical director, unaware that Music was the "genius" writer and performer who eventually voiced the unseen character of "Carlton, the doorman" on the *Rhoda* series.

Also in the room that first day: Jay Sandrich, whom MacLeod described as a "wonderful comedy director. We had a whole series of directors, but Jay stood apart from the crowd, as far as I was concerned. He was responsible for putting much of the show together."

And then there was Mary, who MacLeod called "the leader of a wonderful family. There was no getting away from that. She was Number One. She was so wonderful. You couldn't wait to get to the set. What a gift it was to be able to work with her. Because of her, we all had a nice job. She was so supportive," even when least expected.

MacLeod's hairless scalp may have nabbed him pre-*Mary Tyler Moore* roles like Mel Cooley's bald jewelry salesman on *The Dick Van Dyke Show*. But at one point in his career MacLeod was forced to camouflage his head with what he calls "a second-hand hairpiece" he purchased in New York. This strategic move that won him a role in his first Broadway show, *A Hatful of Rain*, also starring Ben Gazzara, Steve McQueen, Christine White, and Florence (*The Brady Bunch*) Henderson. MacLeod "adored" Henderson, and would later perform with her many times on *The Love Boat*.

But one Sunday night, during his *Mary Tyler Moore Show* days, MacLeod stopped at a department store in the San Fernando Valley, where the show filmed. Upon entering the store, he noticed a display of Zsa Zsa Gabor wigs and hairpieces for men on the main floor. This display, he professed, "I was attracted to right away." He approached the sales clerk, tried on a grey hairpiece, and purchased it. Later that night, he showed it to his wife and children and, as he recalled, "They screamed and thought it was the funniest thing."

The next day, he wore the hairpiece to work, accented with a Hawaiian shirt. As he walked around the set, no one recognized him until they were up close. "And when Mary saw it, she roared," he said. Consequently, they wrote the episode, "Toulouse-Lautrec Is One of My Favorite Artists," which aired Halloween night, October 31, 1970. Here, Ted becomes ill and Murray does the news while wearing a wig. "That just goes to show you how supportive Mary and the entire company were," Macleod said. "You gave them an idea, and they ran with it."

This episode was one of the many "cheerful moments" he experienced while working on the show, including another highlight for him: "Ted Baxter Meets Walter Cronkite" (February 9, 1974), which featured the real-life legendary news journalist. At the time, Cronkite was CBS's evening-news anchorman. When Cronkite walked on camera into the fabricated WJM-TV newsroom, MacLeod said, the studio audience "went crazy!"

But not every day on *The Mary Tyler Moore Show* set was enjoyable.

Chapter

10

Due to her diabetes, Mary would have occasional bouts with blurred vision, slurred words, and issues with her equilibrium. "Everybody was aware of her condition," Ed Asner said on the Reelz Channel. "And they would have broken each other's legs to be the first to offer their lives in defense of her."

Such an opportunity to defend Mary's life arrived one Monday morning, circa 1970, during a production meeting of *The Mary Tyler Moore Show*. That's when her ability to speak was suddenly compromised. To the confusion of the surrounding cast and crew, she burst into tears. "We all heard her screaming in some sort of pain," Ed Asner recalled. "We didn't know what the hell was going on."

It was soon realized that Mary was having a hypoglycemic attack brought upon by her diabetes. One of the show's quick-thinking producers took charge, and poured orange juice into her mouth. Soon Mary was fine.

Mary would eventually become one of the world's leading advocates for those stricken with diabetes. Television writer Rita Lakin called Mary "...a pioneer for women" with *The Mary Tyler Moore Show*. Lakin, who penned episodes of classic TV shows as diverse as *Dr. Kildare* and *Family Affair*, said "Mary was incredible and because of the era when men really dominated everything, I think we always denigrated what we did; and that's true of myself as well. There were a lot of women who did not take their jobs seriously." In turn, Lakin said, they were not taken seriously by the men who worked in the industry. The exceptions, however, included those like director Sidney Pollack who helmed Lakin's episode of *Dr. Kildare*, and David Victor, the show's producer. "Sidney was wonderful to work with, and a wonderful person to know," she recalled. "And he went on to have one hell of a career," while Victor "…was giving everybody their first jobs," despite their gender. "It was really an amazing thing."

Lakin dedicated her memoir to "a whole lot of men, all of whom were kind and helped me and cared," she said. "They were wonderful." In some ways, Lakin's words are uplifting to consider in the post-Harvey Weinstein era of Hollywood, which she described as "the terrible way men treated women in our industry." But beyond her unique experience, Lakin, as a woman writer, along with many of her female peers, never thought that what they were doing was important enough. "That's the era I worked in," she said.

Then along came Mary. "I was inspired by *The Mary Tyler Moore Show* but I didn't know I was inspired," observed Lakin. "I just knew that I kept watching it because I thought Mary Richards and all of the characters were just so wonderful, fresh and so original. There were so many [comedy] shows in that era that were 'thin,' and I was just entranced with the truthfulness of [the *MTM*] show. It had such honesty about it. I was impressed with it."

A good portion of that impression may be attributed to Treva Silverman who, as Executive Script Consultant, had written some of the most beloved episodes of *The Mary Tyler Moore Show*. Gavin MacLeod, among others, held her talent in high regard. "Oh my gosh!" he said on hearing Silverman's name. "I kiss her feet."

Silverman, meanwhile, had been "a major fan" of Mary. "I loved her on *The Dick Van Dyke Show*," she said. "She was pretty, without that *Hollywoodish* 'I-am-pretty' aura. Mary instinctively knew where the comedy was, why and how a line was funny, and never overplayed it. Later on, when she was on our show, and we would have our first table read – no rehearsal, no director – her line readings were just the way you heard them in your head when you were writing them. She had learned so much on *The Dick Van Dyke Show* and our show was all the better for it." Silverman's talent had earned that position of Executive Script Consultant. In the series' first season, Jim Brooks and Allan Burns were executive producers, and David Davis (not to be confused with the same-named editor of *Mary Magazine*) had been the producer. When Davis and his partner Lorenzo Music had their pilot picked up for *The Bob Newhart Show*, Ed. Weinberger (who retained a period after his first name) was brought in as the *MTMS*'s producer. By then, Silverman had already penned a number of scripts, and Weinberger approached her with a request. He needed "another person…another 'head,'" she said.

As a result, Silverman became an executive as well as a writer. She was "enormously happy" with being "exactly at the place" where she wanted to be. She wrote episodes, and edited and rewrote the episodes by other writers. "It was a big deal back then," she said, "...much written about and publicized – because I was the first woman who was an executive on an episodic comedy. It seems like prehistoric thinking now but that was the way things were."

"Most of the drafts that came in were good and needed maybe a moderate amount of work," she explained. But there was one submission that was "so shockingly bad" that Silverman had to rewrite approximately 95 percent of the script. "Out of respect for all writers, the philosophy on the show was to retain the writers' names on their episode," no matter how much rewriting was necessary. After the rewrite, Silverman "gritted" her teeth as she typed the title page and inserted the names of the two writers.

Months later, after the episode was completed and filmed before a live audience which included the two writers, Silverman said that the producer of a comedy show sought her opinion of the two writers, who were fairly new. "They had recommended that he watch *their* show which was going to be on the air the following week." At a loss for words, she murmured, "Well, I'll let you be the judge. Why don't I just send over their first draft?"

The producer "happily agreed," and she in turn "happily sent over....the hideous first draft" written by the two writers. "Ah yes," Silverman said in retrospect, "...how to out-manipulate a manipulator."

Fortunately, such less-than-uplifting experiences were rare on the show which, as Silverman went on to detail, "had a collaborative, supportive atmosphere. The story sessions were the first time I was invited to kind of dig down into myself and find grains of truth that could be expanded into a story. There was a lot of laughing in the story sessions where we would meet together and figure out what I was going to write about – and I could relax because I knew the script didn't have to be funny every single minute. But what it had to be was authentic. No cartoon characters. No larger-than-life stuff. The challenge was in making sure each character was exactly who they should be."

"It was a dream come true," she continued. "I sought the best in myself...the most honest in myself because Jim and Allan had set the bar so high it made me want to reach higher and higher. You got spoiled writing for that series because it was what writing for a series should be, but rarely is. This was because of the collaborative nature of Jim and Allan. No pecking order...no *we're-in-charge-here*. Their goal was to make the best series that could be made."

Silverman's presence was requested when the show first received the green light. Brooks informed her that he and Burns wanted her to write as many episodes as she wished. "So, I felt a sense of security," she recalled. "I didn't feel I had to prove myself, which, of course, led to a feeling that 'I'm terrific and can do no wrong,' which of course led to a feeling of 'Oh, shit, suppose I fail.' But it being a given that you're insecure to begin with…and I speak for myself, but also for most writers I know…I ended up working well, knowing that I was trusted. I felt I was – pardon the cliché – *home*. I got so involved writing my first episode that I think it went nearly a third over the correct length. The characters created by Jim and Allan were so specific, so beautifully drawn, it was hard to resist writing them and writing them – their voices were so clear."

Later on, when Weinberger joined the team, Silverman said, "We all became sort of a family unit. Working with Ed. was odd…that sounds like a children's poem…in that Ed. and I didn't have that much in common as people, but we worked extremely well together. I loved the group – working with Allan was a pleasure – the nicest guy in the whole world, so original and so responsive – and working with Jim, when he would go into what we would call his 'trance' – when lines of dialogue would come out of his mouth like – who is it? – the Oracle of Delphi – in this case not predicting the future, but predicting future lines…lines that would get laughs weeks later with the studio audience. You have to remember this was way before the Writers Room of today. The method was first you'd meet with Jim and Allan and figure out the story."

Many times, Brooks and Burns would present a story concept, "…maybe just a thread of an idea – and we'd figure out the story together," Silverman said. In the show's first season, this would often take an entire week of short meetings until they were pleased with a particular story. Later on, Weinberg would be involved with that process as well. At which point, Silverman would go home and write out a scene-by-scene, beat-by-beat outline of the story. "I never felt secure until I had at least two lines of dialogue that I liked in each scene," she said. "… It built confidence in me that the scene could eventually work."

Often in these story meetings, Burns would throw in what Silverman described as "a wonderful, insightful line" that would make her laugh, or "the Delphic Oracle would do a run of dialogue." But either way, she "absolutely had to have a way into a scene" before fleshing it out beat-by-beat. Next, she would drop off the "sheets of paper off…paper? I remember paper," and once those were approved she would commence writing the actual script.

It was a challenge for Silverman to select her favorite episode, but she chose "Love Is All Around," the pilot segment penned by Brooks and Burns, which she called "brilliant."

"A pilot is enormously hard to write," she explained. "It's all a blank. There's nothing. Once upon a time there was no Mary Richards, no Rhoda Morgenstern, no Lou Grant – well, you get the idea. There was no incredible song reflecting Mary's inner thoughts, her doubts...no dimly seen background story: her friends at the last job giving her a farewell party, the dumb sorta drunk guy leering over her [foreshadowing the concept of Ted Baxter] – you now know she was liked, she will be missed, she's on her way to a new life. And the show hasn't even begun!

"It's a...what's that beautiful Mexican thing that you hit and everything great comes tumbling out...it's a piñata...where you see her past and her future, and meet all her friends-to-be at home and in the newsroom.

"And last but not least, you see the interview scene with Lou. All you need to know about Mary Richards is summed up in that one scene. When Lou asks Mary about her religion, Mary, sticking up for her rights, tells him she's not supposed to answer that, it's against the law. Then, a moment later, giving in to her natural *good-girl-ness* she blurts out, Presbyterian."

"And, of course, the famous line, probably one of the most famous lines to come out of a pilot": the "spunk" line. Silverman preferred to tell it another way.

"There was an opening-night party where we all gathered together to watch the pilot being aired. After it was over, everyone in the group was applauding and congratulating Jim and Allan. A few minutes later, Jim was alone at the buffet table and when I walked up he said, 'Ah, there's an honest face. Hey, are we kidding ourselves? Did Allan and I write an ordinary pilot?' And I said, 'An ordinary pilot would've stopped at Lou saying, 'You've got spunk.' No. Not you guys. Lou *hates* spunk."

Weinberger also wrote "The Lars Affair" (September 15, 1973), an episode that still makes Silverman laugh no matter how often she sees it. Here, Phyllis finds out her husband Lars is having an affair with Sue Ann Nivens. One day, when the script for this segment had just been mimeographed, Silverman arrived to work early. She began reading the material on the stairs, and stopped dead. She "was so mesmerized that people coming into work had to walk around me," she said. "Phyllis...the wannabe sophisticate, losing her husband to – a homemaker; the line 'a damn pie' coming out of Phyllis; Sue Ann treating her soufflé like a baby...hilarious."

Of all the episodes that Silverman penned herself, her favorite is "Rhoda the Beautiful" (October 21, 1972). In this segment, Rhoda loses twenty pounds, but still feels unattractive, while Mary tries to convince her otherwise. Silverman summarized:

> The episode begins with Mary trying to convince Rhoda that she now looks great, having lost all that weight. Rhoda, uncomfortable with her new figure, is wearing kind of loose clothes, and won't accept any compliments. She keeps doing her usual self-put-downs. ("Now I can never say I'd look great if only I lost twenty pounds.") Even when the guys at the office notice her new appearance, she won't acknowledge that she looks good.
>
> She tells Mary that Hempel's, where she works, is having a beauty contest and she's been chosen as one of the contestants. She knows she doesn't have a chance, but she'll do it anyway.
>
> On the night of the contest, Mary waits up for Rhoda to come and tell her the results. Rhoda shows up in a lovely figure-hugging dress, the one she wore for the contest – looking absolutely gorgeous. Mary wants to know, what happened?
>
> What happened?
>
> Well, Rhoda tells her, she came in second. Not first, not third, but a very nice second...which is fine with her. And they leave it at that.
>
> But – it's a lie. She came in first, and is afraid to tell Mary. She's still at a point where she can't admit to herself that it's the start of a new era...a new her...that the world sees her differently.
>
> Finally it dawns on her – it flashes by her in a minute – this is who she is now. And what's more – she deserves it. She, Rhoda Morgenstern from Brooklyn, New York, deserves it. Can she say it out loud? Yes she can – and she then haltingly tells Mary – she won!

There was "another happy ending," Silverman added: "Val won the Emmy for that episode, the genesis of which is compelling. One day, Brooks and Burns told Silverman that Harper had lost twenty pounds over the hiatus, and they wanted her to write an episode that reflected that development with the intention for it to be 'Valerie's Emmy episode.'"

"I'm not sure how it is now," Silverman intoned, "but back then, a series would submit one episode for an actor to be judged on – they win or lose an Emmy based on their performance in that one half hour. So, when you're writing an Emmy episode, you try to write it in a way that shows off all of the actor's different colors...and maybe make the actor stretch a little."

"One thing that a lot of people don't realize," Silverman continued, "is that this episode, along with many, many others, couldn't have been done without Mary's generosity. Very often a star – particularly a star whose name is the title of the show – will insist on having more lines, of being more the center of attention. With Mary, it didn't matter to her who got the spotlight that week. All she wanted was for each actor to shine, and for the show to be good."

The process of assembling *The Mary Tyler Moore Show* clearly involved many variables, but required only one constant: Mary Tyler Moore. And by the time the series aired, Marlo Thomas as Ann Marie on *That Girl* (ABC, 1966-1971), for which Treva Silverman had also written scripts, had paved the way for the independent spirit that both Mary Richards and Mary Tyler Moore became.

The Dick Van Dyke Show writing team of Bill Persky and San Denoff had created *That Girl*, which Mary long acknowledged as a precursor to her series. In the 1980s, Persky directed 100 episodes of *Kate & Allie* (CBS, 1984-1989), a few of which he also wrote. Starring Susan Saint James as Kate McArdle and Jane Curtin as Allie Lowell, *Kate & Allie* centered around two divorced friends who blend their families for comfort and economic reasons in New York City. One episode that Persky directed, titled "Reruns" (March 2, 1987), featured James and Curtin as Mary and Rhoda in a dream sequence. Persky later commented regarding the uncommon thread between *That Girl*, *Mary Tyler Moore*, and *Kate & Allie*:

> As Ann Marie, Marlo was dynamite. She was an exciting 'won't-take-no-for-an-answer- and-wanted-something-more-from-life' woman. And then, Mary [played] this really transitory woman who had a job that was exciting and one that she might not have had five years earlier. And she was on the way to becoming something but she wasn't quite there yet. And Mary [the actress] always said that Marlo [as Ann Marie] opened the door that [Mary Richards] walked through. There would have been no Mary Richards had not there

not first been an Ann Marie. Mary Richards wasn't as aggressive as Ann Marie but Ann Marie was aggressive with a particular innocence in her aggressiveness. She was just really a kitten that wanted to get ahead and get at things.

In his book *My Life Is A Situation Comedy*, Persky describes *That Girl* and *Kate & Allie* as bookends, with *The Mary Tyler Moore Show* slotted in the middle. Each represented "...the progression of what happened to women from 1965 to 1985." On *That Girl* if Ann Marie has an issue with a clogged sink, she calls her father (Lew Parker) for help. On *The Mary Tyler Moore Show* Mary would call the plumber. On *Kate & Allie*, when their washing machine didn't work, they tried to fix it themselves and flooded their apartment. "Then they called the plumber and Kate had an affair with him for eight episodes," Persky commented. "It was the first time on television that a character changed. You can't see any change from episode to episode or year to year in any of the situation comedies before that, really. On *The Dick Van Dyke Show* no character changed. On *The Mary Tyler Moore Show* no character changed. With those shows, you needed people to be the same because that was the chemistry those shows were built on."

It was a point well taken, and shared by CBS executive Perry Lafferty in 1974. "The TV audience is different from the film audience. It won't take change in the characters. In film, people are expected to grow because of external pressures. But the TV audience wants to know what to expect, and when you try something different it upsets them."

"*The Beverly Hillbillies* is a classic case," Lafferty continued. "After a couple of years the writers felt the show was getting a bit monotonous so they had the family buy a motion-picture studio. The ratings dropped instantly. It took us a few weeks to get them out of that situation, but when we did, the ratings went back up immediately."

"A show never succeeds on TV just because it's good," Lafferty said. "One half of all the TV sets in America" weren't tuned into a series like *The Waltons* "just because the show is good. It has to be something else...to fulfill some kind of deep-seated need."

Before, during, and after that *Hillbillies* transition, *Van Dyke*, *Mary Tyler Moore*, and *Kate & Allie* each represented what remains good about television, what Persky described as "the growth of women's independence through the years." After that, there were others like *Murphy Brown*, starring Candice Bergen on CBS from 1988 to 1998, whose main character "did whatever the hell she wanted," Persky said. "And then there was *Friends*" on NBC from 1994 to 2004, which "kind of loosened things up a little more," when it came to female freedoms and human equality. But these shows did it all with style, as opposed to many shows since that have featured characters of any gender seeking "opportunities for have sexual encounters and little else."

In contrast, Mary as Mary Richards on *The Mary Tyler Moore Show*, or as Laura Petrie on *The Dick Van Dyke Show* was, Persky said, "a delightful person and performer," who was "sexy as hell, but…vulnerable. She did ballsy things but never in a ballsy way. She was always a lady at all times. The Laura character remained a contemporary American woman who was exploring new opportunities," while "*The Dick Van Dyke Show* was the first to present a husband and wife as peers." Laura did not have a job away from home, but she certainly worked at home and ran the household like Rob ran the office. "And he was as worried about making her angry, as she was about making him angry," Persky stated. "In all shows previous to that, it was the wife who was always so concerned about what he's going to say. But [on the *Van Dyke Show*] two people were presented as equals and who respected one another."

Mary Richards on *The Mary Tyler Moore Show*, Persky said "…just had that certain way of doing things. You were always on her side. You just always loved [her] even when she squirmed or the way she cried."

Chapter

11

For the career-minded Mary, playing the independent Ms. Mary Richards was not a stretch. "I play me," she told *TV Guide* in 1970. "I'm scared that if I tamper with it, I might ruin it. My forte is not being funny … but reacting in a funny way to those around me."

She did not view herself as "naturally funny." Rather, she said, "I have a natural *love* of other people's senses of humor. I find that probably one of the most important aspects of a human being … [is] to be funny and have a great sense of humor. And I love to be around it … and enjoy it. I think that's why maybe I'm a good 'straight woman,' in essence is that I like to just share in the extra light that comes off that funny person."

Another time, she said, "Humor's important to me, and I enjoy using cutting-edge type of humor. Mary Richards didn't do that. Mary was so…earnest. She was so thoughtful, so careful. She appreciated everybody's humor, but she was not what you would call a funny lady. When I'm with witty, funny people, I try to respond to that."

Working on her sitcom, Mary averred, was the "happiest period" of her life, even as the show struggled to find its voice and viewers during its initial season.

Test audiences did not take to the series. In fact, "… they hated it," acknowledged Bill Persky. "They also hated Rhoda, and Lou, and every character on the show." Although CBS liked Mary, and honored its agreement for an initial 22 episodes, she later confided, "That first year was dismal in terms of ratings." By the end of those twelve months, however, things had changed with the viewers, critics, and her peers – and the Emmys started to roll in. Fortunately, during *Tyler's* gestation period, television wasn't as competitive as it is today. In the 2010s, a series may be cancelled if it doesn't catch on with the viewers in three weeks. In the

1970s, a show was generally afforded the luxury of an entire season to build an audience, which the *Mary Tyler Moore* program did during the summer reruns following its freshman year. During that period, Mary swapped the *Van Dyke Show*'s "Oh, Rob" for the Mary Richard's "Oh, Mr. Grant." From housewife to working woman – it seemed a natural evolution.

According to various sources, Mary's "Oh, Rob" scold/petition was based on the acting style of Nanette Fabray who made countless TV, film and stage performances, including with Sid Caesar, Imogene Coca, and Carl Reiner on their *Show of Shows* variety series. Years later, Mary cast Fabray, who died at age 97 in 2018, as her TV mom on *The Mary Tyler Moore Show*. In one of her last interviews, Fabray talked about working with Mary in the episode, "Just Around the Corner" (October 28, 1972), the first of two *MTM* segments in which she appeared. In "Corner," Mary Richards is less than enthusiastic about her parent's relocation to Minneapolis. In her apartment, she is crying in the hiccupping way she had perfected as Laura on the *Van Dyke Show*. Fabray used her own version of a crying fit in this episode, as Mary's mother.

In 1972, Fabray received a call from Mary, with a request to play her mother on *The Mary Tyler Moore Show*. "I would love to do that," Fabray replied in accepting the role of Dottie Richards.

Once on set, Mary had a second request. She remembered one of Fabray's appearances with Coca and Sid Caesar on TV's hit variety series, *Your Show of Shows*, which had also featured Carl Reiner. Mary was enamored with a particular mannerism Fabray utilized in one sketch with Caesar, involving a diamond ring and tears. "That was one of the funniest things I had ever seen," Mary told her. "Sid had taught me how to do this funny cry," Fabray explained, "… an incoherent talk-through-tears, and Mary loved that. And she said, 'Let's do that on my show.'"

But Fabray was apprehensive about resurrecting the shtick for "Just Around the Corner," the first of two segments she had signed to do for the series. She simply didn't think the scene would be funny. "I felt in my heart that it would not work," she said. Still, Fabray decided to give it a try, to please Mary, who was "in love with [the idea] and she wanted to do it," Fabray said. "And we did it. And it was okay. But there really was no marriage between the shtick and Mary and me as her mother. So, that first appearance was very strained, at least on my part. I don't know if it was on her part."

The second episode in which Fabray appeared, "You've Got a Friend" (November 25, 1972), focused on Mary's father Walter, played by Bill Quinn. "And that was the end of my working with Mary," Fabray said.

Years later, the two reconnected in New York. At that time, Fabray asked, "Why do you think it didn't work between you and me ... that I was not asked to come back, to do any more episodes?" "I have no idea," Mary replied. "I think it was fine. I hadn't really thought about it at all." "And we just left it at that," Fabray said. "I didn't want to pursue it because I didn't want to embarrass her."

"We're two nice people," she added, "... but we didn't have on-the-air [chemistry]. Had there been magic ... if Mary and I had hit it off," Fabray believed she would have been signed to do more episodes. "That's the way it works in our business," she said.

Fabray's less-than-positive experience of *The Mary Tyler Moore Show* did not influence her opinion of the series. She called it "one of the most marvelous things that was ever put on the air. It really was a ground-breaker ... like Sid Caesar's shows."

In many ways, *The MTM Show* continued the spirit of *Van Dyke*, but with a more adult approach. *MTM* added texture to characters and a more modern emphasis on human frailties, follies, and strengths.

When first approached about playing Mary Richards, Mary Tyler Moore was unsure and unwilling to commit to the part. In part she worried that any new role might suffer in comparison with Laura Petrie, already cemented as one of the most popular female roles in TV history. Once the divorcée/failed-romance issue was reconciled and the show made it to the air, smaller hurdles arose – like the right hairstyles.

For example, Mary donned a long black wig – a "fall," like today's hair extensions – to help distinguish Richards from Laura, who had been compared to Jackie Kennedy. Although over the years, Mary would wear her locks in many fashions, she always seemed to revert back to the familiar page-boy hairdo parted on the side. Every few years, she would get bored with that design and cut her tresses short; or make it blonde and spiky (in 1989) or red and spiky (in 1995).

But after the few first seasons of *The Mary Tyler Moore Show*, Mary's mane changed to a layered, more chic form, tinted brown, as her character began to date more. Although she never had an "official" boyfriend, her Richards persona eventually met Joe Warner, as played by Ted Bessell (best known as Marlo Thomas's steady Don Hollinger on *That Girl*) in two episodes: "Mary Richards Falls in Love" (November 22, 1975) and "One Boyfriend Too Many" (December 13, 1975).

Throughout every season, Moore's Mary remains a warm and open-hearted, if strong-minded, independent woman, with a realistic romantic life. As co-producer Allan Burns later observed, Richards was never shown in bed, but she had "a sex life." In the third-season episode "You've Got a Friend" (November 25, 1972), a subtle reference is made to Richards' prescription for birth-control pills. In 1974, Valerie Harper joked about Mary's goody-two-shoes image, in front of and behind the camera. "She's bouncy, she's pretty … she weighs 11 pounds, and is a totally adorable human being. Despite that, I find it impossible to dislike her. Mary's wholesome, but she's not too wholesome. I mean, for example, she likes a great big glass of cold milk to wash down her birth-control pill. She's the kind of person who gives WASPs a good name."

If Harper was talking about Mary Richards, the description also matched the public image of Mary Tyler Moore. Working woman Richards was periodically seen alone on a Saturday night, like her at-home audience. It was the same for Rhoda Morgenstern. This added to the appeal drama when Harper left *The Mary Tyler Moore Show* for her *Rhoda* spin-off series. As she once expressed to *TV Times Magazine*, Harper received a great deal of flak from single women when her new show featured her famously single character getting married. By the eighth episode of *Rhoda*, she was wed to construction worker Joe Gerard, as played by the affable David Groh. "They seem to feel she's letting them down," Harper said of Rhoda fans. One stewardess, for example, told her, "When I'm sitting at home on Saturday night without a date, I don't want to see you married."

But Rhoda was no longer on *The Mary Tyler Moore Show* on Saturday nights. Her series aired on Monday evenings, when being dateless was not the same thing. But the stewardess "didn't seem convinced," Harper said.

Harper then acknowledged another thing which concerned her single fans: "They think we'll fall into that old thinking where success was equated with marriage for a woman," she said, "… where after marriage, a woman gives up her personage."

"That won't happen to Rhoda," promised Harper. She'd been reading the groundbreaking book, *Open Marriage*, by George and Nena O'Neill. "That's the kind of marriage I think Rhoda and Joe will have. Not having affairs, but having the freedom to do things on their own." She continued, "That's the kind of marriage I've had," regarding her then decade-long union to her first husband actor Richard Schaal. Schaal had made a few appearances on *The Mary Tyler Moore Show*, including one episode as Chuckles the Clown (though not in the famed "Chuckles Bites the Dust" segment). In another he played Mary's boyfriend Howard, and in yet another, Howard's twin brother Paul. Schaal had also appeared as Gerard's best friend on *Rhoda*, and as a character named Leo in the first season of *Phyllis*. "You don't stay married for 10 years to Dick Schaal unless you have an open marriage," Harper said. "I've had a great marriage and I think on this show we can prove marriage can be great."

When Harper had been first selected to play Rhoda, producers were initially concerned that she was too attractive to play the self-deprecating, overweight character.   But as an accomplished actress, Harper made viewers believe Rhoda thought herself unappealing.   When it came time to do her own series, Harper was reluctant about leaving *The Mary Tyler Moore Show*, but Mary assured her that if the spin-off did not succeed, Rhoda could always move back to Minneapolis and rejoin the M. Richards family of friends.

"Since we just can't replace Rhoda," Mary once said, "we're looking for a man. But they're hard to find, as they are in real life."

Rhoda never returned to Minneapolis, and the character was never technically replaced on the *Mary Tyler Moore* show.

Such developments were unnecessary.   The *Rhoda* show became an instant hit. It earned big ratings and two Emmys for Harper, the actress eventually divorced Schaal, and the audience conclusively divorced themselves from *Rhoda*, the series, even after Rhoda divorced herself from Joe.   All of this can be examined by referring to an earlier groundbreaking book, Betty Friedan's 1963 *The Feminine Mystique*.

By the time of *Mary* and *Rhoda*, Friedan's revolutionary tale had influenced women, single and career-minded, to join the work force in record numbers. Many such employed females, like those stewardesses who were offended by Rhoda's initial wedded bliss, remained more in tune with Mary Richards' single status. By 1972, *MTM*'s second season, birth control had become accessible to all women, single or married, and *Ms. Magazine*, orchestrated by Gloria Steinem and Dorothy Pitman Hughes, became available in stores everywhere. Women were advocating for the Equal Rights Amendment (ERA) to be added to the U.S. Constitution. The ERA passed both houses of Congress that same year, but fell short of the 38 states required for ratification during a ten-year battle.

Mary Tyler Moore co-creator Jim Brooks later talked with *The Hollywood Reporter* about the show and the era in which it initially aired. "The timing was extraordinary because it was just at the point where the women's revolution was starting and some of our stories came from that. But we knew from the beginning that it was important that the show not just become a polemic of the times and that we just do the character of Mary."

Although Mary Richards would sometimes utter phrases like "I feel like I represent women everywhere" ("The Good-Time News," September 16, 1972), Mary Tyler Moore rejected any direct affiliation with feminism. She defended motherhood, even if her own maternal instincts were not always on the mark with her son. "Gloria thought I was 100 percent on Betty Friedan's train and I really wasn't," she eventually said to *Salon.com* and other media sources. "I believed that women had a very major role to play as mothers. It's very necessary for mothers to be involved with their children and that's not what Gloria Steinem was saying. Gloria was saying that, 'Oh, you can have everything and you owe it to yourself to have a career.' And I didn't really believe in that."

In regard to her own character Mary Richards, Mary echoed Brooks' commentary. She told *USA Today*, "The writers got to know me and, on that, they went to work. I was probably very close in personality to Mary Richards at that point and we agreed that they would never sacrifice character for the sake of a laugh. A lot of subjects that our writers took on were new…We came in at a very good time."

Although Mary Tyler Moore was not a feminist in the *Ms.* mold, her show clearly arrived just in time to benefit from the "Women's Lib" movement. The episodes were mostly about life's small stuff, issues for both sexes. The humor was generated from everyday reactions to regular situations. This elevated the sitcom's level of sophistication even it meant that Mary Richards wasn't a standard-bearer for New Womanhood.

On September 13, 1970, the *New York Times* published a photo spread titled, "Out of the Kitchen, Ladies," which previewed a number of female-skewed programs with the preface, "Is the put-upon housewife and mother becoming passé as a TV heroine? In these four shows, among those launching the new season on CBS, she's been replaced by the career girl." The series covered in the article were *The Storefront Lawyers*, *Headmaster*, *The Interns*, and *Moore*. (As it transpired, Mary's was the only show renewed for a second season.) A few weeks after the *Times* article ran, critic Jack Gould was high on *Storefront Lawyers*, but saw *Mary Tyler Moore* as "…caught in a preposterous item about life as an 'associate producer' in a TV newsroom." Shortly before *Moore's* sophomore year, critic John L. O'Connor believed the sitcom had "potential for longevity, with Mary looking healthy enough to keep cavorting at least until the ripe old age of 45 [because] within the familiar plot points, the viewer can find a good many first-rate bits and pieces [as]…Miss Moore's Mary is a most agreeable bundle of leggy charm."

In 1973, *The New York Times* had more reservations with Judy Klemesrud's article, "TV's Women Are Dingbats," which in part, read: "The much-touted *Mary Tyler Moore Show*, which has shown that the over-30 unmarried woman is not necessarily suicidal, has some of the best writing on television. But why can't the writers find something for Mary to do other than waiting on the men in her office, or worrying about the flowers on her desk, or solving the mini-crises of her friends? Mary works as an assistant in the newsroom of a Minneapolis television station, but she hardly ever gets to write the news or report it on camera – even though she appears to be several times brighter than the men who do."

Klemesrud also had issues with the female leads in shows like *McMillan and Wife*, starring future *Kate & Allie* star Susan Saint James as a dutiful wife to Rock Hudson (*McMillan* also featured *MTM* semi-regular Nancy Walker as their busybody maid). She made further points discussing *Maude* (with Bea Arthur), and *Gunsmoke* (featuring Amanda Blake as Miss Kitty). Klemesrud observed, "Prime-time commercial television has yet to reflect the fact that there is something out there called the women's liberation movement, and that it isn't a big joke after all."

The *Times*' "TV Mailbag" received several letters of rebuttal, including this one from Barbara Wolfson, head of children's programming at a county library in Maryland: "I can't resist pointing out that Shirley Jones in *The Partridge Family* is perhaps the most liberated woman being portrayed on any television program this season. The program may be inane – repetitious and so on – but there at least she is, one mother about whom my son does not assume 'she spends the day shopping.'"

Michael Stern, "Lucille Ball's Number 1 Fan," is a celebrity photo archivist. His best-selling book *I Had a Ball* chronicles his close friendship with the famed redhead. Known for his savvy with film and TV stars at various celebrity events and shows, televised and otherwise, Stern, while in his early teens, attended the filming of a few episodes of *Mary Tyler Moore*. His access came due to his friendship with the late Midge Hurst, wife to Lewis E. Hurst, Jr., the art and set director for Moore's sitcom. "Mary adored him and when he died," Stern recalled "…and she wanted Midge to have a job. So, she created a position for Midge, who was a very glamorous woman … a real Mary Richards-type person, to do things like open and answer fan mail." Midge was able to get Stern tickets to Mary's show.

The Mary Tyler Moore Show was produced on a five-day schedule. Each Monday the cast held a table reading of the script, which was revised on Tuesday. The scenes were blocked and rehearsed on Wednesday and Thursday, and a final run-through closed the week every Friday around 3:00 PM, a short time before filming began in front of a live studio audience. Stern was present for episodes that featured guest-stars Mary Kay Place and Penny Marshall, before their respective regular roles on TV's *Mary Hartman, Mary Hartman*, and *Laverne & Shirley*. He was also in the audience for "One Producer Too Many" (October 30, 1976), the episode in which Knight's TV anchor Ted Baxter describes White's Sue Ann as a pig eating slop in a clip that is mistakenly inserted on screen as he speaks on-air. The studio audiences attending this or any episode of *Moore*, or any other MTM comedies, were always entertained by a small orchestra of five or six band members off to one side of the set, along with whoever was doing the "warm-up" before the episodes began filming. For the segments Stern attended, Les Charles, one of the show's writers, served as the warm-up man.

During one filming, Mary approached the audience, who immediately gave her a standing ovation, after which she joked, "Oh, stop, stop. I already said I was leaving and not coming back." Then she introduced her mother and father, seated in the front row, as "the producers of *The Mary Tyler Moore Show*," a joke she used many times. Like many shows of the era, including *Dick Van Dyke*, *Moore* was filmed like a play, in sequence, differently than sitcoms are produced today. While Stern had access only once to backstage on the *Moore* show, it's an experience he recalled fondly: "Mary and the entire cast, including Ed Asner, Gavin MacLeod, and Ted Knight, would sign autographs for and talk to people. It looked like the big happy family that you saw on the screen and wanted to be with."

Another of Stern's personal encounters with Mary occurred as he stood outside the Beverly Hilton Hotel in Beverly Hills for an awards ceremony on July 21, 1975, at the end of her sitcom's fifth season. Stern was waiting for a glimpse of his favorite star Lucille Ball, only to capture her exit with Mary and Carol Burnett. "It was kind of amazing seeing the three of them together," remembered Stern. He added, "Mary was great with fans, but not the most outgoing. She was very sweet, and always pleasant, but very savvy." Mary was never the type of celebrity who panicked upon any fan's autograph approach. "That was not Mary Tyler Moore," Stern affirmed.

When an older man requested her autograph on an 8-x-10 photo, Mary signed it, "With best wishes, M.T.M." The man was stunned, and told her, "Oh...you just signed your initials." To which Mary wryly responded, "Yeah...that's right," fully aware the abbreviated autograph would be worth less than her full signature. "Even then," Stern said, before the onslaught of celebrity items on sale today, "... she knew that man was probably going to try and sell that photo with her autograph."

Sometime later, upon spotting the actress outside the MTM studio where she filmed her show, Stern said "...she didn't look like Mary Richards. Carol Burnett always looked like Carol Burnett. Lucy, at the time, looked like the Lucy I knew. But Mary had more blotches and lines on her face. On television, and in the photos that I had, she looked younger, but in real life she looked older." The youthful Stern was only one of many who expected a performer's everyday appearance to match her on-screen glamour. Some of those lines were due, in part, to her early ravages of diabetes, exacerbated by alcohol. Also, around this time Mary was experiencing a few personal bumps in the road to her success. Although still wed to Tinker, they had a trial separation during her show's run. And the residue of her first marriage to Richard Meeker still gnawed at her, if only due to the emotional and psychological damage she felt the divorce was having on her son Richie. Her weight had fluctuated during *Dick Van Dyke*, and at times she appeared frail on *Mary Tyler Moore* – due, in part, to diabetes. For Mary, her weight was down, but as with each challenge, she smiled through it all, or at least tried to make the best of it.

In a *Mary Tyler Moore* blooper reel that was periodically enjoyed by members of the show's cast and crew, a very thin Mary joked that she wished she could choose where on her body to gain weight. While rehearsing a scene in which Mary Richards vacuums her apartment in a bathrobe and curlers, Mary sang, off-the-cuff, "Tits. When am I gonna' grow tits?" – part of the song, "Hello Twelve, Hello Thirteen, Hello Love," from *A Chorus Line*. It was a sadly touching improvisation from someone who, like Lucille Ball, did not consider herself a "funny person" in real life, and only knew how to do "funny things" on camera, in character.

In her conversation with *Los Angeles Magazine*, Mary not only addressed comparisons to Ball, but once again, to Carol Burnett: "Lucy is a clown … like Carol Burnett is a clown, and I'm a comedic actress … and there is a difference."

Years later, Michael Stern concluded: "Lucy admitted that she did not know how to be funny in real life. Carol always makes me laugh no matter. And with Mary Tyler Moore, her sense of humor on-camera was equal to how she was off-camera."

Chapter

12

By the mid-1970s, Mary Tyler Moore's comedy style was proving profitable. MTM Enterprises had become a Hollywood powerhouse that generated over $20 million per year, with Mary and Grant Tinker owning most of its holdings. On September 30, 1974, she was the subject of the *People* magazine cover story, "TV's Newest Tycoon." At that time the Tinkers supervised nearly 500 employees at MTM, which had eight shows in development or on the air. Mary had long defined herself as the face of MTM, while Grant tailored the organization with a strategy of respect and encouragement for all creative types, and with as little network intervention as possible.

But all was not well behind the scenes. As Mary later explained in *After All*, by 1971, Dick Meeker, her first husband had remarried and moved to Fresno, California. He asked for their son Richie, now 16, to join him. Richie had thrived and planned for college until his father was transferred out of town. He persuaded his parents to let him remain in Fresno by himself to complete his senior year. Sadly, he became addicted to illicit drugs. It wasn't until February 1973, when Richie called home, frantic and sobbing, begging sanctuary from a cocaine dealer who threatened his life over unpaid debts, that Mary realized the severity of his situation. Fortunately, they found a doctor who specialized in troubled youth. Richie, the now emaciated and frightened prodigal son, found his way home, at least temporarily. Over the next two years he found a measure of peace and finished high school. But because of her show, Mary was unable able to attend his graduation ceremony; in her mind, this was a sign she had failed once more as a mom.

Another time in 1973, during the third season of her series, Mary and Tinker argued during dinner. He thought they should separate because their marriage was "poisoned." Perhaps 11½ years is all they had in them, he said. As Mary also recounted in *After All*, upon hearing these words, she headed to the bathroom, dropped to her knees, and began to cry with big loud childlike sobs, screaming "No!" time and again. She began pounding her fists upon the carpeted floor, even distressing the dogs. After a long time she was able to get up and rejoin Tinker for a drink at the bar. Eventually he requested that she and her belongings be gone within two days.

Later that night, Mary sought the comfort of his arms one last time. He obliged, but the next morning, save for having separate meals, they went to work as usual on *The Mary Tyler Moore Show*.

After six weeks of separation, Tinker called for a truce, and she was nothing but delighted to move into his leased home in Beverly Hills. But that solved nothing. Their lack of personal communication continued, as did each one's growing dependence on alcohol. They didn't travel in separate directions, she later said, "...but that 'taking for granted' attitude" that eventually transpires in most marriages began to happen to them – and they failed to recognize the pattern. They simply stopped caring about each other's feelings and opinions. After several lengthy conversations, the Tinkers remained unsure of how to resolve their issues. It seemed best to part ways, if only temporarily, to see if they would find their way back to one another.

In her later TV interview with Barbara Walters, Mary described this experience as "a really good period," and almost wished "everyone would have that opportunity" to walk away from and then return to a marriage. It was probably a self-rationalization. No ideal marriage includes a break-up.

Meanwhile, her relationship with her son Richie, who seemed rudderless, continued to be strained. She still hadn't helped him foster a sense of responsibility. There might be certain strategies to motivate a child who had everything, but she and Tinker had no idea what those strategies were.

A short time later, Mary and Tinker, together for approximately 11½ years, had formerly separated. "I had heard rumors," Treva Silverman then told the *New York Times*. "And when Grant didn't show up in the control room [one] Friday night for the filming, we knew. The tension was just awful, but Mary was wonderful on the stage. I don't know how she did it."

"Grant moved out of their house in Malibu November 30," said Mary's publicist Dan Jenkins to the *Times*. "I'll never forget that date. That afternoon Mary had to entertain some British journalists. One of them leaned over to her at the end of lunch and said, 'Tell me, Mary, how is it that you have such a marvelous marriage?' Well, Mary gave all the right answers, but when she got up to leave, I could see her put her hand to her mouth, kind of choking back a sob."

In either confronting or cloaking such challenges, Mary continued to release her secret weapon: her smile, which she flashed like a silver shield against what appeared to be the darkest moments of her life. She even found the strength of mind to lampoon her own image in the process. Those private reels of *Mary Tyler Moore* bloopers and outtakes were often repeated to the cast and crew, especially those scenes when Mary blew a line and spoke an unladylike four-letter word. It was all part of the fun.

On-screen she remained the epitome of the liberated, dating single woman, with a likable comic vulnerability. Off-screen she was dealing with the trauma of a failing marriage and less-than-stellar motherhood, while she remained outspoken on topics like birth control, marijuana, gun control, and abortion, none of which pleased conservative viewers.

In 1975, while she made personal smiling appearances on daytime talk shows like *Dinah!* (starring Dinah Shore), to cheer up patients at a hospital in Los Angeles, Mary had also sought a much darker role. She had been considered for the part of Joanne Eberhart in the feature film, *The Stepford Wives*, only to have Katharine Ross win the part. Some years before, Mary had been considered for the lead role of Jennifer North in *Valley of the Dolls*, but Sharon Tate won the part. Now, producers of the *Stepford* film, which featured robotized women, decided against casting Mary. Valerie Harper was likewise under consideration as Bobbie Markowe in *Wives*, a character that was eventually played by Paula Prentiss. According to David Davis, who besides serving as editor of *Mary Magazine*, now administrates Facebook's *Mary Tyler Moore Fan Page*, having Mary team with Harper in the *Stepford* film would have been considered "stunt casting."

Davis had interviewed Harper for *Mary Magazine*, and expressed how much he enjoyed the conflicted relationship between Rhoda and Phyllis, as played by Cloris Leachman. "Originally," Harper told him, "Rhoda and Mary were supposed to be enemies, but the chemistry was so good between us, the writers made us friends and Phyllis became the one Rhoda didn't get along with. Cloris Leachman is nothing like Phyllis in real life, by the way."

Harper felt that she and her Rhoda were likewise distinct, but many critics and viewers did not. Cecil Smith of the *Los Angeles Times* wrote, "There's so much Rhoda in Valerie Harper that it's difficult to separate the character from the actress." But Harper stood by her convictions, particularly upon receiving the green light for her own weekly sitcom –

one that CBS wanted to call *The Valerie Harper Show*, which she rejected. Unlike Rhoda, Harper wasn't Jewish, although she admitted, "I'm Jewish at heart." Harper wasn't born in the Bronx like Rhoda, but was raised in places like Altadena, California, and Ashland, Oregon. Harper had been married "practically all my life," she said in reference to her then-marriage with actor Richard Schaal, as opposed to Rhoda's lengthy single life.

So, although Harper saw many differences between her and Rhoda, that was not how audiences perceived the situation. When the *Rhoda* series debuted in the fall of 1974, the *Los Angeles Times* observed, "The directness, the specific honesty of Rhoda, the openness and candidness of this 33-year-old working girl from the Bronx are among the major reasons the new program shot immediately to the top of the Nielsen charts [that] season and has hovered close to the top ever since."

Even though *Rhoda* later faltered in the ratings, and never found its creative footing once its leading single lady married David Groh's Joe Gerard, viewers adored Harper, still finding it difficult to separate the actress from the character.

The same could be said for Mary. The blurred lines between the performer and the portrayal became more pronounced to fans, a few critics, and even some peers.

Approximately one decade after the original airings of *The Mary Tyler Moore Show* and *Rhoda*, Mary was inducted into the Comedy Hall of Fame, a ceremony attended by Harper. "Mary looked beautiful and seems to be really happy," she told *Mary Magazine* editor David Davis. "I just love Mary. She's a national treasure." Harper then went on to personally thank historians like Davis "…for all you've done for my friend Mary!"

Another time, Harper had acknowledged being a fan of Mary's from *The Dick Van Dyke Show*. "I thought she was adorable," she said. And since the two women had such great chemistry on-screen with *The Mary Tyler Moore Show*, the originally envisioned hostile relationship between Mary and Rhoda was revised, and the duo became best friends.

Such was also mostly the case for Moore and Harper when not on-camera. They would, for example, attend dance classes together, and their relationship off-screen was one of close friendship. But in some instances, it might have seemed like Mary's confidence was sometimes threatened by Harper's presence.

When promoting her memoir, *I, Rhoda*, in 2013, Harper made a radio appearance with Howard Stern, who asked if she thought Mary was ever jealous of her. Harper remained silent. Another time, however, she admitted that, at least, her most famous TV character was partially envious of Mary Richards. "There was a part of Rhoda that was very protective of Mary," Harper said, "…like an older sister. And there was also a part that was jealous of that model's body."

In a later interview, Harper said, "Rhoda wishes she were Mary. But it doesn't manifest itself as jealousy. She knows that Mary may have the great job and the great figure, but Rhoda's from New York. She knows she's got to straighten this shiksa out."

When *The Mary Tyler Moore Show* cast later regrouped for a special segment of *The Oprah Winfrey Show*, Harper once more used the "j"-word, when describing authenticity as the best part of Mary Richards and Rhoda Morgenstern's friendship. "That really was how girlfriends are and that your best friend could be really jealous of your hip measurement, as I was of Mary's, but really be there for her…[to] tell her the truth."

"Beverly Sanders was Mary's best friend," Matthew Asner recalled, "but Mary and Valerie were also very good friends. They had a good relationship. But anytime you have a situation where someone becomes a star, there is bound to be some sort of jealousy there…even though I never saw it. I only saw a solid relationship between Mary and Valerie, and Cloris Leachman, too, for that matter. They were all close, as were the men on the show."

Certainly, that was the public appearance. When talking with entertainment journalist Lisa Kogan decades after *The Mary Tyler Moore Show* ended, Mary and Harper had nothing but mutual praise. When Mary called Harper's initial audition for Rhoda "pure dynamite," Harper interrupted and said she was just "very lucky." "You were not very lucky," Mary returned, "you were very talented."

Of Harper's nurturing charms, Mary said, "Valerie has a very mothering personality. She cares about everybody."

"And Mary wears her strength so lightly," Harper added.

During *Mary Tyler Moore*'s original run, circa October, 1974, *Time* magazine explored the criss-cross chemistry between Moore and Harper:

> Audiences in search of funny girls have learned to forsake the theatre for Valerie and Mary on the smaller screen. Mary opts for the soft approach. Every week, as Mary Richards, the effervescent assistant TV producer, she manages to discover fresh comic possibilities in herself and her supporting cast…[In the episodes] nothing is sacred and few things are profane: sex, inflation, urban miseries and small-time office politics are alive and laughing on prime time…Between them, the two very different, identical comediennes are the season's brightest clowns. On every show they prove that women need not be dingbats or contralto

> foghorns to win applause or affection. Almost alone, they are bringing back the forgotten tradition of the beautiful clown.
>
> From the look of the ladies and the sound of their followers, TV '74 has a glow that extends to viewers who may yet be witnessing television's true Golden Age of comedy – stronger and longer than the one in the '50s. Indeed, Mary Tyler Moore and Valerie Harper are enough to make almost anyone forget the comedies of the past. And even the crustiest nostalgia buffs cannot ponder *The MTM Show* without admitting that all that glitters is not old.

The honest on-screen relationship between Mary R. and Rhoda M. and the real relationship between Mary T.M. and Valerie H. seemed a twin slippery slope. Harper and Moore each kept a protective veil around their on-and-off-screen associations. But a bond of core affection remained firmly in place until Mary's passing.

At the same time, they didn't always get along, which was completely understandable from any perspective. Just because they did not see eye-to-eye all the time, this didn't make them enemies. Conflicts are inevitable in any lengthy relationship, especially in that complicated place called Hollywood, and especially in creative situations. It would not be credible, realistic, or healthy to consider a long-term association without disagreements or even a few hard knocks.

The real issue: The conflicts were never publicly acknowledged by Mary or Harper, neither of whom wanted to burst any fan's bubble. This was noble, but again, unrealistic. It is remarkable that these two masters of art and professionalism were able to cloak and protect their fans' perception of their beloved on-screen characters. That remains a true testament to their ingenuity, integrity, and respect for their admirers. The always warm and friendly Harper once said, "In some ways, I feel as close to Mary as I do to my own family. Mary and I hit it off right away, off-screen and on. She was never one to hog the spotlight and made sure everyone in the cast was used to their best advantage." But while that was and remains the truth, there is more to the story. Mary did enjoy surrounding herself with top-line talent like Harper, but the fact of the matter is this:

Harper's strong performance as Rhoda brought her and the character into the spotlight, and that sometimes meant out-shining Mary. "Even though the Rhoda character was kind of one-dimensional, Valerie's popularity was growing," said writer/producer Rick Lertzman, whose list of best-selling books include *Dr. Feelgood*, the biography of Doctor Max Jacobson, who developed a unique "energy formula" that altered the paths of some of the twentieth century's most iconic figures, and *The Life and Times of Mickey Rooney*, one of television and film's most celebrated stars. "Valerie was becoming more of an influential presence on the show. A lot of the time when some figure in the show gets too big, there's always conflict with the main actor."

Two cases in point: Cybill Shepherd became increasingly annoyed with Bruce Willis's increasing popularity on ABC's *Moonlighting* of the '80s, and again with Christine Baranski on CBS's *Cybill* sitcom of the '90s. In both cases, Shepherd was positioned as the star, while Willis and Baranski were relative unknowns in supporting roles. But due to their appearances with Shepherd, their growing visibility became a popular force to be reckoned with. A similar conflict arose when *Lost in Space* lead Guy Williams, formerly of TV's *Zorro*, was rattled by the fan-base increase and scene-stealing of Jonathan Harris as the eccentric Dr. Zachary Smith on that sci-fi cult favorite of the 1960s.

In that same era, Mary was gaining popularity on *The Dick Van Dyke Show*. While there may have been issues between Mary and Rose Marie in what Lertzman described as a "jealousy between the two of them," he added, "Dick Van Dyke did not have that kind of ego. I always find that the great comics and the people who are truly successful, like Jack Benny or George Burns...they could care less if everyone around them were the funniest people in the world. Whereas people like Danny Kaye, who was a monster, would destroy people around him if they got funnier."

Before finding fame on *The Carol Burnett Show*, comedic actor Harvey Korman performed on *The Danny Kaye Show*. Korman told Lertzman that the temperamental Kaye was easily intimidated by the talents of others. In one dress rehearsal, "Harvey received these great laughs," Lertzman said, "and when it was time to actually tape the show, Danny would make sure to step on those lines to kill Harvey's laughs, which only damaged Danny's show."

Such a situation was different from *The Dick Van Dyke Show*, and *The Mary Tyler Moore Show*. Lertzman observed, "Mary was really more of an ensemble player. I don't know how much Grant Tinker saw an opportunity to create another series with Valerie Harper, or that he thought Mary's show would not be hurt with the loss of Rhoda. But Grant was opportunistic for MTM Enterprises, and he simply felt that spinning-off Rhoda, as well as [Cloris Leachman's] Phyllis would be a benefit to the company."

There was no way around it. Harper always maintained that she wanted to stay on *The Mary Tyler Moore Show*. But CBS wanted a spin-off.

According to what Allan Burns conveyed in the "extras" documentary released with *Mary Tyler Moore's* second-season DVD, Harper had received offers from other networks to do her own sitcom, just as her four-year contract with CBS and MTM Enterprises was up for renewal. MTM Enterprises wanted to keep her in the fold, and that's when the idea of a *Rhoda* spin-off was first generated; Harper could come back to *The Mary Tyler Moore Show* if *Rhoda* failed.

The characters and the actresses did eventually reunite years later in New York for the panned 2000 ABC TV-movie *Mary and Rhoda*, which not only transpired on another network, but apparently also in some other universe.

In an article published April 10, 2009, the *Los Angeles Times* compared Mary and Harper's near-sibling rivalry to that of TV sitcom stars Amy Poehler of *Parks and Recreation* and Tina Fey of *30 Rock*:

> In 1975, Valerie Harper split with her former costar, Mary Tyler Moore, to launch her own spin-off sitcom Rhoda. At the next Emmys, the onetime best pals squared off in the same kind of dishy bout. Everyone assumed that Moore – the Lucille Ball of her day – would clobber Harper. If anyone could topple the TV queen, it might be Jean Stapleton (All in the Family), but not Harper. Harper portrayed Rhoda as a gum-snapping wisecracker. Her character didn't have the emotional depth of Mary Richards, say, or Edith Bunker, right?
>
> But on Emmy night all jaws – including Harper's – dropped when she pulled an Eve Harrington and nabbed the gold prize. At the podium, Harper acknowledged Moore gratefully and gleefully. The L.A. Times noted that she also "felt compelled to thank everyone profusely," including her analyst.
>
> But Moore ended up getting a royal consolation prize at the end of the Emmy ceremony. When the last envelope of the night was opened, it revealed that the winner of best comedy series was The Mary Tyler Moore Show. The news was trumpeted by Lucille Ball in a scene that is remembered today as one of those goose-bump times in Emmy history. When Moore arrived on stage and took the golden statuette from

Ball's hand – looking wonderstruck, taking in the grand context of the scene – we saw comedy's scepter and crown being passed from one generation to another. Hail, hail TV's queens!

One more got hailed last year when 30 Rock won best comedy series for a second time in a row and Tina Fey was handed the prize by Mary Tyler Moore and Betty White.

OK, OK, 30 Rock can easily win best comedy series again, but you don't think Poehler can beat Fey for best comedy actress? You're forgetting how Emmy voting works. It all comes down to the sample episode of Parks and Recreation Poehler submits to the Emmy judges. If it's a doozy, she'll win. That's how upsets happen all the time at the Emmys. That's why Tony Shalhoub (Monk) and James Spader (Boston Legal) keep clobbering hipsters like Steve Carell (The Office) and Kiefer Sutherland (24).

The final irony: Fey and Poehler were shut out, and Edie Falco won Outstanding Lead Actress in a Comedy Series for her role in Showtime's *Nurse Jackie*. Things don't always work out as expected. This was certainly the case with the *Rhoda* and *Phyllis* sitcoms, each given birth by *Mary Tyler Moore*. That mother series and *The Bob Newhart Show* were solid hits for MTM Enterprises and CBS from the onset. *Rhoda*'s ratings for its first two seasons were solid, and *Phyllis* was ranked as a Top Ten show in its first year, even surpassing *The Mary Tyler Moore Show* in the ratings. But their formats kept changing, with new characters and different actors arriving and departing at alarming rates. *Rhoda* was supposed to be about married life, so as not to conflict with Mary Richards' single life. But when Ms. Morgenstern became Mrs. Gerard, not even the charms of David Groh could defer the backlash from viewers. *Rhoda*'s wedded adventures began to falter in the ratings, the Gerards eventually divorced, and the show hobbled along for four seasons.

Phyllis began strong, but a few issues impeded its potential for success. The series featured at its center an unlikable character. Leachman's *performance* was fine, but her *role* was grating. How can a disagreeable leading character sustain itself in a television series, especially a comedy? An unlikable character such as J.R. Ewing, played with great zeal and appeal by Larry Hagman on *Dallas* (CBS, 1978-1991), worked mainly because that series was a drama.

But not so with *Phyllis* which, like *Rhoda*, simply never found its footing. As delightfully ditzy as Leachman was as the unappealing Phyllis, that character was no Mary Richards – or Rhoda Morgenstern for that matter. It didn't much help matters that Barbara Colby, who played Julie Erskine, the owner of a photographic studio where Phyllis worked, was brutally murdered during the show's first few months in production.

In his book, *Ethel Merman: A Life*, Brian Kellow says Colby's career was blossoming. In the mid-'70s, she had made a few well-received guest appearances on *The Mary Tyler Moore Show* beginning with the fourth-season opener. In "Will Mary Richards Go to Jail?" (September 14, 1974), she played Sherry Ferris, a prostitute whom Mary Richards befriends when temporarily imprisoned for not revealing a news source. With her shrewd comic timing and husky voice, Colby won over critics and viewers, which led to her role on *Phyllis*. Although she only appeared in the first three episodes of that series, Colby made her mark, and not even the multiple talents of Liz Torres (later of *All in the Family*) replacing her as Erskine could save the character or the show. Ed. Weinberger tried to make sense of it all in *Los Angeles Magazine*:

"We didn't really have a choice with *Rhoda*, because we couldn't do the show we had set out to do. There's no way you can do a show about married life honestly during the family hour. And with *Phyllis*, we had a written part for Barbara Colby, and she was killed. Good as Liz Torrez was, it just had to be changed. I think there is no question that *Phyllis* is a better show under the new format, and I think the ratings will eventually reflect that. As writers, we did what we had to do."

Unfortunately, no one was watching *Phyllis* or *Rhoda* on Monday nights, certainly not the way they were watching *The Mary Tyler Moore Show* on Saturday nights. Grant Tinker blamed low rankings of the MTM spin-offs on the relentless programming from rival network airings of big-screen movies like *Earthquake*, which aired on NBC opposite *Rhoda* and *Phyllis*. In his comments to *Los Angeles Magazine*, Tinker called the ratings for both shows "atypical," and from a creative standpoint, he had envisioned them doing "very well."

But they never performed well at all; Mary Tyler Moore and her show were the still the ringleaders when it came to the half-hour comedy format within the MTM Enterprises universe. All the while, Mary insisted her involvement with the company was still "in initial only." She told *Los Angeles Magazine*, "I'm interested only in the way a wife is interested in her husband's business."

That was an obscure statement. Driven, yet reserved, both to her credit, Mary admitted the periodic egocentric ways of the entertainment industry, while believing some elements of the "me generation" were healthier than a life of neurotic inhibition. "I'm only going to be here for a very short time," she told one interviewer, "...and I have a right and an obligation to enjoy my life."

And career. By the spring of 1977, she racked up six Emmy awards, two shy of then-all-time leader Dinah Shore. She was the new "Queen of the TV Half-Hour Comedy," as Lucille Ball had not aired a weekly sitcom since the spring of 1974, while Carol Burnett still reigned in the one-hour variety show format. With infrequent talk-show appearances and rare print interviews, Mary was often treated with the awe accorded political dignitaries and royalty. Like Ball and Desi Arnaz, and their successful Desilu production company (which by now had produced hits like *Star Trek*, *Mission: Impossible*, *Mannix* and other TV classics), the MTM wheelhouse continued to expand, if at least with no-hit wonders like *The Texas Wheelers* (ABC, 1974-1975), *Paul Sand in Friends and Lovers* (CBS, 1974-1975), *Doc* (CBS, 1975-1976), and *The Lorenzo and Henrietta Music Show* (1976).

The former was MTM's first attempt with ABC, and the latter was MTM's first venture into syndication which was, as *Los Angeles Magazine* reported, "yanked off the air" in the L.A. area in October 1976. Tinker called the *Music* show "a failure. It didn't succeed. It wasn't good enough. I can't think of anything more I can say after that." But CBS followed up with one-hour surefire winners such as *The White Shadow* (1978-1981) and the epochal *Lou Grant* (1977-1982), which would become TV's first sixty-minute dramedy, and the first spawned by a half-hour sitcom.

Chapter

13

By the spring of 1977, *The Mary Tyler Moore Show* was winding down, MTM Enterprises continued to thrive, and Mary's son Richie was graduating high school – the same year as Larry Mathews, her former TV son Ritchie on *The Dick Van Dyke Show*. As fate would have it, Mathews and Richie found themselves on a combined graduation trip to Europe. It's then Mathews noticed Richie's need for attention, which he did not fully perceive when they were kids. "When our schools went to Europe," he recalled, "Richie and I definitely hung out together. But it's not like we stayed in contact after *The Dick Van Dyke Show* ended. We just happened to run into each other for that trip to Europe."

Richie's continued difficulties were among the challenges which spurred Mary's drinking. As she admitted in *After All*, Mary took to making margaritas in a blender: Her recipe was a quarter of a blender of bottled mix, one quarter of ice, one half of tequila and, "Shake it up, baby! It had the consistency of a milk shake and the effect of morphine."

Despite this horrific reality, she remained dedicated to Mary Richards, a character with whom she formed an intimate bond. As she told Carlos Ferrer, Richards "...has a lot of my mannerisms...my gestures...my timing in conversations. But I'd like to think that maybe someday, if there is such a thing as reincarnation, I could be as good as Mary Richards. I mean, she really was something. She was outgoing and energetic and determined and aware of other people around her. And yet she had her failings, too, and I loved her for that, almost as much."

Mary especially embraced a scene in the first episode of the third season, "The Good-Time News" (September 16, 1972), when Richards enters Lou Grant's office to ask why the man who previously held her job received a higher wage than her present salary. Lou dances around the question until he asks her, "Would it help if I told you that the man who had the job before you was married with three children?" It was how Richards replied that proved especially endearing for Mary. Richards said nothing, exited the office, and then returned with a valid rebuttal. Certain that such an earnest response would not please Gloria Steinem, Bella Abzug, or any of those who Mary called her "women's liberation friends," the scene nonetheless made the actress smile and at least impressed Steinem.

"She really broke through a boundary on TV," Steinem said. "Before *The Mary Tyler Moore Show*, I don't believe there had ever been a woman living alone and having affairs – being independent. I think Mary had considerable influence on the character of Mary Richards, too, for example the episode where she demands equal pay. Ultimately, there was a 'TV solution,' she only gets half the difference. [But] there was a lot of strong, interesting women on *The Mary Tyler Moore Show*. That must be the first time a show with a woman lead spun-off two other shows with women leads [*Rhoda* and *Phyllis*]. I also admired Mary because she suffered a humiliating defeat on Broadway and recovered from it – sort of the Sally Quinn of musical comedy. I met Mary once. You don't feel you're meeting a different person offstage, but you don't feel you're meeting a phony person either. She's shit-free."

After six years of receiving such adoring, if frank, praise, Mary and her sitcom, though still retaining a significant rank in the Top 20, slipped in the ratings to 39th place in its seventh season. The show's producers argued for its cancellation, fearing its legacy of success might be damaged if the show were renewed for another year. To the surprise of the entire cast including Mary, filming for the show's final episode was announced.

According to the November 1976 issue of *Los Angeles Magazine*, Mary felt sad with those closing segments, as would anyone when leaving behind good friends. From an artistic perspective, she believed it was productive to venture elsewhere. "When you play the same character for seven years," she said, "…you know all the facets; all the techniques, and once you reach that niche, it's time to go on." Portraying Richards was simply not as challenging as it was once for her. It's not as if she wasn't satisfied with playing the role – Mary just figured she was "part masochist." "We're successful and we're established," she observed; for that she was grateful. "But success and established is also safe, and safe is only good for so long." She missed the suspense and anticipation of trying a new part; worrying about it, and not being able to sleep at night. "Yes," she added, "…and I guess I miss being sometimes not so successful."

The next few years gave Mary cause to regret her crack about being too successful. Difficulties arose on a consistent basis with her attempts at new weekly television shows. She would fare better with TV movies and on the big screen with *Ordinary People*, but never again would she enjoy the weekly success of another character like Mary Richards or Laura Petrie.

But Mary was not alone in deciding to end *The Mary Tyler Moore Show*. "There were a number of creative people who felt, as I did," she said, "...that we had done everything within the form that we had...the lady in the television newsroom...and [her surrounding] characters who were part of her life. We felt that we met all the challenges and that it was time to go on." She told Carlos Ferrer, "It was time. It was seven years, which back then was a lot. And I knew it was right...to move on. I did *Ordinary People* and a play on Broadway [*Whose Life Is It Anyway?*]. So, those were all good things."

Grant Tinker told *Los Angeles Magazine* that the decision to end the series was based on several factors. "The creative side, of course, was. . .to quit while the audience still thinks we're good," but then there was the additional attraction of syndication, which was "a big drawing card." Mary's show, he thought, was going to be "one of the all-time" big hits that "will sell better than any situation comedy ever has."

But as Ed. Weinberger observed in that same article, "...the show was running out of credible stories. We're trying desperately not to repeat ourselves...another season would have been stretching it."

For Mary, in the final countdown, leaving the show "...was like losing my family." Mary Richards, Lou, Ted, Murray, Rhoda, Phyllis, Sue Ann, Georgette, and all "...became part of me," she said. "Saying goodbye to them," and the actors who portrayed them, "...even though we all knew we weren't going to different continents, the likelihood was that it would never be the same. And it hasn't been. We see each other from time to time. I live in New York, and they live in California. It's a very special occasion when we get to see each other." It wasn't just the show's actors who became like close relatives. "[T]he prop men; and the assistant director. All of those people who become your buddies."

That company of friends had also become our pals; after seven years, they would be disbanding. Mary was the leader of that gang, "our gang," as Ed Asner said. According to him, Mary, the actress/employer/business proprietor, didn't often act like a pushy boss on the *Mary Tyler Moore* set, which could have easily happened due to her status as more than just the face of MTM Enterprises. Although Mary was and remained chairman of the company, she consistently claimed throughout her MTM reign that she had no real executive power with the company.

Matthew Asner was only seven years old when his father began working on *The Mary Tyler Moore Show*, and fourteen when the sitcom ended. Years later, Matthew had partnered with producer/director Danny Gold to form Mod 3 Productions, which was instrumental in the early DVD release of the *Moore* series. "I have two sets of memories of Mary," Matthew recalled. "The first set of memories is of a young child being around this iconic figure, and having Mary always being incredibly warm with me. The other set of memories is when we did the DVD for *The Mary Tyler Moore Show*, and dealing with her in terms of business. And bringing business into that relationship was complicated to say the least."

By that time, Fox owned the rights to the *MTM* series, and Asner and Gold made arrangements to speak with the studio about packaging the DVD and producing a documentary that would be incorporated into the release. "They seemed excited at the prospect of us delivering decent *extra* material for the project," said Asner. "And we convinced them that we were the right people to do it."

One of the next steps was to contact Mary, inform her of the proceedings, and schedule a taped interview that would be edited into the DVD documentary. But according to Asner, this idea took Mary by surprise. When he first phoned her, Mary was caught off guard. There had been little conversation with her about doing the interview. "And she balked at first," he said. "She seemed to be rubbed the wrong way. She wanted a full understanding as to what was going on, business-wise. And she reacted in an appropriate way that I was unfortunately in the middle of. It was uncomfortable for me. But we navigated through it, and she came around, and was a doll...a wonderful, beautiful professional person when we finally did the interview."

Mary's business acumen remained in full force throughout her career. She consistently wielded her power for the highest good of any project with which she was involved, especially when it came to *The Mary Tyler Moore Show*. But she was always fair-minded in doing so. "She delegated and she let people do their jobs," said Asner, who understood her position regarding the DVD release of her *MTM* series. "Any time something is sold out from under you," he observed, "you still want a piece of it because it has your name on it. And I believe MTM Enterprises had sold the show to Family Channel, and then it was purchased by Fox."

In which case, Asner and Gold were dealing with Fox and, as Asner surmised, "Mary was probably being told very miniscule details about [MTM Enterprises] by then, and was not really involved in the day-to-day operations of anything. And she most likely wasn't getting much money from it either because they probably paid her and moved on. Any time you have your name on something and someone else is making money from it…that can be kind of disconcerting."

For his part, Asner viewed himself as "a young producer who just really wanted to do this DVD for obvious reasons. Not just for my wallet, but I really wanted to do it because it was a huge part of my life and a tremendous part of my father's life. My father's career was made because of *The Mary Tyler Moore Show*. So, to be able to produce something of value in that area, to me, was very attractive."

That meant interacting with Mary in a new way – much different, of course, from their previous interactions when he was a child on set. "She had two hats on when she was talking with me," said Asner. "One was the warm person that I saw on the set of *The Mary Tyler Moore Show*," when she was nurturing at arm's length, but interested in Asner's welfare as a child. "That Mary still existed when I contacted her as an adult," he said, "but it was a business call. Mary was at first talking to me as that child she hadn't seen in twenty-five to thirty years, and all of sudden, the conversation took a very sharp veer off the road into business territory. She wasn't prepared for that."

That's when Mary forwarded Asner to her attorney, David Begelman who, as Asner recalled, "…was an extremely nice man who really helped navigate her understandable ego about the situation and we got it done."

However, Asner's most challenging moments of work on *The Mary Tyler Moore Show* DVD involved his dealings with Mary's husband Robert Levine. "I had a negative experience with him," he said. "But in hindsight he was probably doing what he could to make her look the best she could in the situation. So, I can't fault him for his dedication to her. But he was not an easy man to deal with when we went to her house and filmed."

Here's what happened:

Asner and Gold had taken a red-eye flight from Los Angeles to meet with Mary in her New York home for a shoot that had been planned weeks earlier. But just as Asner and Gold deplaned in New York, Asner's phone rang. It was Mary. "Hi, Matt," she said. "I'm just checking in. When are you coming to New York to film me?"

"Well," Asner replied, "we just landed. We're going to hop in a cab and come over to you right now."

"But I'm not going to do the interview," Mary stated firmly.

Asner was stunned. "What? Why?!" he asked.

"Fox hasn't come to a deal yet," she replied.

At that point, a flustered Asner disconnected from Mary, called Fox, and said, "What the hell is going on here?"

A studio representative told him, "She wants a certain amount of money to go to her charity, and we really don't want to do that."

"It's going to charity!" Asner recoiled. "Just do it! You're Fox!"

The studio ultimately consented, but formal arrangements were not decided that day. In the meantime, Asner called Mary back and said, "Look – we're going to come and interview you. I have a make-up person who will be arriving at your house in about an hour. Let's just do the interview. We'll keep it in the can, and I promise you that [the footage] will not be used if we don't come to terms. And at least we won't have wasted a trip here."

"Fine," Mary said. "That's fine."

"So, we ended up getting in the cab, and going to her house," Asner explained. "And that's where I kind of had a run-in with Robert, who was probably annoyed with what was going on, which is probably why he wasn't very nice to me."

In preparing to film Mary, Asner and Gold were positioning camera angles. "We had set up our shot and invited Robert to look at it," Asner recalled. "Levine did so, and said, 'Oh, no, no, no. This is all wrong.'"

At which point, Mary instructed Asner and Gold, "Turn the monitor around and let me look at it."

After perceiving the shot, she paused and said, "I think it's beautiful."

In the end, the shoot with Mary went remarkably well. Fox made the necessary donation to her charity, and *The Mary Tyler Moore Show* DVD was released with much fanfare and to critical acclaim.

Interacting with Mary and those in her inner circle could periodically prove challenging, especially when it came to business. But her guardedness was based on the need to protect her "brand," her marketability. This contributed to her success even when she camouflaged such fierce occupational savvy.

In 1974, Helen Gurley Brown, founder of *Cosmopolitan* magazine, and a discerning businesswoman in her own right, referred to Mary, Carol Burnett, and Dinah Shore as "living examples of how you can be a mogul and not have to act that way. All three of them run empires, but you never hear a bad word about them because they're such pussycats. I don't know Mary personally, but I like her by reputation. I even like the way she and Grant Tinker act about their marriage. If there's trouble, they admit it, and when they're back together they let you know. They don't keep up a phony façade. They don't pretend there's something there when there's not or there's nothing there when there is. I consider Mary a *Cosmo* girl, both [on the *Mary Tyler Moore* show] and in her personal life. On one hand, she's very feminine and susceptible, but on the other hand, she and her husband run a multimillion-dollar empire. She just exemplifies the *Cosmo* girl in every way."

In retrospect, Ed Asner said the original *Mary Tyler Moore Show* cast and crew respected Mary's authority. "We were all in awe of her and her position, and she never did anything to trigger anything differently in us. She was in the hands, at least on the surface, of the producers, writers, directors and her husband…up in the big office, and yes, there would be some conflict at times. But it was always wrapped in humor and warmth to remove any sting." Mary refrained from telling fellow cast members how to interpret their characters or say their lines. "I never saw any of that openly to my knowledge," Asner said. "If she did say something I would listen, but I never did anything against my grain."

Years after her sitcom ended, Mary said, "During the time of *The Mary Tyler Moore Show* I thought I had to be exemplary because the company bore my initials – MTM. On paper, anyway, I was the boss. So I never really shared very much of importance with anybody. But I've changed, really. Now I don't think it's all that critical whether or not everybody loves me."

But behind the glare and glamour of the *MTM Show* cameras, Mary may have been perceived by some as indifferent. She became known within the show-business community as a tough, savvy businesswoman who carefully guided and protected her personal and professional life. Many of her peers, friends, and colleagues led active social lives, but she and Grant Tinker played it cool. Even Asner, the other "Grant" and father figure in her TV life, once referred to her as "a closed corporation."

Asner, however, was still party to her inner circle. He continued to play Lou Grant in the one-hour dramedy of the same name that would debut in September 1977 after her *Moore* show ended. As he explained in November 1976 [to *Los Angeles Magazine*], "There'll be a greater concentration on drama, with Lou going back on a newspaper, and we'll be doing it without an audience, which I'll miss."

"Everyone will be sad not to come in on Monday morning and see the same familiar faces," a staff member added. "But in every case, the cast is going on to do wonderful things to enhance their careers."

Meanwhile, Betty White was gearing up for CBS's *The Betty White Show*, co-starring Georgia Engel, even if the premise hadn't been settled. "I don't know yet whether it will be about Sue Ann," she said. "But it undoubtedly will be a character with some of Sue Ann's qualities, or lack thereof, if you want to put it that way."

Ted Knight, who once musingly sang, "Here she is…Mrs. MTM," when Mary walked into a rehearsal, was also under exclusive contract with CBS, and even though there was no certain series in his near future.

As the actor conveyed in *Los Angeles Magazine* in 1976, he was "looking forward to a consistent level of involvement." "It's been harder for Gavin [MacLeod] and me," he added, "because some weeks we have had substantial parts and other weeks it's been a pittance. It's hard to be a star one week and subservient the next. I've had to make compromises, do dumb things that I didn't want to do, for the sake of the role. I've prostituted myself, hating it all the time and I just hope I haven't drawn all the curtains – that the creative juices are still flowing."

Nothing ever came of his contract with CBS, but Knight eventually found success again, this time, with ABC in the half-hour "jiggle" comedy, *Too Close for Comfort*, which later switched to first-run syndication as *The Ted Knight Show*. Of his exit from the *MTM* series, he concluded in *Los Angeles Magazine*, "I'm going to miss the steady paycheck, Gavin MacLeod, and the man who makes the coffee. Maybe the rest of the remorse will catch up with me later."

But it was those kinds of statements that led Mary, who had been tight with Knight, to say things like, "He wore his heart on his sleeve."

Years later, *Too Close for Comfort* co-star Lydia Cornell made similar observations. She played daughter Sara Rush to Knight's Henry Rush. Also starring in the series were Nancy Dussault as Knight's wife Muriel; Deborah Van Valkenburgh as their other daughter Jackie; and Jim J. Bullock as family friend Monroe Ficus. "Ed Asner came and visited us on the set a couple of times," recalled Cornell. "And so did Gavin MacLeod. We all hung out together. They visited the set a lot. They all loved Ted. He had a really good camaraderie with everyone. They were very proud of him and I got the impression that they wanted him to know how much they were proud of him."

On March 13, 1977, Asner penned a poignant article for *Family Weekly* magazine to coincide with the last season of *The Mary Tyler Moore Show*. He wrote, "Gavin, Ted and I have become good friends off and on the set, and working together has been a pleasure." With regard to the show's entire cast, Asner further observed, "Of course, we weren't perfect darlings, and sometimes we indulged in the sulks, but we tried to heal our differences."

According to Matthew Asner, "Ted was my Dad's best friend. And then I guess they had a falling-out and their friendship went south. They didn't communicate for about six years. But when Ted was very sick and dying, my Dad visited him and they reconnected."

"Maybe there were some personality conflicts early on," Cornell said, "…and having Ed Asner and Gavin MacLeod visit our set was their way of making amends. I don't know. But if there was any rivalry, I didn't see it. I do know Ted was competitive and very hard to deal with at times. But he never told me about any conflicts on the *Mary Tyler Moore Show*. I only knew him later. And all I saw was that Ed and Gavin were thrilled for him that he had a hit show. He had failed with his CBS sitcom right before our show. And he was devastated. And he thought he was the star of *The Mary Tyler Moore Show*. He really did. So, not getting a hit show right away really crushed him. Ed went on to *Lou Grant* and Gavin went on to *The Love Boat*. So, Ted needed a hit and he finally got one and that's when he came to congratulate him."

Cornell said Knight believed he was the "big draw" on the *Mary Tyler Moore Show* "because his character was such a buffoon, and once he stepped into that fate, he became the big draw. Without Ted it wasn't that funny, really. I mean, there was a lot of warm interaction on the show with the other characters. But Ted added the element of excitement and craziness. And he assumed he was going to get a big hit series afterwards like everyone else did. But he didn't and he was freaking out about it. And then he was so over-the-moon happy that he had a hit show [with *Too Close for Comfort*], and a lot of that may have been due to the interaction between him and me in my bikinis. It was a good chemistry, all of us together."

However, Knight later became upset with Cornell. She recalled, "He didn't want the girls to have bigger parts in the show. But the ratings would go up when we would have more airtime. So, it was really upsetting. Ego crushes so many dreams of people. Deborah and I could have had a spin-off but he wouldn't allow it. And he would have been a co-owner but he didn't want anyone to outshine him. At the time he was the star of our show, and he was highly paid, and that's all that mattered."

Knight became so ruffled by Cornell's increasing popularity that he had her character removed from an episode of *Comfort*. Robert Mandan, best known as Chester Tate, husband to Katherine Helmond's Jessica Tate on ABC's *Soap* sitcom (1977-1981), had been hired to play Knight's brother in one episode. "And they wrote me out of that episode," said Cornell, "and they wanted Robert to be the father of Cousin April [played by Deena Freeman], who they wanted as a substitute for my character. But that was all a ruse to try and get rid of me, because they thought my manager was asking for more money. But I wasn't. I would have done the show for free. But my managers were throwing my weight around like I was the star, and it pissed everybody off and they tried to write me out of the show. It was a really bad year for me. I had no idea what was going on."

As a result, Cornell continued, "Ted was always angry at me for that – until we had it out one day in the dressing room, and I cried…hard. And then we became closer. He took us all to the Ivy [restaurant in West

Hollywood] to celebrate the fact that Metromedia picked up our show for ten more years, which was pretty amazing. And then when we were all negotiating our contracts, Deborah decided she did not want to do the show anymore, and then they cut me out, too, and said, 'Ok … let's create a whole new show with Jim Bullock and Pat Carroll, and call it *The Ted Knight Show*.' It was pretty shocking. At the very end there was an added betrayal. So, I don't know what to think of that," Cornell said.

"But," she added, "…Ted and I made peace with each other before he died," in 1986.

Although Knight at one point wanted to leave *The Mary Tyler Moore Show*, he never caused as much ruckus as he would later create during his ABC series years – perhaps because on *Mary Tyler Moore* he was a supporting player, not the headliner. And he certainly never behaved badly with Mary, whom Cornell finally had a chance to meet, if under unpleasant circumstances, at Knight's funeral.

"Mary never came to our set like Ed and Gavin," Cornell said. "But I wish she did. I loved Mary. But by that time, she had increasing issues with diabetes and alcoholism, and she had just been married [to Robert Levine]. So, the only time I met her was at Ted's funeral, where we hugged. Mary Tyler Moore was a big girl-crush. She was so humble and demure, and her comedy was clean. There was just something so pure and innocent about her. She just seemed so innocent, and that's kind of what I emulate; that's kind of how I am in real life. Every woman looked up to her."

Cornell, who also battled and conquered her own alcoholism, had "…bonded with Mary on that level," she said. "I identified with her. It's like we both knew we had that secret part of ourselves. She was sober by the time I met her, even though I wasn't sober by that time. I got sober in 1994. But she was one of the reasons I got sober."

At Knight's funeral, Cornell "cried the hardest. I had to get up and give a eulogy. And everyone from *The Mary Tyler Moore Show* was there including Mary, Ed, Gavin, Cloris Leachman, Betty White. I sat in the first row, and we were all crying. It was a big funeral."

For Gavin MacLeod, leaving *The Mary Tyler Moore Show* and going on to his own show, *The Love Boat*, was not as traumatic as it had been for Knight. MacLeod took things more philosophically. "Life is full of different times," he told *Los Angeles Magazine* at the *MTM Show*'s demise, "…and this has been one of the most fruitful times in my life. It doesn't seem like seven years. When I started this show, my oldest girl couldn't even pronounce it. She called it *The Tiny Miley Moore Show*. Now she's in junior high." He said the series changed his life, and that he was offered a "surprisingumber of pilots."

In another interview, MacLeod mentioned looking forward to once again playing "heavies," or villain roles. He wanted to trade Murray's typewriter in for "a tommy gun, or a knife or any blunt instrument." But when that appeared in print, he said, "Did I get letters!"

MacLeod had also said that the show had influenced his life for the better. He became interested in a healthier diet, and believed the entire cast looked more physically fit than they did when the series debuted in the fall of 1970.

But for those like Ed. Weinberger, the most significant change on the show transpired with the character of Mary Richards. "She's grown up," he said. "We started out with an almost virginal girl, very concerned with dating and her love life, and then the show began to make statements about a woman [alone], having a good life, having a career, without always having to have a guy around. The other changes have been more subtle. The character of Lou Grant could have just been a cliché, but we've shown other sides of the man."

Another member of the show's staff said that Tex Baxter started out as a two-dimensional character that became "a very real person who can choke up when he's in trouble, or break you up with just a walk."

That became the case with most characters on the show. But as the end drew near, the question became: Would Mary Richards remain single? "A lot of people ask that question," observed David Lloyd, the show's executive story editor, in *Los Angeles Magazine*. And when he polled the studio audience attending one of the show's final episodes, the response was mixed. There was even some talk of having Mary and Lou Grant get married.

But according to Allan Burns, that only would have worked if, in the last scene of the series finale, Mary would have turned to Lou in the dark of their bedroom, and said, "Oh, Mr. Grant!"

Although such a stunt would have made a devastating tie-up to the show, Mary Tyler Moore never envisioned marrying off Mary Richards to anyone. She didn't want to end the series "all tied up in a ribbon," she said. The actress envisioned the last segment as "a farewell show, with a tearful goodbye, so that we won't all be working with tears in our eyes in an episode that's supposed to be upbeat. To have Mary Richards get married and live happily ever after would be to turn our backs on all we've said on this show, and all the good we've done. Society says marriage is the ultimate goal, and it is the most wonderful state for many people. It certainly is for me. But it's not for everyone. In terms of asserting the right of a woman to be single and to have a career, we've said a lot in this show and I wouldn't want to undo it now."

Weinberger had planned to end the series just as *Variety's* Army Archerd had reported; having the WJM-TV staff exiting the newsroom – each one fired, except for Tex Baxter. Weinberger thought it would be "a nice ironic touch. Mary would be doing a documentary that would take her out of the country, and Lou would be going to a newspaper, and Murray getting another job in Minneapolis. We wanted to duplicate the emotions we would feel actually, to make a situation where it appeared unlikely that they would ever see each other again, so that their on-the-air goodbyes would be their personal goodbyes. In a way, I'm a little sorry that it's been discussed. But it's probably still the way we're going to go."

The sitcom's final half-hour, aptly titled "The Last Show" (March 19, 1977), featured group hugs, in front of and behind the scenes, and became the most-watched program of the week. That season the show earned an Emmy for Outstanding Comedy Series, which merely added to its arsenal of accolades from previous semesters. The segment also represented another milestone. At its close, Mary broke character to feature a curtain call in front of the live audience where she introduced her castmates right before the end credits rolled for what became the final time. That was the first time in history that an American TV network show had ever done anything like that.

"I will miss Mary," said social activist Shirley Chisholm. "One of the delightful aspects of the show is that it has featured a single woman making it in a male-dominated occupation." Although she still wondered, why Mary Richards always called her boss, *Mr. Grant*, while her male colleagues refer to him as *Lou*?

Ed Asner, the actor who brought Lou to life, said, "I am inordinately proud and delighted that we at the show never settled for less than the best, both as a group and as individuals. I guess a lot of it had to do with Mary. This woman is one of the most talented, beautiful and intelligent people I've ever been associated with. But I still can't forgive her for finking on me in the episode where I [as Lou] slept with Sue Ann [Betty White] and didn't know it."

Barbara Walters had named *The Mary Tyler Moore Show* her favorite program, mostly because of its star. "There's nobody like Mary Tyler Moore. She's fresh without being icky-pooh. And there's enough reality to all of the characters to make them believable to those of us in the [entertainment/news] business. I think one roots for all of them. In his own way, each one of them is a loser who somehow comes out ahead. Ted, of course, is an exaggeration, but he's recognizable as that old-school brand of actor who reads the news. What Mary Richards goes through with Lou, that kind of apology for blurting things out – there's nothing-personal, it's-not-something-I'm-asking-for-myself – every woman in the industry still goes through that. But leaving all that aside, it's just a marvelously funny program, and essentially what makes it so is the charm and humor and the straightforwardness of Mary Tyler Moore. Someday, I hope Mary Richards gets my job."

"If Mary needs a job," legendary news anchor John Chancellor once posed, "send her on over to the NBC newsroom."

"It saddens me that I won't be able to see Mary regularly anymore," said Carl Reiner, her former boss and co-star on *The Dick Van Dyke Show* who'd become a fan of *The Mary Tyler Moore Show*. "I liked being able to visit with her, knowing exactly where she lived. It was a special show and one that was important in the evolution of television comedy. It took the original *Van Dyke Show* – where working life was an integral part of the show – and went a step farther; they made working life the focus of most of the action. Also, they did less story and more character, which was an important development. It gave the show a backbone. Even when they had a poor story, the characters always worked."

"It's not as though we're saying goodbye to Mary Tyler Moore forever!" exclaimed Cloris Leachman. "After all, the show will go into syndication forever; and Mary's going right into other projects."

When *The Mary Tyler Moore Show* came to a close, its leading lady was definitely ready to move on to other roles on-screen and in life. In commentary reported by both the *New York Times* and the *Washington Post*, she said, "After *The Mary Tyler Moore Show*, I decided I was not going to play any more characters with whom I was totally familiar...I can't live with [the women's liberation label]. I can't carry it around anymore."

ACT IV

Extraordinary People

Mary earned an Academy Award nomination for *Ordinary People*, released in 1980 by Paramount Pictures, and co-starring Timothy Hutton (seen here). [Credit: Ronald V. Borst/Hollywood Movie Posters]

Chapter

14

The Mary Tyler Moore Show had ceased production, but the success of its leading lady soared, despite a few less-than-successful TV, film, and stage productions. Mary's continuous struggles with her health and well-being, particularly with diabetes, certainly did not help matters. She once observed, "The hardest part about being a diabetic is every day you wake up and think, *Is this the day the kidney will give out? Is this the day I'll have a stroke?*" But she remained stoic, despite the challenges. When first diagnosed, her blood sugar level had been 750, when it was supposed to rest within the 70 to 110 range. "The doctors were quite amazed I was alive at all," she said. "In fact, I made it into a medical textbook as an 'extraordinary case.'"

In many other aspects of her life and career, Mary was extraordinary, but she was no textbook example. She broke the mold.

The Mary Tyler Moore Show had sealed her status as a star. She now enjoyed the luxury of picking, choosing, and producing her own projects. She expanded in a long-desired musical direction when, in 1976, one year before her famous sitcom ended, she began to reinvent herself with *Mary's Incredible Dream*, a peculiar TV-movie musical.

Around the same time, Dick Van Dyke had developed and then aired a new variety show called *Van Dyke & Company*. Though innovative and Emmy-winning, it was short-lived. Much of his show was taped and sometimes filmed on location, while the studio interior scenes, including intros with Van Dyke, appeared to be taped in front of a live audience.

But Van Dyke's *Company*, and Mary's subsequent specials and weekly variety shows, achieved nothing like the success of their combined 1969 well-crafted and well-received one-hour delight called *Dick Van Dyke and the Other Woman*. The special was so popular that CBS aired it three times until 1972. Variety-show archivist Tom Wilson explained why:

"There were several well-done segments that featured him, her or both of them." In this case, the material and the performances matched. "The show was solid," Wilson said.

Such was not the case with *Mary's Incredible Dream*, which was originally titled *The History of the World as Mary Tyler Moore Explains It*. That idea changed when the producers decided to add wraparound segments of Mary sleeping, presenting the special as one long dream sequence. "People are going to see a different Mary Tyler Moore," promised the now 38-year-old star. She called this special "the biggest undertaking TV has ever attempted," which was a tall order with lofty words.

Years later, pop-culture enthusiast Jaime J. Weinman shared his thoughts about her *Dream* on his website, *Something Old, Something New*: "Of all the many variety shows and specials on network TV in the '70s, the strangest may have been *Mary's Incredible Dream*," which he described as this "bizarre mish-mash of music, religion, philosophy, and high-in-every-sense-of-the-word camp."

In some ways, *Dream* was "a standard variety special...glitzy, cheesy musical numbers, and a song list that spans about five decades...But it has no sketches or...dialogue for anyone except the narrator," except for a line from Mary at the opening. Around the middle of this wild trip, Mary speaks a line which is supposed to tie the whole thing together: "I can't talk now. I'm having this incredible dream."

Beyond that, the special linked its musical numbers with what Mary called "...a story of the eternal cycle of man. If viewers don't want to follow the story they can just enjoy the music and dancing."

The special was highly touted in the press, with several big production numbers featuring Mary and guest-star Ben Vereen. Tom Wilson remembered watching *Incredible*'s first run. "It started out as a bizarre show, and got weirder and weirder." "I think people must have been turning it off," Wilson said, "because I'm pretty sure the ratings ended up being less than significant." (In fact, CBS instructed Mary not to pursue the musical-variety show route.) "But obviously," Wilson said, "she was a big star and kept pushing for it, and she ended up doing one other special, and two weekly variety shows."

Co-directed by Eugene McAvoy and Jaime Rogers, and created and written by Jack Good (The Monkees' *33 1/3 Revolutions Per Monkee* TV special), *Dream* may have been a nightmare for some viewers, but for Mary it was a joyful vision of more things to come. Usually shy of the press, she got busy promoting the special. She told Hollywood columnist Marilyn Beck, "As a performer I can go to my grave happy now. I've done everything I want to do. I'm talking to Jack Good about doing a weekly musical variety show. Since he created and produced my special, I'm convinced he can do anything."

Beck noted Mary's excitement about *Dream*: "Mary's so convinced the special is the best thing ever to hit the airwaves she's been talking it up to anyone who will listen. And has been cornering so many of her friends for preview cassette-unit glimpses of the all-musical hour that actress Betty White finally told her teasingly, 'It's a shame you don't put it on TV, instead of showing it door to door.'"

In speaking with UPI's Vernon Scott, Mary credited *Dream* as Good's brainchild. "When he came to me with the idea, I told him he had carte blanche. Without any structure or guidelines from me, Jack produced a unique, no-holds-barred musical happening."

Whether Mary attempted to "talk-sing" her way through "I'm Still Here" or made a valiant attempt with the Cy Coleman and Dorothy Fields tune, "Nobody Does It Like Me," Weinman for one said *Dream* was "probably a better showcase for Ben Vereen." It was one of his first big television performances, and right up his dancing alley. In contrast, Mary "gets to do all the stuff she's only OK at and little of the stuff she's great at [delivery of and reaction to dialogue]."

"But it is what it is," Weinman decided, "...and I can't help enjoying it just for the strangeness of it all. This is a special that ends with Mary Tyler Moore as a pink angel, floating and spinning in front of religious symbols and clouds while singing 'Morning Has Broken'...with Arthur Fiedler conducting the 'Hallelujah Chorus' in heaven...a historical version of 'Sh-Boom,' and Jerome Kerns' 'She Didn't Say Yes' retrofitted as a song about the temptation of Eve."

"TV really could be pleasantly insane in the mid-'70s," he added. "[And] any special that begins with the 'CBS Special' logo and ends with the MTM kitten is a special that gets a few extra points just for logo coolness."

That same logo soon appeared on other, less fanciful MTM productions, like *Lou Grant*. The series debuted in the fall of 1977 with Ed Asner in his benchmark role, with an increase of 30 minutes and a dramatic twist on the side. The smooth relationship Ed shared with Mary during their previous sitcom days continued during production of the new *Grant* show, despite her conservative Republican edge, and his liberal ways. The new program's one-hour dramatic format was more likely to stir controversy; political tensions later surfaced off-camera.

The ratings remained high for *Lou Grant* in its first mid-season. In contrast, the reception for Mary's second variety special, *How to Survive the '70s and Maybe Even Bump Into Happiness*, was lukewarm. The title can be seen as wishful thinking on behalf of its star. It was a brave attempt to face the rapidly changing world with a courageous smile, with a great deal of support on and off-camera. Mary assembled such performers as Dick Van Dyke, Bill Bixby, Harvey Korman, Candice Azzara, Gino Conforti, former *Dick Van Dyke Show* and *That Girl* writer/performer Sam Denoff, and good friend Beverly Sanders. "This special wasn't as flamboyant as the first one," Tom Wilson observed. "It was more topical of the '70s and its fads."

The *'70s* special also featured John Ritter (son of musical cowboy Tex Ritter), who by then had become a major TV presence via his hit "jiggle" ABC sitcom, *Three's Company*, which also made stars of Suzanne Somers and Joyce Dewitt. Pre-*Company*, Ritter had worked with Mary on an episode of *The Mary Tyler Moore Show* called "Ted's Wedding" (November 8, 1975), in which he played the priest who presides over Ted and Georgette's wedding in Mary's living room. During *The Dick Van Dyke Show* years, when he was just a teenager, Ritter had a crush on Mary along with the rest of the viewing world. But unlike most of the population, he somehow obtained her phone number. On the front page of his loose-leaf school notebook was written the words "Mrs. Grant Tinker," alongside her number. When he finally gathered the courage to make the call, it was Tinker who answered. John asked to speak with Mary, Tinker asked who was calling, and then John hung up. When he later shared his teen memory with Mary, she joked and said, "So, that was you!"

It all sounded like a skit that could have appeared on any one of her variety ventures, including *How to Survive the '70s*, which took a lighthearted look at the stress of life in the 1970s. Special attention was paid to the proliferation of self-help books that promised success in life – if you bought the book. One of its writers was classic TV legend and prolific writer Sam Bobrick, who penned acclaimed variety shows such as *The Smothers Brothers Comedy Hour* and *The Kraft Music Hall*, as well as episodes for sitcoms like *The Andy Griffith Show* and *The Van Dyke Show* from 1988. Bobrick later created the *Saved by the Bell* TV sitcom, which became one of the most successful ongoing youth-geared platforms in TV history. He called Mary's *Survive* special "a pretty nice show…pleasant, but not spectacular." "It went very smoothly, and nobody was disgruntled," he said, including Mary, whom Bobrick described as "a very nice woman" who "started out as a dancer. That's why she wanted to do a variety show. And she trusted Billy very much."

"Billy" was Bill Persky, Mary's dear friend. Perksy's writing partner Sam Denoff and Bobrick had roomed together when they first moved to Los Angeles. "We all knew each other pretty well," Bobrick said.

As with *Incredible Dream*, Mary intended that the *'70s* special should showcase her musical and dance abilities; she approached Persky to supervise the festivities as director, producer, and head writer. "My thought was that the '70s were just over and they were ridiculous and it would be great to make fun of them," he said. "And there were all those self-help books, and that essentially is what the set was…piles of self-help books."

Two sketches were standouts for Persky, the first of which, with Van Dyke, wasn't rehearsed. "I ran it with Mary and Dick just once. I told them what I wanted them to do, and they did it and it was wonderful. It was about relationships, and how they take a long time and how they could happen in a moment's time. And the relationship between their two characters took place five floors up on an elevator from the second they got on to the second they got off, and by the time they did get off, they were madly in love. And then after that, each of them met the person they were married to or with. But Mary and Dick carried the scenes off with pure brilliance."

The second skit took place at a singles club, showcasing the talents of Bixby, Korman, and Ritter. Persky explained: "They were all people-watching and Mary was playing a woman who had recently been divorced. But it turned out her husband [Bixby] was there. And they ended up sitting next to each other and talked really snippy. She said things like, 'So…are you still going out with that other woman? How old is she now…seven or eight?' Things like that. And then when they each started to leave, he said to her, 'You're the best thing I've seen all night.' And it was really lovely."

The special ended with the segment, "This Is the Rest of Your Life, Mary Tyler Moore," featuring Mary, Korman, and Ritter, projecting what her career might become. The skit began with Mary returning to television with a show called *Welcome Back, Mary*, "which doesn't do very well," Persky recalled. "She comes back two years later with another show called *Mary Again*, which also doesn't work. In her late '70s she does yet another show called *Oh, That Mary*, and that doesn't last very long either. When in her 80s, she does *There Goes Mary*, in which she's photographed only from the back." At which point, she turned to John Ritter and said, "Have I no shame?" To which he replied, "Apparently not."

In effect, the climax of *Surviving the '70s* special became, as Persky described it, "…the precursor of what followed in Mary's career [in real life]."

The following fall, Mary convinced CBS that she could headline a weekly variety show but, as Persky said, "It never really worked." No matter how hard she tried, and try she did.

Come September 1978, she tamed the surreal premise of her *Incredible Dream* and *Surviving the '70s* specials into two full-blown attempts to recreate the female-driven weekly variety format which had reached its apotheosis with *The Carol Burnett Show* (CBS, 1967-1978). With her love for song and dance, Mary believed the home audience was ready to re-embrace the variety genre on a regular basis.

Unfortunately, viewers disagreed. Neither of her efforts in this category succeeded. First came a sixty-minute show simply called *Mary*, which co-starred Dick Shawn, Swoosie Kurtz, future talk-show legend David Letterman (who doubled as a writer), and Michael Keaton, a few years shy of his movie-star status with films like Ron Howard's *Night Shift* (1982) and Tim Burton's *Batman* (1989).

Writer Arnie Kogen was the head writer for this *Mary*, and its subsequent revision, *The Mary Tyler Moore Hour*, both of which he said "had some very funny sketches and material...but this was an edgier Mary. She sang songs like 'Dead Skunk in the Middle of the Road' and once introduced the Ed Asner Dancers, six chubby Lou Grant look-a-likes in shirts and ties disco-dancing around the stage."

"Mary Richards was loved worldwide," Kogen continued, "...and Mary Tyler Moore was America's sweetheart...probably Canada's sweetheart and Bulgaria's sweetheart, too. But America and Canada and Bulgaria...did not like this 'new' Mary. And Mary Tyler Moore was not thrilled with the series either. Neither was CBS. The show was cancelled after three episodes."

After the trio of disappointing segments *Mary* was re-tooled in January 1979 as *The Mary Tyler Moore Hour*, a backstage show-within-a-show. At one point, other titles were considered like *The New Mary Tyler Moore Show* and *The Musical Side of Mary*. But whatever it was called, the reviews were brutal. One critic for *United Press International* wrote, "It was so bad even the commercials for it got bad ratings."

The new concept, which harkened back to the old Jack Benny-George Burns-Gracie Allen format, was a failure. Mary played Mary McKinnon, a character who, well, heads a weekly TV variety series.

Guest stars included Lucille Ball, whom as Mary later told Barbara Walters, discovered "to be a very serious lady...[a] no nonsense" type. There wasn't "a lot of bantering. It was wonderful to watch her. But once she got on that set, and starting rehearsing [in character], she was a funny, funny person."

Mary found it hard to contain her laughter during one scene in which Ball eats baby eel and octopus. But according to Jim Brochu's book, *Lucy in the Afternoon*, the famed redhead failed to find anything amusing about working with Mary. Mary's staff claimed they had been cordial with Lucy, but that wasn't Ball's perception. She believed Mary, in particular, was not at all fond of her, and was nothing but frosty and distant. Lucy complained, "I'd say something to her, and she'd smile that big, toothy smile and walk away."

If true, the "walk-away," minus the smile, was a maneuver Mary had employed a few years earlier during her original *Mary Tyler Moore Show* days. According to one source who requested anonymity, there was a similar brief interaction with her during an entertainment industry event attended by several showbiz professionals:

> We spent much of the day huddled together. Mary never spoke to or looked at anyone in the eye. For that matter, she never even glanced at anyone in the room. The rest of us respected her obvious need for privacy and left her alone. In fact, there had been very little conversation other than a couple of people who knew each other saying hello.
>
> Finally, about midway through the event, while everyone was getting coffee, tea, whatever...someone approached her and said something about them having a mutual friend. Without looking up or, again, glancing at him, Mary sort of shrugged and walked away.
>
> The guy who'd spoken, who'd obviously taken hours psyching up to say hello, looked after her, and to me his face showed nothing less than total relief. Not another word was spoken between any of us for the rest of the day.
>
> It should have been a learning experience, I suppose...except that I couldn't figure out what I was supposed to learn. I finally decided that the lesson was to never again try to communicate with someone who obviously does not want to communicate because, man, it was as uncomfortable for everyone as it could be.

Flash forward to Ball's visit to the new *Mary* set and Brochu's assessment: Lucy was to perform the song, "The Girlfriend of the

Whirling Dervish," which she loathed and asked Mary to change. But Mary refused, which riled Ball, who was used to getting her way. She had literally run each of her hit sitcoms (*I Love Lucy, The Lucy Show*, and *Here's Lucy*) and was infamous for not only directing cast members, but directors, too. Even so, Ball consented to perform "Whirling." She entered the music studio for a prerecording, and braced herself for a confrontation. She made it clear to all those concerned that she would deliver only one rendition of the song, and that would be it. If any technical glitches arose, they needed to be addressed on the spot because Ball would do "one take and one take only!"

She performed "Dervish" and, after a moment, the sound engineer politely requested another take. Stan Freeman, the show's pianist, kept an observant eye. He described Ball as acting like a child. "She threw herself down the floor kicking and screaming and yelling, 'I won't! I won't!'" Happily, after the tantrum ended, Ball literally rose to the occasion like the pro she ultimately was and gave the tune another go.

This awkward behind-the-scenes conflict between Ball and Mary was particularly disturbing in light of other public, positive interplays between the two on TV. In public, they were nothing but cordial when they met at various industry events (some of which were televised). When going on the record, they spoke fondly of one another, as Mary did about Ball during a Barbara Walters special.

The alleged Mary-Lucy conflict is also unsettling in view of the early behind-the-camera days of *The Dick Van Dyke Show*, when Ball would monitor rehearsals of that series at her Desilu Studios. She would sit in the rafters above, looking down on the players like a supervising surgeon in an operating theatre. After one *Van Dyke* rehearsal, Ball told Mary, "Baby, you're good," and then walked away, elating the younger actress. "That was the greatest gift I ever received in this business," Mary later told *ABC News*.

But the balance of power had shifted when Ball approached Mary with a creative suggestion on the set of her variety show. Again, if what Brochu reported is true, Mary's response was disrespectful, unfair, and hurtful; overall, very un-Mary-like.

Thomas J. Watson worked for Lucille Ball in the publicity and business-affairs department. He also co-authored with Bart Andrews the acclaimed book, *Loving Lucy: An Illustrated Tribute to Lucille Ball*. Watson was working at CBS in New York, when the network moved him to Los Angeles. There his office happened to be situated next to Mary's, which was basically operated by Mary and her assistant Frank Adamo. Due to the close proximity of their offices, Adamo and Watson became friends. Consequently, Watson was privy to much of what transpired behind-the-scenes of the *Mary* variety show, for which he also eventually worked in the research department.

As opposed to what Brochu reported in his book, Watson did not recall any controversy or conflict between Mary and Ball. But Gary Morton, Ball's husband at the time, did have some interesting insights regarding what transpired at the first table-read of the script from Lucy's appearance on *Mary*. "Lucy was constantly changing things," Morton told Watson. "At least the scenes that she was in," Watson later assessed. "And Mary basically went along with it because who better to teach you sitcom that Lucille Ball."

"Lucy was very hard on everybody, as far as doing their job," acknowledged Watson, who attended a rehearsal of "The Girlfriend of the Whirling Dervish." According to Watson, that song was not performed in front of the audience, as was the case with most of the musical numbers for the show. "They didn't want to do them in front of an audience for whatever reason," he said. Subsequently, the "Dervish" tune was taped the night before without an audience save for a few fortunate attendees, including Watson, and the necessary cast and crew.

According to Watson, "Dervish" was performed a few times when at one point, the director, who was stationed up in the booth, said, "That's good, ladies. Let's move on." At which point, Watson continued to recall, "Lucy turned and sort of stamped her foot and said, 'No! I was a half a beat off through the whole damn thing! Let's do it again!' She wasn't happy with it. And so they did it again. She knew herself and she felt like she was off. And she wanted to be as good as everybody else. And that's the only thing I knew about as far as that number was concerned."

As fate would have it, Thomas J. Watson had attended the same college a few years earlier with David Letterman. "We knew each other," Watson said, "but we weren't what you'd call close buddies. We just shared the same classes." By the time Letterman was cast as a regular on Mary's variety show, Watson had become involved with audience participation and research, otherwise known as *program testing*. In such cases, various TV shows are presented and previewed to sample audiences before the program's debut. "And the audience response for Mary's show was not fabulous," Watson said. "So, everybody was holding their breath when the show went on the air."

One of the last conversations that Watson had with Letterman took place when the day after Mary's show debuted. Letterman bounced into Watson's office and asked, "How'd we do?" Watson's face said it all. "I didn't even have to open my mouth," he recalled. At which point, Letterman responded with, "Oh, damn!" "And he just turned around and walked out," Watson said. "Indeed, we only did three or four episodes, and they yanked it. But Mary and Frank [Adamo] stayed in that office, because they only took about a month or two off, but not much more. Because then they want back into production with what became *The Mary Tyler Moore Hour*, which was more of a sitcom/variety show type of thing…and that's the one where Lucy was one of her first guests. But, of course, that show didn't last that long either."

In the end, Ball's appearance on *The Mary Tyler Moore Hour* did nothing to heal or alter that show's dire prognosis. An additional dose of energy, by way of guest-star Dick Van Dyke, also proved futile. These and other noble attempts at reprogramming, nostalgic or otherwise, simply could not save *The Mary Tyler Moore Hour*, which was canceled within three months.

Why didn't it work? Why did Mary fail with each of her attempts at the musical variety format, whether as specials or a weekly series? Television variety shows had a long, successful history through the '50s and '60s. So why did most of the shows of the late '70s and beyond fail? Rick Lertzman offered this observation:

"The variety-show format was running down weak by the time Mary tackled it. But more than that, Mary didn't have the chops to do a variety show. She wasn't the caliber of Lucille Ball or Carol Burnett. She was not a sketch comedian like Carol, who had worked on *The Garry Moore Show* and on the [first] *Bob Newhart Show* in the '60s. Carol could carry it off. Mary was an actress that had to have lines. You couldn't look to her for improvisation. That simply was not her milieu. She did not have those kinds of skills. She had a lot of weaknesses as an actress. Carol Burnett could run the range from burlesque comedy to pathos, but Mary could not. Mary was a pretty face, and a lot of her success was based on her looks. I always liked her and still love to watch her, and this is just my opinion, but you could easily plug someone else into the roles that she did."

On the other hand, Treva Silverman once said, "Mary is brilliant. A person has to be to respond so appropriately to everything she does. Comedy really is a form of perception. Mary is quiet about it, but she knows everything that's going on around her."

Allan Burns once said that he, Jim Brooks, and the other scribes of *The Mary Tyler Moore Show* tried to write good "attitude lines": "She's funny when she's in a situation where she is vulnerable, tired, angry, surprised – she can play those attitudes with a very funny slant. And she surprises us. We don't write the attitudes into the script; sometimes she just comes up with completely off-beat responses."

Such unique retorts were usually directed towards a bumbling Ted Baxter, as when in 1972's "The Good-Time News," Mary Richards gives him a well-deserved "shut up!" Or in "Will Mary Richards Go to Jail?" (September 14, 1974), when Mary hands Ted a news bulletin to read; Ted looks it over silently, forcing her to scream from off-camera to read it "OUT LOUD!"

Rick Lertzman's viewpoint was similar to *Newsweek's* Malcolm MacPherson who, in 1973, assessed, "It may be that Moore is a limited actress. It also may be that her other vehicles did not make as good use of her talents" as CBS did with the original *Mary Tyler Moore* show. "Despite that big smile and those lithe-gawky gestures, her humor is private and subtle."

"There is a small temptation to conclude that *The Mary Tyler Moore Show* owes little of its success to Mary Tyler Moore," MacPherson continued in his survey of Mary's and Dick Van Dyke's attempts to return to weekly TV. "Mary's first big hit was the role of Laura Petrie in the old *Dick Van Dyke Show*, and that series was a lot funnier" than the "Moore-less" *New Dick Van Dyke Show* of 1971-1974. "But when Mary tried to cash in on her TV fame, the results were disastrous. On the stage, she starred in *Breakfast at Tiffany's*, which closed in previews. Her movies, including *Thoroughly Modern Millie*, were, by her own account, 'bombs.'"

That same word could be applied, however ungraciously, to Mary's weekly variety attempts in 1978 and 1979. But it wasn't all her fault. Reverberating Lertzman's appraisal, writer Sam Bobrick said that TV comedy sketches had by then "fallen by the wayside." "There was no better sketch comic than Carol Burnett," he said. "Her show was brilliant." But after Burnett's series ended in 1978, the musical-variety format was dead in the water. "The people watching *The Carol Burnett Show* were adults," said Bobrick, "...and not so much the kids," an all-important demographic for advertisers.

The last variety show Bobrick worked on was *The Tim Conway Comedy Hour*, which debuted on CBS in the fall of 1970. To keep up with the times, Bobrick said, "We really tried really crazy sketches." Because the Conway series was scheduled after shows like *Gomer Pyle, USMC*, "we didn't inherit the lead-in audience," Bobrick said. "We were losing our adult audience, but gaining our young audience." Fred Silverman, then president of CBS, "tossed us out just as our ratings were changing," Bobrick said. "The network really didn't give us a chance, and they should have. We were keeping up with the times."

But it was too late for *The Tim Conway Comedy Hour*, even with cast members like Sally Struthers (a year before her career-changing role as

Archie Bunker's TV daughter on *All in the Family*). "We gave Sally her first job," said Bobrick. "And we had three comics who were our writers, and I loved them. They were wonderful. We called them 'The Third Bananas,' who consisted of Craig Nelson, Barry Levinson, and Rudy De Luca. And Craig became a big television star [in ABC's 1990s sitcom *Coach* and other shows], and Levinson became a big director. And Tim Conway, of course, was brilliant and wonderful to work with. It was one of the best jobs I ever had and I just loved the show," Bobrick asserted.

The half-hour sitcom format continued to thrive. Innovation arrived in the guise of *All in the Family*, and *The Mary Tyler Moore Show*. The one-hour drama format continued to succeed, led in new directions by MTM's production of *Lou Grant*, and later *Hill Street Blues* and *St. Elsewhere*. But with the onset of irreverent late night programming such as *Saturday Night Live*, and prior to the MTV music video craze of the 1980s, the musical-variety format was a dying breed.

"The variety-show format had run its course," observed Tom Wilson. The material presented was "just the same kind of thing...a mixture of duets and skits," a configuration that had been showcased for over twenty years. "When they tried to come up with something different, like *Mary's Incredible Dream*, sometimes they worked and sometimes they didn't. And in that instance, it didn't."

Additionally, there were several veteran stars of specials from the '50s and '60s, who were now making occasional guest spots in the '70s. They had all that vaudeville training," said Wilson, but their style was out of style. "So they were out of the picture," he said. "What you had now were these younger performers that didn't have the stage background trying to do what their predecessors had done, but without the experience. Many of them had come up in television but they didn't know how to perform in front of a real audience and suddenly they're thrown into these variety shows where they're performing in front of an audience."

"Sometimes, too," Wilson said, "...even members of the production team involved, including the directors, didn't have the know-how to make things run smoothly." Or the lead performers were hired as a form of "stunt casting." Either way, "...it wasn't working."

Stars of dramatic shows were sometimes signed for one-hour musical-variety specials simply because it became the "in" thing to do. Cheryl Ladd (*Charlie's Angels*), Lindsay Wagner (*The Bionic Woman*), and Lynda Carter (*Wonder Woman*) each blazed the TV screen with one-time musical variety shows. Or pop-music stars like Tony Orlando & Dawn and the Captain and Tennille had hit records, which network executives, somehow felt would automatically translate to TV stardom. (Of course, *The Sonny & Cher Comedy Hour* and *The Donny & Marie Show* justified these hopes.) The latter worked, Wilson said, because the Osmonds "were really young, and it catered to a young audience that the networks were always interested in. But also they made sure that their show was populated with a lot of veteran performers; every episode usually had a current star like Farrah Fawcett but also someone like Milton Berle."

While even youth-geared programming such as *The Brady Bunch Variety Hour* aired and bombed after only three episodes were aired, according to Wilson, "Other big names started saying, 'Well, hey, I have a musical background. I want to do a variety show or special, too.' And the networks catered to these whims because they wanted to keep their stars happy, but in most cases the specials weren't that good."

Exhibits A & B: Mary's two weekly music-variety excursions. According to Wilson, "The first show, *Mary*, was kind of an ensemble show with a lot of up-and-coming performers in its cast, patterned to some extent like *Saturday Night Live*. Shortly after that, it merged into *The Mary Tyler Moore Hour*, which was more of a show within-a-show."

Wilson described the latter as "cliché-ridden" with "annoying characters...a nervous, loud, obnoxious producer...a bitchy secretary that's always interfering....the ditzy character played by Dody Goodman, who worked at Mary's house, screwing things up. And Michael Keaton was a page, overstepping and noisy."

"It was challenging to sit through the show," he said, "...because there were so many unlikable people around Mary who was essentially playing Mary, the one who's trying to keep everyone happy. It just seemed like every episode was the same. Every week they had a guest star who had some problem. And then there were some scenes in the dressing room where Mary has to deal with the secretary or some issue at home or having a fight with the producer about some other problem. The point is the writing was bad. Mary wasn't bad. But the material was substandard."

"A good variety show or special," Wilson declared, "...starts with featuring people who are very likable. But you also must have good material that doesn't seem forced or cutesy. And if the musical numbers aren't staged well they fall flat. You need a good choreographer, director and musical director, and a strong rapport between the performers, even if the skits are weak. You need a good variety of elements to make a good variety show," Wilson concluded.

Bill Persky felt that Mary's variety TV ventures failed, especially her weekly editions, due to a combination of factors. "Maybe the timing was off. The time had passed. Or maybe she couldn't carry a variety show every week. I don't honestly know. But she went on to do movies like *Ordinary People*, and after that she could do whatever she wanted."

Chapter

15

From the extravagant, bright, and flashy, to the dramatically sublime:

On the original *Mary Tyler Moore Show*, Mary delivered a comedic take on fictional journalism. With *First You Cry*, a CBS TV-movie from 1978 in which she cast herself and produced, Mary played it realistically straight. Based on the true story and bestselling book of the same name (but with a comma), *First You Cry* was written by NBC television news correspondent Betty Rollin about her battle with breast cancer, and how her subsequent mastectomy changed her marriage, philosophy and life. Exterior scenes were shot on location in New York City, while interiors were filmed at CBS Studio Center in Studio City, California. *Lou Grant*'s set doubled as the NBC newsroom where Rollin worked. *Cry* won rave reviews, and Mary gained an Emmy nomination as Outstanding Lead Actress in a Limited Series or a Special. She also earned new respect as a "serious" actress. The moments of wry humor, credited by Rollins as part of her eventual healing, didn't seem out of step when brought to life by Mary.

"I cared a lot about the project," Mary said in *Interview Magazine*. "I felt from having read the book it was based on that if it [breast cancer] were to happen to me or somebody close to me that I would handle it much better. I wanted the film to reach many more people which I felt could only be done through television."

Rollin had leavened her book with humor, which Mary thought was equally imperative for the TV adaptation. In this way their vision for the film was the same. Neither wanted it to be, in Rollin's words, "a dreary story in any way," while both she and Mary thought "it might help people."

Truth is – real life has both laughter and tears. Any effective book or script must reflect both, especially when dealing with such a sensitive issue as a health crisis. A successful project about such a topic must balance humor and heartbreak. Such perspective, said Rollin, an admitted atheist, "contributes to any healing." Much of her mail "was funny" and subsequently productive and health-inducing. Compassion, authenticity, and maturity were shown through the project.

Following her recovery, Rollin served as a primary caregiver to her mother, Ida Rollin. She had brought her mother to the set of *First You Cry* in Los Angeles. "I have this cute picture of the three of us," Rollin recalled. Mary "...couldn't have been nicer to my mother."

Rollin had also visited one of the New York location shoots for *Cry* at Rockefeller Center near NBC where she worked, and attended a press junket for the film. Though not privy to Mary's interactions with the film's cast and crew during this period, Rollin said the actress was "quite pleased" with *Cry*'s director, George Schaeffer. "As much as Mary wanted to do the movie, it was very important to her to have the film retain its sense of humor and romance. Yes, the plot had to do with breast cancer, but it was really about romance and a young woman's life."

As further proof of its success, the film was parodied in 1979 with a sketch on *Saturday Night Live* (*SNL*) called "*First He Cries*," with guest-host Bea Arthur portraying a consoling doctor to Bill Murray's character after his wife, played by Gilda Radner (who would later die of ovarian cancer), undergoes a mastectomy. Although *SNL* by definition is irreverent, this skit came across as more tasteless than usual. Still, a certain measure of public awareness was signified by being the target of *SNL*'s sights. According to Rollin, Mary believed *First You Cry* would serve as a positive and educational vehicle that would inform viewers about this disease, "...to let them know that it's not the end. Sometimes it is, but not necessarily."

In 1974, *Bewitched* star Elizabeth Montgomery, a contemporary of Mary's, starred in *A Case of Rape* which, like *Cry*, was one of the first issue-oriented TV-movies. *Cry* and *Rape* were groundbreaking showcases for both performers, at least in acknowledging some of the more unsettling sides of modern life. When Rollin wrote *Cry*, first published in 1978, she "wasn't thinking about 'doing good,'" but rather, "telling the truth and about what this experience was like for me."

Breast cancer was not part of the mainstream conversation, and Rollin wondered if viewers would accept Mary in such a serious role. Because

Rollin was in the public eye, she was warned not to write the book. When she was diagnosed with breast cancer, no one else, "except for the very brave Betty Ford and Shirley Temple," had acknowledged their battles with the disease. Temple, in particular, Rollin observed, "never received enough credit for speaking out about it." For Mary to have tackled the issue on-screen "was kind shocking for people but it was a good kind of shocking that she pulled it off."

It was just as shocking when Montgomery appeared in *Rape*, or in the 1975 TV-movie *The Legend of Lizzie Borden* about the famous ax-murderess. But the very un-*Bewitched*-like characters in both films were relished not only by viewers and critics, but Montgomery's peers (she was Emmy-nominated for both films). In like manner, only an accomplished and respected actress like Mary could have taken the lead in *First You Cry*. "It had to be someone who was as powerfully loved and respected," said Rollin, and Mary fit that bill. She agreed to star in *Cry* because it was so different from *The Mary Tyler Moore Show*. "She loved the danger of it," Rollin said. "It was brave of her and, particularly at that moment in her career where she had enjoyed so much success but only on one note."

Carol Burnett, another of Mary's contemporaries, appeared in the April 1979 ABC TV-movie *Friendly Fire*. Like *Cry*, *Fire* was a true story of a middle-age woman in crisis. Burnett played Peg Mullen, a woman who lost her son to American "friendly fire" in the Vietnam War. That year at the Emmys, Mary and Burnett were both nominated for Outstanding Lead Actress in a Limited Series or Movie. (Bette Davis won for *Strangers: The Story of a Mother & Daughter*). Burnett, Mary, and Montgomery had finally earned recognition for dramatic roles – even if some critics felt comedy was easier than drama. Or as Rollin said, "…especially comedy about something you could die from."

Before becoming a writer, Rollin had studied acting briefly, early in her career. So, she spoke with a measure of authority when addressing Mary's talent. "It's kind of silly to think people are serious actors only when they do a serious role or when their character is placed in a serious situation. Mary had long proven her skills but she liked the idea of doing something serious that other people would think was serious, even though, as far as she was concerned, she had always taken her work seriously, including comedy."

Rollin, however, found Mary to be relatively solemn off-camera, just as Mary had described Lucille Ball when they worked together on *The Mary Tyler Moore Hour*. "I didn't know her very well," Rollin said, "…but I did get to know her a little bit. We went out to dinner with our husbands and two other friends and we had some contact during the making of the movie and somewhat afterwards. She had a sense of humor, but was disciplined, and I would say formal. It's a funny word, but she was also very correct, not at all flighty, silly or giddy, or any of those things. We liked each other, and it pleased me that she liked my mathematician husband Ed [Harold Edwards], because he's very serious, smart and as formal."

When First You Cry initially aired, Edwards was a professor at New York University, and oblivious to popular television programming. "Frankly," Rollin recalled, "he did not have any idea who Mary Tyler Moore was. I don't think he ever saw her show or *The Dick Van Dyke Show*. Ed has a sense of humor and a light side but [TV sitcoms were] just not on his radar."

But Rollin was on Mary's. When MTM Enterprises acquired the film rights to *Cry*, the author later said that she was "in kind of an awful moment in my life. I had just broken up with somebody and my father had just died and I had come back to New York and I was staying with my mother, temporarily."

At this point, the phone rang. She picked up the receiver and a female voice said, "Hi, this is Betty Rollin." Rollin remained silent and then stunned for a few seconds. Who was this strange person calling and identifying themselves by her own name? And then Rollin realized that voice belonged to Mary, who was joking with her from the other end of the line. Rollin was "amused and delighted at this discourse and thought it was so adorable, and extremely charming." Mary calling and claiming to be Rollin while actually speaking to Rollin was Mary's way of expressing just how delighted she was in deciding to play the journalist on-screen. In making that call, Mary provided much-needed comic relief at a serious time in Rollin's life, validating the pertinence of humor during challenging times.

In 1988, years after *Cry* aired, Rollin authored another book, *Last Wish*, about her mother's battle with cancer and subsequent assisted suicide, in which Rollin participated. At this point she received another call from Mary who, Rollin said, "could have just as easily written a note or an email. But she loved the book, and wanted to tell me just how much, and how she felt about it, which I thought was very formal." Yet Mary had no interest in adapting *Last Wish* into another TV-movie. ABC did that in 1992 with Patty Duke and Maureen Stapleton. Mary's call was simply to express comfort and appreciation.

Don Johnson, future star of NBC's groundbreaking *Miami Vice* music-TV-hybrid series of the 1980s, had played Rollin's boss in *First You Cry*. At the time he was in the midst of substance abuse. And while Johnson eventually checked himself into rehab after the movie completed filming,

Mary's sister Elizabeth Ann Moore, just beginning a career in TV news, died of a drug overdose near the end of *Cry*'s production.

In his book, *You're Gonna Make It After All*, Marc Shapiro says Elizabeth had apparently ended a relationship with a boyfriend. Upset, she drove to her parents' home, and discovered her mother was intoxicated. As Mary would do whenever she felt unsettled, Elizabeth reached out to her Aunt Bertie. What transpired next remains unclear, but the following morning, Bertie found Elizabeth lifeless in bed. At first, the coroner ruled her demise a suicide, due to an overdose of painkillers and drugs. Mary, however, insisted that this could not have been the case, just as she would later refute similar suicide rumors surrounding the loss of her son Richie, who died three years later from an accidental self-inflicted gunshot.

Shockingly, Mary would later admit in *After All* that she herself contemplated suicide. When inebriated, she would play a horrid game of Russian Roulette with her car, which she would recklessly navigate through her neighborhood streets, ignoring stop signs. In case there was any doubt of her "acute state of alcoholism and the insanity it produced," Mary recalled "with sickening clarity that on more than one occasion," she would play such terrorizing games with her vehicle but without any concern for her "own safety and the safety of others."

When she phoned Rollin about *Last Wish*, Mary's brother John Moore was quite ill. In hindsight, it was a devastating time on several levels, and Mary may have been reaching out to Rollin for help to more productively assist her sibling's exit from this world. "I really don't want to comment on euthanasia as a subject," Mary later said. She could only relate to the experience through her brother, who had called her from California when she was in New York. "He had stashed a lot of pain medication," she said, "and…he was going to make yet another attempt at suicide which he had done before and failed." She pleaded with him to wait until she could reach him. When she eventually arrived at his side, he asked for her help, and did not want to fall asleep until he got it.

But her assistance at the attempted suicide did not work. Her brother lived another three months. He underwent surgeries to sever the nerves in his spinal column and both arms, and died with a relative sense of peace. Mary called his death a "blessing…that he was able to go with serenity," because he told her that God appeared to him that morning and said, "You're going to a place where you're going to feel normal."

She had by then performed in *Whose Life Is It Anyway?* – her hit Broadway play about a patient fighting for the right to control their own life, including its ending. But it never occurred to Mary that John would be dealing with that same issue, just as Rollin was unaware of Mary's issues with John. "Mary didn't say anything about him in that call," Rollin said. "I'm learning something I didn't know."

Many fans of *First, You Cry*, the book, and *First You Cry*, the movie, may have thought the same after reading or watching Rollin's story. However presented, the franchise became an educational tool utilized by the publishing and entertainment industries beyond directly academic venues such as the library or public-TV programming. "When art is done well, it's always instructive," said Rollin. "Whether or not it's happy or sad, if it has real merit it's bound to be instructive in some way. I don't think it's the duty of television to be instructive. But it can be. It definitely happens."

You could even say that Mary's portrayal of Laura Petrie as TV's first truly independent home engineer was similarly instructive. And her role as Mary Richards blazed the trail for free-thinking, career-geared women, single or otherwise. Although such concepts were not consciously developed as groundbreaking elements for *The Dick Van Dyke Show* or *The Mary Tyler Moore Show*, that's essentially what they became. And the same may be said for *First, You Cry*. Rollin wanted "to tell the truth" of her life experience, while the film's social influence was unmistakable. And she received the mail to prove it; lots of it. And she continues to receive heartfelt messages, now mostly via email, professing things like, "*First, You Cry* saved my life," or "I never would have gotten through my health challenge without *First, You Cry*."

"And they sometimes refer to the movie and sometimes not," Rollin said. "But I think what the movie did, was widen the scope. More people watch television than read books. The movie had a kind of reach that the book could never have. Sometimes, I run into people who know or read the book because they have seen the movie."

Rollins is content with the result. "I received something I didn't deserve," she said. "I didn't have altruism in mind when I was writing the book. I merely had something remarkable happen in my life and, as a writer I wanted to make something out of it. I had a sense of art about it. I didn't have a sense of mission."

At first, Rollin was surprised by the intense public response for the original book and its subsequent film. If she had set out to "make a statement," she doesn't think it would have turned out as well. "If you'll pardon my lack of modesty," she said, "I just wanted to write a good book, and I wanted it to be funny. I wanted it to have life. I wasn't at all thinking of it as a self-help book in any way. What made it work for me, Mary, and for others…was that it was not a self-help book, even if that's what it turned out to be…to my utter surprise."

Such significance is also attached to Carol Burnett's *Friendly Fire*, and Elizabeth Montgomery's *A Case of Rape*.

There are more than a few connections between Burnett and Montgomery, as there are between Montgomery and Mary. Mary was friends with Burnett, who was close to Montgomery. Although Montgomery and Mary never traveled in the same social circles, all three starred in iconic TV shows produced and/or directed by their husbands. Mary was with Grant Tinker. Burnett was wed to Joe Hamilton; Montgomery's husband was William Asher; the couples were also business partners. When each of their selective shows ended, apparently, so did their wedded bliss. At least that's the way it turned out, give or take a few years: *Bewitched* ended in 1972; Montgomery and Asher divorced in 1974. *The Carol Burnett Show* ended in 1978; Burnett and Hamilton divorced in 1984. *The Mary Tyler Moore Show* ended in 1977; Mary and Tinker divorced in 1981, shortly after the failed *Mary* and *Mary Tyler Moore Hour* variety shows.

Rollin, meanwhile, never sensed any tension between the Tinkers, even though "there was really no way for me to have seen that," she said. "We had a nice dinner, and they were certainly nice to each other at that dinner." But Rollin did not have the kind of intimate friendship with Mary that would have allowed for a more in-depth observation of her personal relationship with Grant.

Either way, once the Tinker union ended, Mary wanted the new face she had long considered, and her obsession with plastic surgery began. *First You Cry* became her final scripted dramatic performance on television before transitioning to feature films like *Ordinary People* and *Six Weeks*, after which she began to experiment with dental implants, new cheekbones, and other facial reconfigurations. "I hate my teeth," she once said. "I should have had braces on them. They're too big. A hint of having teeth like Gene Tierney is all right, but mine really are buck."

Mary also wasn't that crazy about her wide mouth. In her pre-teen years, she would purse her lips in public to give the illusion of having a smaller mouth. "I suppose we all have different images of ourselves and what we'd like to be," she said in one early magazine interview. "The only good thing about me is my nose. I have one of the world's greatest noses. The rest of me is just average. My figure's all right. I don't mind it. It can get a little out of hand after a three-month vacation when you just sit down around the pool getting tan and fat. Then I have to go on a crash diet. I just simply can't afford to gain too much weight because I have such an investment in a whole lot of stretch pants. And they all fit within an eighth of an inch and if you gain more than a half-ounce you've had it. You can't wear them."

In 1991, in coverage celebrating *TV Guide*'s 2000th issue, Mary addressed her first appearance on that magazine's cover, on December 9, 1961. "I felt like I had arrived; it was a big deal in my life. I have never seen a picture of myself that I liked. But as I recall, it wasn't one of the humorous pictures. When it's comedic…I don't have so much a problem with it. But when it's a glamour head shot…I'm less satisfied."

Another time, she said, "I only ever had confidence in two things: my nose and mouth. I knew they were OK. In fact, I got furious when I read something in one of those [tabloids] that referred to me as having a nose job. The story also said I had had a facelift and eye work. And without saying anything further, I will just say that I was upset over the nose job," she laughed.

Mary may have been referring to a statement by Dr. George Lefkovits, who once said, "[Her] face is very plastic-looking. I think she had a full face and neck lift and some laser treatment giving a shiny look. Her nose looks pinched."

A second doctor's opinion suggested that diabetes had contributed to her thinning skin, which makes cosmetic surgery more challenging. The physician also believed Mary had too much pull at the corners of her mouth, giving her an unnatural appearance. As a remedy, he suggested collagen injections to fill out her face. But that would have been counterproductive to Mary's objective. As she once told Entertainment Weekly, the "baby fat" in her cheeks had been surgically removed.

Another doctor opined, "Judging from the way Mary's ears melt into the sides of her face, she has had a face or neck lift. Her wrinkles have gone although her skin looks too tight in places. The disappearance of her eyelid creases is a telltale sign that she has also had upper eye-lid work. Her eyebrows are unusually high now. She must have had them lifted, too."

There were also rumors of breast implants and facial cheek implants.

Although Mary would eventually become strong-minded with her advocacy against diabetes and for animals, she, like many performers, still lacked the assurance and self-esteem required to battle age without plastic surgery.

Things like her losing an Emmy for *First You Cry* didn't much help matters, but she never fully understood why her work beyond the *Dick Van Dyke* and *Mary Tyler Moore* shows was not more readily embraced by critics or her peers. She should have won more awards, and she once compared increasingly brutal reviews to "drop-kicking a puppy."

But one reason why Mary never received more critical accolades or Emmys, Golden Globes, etc, beyond playing Laura Petrie and Mary Richards, may have been because she refused to play the game. Like Elizabeth Montgomery, who never won an Emmy (even after multiple nominations), Mary did not enjoy the social side of Hollywood, a necessary part of what is now called "networking." Due to Mary's exquisite taste in clothes, she did enjoy figuring out what to wear to a social gathering. But as she once told *Newsweek* magazine, "I hate parties. It's a hangover from childhood insecurities. Feeling that nobody really likes me and I won't have anything interesting to say."

Fortunately, when she would win an award, Mary never let loose at the podium or blurted anything like Sally Field's "You like me! You like me!" speech (following her lead Oscar victory for 1985's *Places in the Heart*). But at least Mary was not alone in her artistic loss for *First You Cry*. In addition to her losing an Emmy for Outstanding Lead Actress in a Limited Series of Special, the film also failed to win in three other categories: Outstanding Drama or Comedy Special; Outstanding Film Editing for a Limited Series or Special (for James Galloway); and Outstanding Music Composition for a Limited Series or a Special, for Peter Matz.

Chapter

16

Despite Mary losing the lead actress Emmy for *First You Cry*, the film became a tremendous benchmark in her career, as she continued to support the achievements of others, namely Ed Asner and Fred Astaire.

Asner was her dear friend and former co-star. Astaire was one of the stars she had longed to work with, after being inspired by his movie musicals when she was a child.

In 1978, she and Astaire did finally appear together at a star-studded live stage tribute to the song-and-dance man that was hosted by the Academy of Television Arts and Sciences in 1978. Mary presented Astaire, then 78, with a plaque at the event where he received a standing ovation from a crowd of approximately 750 people.

On March 7 of the following year, Mary was there to help honor Asner when he received the *Man of the Year* award from the Hollywood Radio and Television Society at the Century Plaza Hotel in Los Angeles.

On the other side of the country, Mary and Grant Tinker moved to a spacious new $2 million house in the hills of Los Angeles, which she marked as their fifteenth place of residence. The couple frequently switched homes to accommodate the constant changes in their family dynamic, which included his four children from a previous marriage, and her son Richie. They were never quite sure which offspring would be living with them at any given moment or month.

Sometimes, they would purchase a home and view it as a secluded home for two, and then one of his children would call and say, "Hey, Dad…I want to come live with you and Mary for a year." No child was ever turned away, but the hideaway was now too small, and the family would be forced to move into a larger residence. The following year, that same child would want to move out, and two more of Tinker's children would want to move in, or Richie would want to go live with his father. There was also a brief relocation to New York, which lasted just six months. At which point, Mary and Grant returned to Los Angeles to live in a temporary home.

She wanted to work, but was hesitant about tapping the built-in potential of another sitcom. "That would certainly seem to be the road to take," she said. "On the one hand you want that to happen, and yet, as an actress…it is death…especially if you played a character that the audience loved, and I think they really did love Mary Richards. And as they see her every afternoon or morning wherever it's shown in whatever market, it makes it that much more difficult for you to develop a new character."

Mary was consistently enthusiastic about expanding her career with movies, both for TV and the big screen, but she remained cautious about the possibilities. "I don't think I'm a box-office star at all," she would reiterate time and again. "But I could do a credible job in a secondary role. That would be wonderful. I would love to do that." She also regretted not having more children, biologically or by adoption. "I often wish that now, if the situation was such that I could have another stab at motherhood," she said, "…because I could give so much more to that child now, because I'm through looking at myself."

"I like being me for the most part," she once asserted. "But if I could change some act, I would have had more children. Having just one child and losing him has left me bereft," she said with misty eyes, "…that I would change."

Reflecting on Richie's birth during an earlier interview with Barbara Walters, Mary believed she was as good a mother as possible, but was so wrapped up in herself, "as you must be…at 18, 19. That's still a very precious, growing period for [anyone], and there I was with a baby who was demanding full attention." She didn't get all the enjoyment out of it that she could have. "I don't think I screwed him up and I'm grateful for that," she said. But she did the best she could. She honored fidelity, but understood "the desire…to know somebody better…to see somebody who appears to be very exciting." But she didn't pursue such desires; if she had acted upon those feelings, it would have ruined "one of the most valuable aspects" of her marriage, which she called "complete confidence and trust."

A similar confidence and trust may have been broken between Mary and some of her more straitlaced fans who read that she and Tinker had smoked marijuana. It was said that for her, it was little different from drinking a martini before dinner. Mary was infuriated by that report, which she labeled inaccurate. "I got steamed," she said, "...because what I said was that I *had* smoked marijuana, not that I *did* smoke marijuana [on any regular basis]. And I feel I do have a responsibility to a lot of young people who look to me for, if not leadership, than some sort of trend-setting. And I would not want to lead anyone to the kind of life where you are dependent on any kind of relaxation that's artificial...whether it's a martini...or Librium or...marijuana."

When used judiciously, marijuana was "...not any more harmful than a martini used judiciously," she said. "But I'm not for either one."

It was her life, anyway, wasn't it? Or maybe it was Brian Clark's, whose play, *Whose Life Is It Anyway?* opened on Broadway in 1979. At the time, the starring role, a paraplegic sculptor, was portrayed by Tom Conti, who won a Tony Award over Jack Lemmon in the play *Tribute*. One year later, Conti completed his contract, and *Life* producers altered the gender of its lead character and cast Mary who, according to the *New York Times*, "...assured the continuance of the play."

Mary's performance in the role was lauded by other critics, as well as friends and colleagues like Robert Redford, her director of *Ordinary People*. He caught an early performance of the play and raved, "I feel like a proud father."

Life, now co-produced by MTM Enterprises, became Mary's triumphant live-stage return to Broadway, fifteen years after the indigestible *Breakfast at Tiffany's*. The show had been scheduled for a three-month run but became so successful it was extended an additional three months. Opening at the Royale Theatre on February 24, 1980, *Life* ran for 96 performances, and earned her a special Tony Award for a leading role that was initially written for a male actor, the year Phyllis Frelich won as lead actress for the play *Children of a Lesser God*.

Mary was ineligible for a traditional Tony nomination because she was classified as a replacement performer. *Los Angeles Times* arts and theatre editor Craig Nakano provided some clarity with the article, "Why Mary Tyler Moore Received Her Special Tony Award in 1980." According to the Tony Administration Committee, records did not specifically mention why Mary was recognized with theatre's most prestigious accolade. But according to the winners list published June 10, 1980, she received the award "...in appreciation of the appearance in live theater of a major television star."

MTM Enterprises produced five other plays in New York including *Noises Off*, *The Octette Bridge Club*, *Benefactors*, *Safe Sex*, and a revival of *Joe Egg*, which won a Tony in 1985, by which time Mary was residing in Manhattan following her separation (and subsequent divorce) from

Grant Tinker in 1981. She attended New York premieres of Broadway musicals like *Grind*, starring Ben Vereen, and *The Glass Menagerie* starring George C. Scott; hung out at Studio 54 with people like Grace Jones; and continued to build a new life. At the same time, as she chronicled in *After All*, she was seeking "a new face," with plastic surgery.

Around this time, her relationship with Richie had gotten worse, and she continued to drink heavily. But she did not allow such personal turmoil to take its toll in public. All the while, her artistic integrity, professional and personal decisions, and general thought process in choosing non-Mary-like characters, became complicated and intriguing. She was open to playing any role, unless the "really scary" or the difficult-to-accept characters of a given movie or a TV show were gratuitous. She didn't want stunt casting to merely drum up business from young healthy males – which, she joked, by then was not requested very often. She was attracted to credible and realistic characters that did the best they could with the cards they were dealt. This was "true of every human being," she said.

After all, "Adolf Hitler believed that what he was doing was right and that God was on his side." She added, "I always go into a role, fortunately, not having to play Mr. Hitler, believing that the truth will come out...the truth of the performer played through the reality of the character will emerge, and be acceptable; if not understandable, at least recognizable."

Mary was always happy to perform a comedy or drama on television, film, or the stage. But any potential characters had to be absent of clichés. She rejected scripts that lacked the element of surprise. "You have to be surprised," she said. The story or character had to be "real" and "human," and she looked for moments in a script that she personally connected with, somehow.

With another nod to the macabre, Mary said, "For example, in order for me to play a murderess, I don't really have to murder someone. I just look for freshness [in a character]."

According to her interview with *Newsweek's* Ramin Setoodeh, the dark reference was generated from a "private little joke" she would share with a friend whenever they found themselves on an elevator. Upon the elevator's arrival at their requested floor, and seconds before the door opened, one would say to the other, "She killed her husband, you know," just to freak people out.

Future *Mary Magazine* editor David Davis saw Mary perform twice on Broadway, once in late 1979 for previews of *Whose Life Is It Anyway?*, and in 1986 during the first week of *Sweet Sue*. Davis shares his memories of her *Life*:

> When the curtain went up, Mary got a huge round of applause and grinned broadly, temporarily breaking character. She was playing a quadriplegic sculptor fighting for her right to die. Her performance was electrifying. Ordinary People hadn't been released yet, so people weren't fully aware of her abilities as a dramatic actress, except maybe from the 1978 TV-movie First You Cry. There were so many people in the audience coughing throughout, it was beginning to get annoying, especially during the quiet moments of the play. It was a Saturday matinee we attended. The woman sitting next to me fell asleep and was snoring by the end of the play. Another annoyance, but I was still thrilled at seeing Mary live. I couldn't believe how three-dimensional she looked after seeing her on a flat screen for so long.
>
> At one point during the show, Mary's character was arguing combatively with her doctors, and some phlegm got caught in her throat mid-sentence. She cleared her throat before continuing the dialogue. She was such a pro. At the curtain call, Mary received a standing ovation. She was wearing an orange terrycloth robe and looked absolutely thrilled at the reaction. You could tell she knew she hit a homerun. As she walked off the stage, she wiped a tear from her cheek.

Despite her sometimes distant persona, Mary was sensitive to the core, and she reveled in the art of surprising others. She continued to select non-Laura/Mary parts for television and film, none the least of which was her Oscar-nominated role in 1980's *Ordinary People*. Her Beth Jarrett character was described by the *Los Angeles Times* as "unsympathetic, nearly bloodless." In another review, the *Times*' Justin Chang defined Jarrett as "a model wife and mother permanently warped by tragedy. Still grieving the untimely loss of her firstborn child, Buck, she withdraws emotionally from her husband [Calvin, played by Donald Sutherland], and turns her fury on their youngest son, Conrad [Timothy Hutton]."

Chang continued:

In Moore's performance, every curt remark and slight becomes an act of passive aggression, a way of withholding a mother's love. Unable or unwilling to comfort Conrad in his own troubled moments, she stiffens like an automaton when he tries to hug her. When he's not hungry enough to eat the French toast she's made him, she whisks the plate away, repaying one form of rejection with another.

Moore doesn't entirely extinguish that dazzling smile; we even see Beth laughing along with Buck, in a brief flashback to happier days. But she does put it to coolly subversive use. At social gatherings she turns her grin into a shield, a mask of contentment that can clench, without warning, into a reproving stare.

Ordinary People is an easy enough film to dismiss today partly because it beat Martin Scorsese's *Raging Bull* for the best picture Oscar, and partly because its insights into suburban malaise soon became widely circulated clichés. (The ambitious tortured wife played by Annette Bening in *American Beauty* is merely the most obvious of Beth Jarrett's many descendants.)

While other critics at first failed to embrace *Ordinary People* or what Chang called Mary's "un-showy transformation," Pauline Kael wrote, "As this WASP witch, whose face is so tense you expect it to crack, Mary Tyler Moore…seems to be doing penance for having given audiences a good time."

"There is indeed a kind of pertinent, self-flagellating quality to Beth," Chang wrote, "and Moore's performance is powerful in part because it represents such a cruel negation of her comic persona. After the actress' transformation from a fulfilled housewife on *The Dick Van Dyke Show* into a single career woman on *The Mary Tyler Moore Show*, Beth Jarrett was a terrifying reversal, a version of Laura Petrie gone mesmerizingly wrong."

One could only wonder what Chang, or other film critics and moviegoers would have thought had Mary, and not Kathy Bates, played the role of Annie in the 1990 film adaptation of Stephen King's *Misery*. Mary had been up for that part, but lost out. Still, Mary's maturity as an actress and as a woman had prepared her for her role as Beth Jarrett in *Ordinary People*; her time had come, and her craft was honed.

Writer Rita Lakin always perceived Mary's acting as "really honest. I don't know how she dug that deep for *Ordinary People*. My God, her guts were spilling when she did that film. I was in awe of her and the movie, and I wondered how much of it was true to her life…how much angst she had…how much she might have experienced in her real life that allowed her to be able to play that kind of character."

Since *Ordinary People* was about a mother's loss of her eldest son by suicide, director Robert Redford wanted a likable actress for the role because "Beth is likable on the surface." And while Ann-Margret and Lee Remick were apparently strong contenders to play the part, Redford selected Mary because she was "the all-American girl."

Co-starring Sutherland as Beth's understanding-husband Calvin, and the Oscar-winning Hutton as her troubled son Conrad, *Ordinary People* broke new ground for Mary. In a videotaped conversation with Carlos Ferrer, she called working on the film "…breathtaking. Donald was so rich in his performance, and so giving, off-stage. Timothy Hutton was a joy…a delight to be around. He was just maybe 18 at the time. But you could see him [bloom as an actor] like a flower in slow motion or fast motion, when it just emerges right before your eyes."

But to remain in character, Mary kept her distance from Hutton while making the movie. "The most that was ever exchanged between us was 'Hello' or "Good morning' or a nod," Hutton later professed. "But she was so prepared and professional."

"I think I understood Beth Jarrett…much better than I thought I did at the time," Mary once revealed after playing the character. "I was surprised that Robert Redford wanted me to play the role. I thought it was a bigger stretch than, in fact, it was."

Mary called Redford the best director she had ever worked with. "He was amazing with me. He had done his homework. He knew what he wanted."

This may have been true, but Mary was prejudiced. She once had a crush on the actor, and was slightly in awe of his good looks, which only added to her appeal in the public eye. She was human. Just like everybody else, she had celebrity crushes, too. Others were Dick Van Dyke and Carl Reiner while working on *The Dick Van Dyke Show*, and David Letterman and James Garner after *The Mary Tyler Moore Show*.

While attending Immaculate Heart High School in Los Angeles, Mary had a thing for Jerry Lewis, whose photo she had pinned to her wall, while she slept with his autographed image under her pillow – and the youthful and muscular Marlon Brando. "God, he was the greatest-looking thing that ever lived," she had said. Mary and her schoolmates would drive down Mulholland Drive and park in front of Brando's house waiting for him to appear. He finally did, only to warn the young school girls to leave him alone. Years later, Mary was introduced to the moody actor at an airport lounge, and to her dismay he didn't recall their Mulholland Drive exchange.

In 1974, Mary could hardly forget her encounter with Cary Grant, another celebrity crush. She had been sunbathing on the beach in front of her house in Malibu, where Grant also held residence. While on her stomach with the back of her bathing-suit bra undone, Mary heard Grant's unmistakable voice. "I just wanted to tell you I think you're a wonderful actress." She leapt up and grabbed her top, and plunged back down into the blanket. As she later told talk show host Conan O'Brien, "I don't remember what I said, but there was certainly no vowels."

In 1981, following her divorce from Tinker, Mary now single in New York, fantasized about having an affair with the slight-in-stature talk-show host Dick Cavett, then married to his first wife actress Carrie Nye. But as Mary revealed in *After All*, she was a "height bigot" and couldn't imagine any potential first kiss where she would have to stoop down in order for her lips to meet his; or waking up with Cavett in the "spoons" position with his toes pressed against the back of her knees.

Mary also teased about her fantasies of yet another talk-show host. David Letterman was part of her first weekly *Mary* variety series, early in his career. She had often spoken of her fondness for Letterman, and enjoyed a funny, flirty relationship with him, if only on the air. And she would love to shock her fans with outrageous jokes that she would bring to the various incarnations of Letterman's shows

In reality, there were no romances at all with any of these gentlemen. But Mary did have her share of true relationships after Tinker and before Robert Levine. In 1980, she briefly dated her *Whose Life Is It Anyway?* director Michael Lindsay-Hogg, son of actress Geraldine Fitzgerald. In 1981, she dated Sir Gordon Lindsay White, known for his former relationships with Marilyn Monroe and Jackie Kennedy. Even though Mary and Robert Redford were seen at places like the famed Sardi's restaurant in New York, those kinds of appearances were for promotional purposes only, regarding *Ordinary People*.

But as Mary alluded to in *After All*, there was an actual affair with a man that began on the (anything but) *Ordinary* set, shortly after the movie began filming. Whoever this person was, he and Mary viewed their mutual attraction, however sincere, as the temporary happenstance of location moviemaking. He had long been involved with another woman, and had little inclination to change that part of his life, even though her marriage to Tinker was kaput. At the moment, Mary was welcomed by the new man in her life, while allowing her Catholic guilt to condemn her for committing what the Church viewed as a mortal sin. But "on the other side of the ledger," she wrote, "was the undeniable affirmation that I was an appealing woman," which she had apparently "forgotten."

Through the course of *People*, Mary's keen professional eye was squarely on Redford. She respected him as a director because, among other things, he was open to suggestions from other creative individuals on the set. "If the cameraman went to him and said, 'You know what? I think maybe this angle would be a little better and I'll tell you why,'" she told Carlos Ferrer. "He would listen to them and say, 'Yeah…you're right. Let's bring the camera around and do this and do that. He also gave a wonderful gift to the performers. After almost every scene he would say to us, 'Ok, guys…*play.*' And by that he meant, 'Take the same words, but do anything you want with them; keep the same blocking. Move in the same places you moved but, just so you know, if you want to scratch a place that you shouldn't be scratching go ahead and do it. If [your character] wants to be angry instead of happy to see some [other character, well then] do it.'"

It was a theatrical strategy Mary found productive. As a result, Redford received what she called "…some wonderful reactions, and interesting performances." It was also a form of acting that she was familiar with due to the multi-camera film technique used on most movies and TV shows, as well as the psychological "community effort" where "everybody pitches in…with the director of course always at the helm."

A similar method and work ethic had transpired during her *Dick Van Dyke* days when Carl Reiner told her: "I will take a suggestion from the man who makes the coffee if it's a good one. It doesn't matter…because it can only make you look better."

In contrast, one director with whom Mary vowed never to work with was Reiner's son, Rob Reiner (*When Harry Met Sally*, *The Princess Bride*, *Stand by Me*, and more). He began his career as an actor, most famously as Michael "Meathead" Stivic on TV's landmark series *All in the Family*. As Mary explained one night on TV's *Larry King Live*, when not in school, the young Reiner son was a frequent visitor to the *Van Dyke* set. "He was a shy, retiring [little] kind of guy, Rob was," she observed. "But you could tell there was an imp in back of those eyes yes just waiting to come out. And one day, he passed me and reached out and affectionately gave me a swat on the behind. And I was in my most Kathryn Hepburn stage, early on it was, and I went straight to Carl and said, 'Your son whacked me on the behind,'" fully expecting him to take Rob to task. "And apparently, what he did was he said, 'Rob…is this true?' And he said, 'Yes, I did, Dad.'"

At which point, the father Reiner instructed his son, "Well, don't do that again."

"Isn't that great?" Mary remarked in retrospect to King. "I feel like a lady of the evening telling of the transition from boyhood to manhood that I facilitated for Rob Reiner."

The younger Reiner eventually made joyful peace with Mary years later on the set of *The Dick Van Dyke Show Revisited* reunion special. And as he later explained to talk-show host Stephen Colbert, time healed all wounds, and maybe, too, ignited a few new ones. For on that *Revisited* set, Mary allegedly bent over and apparently now invited Reiner to slap her derriere.

Shortly after *Ordinary People* premiered, Mary was forced to face one of the most challenging times of her life. While she retained composure in public after her son's death following the movie's release, Timothy Hutton had also suffered the loss of a close family member. His father, actor Jim Hutton, died of liver cancer at only 45 years old on June 2, 1979. Because Mary felt she had slighted the younger Hutton for remaining so uniformly in character as Beth Jarrett while working on *People*, she eventually made an effort to balance the scales. She would defreeze her cool manner towards Hutton when they would get together and do things like go hot-air ballooning together after the movie wrapped.

At the same time, too, handing Hutton the Oscar for his Best-Supporting role in *People* at the Academy Awards telecast that year could not have been easy for her. She was nominated in the dramatic lead actress category, but lost. "She opened the envelope and just gave me this look," Hutton had said.

Whereas Mary did the best she could to make amends with her movie offspring, she had continued to neglect the relationship with her real-life son Richie Meeker.

Shortly before Richie, at only 24 years old, mistakenly shot himself with a sawed-off shotgun on October 15, 1980, Mary granted one of her most revealing interviews on record. She sat down with Rona Barrett for a prime-time television special. She discussed the end of her marriage to Tinker, her struggles with diabetes, and her rocky relationship with Richie.

But then Richie died on the day the special was to air. Tinker, then-president of NBC programming, pulled the show from the schedule. According to MTM archivist David Davis, Tinker was "uncomfortable with Mary discussing their marriage and asked Rona Barrett to bury it, for that reason, and also out of respect for Mary's personal tragedy."

Death is always tragic for anyone, celebrity or not. A death in the family is worse, whether it be a parent, child, uncle, aunt, or cousin. But when a parent dies young or a child dies in general, that beggars words.

At the very least, Mary and Hutton bonded in their shared grief, no matter how or when their loved ones died.

A formal investigation by the Los Angeles Coroner's Office listed Richie's demise as an accidental death. He collected guns and kept a few on his bedroom wall. He had been toying with one model, a "Snake Charmer," and it went off. The weapon was eventually removed from the market because of its "hair-trigger" instability.

"God almighty," Rita Lakin remarked upon hearing how Mary to some extent played out in real life what she had experienced on-screen. "She did that movie before a tragedy, and I began my entire career after a tragedy. I had to start to work right after my husband died." Lakin had penned her first TV script, an episode of *Dr. Kildare* titled, "A Candle in the Window" (November 5, 1964), about a woman (played by Louise Sorrell) who had been recently widowed. Lakin wrote about what she knew. "I had to dig into my unhappiness and write about my own experience," said Lakin, while Mary's life sadly imitated her art when Richie died on October 15th, 1980 after *People's* premiere on September 19th.

Lakin had also penned a 1975 TV-movie called *Hey, I'm Alive* which featured Sally Struthers and *MTM Show* co-star Ed Asner. She had co-written with Gavin MacLeod, another MTM veteran, a live-stage musical called *Saturday Night at Grossinger's*. *Night* never made it to Broadway, but played several small theatres.

Mary was experiencing additional pangs, with her troubled marriage to Tinker, which would soon end in divorce in January 1981. Her tumultuous relationship with Richie could never have fully prepared her for his death. She spoke of losing him with entertainment journalists Marilyn Beck and Stacy Jenel Smith for the *National Ledger*. "It came from out of nowhere," Mary said. "He was doing well. Unfortunately, there were terrible rumors that Richie killed himself." But as a collector of guns, her troubled son was cleaning one of them, which "went off and shot him in the head."

According to David Davis, however, Richie's roommate Janet said he "…was playing Russian Roulette."

Richie's death "was ruled an accident and not a suicide," said Bill Persky. "I knew Richie but not well enough to decide his mental state. He was always a nice kid, and you wouldn't have expected that there was anything wrong. But I don't know. And Mary didn't know either."

Losing Richie marked a dismal period in Mary's life, and deepened an already dark side of her personality. She told Larry King, "Everybody has dark sides," something she "felt good" about having. Mary viewed herself as "basically a good person, in spite of and maybe because of some of those dark sides…Most people in the world are well-intentioned [with behavior that goes] wrong. But the thoughts are pure to begin with."

Redford had seen her dark side when casting her in *Ordinary* in the first place. They lived close to one another on the shores of Malibu Beach, where the director periodically observed the actress strolling in gloom. Much later, Redford called Mary "brave and enormously powerful" for taking on what he considered her most somber role. As chronicled in *After All*, Mary had tapped into past, unhappy real-life memories, beyond Richie, to interpret the icy-veined Beth. She thought of her family history, how they "missed the mark" of being everything people thought she was supposed to be. She addressed her issues with her demanding father and his high expectations, how her low academic performance disappointed him.

The similarities between Beth and Conrad and Mary and Richie were staggering, and could not be denied. Neither relationship was solid. It was indeed a harrowing example of life imitating art, just as Richie's life was on the upswing. Shortly before Richie's accident, Mary secured for him a job in the entertainment industry, beginning in the CBS mailroom. It was a menial position, but a good start for what might have been a lengthy career, and led to a more productive relationship between mother and son. But it was not meant to be.

According to Tom Watson, the turnaround in the CBS mailroom was rapid; but in a good way. "We were always getting new mail personnel," he said, "…because they tended to hire people who wanted to work in the industry. You push a cart around the building and you get to know the business or what's going on in that [given] building and a lot of times people were absorbed into other jobs. So, being in the mailroom was a great starter-position."

Then, one day, Richie Moore showed up on the job. "He was very nice, very sweet, very professional," Watson said. "And he did his job."

Sometime after Richie's first twenty-four hours working for the mailroom, Watson learned from a colleague that Richie was Mary's son. And Watson was warned not to acknowledge that fact in Richie's presence. "I'll make an agreement," Watson mused to the colleague, "… I won't mention my mother. And Richie won't mention his." As Watson later recalled in retrospect, "It was no more appropriate for someone to ask me about my mother, who was not in the business, and a housewife in Indiana. She had no more to do with my job than Richard's did with his."

However, Watson further assessed, "Richie eventually learned that we knew because we sort of let on to it all," Watson said. "It was kind of a passive agreement. 'You do your job and I'll do mine and we won't discuss our parents.'"

Mary taped her variety show at CBS Television City Studios, at the corner of Fairfax Avenue and Beverly Boulevard. "In those days you didn't have all the guards and barricades around," Watson said. "There was just an open parking lot around the building and everybody parked someplace. Many nights, we basically worked from around 9:00 AM to 5:30 PM, which meant you usually arrived between 8:30 and 9:00 AM, and stayed until somewhere between 5:30 and 6 PM."

On more than one occasion, Watson and Richie would leave at approximately the same time, "He'd wave from the car and that sort of thing," Watson said. "He would be driving up Fairfax, and I'd wave back. There was absolutely no hint that there was anything wrong."

One night, however, something was very wrong. Watson arrived home and a few hours later, heard the news of Richie's death on the radio. He thought, "Holy shit! I just saw him this afternoon."

Watson immediately phoned Frank Adamo, who told him, "It's not a good evening."

"If there's anything I or anyone else at CBS can do," Watson offered, "…be sure and let us know."

"But of course they didn't let us know," Watson later recalled, "…because what can you do when tragedy strikes…when someone loses their son?"

In all, Watson said, "Richie was very friendly and open. You would never think that there was anything bubbling underneath," in reference to unfounded rumors that Mary's son had committed suicide. "Everyone said he killed himself…and that he was so depressed. Well, not to me he wasn't. I didn't know him on a personal level. But on a professional level, he was an ideal employee…exactly what anyone would want. I never saw anyone other than a really nice young man doing his job, and he seemed up and happy. It was said he was cleaning his gun, and that it went off by mistake, and I have no reason to believe that his death was anything but a horrible accident."

Meanwhile, Grant Tinker was apparently disinterested in raising Richie.

"From what little I did know of Grant," Watson said, "…it didn't seem like he was kid-oriented at all. He was very much more the Hollywood-executive type. And I don't know if there was any room in that psyche for a youngster's problems. I really can't address that."

But Watson was certain that Grant and Mary were best friends with Betty White and Allen Ludden. When Allen and Grant were young, they had served in the army together, and remained friends through the years after their subsequent marriages to Mary and White. "They all went out to dinner together and were very much Hollywood socialites," said Watson. "And that's the image of Grant that I've always had." In reference to the fabricated perfect family portrayed by Robert Young, Elinor Donahue, and Laurin Chapin on TV's *Father Knows Best*, Watson said, "Grant wasn't Jim Anderson at home with his kids Betty, Bud and Kathy."

As Mary further expressed in *After All*, she held a service for Richie in Los Angeles on a sunny day, outdoors, where his casket rested under a vast oak tree. The next day a funeral director delivered his ashes to her. Dick Meeker and Tinker joined Mary, who held close to her heart Richie's remains. They boarded a private plane and flew north to Mammoth Airport, where a rental car was waiting. Meeker drove them to a place near the Owens River, where they walked to a small bridge on which father and son had spent some happy times. Meeker and Tinker stood together on the bank as Mary made her way to meet them.

In her description of the event, she said the water was clear and high as she knelt over it. She opened the container and emptied it into the rushing waves. What was meant to be a prayer became an outraged demand. To the heavens she screamed, "You take care of him!"

Mary then flew back to New York, where she met with Bill Persky for dinner. "She really went through some doubts and questions of loss that you would expect," Persky recalled. "It affected her deeply, in terms of losing her son, and in terms of the loss of her participation [in motherhood] and how it might have made a difference in his life. Her parenting was not a hands-on kind of thing. She certainly was there for him as a mother, but being that mother was not a major aspect of her life."

Mary, now 44 years old, was living in New York, a major film star, divorced and childless. Her personal and professional bonds were strengthened with friends like Persky, and actresses Beverly Sanders and Hope Lange (who, like Mary, was also newly single). Lange, best known on television from *The Ghost and Mrs. Muir* (NBC, 1968-1970), and *The New Dick Van Dyke Show* (CBS, 1971-1974), felt compelled to befriend Mary because they both played Van Dyke's wife in their respective sitcoms.

Sanders was best known in Mary's circle as Rayette, the waitress from episodes of *The Mary Tyler Moore Show*. She had starred with Dom DeLuise in the short-lived sitcom *Lotsa Luck* (NBC, 1973-1974), and later in her recurring role on *Rhoda* as Susan Alborn, mother of seven and nicknamed "Easie Suzie," in high school. She also appeared in hundreds of commercials and sitcoms, and in the feature films *...And Justice for All* (1979), and *Just Between Friends* (1986), starring Mary. Off-screen,

Beverly was Mary's best friend on the West Coast, while Bernadette Peters was Mary's best friend from the East Coast. Even though the character Sanders played on *Rhoda* was almost always pregnant during the run of that show, in real life getting pregnant was not so easy for Sanders. In 1998, Sanders starred in the critically acclaimed one-woman show in Los Angeles, *Yes Sir, That's My Baby*. She wrote it herself, detailing her heart-wrenching experience adopting her daughter, Laura Newmark, upon learning she could not conceive.

Bill Persky knew of Mary long before they met and worked together on the original *Van Dyke Show*. Well aware of her roles as the Happy Hotpoint girl and on *Richard Diamond: Private Eye*, Persky mused, "I was in love with her legs even before I knew there was a body attached to them. And I was madly in love with her like everybody else."

In truth, they were "just really good friends," he clarified. "We were very close. And we continued to be over the years. But it wasn't anything more. I wasn't exactly the romantic eyeful of her life. I was just the person that it was easy for her to be with without anybody saying anything. And when she moved to New York, I was the only person she really knew, and I took her everywhere and we spent a lot of time together, and our friendship grew from there."

One night, a romance may have blossomed between the two. He explained: "I took her home from some event, and we were in front of her doorway, longer than was sort of necessary and we kind of looked at each other and I said, 'I think we better call Carl,'" as in Carl Reiner from the *Van Dyke Show*, "...and we both laughed and that was it."

It was a moment that mimicked a scene not between Rob and Laura on *Van Dyke*, but Mary Richards and Lou Grant on *The Mary Tyler Moore Show* when in the episode, "Lou Dates Mary" (March 12, 1977), the two characters attempt to court and kiss. But when that crucial second arrived, it was cut short due to their shared laughter. "I didn't make the correlation at the time," conveyed Persky. "But yes. It was like that."

Mary and Persky would also spend time in the Hamptons, where he shared a home with friends, and where she had rented a home close by with Lange. "They used to come over to our house and we'd play charades," Persky recalled, "...and it was a great time. Unfortunately, she was drinking at the time and still dealing with many problems, which thankfully she eventually resolved, if never getting over losing Richie."

Mary smiles with date Valentine Peyton at a Peyton family wedding in June 1953. [Credit: Patty Barry]

Upon graduating high school at 17, Mary wed Richard Meeker in 1955. [Credit: Richard A. Lertzman Collection. All rights reserved.]

A mid-teen Mary performs in a dance recital with fellow classmates at the Ward Sisters School of Dance Arts in Los Angeles, circa 1954. [Credit: Ronald V. Borst/Hollywood Movie Posters]

Mary makes with the maracas in one of her early modeling jobs for Latin album covers, circa 1957. [Credit: Classic TV Preservation Society]

Mary meets the press for only-her-legs-on-screen/voiceover role as Sam in *Richard Diamond: Private Detective* (CBS/NBC, 1957-60). [Credit: Ronald V. Borst/Hollywood Movie Posters]

Mary with Dean Fredericks and Yvonne Preble in the "Strike Force" (1-14-59) episode of his *Steve Canyon* TV series. Mary was billed as Mary Moore for the role of Second Spanish Girl; Preble was the First Spanish Girl. [Credit: Ronald V. Borst/Hollywood Movie Posters/NBC Publicity]

In "The Mask of Jason" (3-3-60) episode of John Cassavetes' *Johnny Staccato* TV show, Mary plays an actress Johnny must protect from a man with a scarred face. [Credit: Ronald V. Borst/Hollywood Movie Posters/NBC Publicity]

Mary with Ron Ely in the "Killers in Paradise" episode of his TV show *The Aquanauts* (1-25-61). [Credit: Ronald V. Borst/Hollywood Movie Posters]

Mary starred with David McLean and Lizabeth Hush in *X-15*, her first feature film, in 1961. [Credit: Ronald V. Borst/Hollywood Movie Posters/United Artists Publicity]

Left to right: Mary, David McLean, and Lizabeth Hush. [Credit: Ronald V. Borst/Hollywood Movie Posters/United Artists, 1961]

Many people thought Mary and Dick Van Dyke were married in real life. They make light of that assumption in the 1969 TV special, *Dick Van Dyke and the Other Woman*, which paved the way for Mary's foray into *The Mary Tyler Moore Show*. [Credit: Classic TV Preservation Society]

According to what Richard A. Lertzman learned from Grant Tinker, after Mary met and married the Benton & Bowles ad-man in 1962, it was he who placed her in the driver's seat on *The Dick Van Dyke Show's* road to success. [Credits: Ronald V. Borst/Hollywood Movie Posters]

Mary loved her son and her career, and was frequently torn between the two. Here, she poses with Richie in 1966, when she and Grant Tinker had just relocated to New York. [Credit: Richard A. Lertzman Collection.

In 1966, Mary performed with Richard Chamberlain in the failed Broadway musical *Breakfast at Tiffany's* (a.k.a. *Holly Golightly*). [Credit: Ronald V. Borst/Hollywood Movie Posters]

George Peppard and Mary star in *What's So Bad About Feeling Good?* [Credit: Ronald V. Borst/Hollywood Movie Posters/Universal Studios Publicity, 1968]

Mary starred with Robert Wagner in *Don't Just Stand There!* [Credit: Ronald V. Borst/Hollywood Movie Posters/Universal Studios Publicity, 1968]

During and after *The Mary Tyler Moore Show*, Mary failed in various attempts to return the variety show to television, either as one-time specials (such as *The Incredible Dream*, 1976, pictured here; and *How to Survive the '70s* and *Maybe Bump into Happiness*, 1978), or as weekly ventures (*Mary*, 1978, and *The Mary Tyler Moore Hour*, 1979). [Credit: Classic TV Preservation Society]

Back row: Ed Asner, Gavin MacLeod, Ted Knight. Middle: Mary Tyler Moore and Georgia Engel. Front: Betty White. [Credit: Classic TV Preservation Society]

In 1980, Mary makes an appearance with her parents and acclaimed dancer, Gregory Hines, for the National Dance Institute. [Credit: Richard A. Lertzman Collection.

In 1982, Mary starred with Dudley Moore in the feature film *Six Weeks*. Here, they attend the film's New York premiere. [Credit: Classic TV Preservation Society]

Mary married Grant Tinker, the Benton & Bowles ad-man in 1962. [Credit: Classic TV Preservation Society]

In 1983, Mary met and married Dr. Robert Levine, who remained loyal, loving, and dedicated to her until her passing in 2016. [Credit: Classic TV Preservation Society]

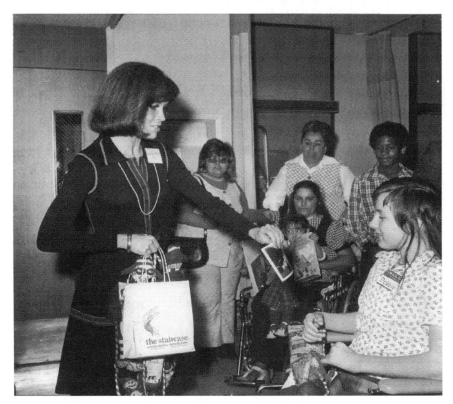

Mary visits a children's hospital in Los Angeles in the fall of 1973.
[Credit: Ronald V. Borst/Hollywood Movie Posters]

"THERE'S A CURE, AND WE'LL FIND IT."

Mary Tyler Moore

JDF Juvenile Diabetes Foundation International

For information or to make a donation:
60 Madison Avenue, New York, N.Y. 10010
1-800-223-1138

One of her many print ads for the JDF. [Credit: Classic TV Preservation Society]

Mary (CBS, 1985, with James Farentino), an edgy, half-hour sitcom incarnation of *The Mary Tyler Moore Show*. [Credit: CBS Publicity, 1985]

Mary starred with Christine Lahti (pictured), Ted Danson, and Sam Waterston in *Just Between Friends*. [Credit: Greg Gorman, 1986]

In 1986, Mary is back on the stage with *Sweet Sue*, co-starring Lynn Redgrave, and seen here on the cover of the March 1987 issue of *Playbill*. [Credit: Classic TV Preservation Society]

Mary makes a semi-happy return to TV-movies in *The Last Best Year* (ABC, 1990), co-starring her good friend Bernadette Peters. [Credit: Classic TV Preservation Society]

Mary takes the lead in *Annie McGuire*, a 30-minute dramedy which premiered on CBS in 1988. [Credit: Ronald V. Borst/Hollywood Movie Posters]

In 1991, Mary attended a fundraiser for the Pennsylvania Ballet with her husband Dr. Robert Levine. Her generous donation helped keep the company going, as it was facing closure. Of course, she chose to pose with this sculptured lion, due to her love for animals. [Credit: Victor Malafronte]

Carl Reiner, Rose Marie, Mary Tyler Moore, and Dick Van Dyke on the set of *The Dick Van Dyke Show Revisited*. [Credit: David Van Deusen/*The Walnut Times*.]

Larry Mathews, Dick Van Dyke, Rose Marie, Mary Tyler Moore, and Carl Reiner at the 2003 TV Land Awards. [Credit: David Van Deusen/*The Walnut Times*.]

Mary was best-known on-screen as Laura Petrie and Mary Richards, but no one will ever forget her generous heart and soul off-screen.   [Credit: Ronald V. Borst/Hollywood Movie Posters]

[Credit: CBS Publicity, 1976]

ACT V

High Society

Mary's real and reel lives – filled with struggles and victories,
amidst the backdrop of the elite. Here, she played Mary Todd
Lincoln in the acclaimed NBC-TV miniseries *Gore Vidal's Lincoln*
(1988), which also featured Sam Waterston. Waterston also
appeared with Mary in the HBO-TV-movie *Finnegan Begin Again*
(1985), the feature film *Just Between Friends* (1986), and as a judge,
uncredited, in the Lifetime TV-movie *Stolen Babies* (1993), which
later aired on ABC (after Mary won an Emmy). [Credit: NBC, 1988]

Chapter

17

On December 31, 1980, and at 43 years old, Mary formally filed to end her 18-year marriage to Tinker. At first she rented an apartment at the New York Waldorf-Astoria Hotel, and later leased a home on East 64th Street. That Christmas, she told everyone that she didn't want any gifts. Not receiving presents was her gift. "I would like to have the ability to convince my family and friends not to give me anything for Christmas," she said, "because I just moved to a New York apartment and I don't have the space for anything else." It had taken her 18 months to get the apartment "in shape and the list keeps growing of things that needed adjusting. I think I will be here for quite some time."

Around this time Mary had also begun a more concerted effort for the social causes and issues in which she believed – chiefly her charitable activism for animals and those stricken with diabetes. Before moving to New York, "…there wasn't really the kind of time required to take seriously any crusade," she said. Living there, and now working on what she called "short-term projects," as opposed to weekly TV shows (some of which, sadly, became short-term projects themselves) had afforded her the time to focus on what she wanted to do and become involved with. "I help wherever I can," she said. "Whether that means going to Washington to lobby Congress, or just showing up for a benefit and signing autographs. Whatever needs to be done, I do happily."

Before, during, and after this period, Mary would still make time to attend dance classes, some of which were attended in Los Angeles by actresses BarBara Luna and Sherry Diamant Schaffer, who had performed together on Broadway in *West Side Story*. Both would work a great deal in television, with Luna making countless guest-star appearances on everything from *Bonanza* to *Star Trek*. Schaffer's credits include a guest spot on ABC's *The Young Lawyers*, a semi-regular role as the babysitter to Brandon Cruz on *The Courtship of Eddie's Father*.

When on the West Coast, Luna and Schaffer, who remain good friends today, attended Rolland Dupree's ballet dance class in Hollywood, which was open to the public. But according to Schaffer, "mostly everyone in that class was in show business. And whenever we would go to class, we would see Mary Tyler Moore. There were most likely other stars in there, but I distinctly remember Mary, and the visual of what she looked like. She was tall and trim with beautiful thin legs, and a very slender ballet body."

Each time Luna and Schaffer attended class, mostly between 1969 and 1972, they seemed to see Mary. Schaffer recalled the actress "...was always at class and there before us when we arrived, or she would arrive already sweaty as if she had been working out beforehand. She would run up to those she knew, like BarBara, say hello, and then she didn't interact with anyone else in the class. She was there for the dance. She would quickly move to her spot in front of the class, closest to mirror and the instructor, whereas I stayed further back in a spot on the floor where we could follow those in front along with the instructor. And she was very good and probably a little better than most of the people there. Her demeanor was so much so that she was there to work out. She was a pro. She was very, very businesslike when it came to dance."

"For those who have had ballet lessons since they were two years old," Schaffer continued, "there's a certain way of dressing. And Mary dressed in a way that was common to professional dancers. She wore pale pink tights with wool leg-warmers scrunched around the ankles and calves, and soft Danskin jazz shoes with a slight heel when rehearsing for something that required shoes with a heel during performance or soft ballet slippers for daily workout. She wore a small ballet skirt wrapped and twisted in a professional manner and a hand towel around her neck. As her hair was short her sweaty bangs were clipped away from her face."

"Ballet is not something that you acquire even as easily as a musical instrument. It has to be something that you've been doing your whole life. And your bones grow into it."

It was obvious to Schaffer that Mary fit that description. Mary once described dance as "an old friend, classic and unchanging. I like to work on things like getting my leg just another inch higher. In fact, I fault myself that I don't take jazz classes because they require so much self-expression."

When Mary later made the formal move to the East Coast, she remained dedicated to retaining the look and stamina required for her own interpretive dance regimen. As she explained to Andy Warhol in *Interview Magazine*, a typical New York day for her included the continuance of dance classes and more. Depending on how late she had been out the night before, she would awaken anywhere from 9:00 to 10:30 AM. On those days when she arose earlier, she would take a dance class. After class, she would return home and periodically take a business luncheon meeting to discuss a script or a potential creative project. She would also at times return home to have a session with a tutor in various new areas such as political science.

"It's just an interest I'm pursuing," she said.

Beside these activities, three times a week, she would have a session with her analyst, return home, answer mail, return phone calls, and then have dinner with friends." And her interactions with the analyst and her friends were clearly two different experiences. "A friend will give you immediate feedback and that will be that friend's opinion," she said. "An analyst often remains quiet and you hear what you've said and you gain your own insight."

Mary was basically designing her own life as she saw fit, but didn't take such luxury for granted. She was blessed with her abilities, and felt not taking advantage of that talent would be "a crime." Of course, she was also adjusting to the emotional and psychological aspects of being newly single. How did her own life in 1981 compare to the fabricated life of Mary Richards from 1970 to 1977? "Her life focus was on things other than a permanent sexual romantic attachment, which in a way parallels my views these days," Mary said of her former TV persona. "I've had that and now I'm about other things."

Mary later conveyed in *After All* that she lacked the kind of life experiences that her fictional self was accustomed to on *The Mary Tyler Moore Show*. For the first time, Mary, and not Mary Richards, was an independent woman carving out a career, and "...finding her way in a strange city, making new friends," doing exactly what she wanted to do, "...alone!"

In 1981, Mary did not have a significant other. She refused to address her previous alleged liaisons, particularly with Warren Beatty, other than to say, "Warren and I are friends." She spent most of her working life as a married woman, "So any of the personal questions were fairly easy to respond to because there was never any question of my privacy, his privacy; that was no book, we were married," she said, in reference to Grant Tinker. "There were certain private areas. But now that I'm a single woman and I do have relationships with people from time to time, I find I can't respond to questions about those personal relationships."

Mary wasn't in search of a third husband at this time. She said, "I think marriage, in its loosest sense, is people committing to each other saying 'I love you' and 'I like being with you' and that is wonderful. I don't see the need for formalizing it unless you plan to have children and you want the fair distribution of assets. I also don't think you should ever expect forever in anything, in either platonic friendships or sexual friendships."

Mary was so intrigued with her new life in New York and being a single woman almost for the first time, that she wanted to "experiment a bit." She was living on her own and making her own decisions. "I began dating," she said, "...you know the good and the awful...I was so inexperienced, I began spending a lot of time with people in the fast lane. Drinking too much, staying up too late, and dwelling on a lot of superficial trappings of life."

She was in her forties, living it up as many do in their early twenties. "Plus," she said, "I had the aura of celebrity, which is very attractive to people who are not necessarily the best kinds of people for you. And then, thank God, I met Robert and we married."

There was also her relationship with animals, which was an entirely different matter. Mary had hoped to one day be able to say that she had changed the way people think about animals in the same way that *The Mary Tyler Moore Show* helped alter individuals' perception of women in the workplace. "I'm convinced, with heightened awareness," she said, "that there will come a time when we look back and say, 'Can you believe that people used to eat animals?' A human being has been given an intellect to make choices, and we know there are other food sources that do not require the killing of a creature that would protest being killed."

She would not become a vegetarian until around 1992, and never became a full vegan due to certain nutritional needs, but she would eventually stop wearing leather products. "Although my shoes might have leather soles, I guess," she once said, "...I will not wear anything for fashion that's made of an animal." And she would soon be wearing fabric shoes with fabric belts and handbags.

But before those transitions began, Mary was doing the best she could with being an early forty-something living on her own in a rented house on East 64th Street. She began to realize the fortunate fictional aspects of her TV alter-ego's life.

She scrutinized herself with true soul-baring, and continued to address the grayer shades of life, career, characters, parenthood, childhood, and marriage. As she continued to assess in *After All*, Mary tended not to be as buoyant as Mary Richards. She had a kind of anger that she lugged from a less-than-cheery childhood. She held herself to a high standard, and found it a challenge to show herself any measure of compassion. She was profound, even when she forgot the extent of her wisdom.

She had once said, "Sometimes you have to get to know someone really well to realize you're really strangers." But when Carlos Ferrer reminded her of that quote, Mary was bemused, and wondered, "Did I say that? That's a little too profound for me." But upon reflection, she thought it a valid and "interesting premise." "When you fall in love," she said, "...and you marry, you really don't know very much about each other, and [some] twenty-five years later, you're intimate, God knows, after all those years, and you realize more and more as that time goes by, that you really don't know a whole lot about [one another]...you are still discovering new facets...new aspects of each other."

No formal third party was officially documented as responsible for Mary and Tinker's breakup. But besides Mary spending time with platonic pal Bill Persky, other friends told UPI News that she was indeed keeping amorous company with Beatty. A fellow actor and New Yorker, the famed movie star (who began his career in early episodes of classic TV's *The Many Loves of Dobie Gillis*, 1959-1963, CBS), was known for his high-profile liaisons with other actresses such as Julie Christie, Diane Keaton, Michelle Phillips, and Leslie Caron, one of Mary's idols. So, other than her three husbands, besides the affair she documented in *After All*, and despite her denial to the contrary, Beatty was allegedly the only man, famous or otherwise, with whom she became romantically entangled.

More than anything, Mary was selective and loyal; while the first two of her marriages did not last nor were they nearly as successful as her final union with Robert Levine, she continued to move forward in her usual buoyant manner. As she once suggested to an interviewer from the Sunday edition of the *New York Times*, "Couldn't you just slap my face for being so positive and optimistic?"

Serious and funny, open and honest, happy and depressed, yet always on guard, and sometimes off-color, Mary was a puzzle. In that same article, she observed, "I don't share my innermost feelings with my friends."

Or apparently, not with anyone else either. While making the *Mary Tyler Moore* sitcom, a reporter from *Esquire* magazine had once wanted to interview Mary. As she recalled in the *Times*, "He liked the show and wanted to do a story, but after awhile he said to me, 'You know, I think everyone is trying to protect you; that there's something about you that isn't your image.' Then one day, he just left, without cancelling his appointments or anything."

Her then biggest defender, Grant Tinker, also said to the *Times*, "Basically, we're dull people. But I raised the red flag about that guy from *Esquire*; weird people want to find something weird, even if it's not there."

Mary also shared an encounter with another reporter, a woman who once called her aside with what Mary described as a "a very confidential tone," and said, "Tell me, Mary…tell me that you aren't Wonder Bread."

Another time, Mary acknowledged, "There are certain things about me that I will never tell anyone because I am a very private person. But basically, what you see is what I am. I'm independent, I do like to be liked…I do look for the good side of life and people…I'm disciplined, I like my life in order, and I'm neat as a pin."

She had also professed in the *Times*, "I love order and discipline. God, I sound like a Nazi, don't I?"

But to Tinker, Mary was "a very gutsy lady…single-minded" and had "an amazing ability to concentrate." He also called her "ambitious," but for her talent, not necessarily for power or control over the *Mary Tyler Moore* sitcom.

In the eyes of the mainstream public arena, meanwhile, Mary appeared to be a moderate liberal throughout the 1960s and 1970s. According to author Marc Shapiro, shortly before 1990, she was "perceived as a 'born again' Democrat by many political observers. But much of her political and social activism would continue to be of a stealth nature. She would, unbeknownst to many, contribute to left-leaning/progressive causes."

Although she had endorsed President Jimmy Carter for re-election in 1980 with a television ad campaign, Ed Asner later said, "Mary was always a Republican." For one, "She was a big Nixon supporter, just before Watergate."

Asner himself, of course, was no stranger to politics. He served as spokesman during a three-month television and theatrical strike of the Screen Actors Guild in 1980, a period of work stoppages aimed at improvements to SAG contracts. The next year, he became the Guild's president, serving for two terms, the second of which came to a bitter conclusion due to national politics. He was opposed to U.S. involvement in Central America, suggesting that guild members contribute toward opposing U.S. foreign policy. But he clashed with political conservative Charlton Heston, who won the office in a highly publicized power contest with Asner, who later supported other liberal causes including gun control. While Asner was selected for membership in the Gun Control

Hall of Fame, Heston would go on to be named president of the National Rifle Association.

Asner grew up as the youngest child in the only Jewish family in his Kansas City neighborhood where, in a foreshadowing of his Lou Grant character, he edited the high-school newspaper, acted in a few plays, and was voted an All-City tackle in football. He was both diverse and tough as nails.

Just like Mary. As the woman behind the man behind the woman of MTM Enterprises, she demanded order, if in subtle ways, on the set of any show her company supervised, whether her own sitcom, or any of its sequels, including *Lou Grant*. When Asner's own politics, in the form of liberal views, became too much to handle for her, MTM, and CBS, his hit show was cancelled before its time. He later shared his perspective of the events that led up to that unfortunate decision, beginning with a memory of his early days as an actor, when he was careful not to allow himself to "…be caught up in the Blacklist or the Red Tide":

"When I came to New York, being a member of both SAG and AFTRA, I had signed a Stockholm peace pledge." This was a 1950 international petition drive calling for an absolute ban of all nuclear weapons. "I had heard of people being denied," Asner continued. "I had to fill out my loyalty oath and that apparently applied across the board. I wondered if they'd catch me up on signing this Stockholm peace pledge. That's how fearful I was. It didn't reflect on me. Most of those years, the issues surrounding Central America and El Salvador, I kept my mouth shut not willing to be identified, not willing to be tagged. And when I spoke out on El Salvador – what I considered to be a humanist position…it produced a hailstorm of opposition."

He found himself questioned in Washington at a large press conference, during which he was asked, "Are you for free elections in El Salvador? What if those elections lead to a Communist Government?" It was like a freight train hit him in the face, Asner later recalled. He delivered what he called "wimpy" and "cockamamie" answers. In his mind, he thought, "'I've come all this way for *this*?! All this distance and I'm going to waffle?!" He then clarified his responses, particularly to an initial question of whether or not he supported free elections in El Salvador by saying he would do so "…if it's the government the people of El Salvador choose."

Because of this reply, Asner "…felt it was the end of my career…the beginning of resounding provocation that led to all the attacks. I was labeled a commie, among other things, and the *Lou Grant* series got cancelled." His relationship with Mary, though lengthy and loyal, remained solid, professionally. They would see each other at MTM-planned parties or events, but other than that, they did not socialize. This was different from Mary's interactions with other MTM colleagues, such as Ted Knight, who frequently dined with Mary in Beverly Hills, as she and Tinker had with Betty White and her game-show-host husband Allen Ludden. Tinker and Ludden had known one another for years, as friends and business partners, once teaming on a game show.

But it was no game when CBS cancelled *Lou Grant*. That decision brought a blow to MTM Enterprises and Mary's pocketbook. But she was never upset with Asner. "She pretty much stayed quiet through all of that," Matthew Asner recalled. "*Lou Grant* was cancelled because William Paley decided that he didn't want Ed Asner on his network anymore."

Paley was the CBS chief executive who built the network from a small radio station and transformed it into one of the foremost radio and television networks in America. "It's been told to me and many other people," continued Matthew, that at some point, "*Lou Grant* was on the schedule and William Paley walked into [a meeting] and said, 'What the hell is *that* doing on there?' And he took the show off the schedule. And that's kind of the story that has been running around because he just didn't want that kind of controversy on the network."

However, those at MTM Enterprises, "for the most part," continued Matthew, "were in shock. They had a Top 20 show that all of a sudden was cancelled. And of course there was only one person to point the finger at, and that was Ed Asner. So, it was a very difficult time for my Dad. And Mary was very respectful to him during that time, while on the other hand, Mel Blumenthal, one of the MTM studio heads, was not so very nice to my father. He told my father that he had about a week or two to get off the lot. But through it all, Mary and my father kept their friendship strong. And she never went after him in terms of talking negative about him or anything of that nature."

Nevertheless, the cancellation of *Lou Grant* was nevertheless a painful professional step backwards for Mary, just as two major personal events transpired, both having to do with her parents: Her mother suffered a stroke and her father an abdominal aneurysm. Despite Mary's troubled early relationships with them, she remained a dedicated daughter, loyal and sincere even in the midst of what became her discontent. Her strong will and sense of independence still rang true for all to see.

On March 21, the first day of spring in 1982, Mary delivered an emancipating portrayal of Mrs. Stephen Douglas, the famed independent female of American history, on the ABC TV special, *I Love Liberty,* which was developed by Norman Lear. The special was produced by People for the American Way, a non-profit organization formed by

Lear to advocate against the increasing influence of right-wing religious groups.

An all-star special paying tribute to America in commemoration of the 250th anniversary of George Washington's birth, *I Love Liberty* was filmed at the Los Angeles Sports Arena before an audience of 10,000. It featured variety acts like *Sesame Street's* Big Bird, who introduced a pre-taped skit by the Muppets about the Second Continental Congress; Barbra Streisand singing "America the Beautiful" with the United States Air Force Band; and Robin Williams performing a monologue as the American Flag. Other participating celebrities included Mary's friend and co-star Valerie Harper, Desi Arnaz, Jr., Valerie Bertinelli, LeVar Burton, Patty Duke, Erik Estrada, Peter Falk, Jane Fonda, Bonnie Franklin, Barry Goldwater, Burt Lancaster, Hal Linden, Shirley MacLaine, Walter Matthau, Kristy McNichol, Helen Reddy, Christopher Reeve, Kenny Rogers, Frank Sinatra, Dionne Warwick, Dick Van Patten, and Henry Winkler.

Also included was the remarkable actress/comedienne/writer Geri Jewell, born with cerebral palsy. Jewell never allowed her disability or any challenge to keep her from success. In her critically acclaimed memoir, *I'm Walking as Straight as I Can*, Jewell describes *I Love Liberty* as "spectacular." "In a way," she writes, "...it was Lear's response to Jerry Falwell," the fundamentalist preacher who seemed to spend much of his time advocating against various freedoms. "*Liberty* was a creative effort to honor the values of all American people," Jewell continues, "...not just the religious right, who were claiming that their values were the only ones that mattered. In fact, looking at how the world is today, with America polarized once again, I would love to see an *I Love Liberty II*."

On the day of the original *Liberty's* premiere, the *New York Times* wondered, "Is This Entertainment Special Promoting a Special Interest?" In the article, Richard Zoglin addressed the controversy surrounding the special's political viewpoint: "Although *I Love Liberty* has styled itself as a non-political and non-controversial salute to such American values as freedom, patriotism and tolerance, Moral Majority officials [led by Falwell, who had not yet seen the show] have already attacked it as a thinly veiled effort to promote Mr. Lear's liberal political views...In a typical segment, six actors appear on stage to articulate some of the complaints of ethnic and minority groups. 'I am an angry black,' says LeVar Burton, portraying a working-class black man, who is unhappy over the high unemployment rate. 'America hasn't worked that well for me,' he concludes, 'but I love my country.' He is followed by a Hispanic, an American Indian, a woman, a homosexual and a middle-class white male – all of whom tell why they are angry and why, despite dissatisfactions, they still feel a strong allegiance to the United States."

In addressing *I Love Liberty* in an interview, Lear once said the special attempted to prove that having a diverse perspective is part of the American way. "This country has lived in turmoil, and our strength comes out of that turmoil," he said. "The show's patriotic theme," he continued, was an effort to display that taking pride in one's country was "not the private province of the far right."

Also in 1982, Mary paired with actor Dudley Moore (no relation) for the feature film *Six Weeks*, directed by Tony Bill, who began his career as an actor. One of his first TV appearances was for an arc of episodes for the fifth season of *Dr. Kildare*. Once switching careers to directing, Bill's sensitive artistic touch was evident in TV shows like *Chicago Hope*, and with feature films such as *My Bodyguard* (1980), and 1990's *Crazy People*.

Like *Ordinary People*, *Weeks* has a dire premise about the death of a child. She's the ice-dancing daughter of Mary's character. Real-life figure-skater and ballerina Katherine Healy played Nicole Dreyfus, the role of an aspiring dancer stricken with leukemia. After screening several thousand girls without success, director Tony Bill tried the opposite approach and asked the New York City Ballet's Jacques D'Amboise to help him cast a dancer who could act. D'Amboise did not think twice about suggesting Healy, then a 13-year-old, five-foot, 85-pound pixie whom he called "one in a million."

Since Healy dedicated most of her time to ballet, she had little time for TV or films and, as a result, she had never seen either Mary or Dudley Moore. But following direct in-person conversations with them, Healy did a screen test and won the role of Nicole opposite Mary as her mother Charlotte, and Dudley as politician Patrick Dalton.

The combined flare for comedy provided by both Mary and Dudley slightly lightened the heavy burden of this plot, but it was not enough to satisfy the box office. This second consecutive maudlin story was an odd selection for Mary following the loss of her only son a mere 24 months before. She addressed this observation in an interview with entertainment reporter Bobbie Wygant shortly after the film's Los Angeles premiere bash (which doubled as a benefit for the Juvenile Diabetes Foundation):

"Everyone has this conception of there being a thousand wonderful scripts out there to choose from, and that's not the truth. In fact, a good script is very hard to come by. And so it was just coincidence that there were two dramatic roles. I'd love to do a comedy again. I have in fact two in development now; I hope one will be ready in the spring. I'm anxious to get back to [comedy]. I miss it. Although I must say, it has been great excitement for me doing something different."

Escorting Mary to the film's premiere was actor/comedian Steve Martin. Upon seeing Mary and Martin together, the press had a field day; and naturally, there was yet another speculation of a new romance for Mary.

Wygant began to discuss Hollywood romances; how they are periodically misrepresented in the media. She suggested to Mary that photos of her and Martin together might soon be splashed across the tabloid press. "They don't miss a trick, do they?" Mary said wryly of the possibility. "That's one aspect of my life that I really loathe…that invasion of personal privacy."

When Wygant described Mary and Martin as "the most handsome couple" at the *Six Weeks* premiere, Mary offered a near-passive-aggressive response. "Oh, thank you," she said. "But I think my mother and father would argue the point…they think they are."

Mary's association with Martin was platonic, but that remark about her parents was an awkward and insightful comment that seemed to kill two birds with one stone:

Mary still held a measure of resentment towards her parents. She felt they were so self-absorbed that they hadn't supported her aspirations as they should have. It was a bitter juxtaposition with Mary's film character emptying herself to help a sick daughter.

The young performer had reminded Mary of her own youth. It took her back to a decision she made when she was Healy's age. The life of a ballet dancer is very restrictive, and Mary wasn't prepared to dedicate herself to the art of ballet the way Healy had. "She truly wants to be a ballet dancer and not an actress," Mary told Wygant. "It could change. But I doubt it. [Ballet] is a very isolated kind of life, and one that I wasn't suited for." So, she "threw away the point shoes and started to take tap."

Mary reflected further on her childhood and early career choices. She'd addressed these topics many times before, but now with additional insight and maturity. Acting had replaced dance as her number-one aspiration. She recalled how she started out in the chorus on TV variety shows, and was given a line "now and then with little tiny parts"; how her dream of being "a dancing-actress was just not going to come to pass because they were not making those kind of movies anymore"; how she told herself, "Well, kid – you better get yourself an agent and fake your way through it."

Although she lacked formal experience or training, Mary was "…an observer of life," free enough to express herself. And she "got lucky" and "worked a lot."

Mary's life was a testament to the various adages that define success as a combination of luck, timing, talent, determination, and hard work. All of these were what ultimately prepared her for what Wygant called "very heavy scenes" in *Six Weeks*. Those scenes, Mary said, "got to be as heavy as it would be in real life. And we must as an actor always make it that. You look at the situation and you completely submerge yourself in it. And it must be painful...the tears must be real. Actors use different techniques. Some actors draw on experiences or something they've read or been told. But I like to work with just the situation at hand, and really lose myself in it...which I did. So, yeah...[working on *Six Weeks*] was painful...and that's as it should be...[those are] appropriate feelings."

Fortunately, Dudley Moore was there to break the tension. "He was wonderful fun," Mary said.

Her perspectives on life, privacy, and *Six Weeks* collided on the night of the movie's premiere. She enjoyed herself though such an event was "not the kind of thing" she looked forward to, due to the attention and spotlight. She was "not always comfortable" in those situations. "But that was kind of a special group," she said. "I had a good time."

Unfortunately, most critics did not. Janet Maslin of the *New York Times* claimed the film "aims directly for the heartstrings, but it may put you in a mood that's more quizzical than sentimental. Consider the story, which begins when Patrick Dalton [Dudley Moore], a California politician, encounters...Nicole [Healy], who is smart, toothy and utterly self-assured – kind of a miniature Susan Anspach" – an odd reference, considering Healy's similarity to Mary.

"Somehow," continued Maslin, "Nicole so captivates Patrick that he forgets all about his Congressional campaign to become fast friends with her. Is this the way a would-be Congressman might really behave? And incidentally, are there many would-be-Congressmen with accents like [Dudley's]?" Patrick likewise became captivated by Nicole's mother, a cosmetics tycoon named Charlotte Dreyfus [Mary], who lives with Nicole in a swank apartment above the make-up factory."

"There are quite a few peculiarities to their living situation," wrote Maslin. "For one thing, Nicole is first seen in a suburban area, walking toward a house she says is a neighbor's place. And the factory itself is in an industrial spot downtown. For another, the place has a dance studio and an artists' workroom for neighborhood folk to use. Isn't it odd that a woman of Charlotte's obvious handsomeness and generosity has absolutely no friends? Not only isn't there anyone else in Charlotte's life when Patrick comes along, there is not even a reference to any other parent Nicole may have had. Isn't it customary, in circumstances like these, to make at least a passing reference to the father?"

True, *Six Weeks* has extensive holes in its plot. But it has undeniable charm. The drama has its flaws, but the entire movie enchants, despite its slow pace in comparison to modern films. The three lead performances by Mary, Dudley, and Healy are as pure and real as their on-screen chemistry; they play off one another well. Dudley was dignity personified on-screen, while Healy was a natural in front of the camera. Although Mary's character, Charlotte Dreyfus, is cold and distant at first, this does not detract from her pre-plastic surgery natural beauty. Charlotte's transition from alleged hard nose to soft heart is elegantly moving.

What is particularly striking is Charlotte's similarity to Mary's real-life work as the head of MTM Enterprises. Both women were in powerful positions. Though Mary never publicly acknowledged just how much executive veto she held with MTM, Grant Tinker trusted her, and accepted her input for various business and creative decisions. As Maslin pointed out, Charlotte apparently had no friends. But as Mary admitted on more than one occasion, neither did she. Mary had very few intimate friends beyond her three husbands, and actress Beverly Sanders. Only later in life did she establish additional lasting bonds, as with Bernadette Peters.

Maslin's description of Charlotte's "handsomeness" was equally curious. As Carl Reiner had said, "handsome" was the sole compliment Mary's cold and distant father, George Tyler Moore, once granted to her when she dressed for prom night as a teen. Maybe all of that spoke to Mary, consciously or subconsciously, when making the initial read of the script for *Six Weeks*?

At least the Charlotte character softens a bit as the film continues. Ironically, she seems "colder," more distant, in California. Charlotte warms up, personality-wise, in the big city New York. There is a glimmer about Mary in the film's Manhattan moments as opposed to the Sacramento scenes. What really shows through is that Mary loved New York more than California. She looks radiant in the New York scenes, resplendent in a bright orange cape and frock, which reflects an "inner glow."

Due to Mary's history with dance, and her long desire to appear in a movie musical, she also seemed particularly pleased to take part in a ballet dance sequence in the film, the first time she moved with any kind of music on the big screen since *Thoroughly Modern Millie*. Of further note: the difference in height between the stars, though Dudley's slight stature is never mentioned. Instead, they are presented as two people who meet and ultimately fall in love under very unordinary circumstances.

Frank Adamo, Dick Van Dyke's assistant and an extra on *The Dick Van Dyke Show*, and subsequently Mary's assistant behind the scenes of *The Mary Tyler Moore Show*, has a small role in *Six Weeks*, while a photo of Mary as Laura Petrie rests on Charlotte's piano.

MTM historian David Davis, "Mary's Number One Fan," offers his unique insight into *Six Weeks*:

> In November 1982, when I was 17, I was flipping through the Sunday edition of the New York Times and came across a full page ad for the movie Six Weeks, stating that a charity premiere was going to be held in New York at the Rivoli Theatre with a black-tie after-party at the Waldorf-Astoria, and people could order tickets to attend. It was all to benefit the Get High On Yourself Foundation, an organization founded by producer Robert Evans as part of the conditions of his community service and probation after his arrest for cocaine possession. I begged my dad to get me a ticket, and he agreed, as an early birthday present. At $250 apiece, we could only afford one ticket, so I attended the event by myself, but my dad drove me there. He was planning to meet my cousin in the city and have dinner with her, and then pick me up afterwards.

> I eagerly took my seat in the movie theater, where I was surrounded by such celebrities as William Katt, Morgan Fairchild and Cathy Lee Crosby, who hosted the event. I had read the book the movie was based on first, so I was disappointed with all the drastic changes that were made in the screen adaptation, but I was still dazzled by the movie, and the excitement of being there, and the anticipation of possibly meeting Mary afterwards. Shuttle buses were waiting outside the theater to take us to the Waldorf. There was a room set up for cocktails and hors d'oeuvres, where I saw Susan Anton, who was dating Mary's costar Dudley Moore at the time, sitting at a small table drinking champagne with two men. I waved at her from across the room, and she smiled and waved back, then gave me a look like, "who the hell are you?"

> Then the film's young star, ballerina Katherine Healy walked in with her mom. I waved at her too, and she gave me a reluctant smile. I walked over to the main banquet room to find my seat. I introduced myself to

the people at my table, one of whom was the editor of Essence magazine. I found out later that Barbra Streisand [was there. She was] involved with the film's producer, Jon Peters, but I never saw her. I don't think she stayed very long after making a brief appearance on the red carpet and in the lobby of the theater.

Then, it happened. I saw Mary standing next to her assistant, Frank Adamo, trying to figure out where they were supposed to sit. I smiled at Mary as I walked past, and she smiled back. Then, to my surprise, my dad walked in. He had somehow convinced them that he was on the guest list and they allowed him inside. He told me he had just spoken to Mary and that she agreed to talk to me. I suddenly got very nervous, and hesitated. He said there's no way you're leaving here without meeting her, and walked me over to her table where she was canoodling with her future husband, Dr. Robert Levine. He looked to be about 20 years old at this time, but he was almost 30. "Mary," my dad said. "This is my son David. He's your biggest fan and has been following your career for years. He writes for his high school paper."

"Hello, David," she said with a smile, and asked me, "How old are you?...What grade are you in?...Do you want to be a writer?"

I answered, "I'm 17...in 11th grade...yes I want to be a writer. I understand your dream was to be a dancer."

"That's right," she beamed. "I started out as a dancer."

Then my dad walked away so we could have privacy. I wished he hadn't done that, because then he could've taken a photo of me with Mary, but I'm still grateful, believe me. I asked her if it was okay if I took her picture. She said "sure." Then her manager spoke up and said, "no, Mary." Her face turned grim and she suddenly looked very annoyed with him, and snapped, "Marty!! It's all right." He mumbled something inaudible. Then she turned to me and gave me the biggest, broadest smile for what seemed like five minutes. I held the camera up to my face, and she said "hurry up." It was just like that scene in Ordinary Peopl

I tried to say thank you and goodbye, but she had already turned her head away. At first I was disappointed, but immediately got over it. She's Mary Tyler Moore, for God's sake, and she took the time to talk to me, which was more she did for any of the other fans in the room. She ended up leaving with her entourage before dessert was served. I wrote an article about this experience for my school paper, along with the picture of Mary that I took, which helped me get promoted from feature editor to editor-in-chief at the start of my senior year.

Years later I met Mary again and spoke to her on the phone a couple of times and she was much more receptive, especially after I started an international fan club on her behalf.

Davis' story conveys the starstruck feelings of many of Mary's fans. Her gracious acknowledgment of his appreciation is a touching illustration. She did indeed understand that this brief encounter might become a life-changer for her young fan. It's a wonderful reflection of her sincere, periodically tormented soul.

Chapter

18

In the years after her divorce from Grant Tinker, Mary dated father figures like Sir Gordon White, a British millionaire, and comedian Steve Martin, each of whom were reminiscent in some capacity, age, or stature to Tinker, as well as Richard Meeker and George Tyler Moore. Then she met the 18-years-younger Dr. Robert Levine, for whom her love "evolved quickly," she said. It started as a strong attraction to a wonderful guy, and before she knew it she was in love. They married soon after.

Their wedding took place at New York's Pierre Hotel, where Levine treated her mother for bronchitis on a weekend house call. This was after she and her parents returned from the Vatican and a personal audience with the Pope John Paul II, whom she once described as a "moving individual." "When he looks into your eyes," she said, "…you are convinced he's seeing your soul, and he probably is. It was a wonderful experience."

But a different kind of religious experience was awaiting her at the Pierre Hotel. Her mother had become ill during Yom Kippur and their Jewish family doctor was unavailable. Another physician, Dr. Robert Levine, was on call. While phone-chatting with Mary, Levine suggested bringing her mother to the hospital for an examination. Upon doing so, Mary was taken with Levine, who she later described as a "thoroughly gorgeous cardiologist…a dream from childhood…who turned out to have a sense of humor…to be sensitive and sweet and caring."

She was charmed by how gentle Levine was with her mother. Levine conducted his final exam, and apparently also passed Mary's litmus test. After releasing her mother from the hospital, Levine made a few subsequent house calls to Mary's apartment, where her mother was recuperating. When he instructed Mary to contact him in case of an emergency, she asked, "Does acute loneliness count?" To which he replied "Yes," with a smile.

A short time later, the Catholic Mary and the Jewish Levine went on their first date, which surprisingly was also attended by Bill Persky, who made Mary feel safe and protected. Persky explained: "I was the person she would be able to go out with without there being any talk or gossip. Without anyone saying anything at all…because we were just friends, and nothing more. So, one Saturday night we went out to dinner, for Chinese food, and she said, 'I invited someone to join us. He's a doctor.' And that was Robert. And he came to dinner and that was the beginning of that."

From there, Mary's relationship with Levine became serious, despite differences in age and religion; their feelings were strong enough to defy convention. She later told talk-show host Larry King that her generation gap with Levine was a topic of discussion early in their relationship, later, and "always." They realized how unimportant such trifles could or would be "in light of the other good things we bring to the union," Mary said. "He loves what I do. In his secret heart of hearts, he would love to be a performer." Levine also had no issue being referred to as "Dr. Moore." "He would just laugh it off," she added, and be ready with a pen in hand for any autograph seekers.

With nothing to come between these two lovebirds, they planned to marry. As documented in *People* magazine, the festivities began with an elegant bridal shower held in October 1983 at the Park Avenue apartment of producer Dasha Epstein, who partnered with Mary for the re-gendered Broadway edition of *Whose Life Is It Anyway?* The few guests at the in attendance included actresses and good friends Linda Gray, Pippa Scott, Beverly Sanders, and Hope Lange, each of whom doubled as bridesmaids, with Lange gifting Mary with an array of alarm clocks, stethoscopes, and lingerie designed in humorous homage to *Whose Life* and the newly crowned doctor in the house.

The wedding was set for one month later on November 23, 1983. "There was a road [for us] to travel to gain acceptance," Robert Levine said at the time. "[We] all have a soul-mate, and it's very hard to find that person." The ceremony was held at the Pierre and officiated by a rabbi. The marriage was the first for Levine, who was formally described in a *New York Times* announcement as a senior fellow in the division of cardiology at Mt. Sinai Medical Center, with a medical degree from the Stritch School of Medicine at Loyola University in Chicago. He was the son of Irving and Marion Levine of Port Washington, Long Island; a national director of domestic affairs for the American Jewish Committee in Manhattan; and an executive director of the North Shore Child

Guidance Centers in Nassau County. (Later that year, Mary served as a cheerleader for a celebrity charity softball game, at which rock star Meatloaf served as pitcher.)

Those attending the wedding were Mary's parents, Sanders, Lange, and of course Persky, who sat with Cloris Leachman. "The funniest part of the whole thing," he recalled, "...is that it was a Jewish wedding, and Mary's father was the most Catholic person on the planet. I mean, he could neutralize an entire synagogue just by walking past it."

As a result, Mr. Moore had issues with standing under the chuppah, the canopy under which a Jewish couple traditionally stands during a wedding ceremony. "He just couldn't stand under it," said Persky with a laugh. "He was sort of half under it and half out of it."

But there were no such half-hearted measures for Mary and Levine. They were unconditionally dedicated to each other. Valerie Harper told *People* that he made Mary feel "cherished," that the couple's religious beliefs were of little issue, and that both families were happy about the marriage. "Mary's filled with joy because she and Robert are friends as well as loving each other [romantically]." Harper also joked that "Rhoda would be jealous that Mary married a young, handsome Jewish doctor."

Another friend said, "You'd never know this is her third wedding. All [Mary] talks about is her dress and how excited she is."

Emanuel Azenberg, a producer of Mary's play, *Whose Life Is It Anyway?* called Levine "one of those doctors they wrote movies about 30 years ago. He's genuinely caring. There's no question they're in love. They both have too much integrity to stay with the relationship if they weren't."

Yet another friend of Mary's thought she married Levine to spite Grant Tinker. Now 57, Tinker had been dating Melanie Burke, a former secretary in her twenties who some suggested resembled Mary. The friend said Mary was "devastated" by her second divorce.

As *People* pointed out, Mary had officially joined the "cougar club," made up of older women's liaisons with younger men. Other members of this group included twosomes like Olivia Newton-John, 35, and actor-dancer Matt Lattanzi, 25; Carly Simon, 38, and actor Al Corley, 27 (of TV's *Dynasty* fame), and more. New York psychologist Penelope Russianoff, who portrayed Jill Clayburgh's therapist in *An Unmarried Woman*, the 1978 groundbreaking, women's liberating movie, told *People*, "Young men are taken by the honesty of a woman who has the guts to go against cultural clichés."

No doubt about that. Mary had courage, every ounce of which she used to battle the several challenges she faced, including diabetes.

During her interview with filmmaker Carlos Ferrer, she called the disorder "a strange killer. It's the side effects…the consequences…so life-threatening…It's a really devastating disease. It's the leading cause of non-traumatic amputation. So, it's no fun and games. But I do the best I can to keep myself in control," with daily blood checks and insulin injections. "And that seems to be keeping me on the straight and narrow," as did a strict diet and exercise program, from which she periodically teetered.

In a previous conversation with pop-culture icon and artist Andy Warhol for *Interview Magazine*, Mary acknowledged her cravings for pizza, diet soda like Tab, or even Coca-Cola. Shortly before the article was published, she had recently ingested a can of Coke "by mistake," and decided "…it tasted very strange." Although Tab was marketed as sugar-free, Mary would overdo it. "I should own stock in Tab," she said. "I go through about six [cans] a day." She may have deemed her Tab intake safe for her strict diabetic diet, but there was no denying the fact that pizza and Coke were not the healthiest of choices. She also admitted to breaking her discipline every so often to have a bit of Sweet'N Low in her coffee, or a dessert like chocolate mousse.

But her real weakness was pizza, or as she told Andy Warhol in 1981, "any form of carbohydrate. I like junk carbohydrates. I like cheap, greasy cheeseburgers, quality French fries." One night that year in New York, she visited Max's Kansas City restaurant. "They have wonderful French fries that actually have the hint of a taste of a potato in them," she said.

Joyce Bulifant remembered Mary periodically veering from her diet during their *Mary Tyler Moore* days. "Sometimes she was naughty," Bulifant mused. "She would sneak in one too many candy bars every so often."

But in 1984, supported by husband Levine, Mary began a strict, new, sobering journey. At 46 years old, she checked into the Betty Ford Center to help her combat alcoholism, the disease she shared with her mother, then still living; a condition that, in combination with painkillers, had taken the life of her younger sister Elizabeth. Her brother and son had ultimately lost their battles in part due to substance abuse.

Larry King once asked why Mary drank, and she replied, "…because it smoothed the edges of life." But she would refrain from drinking at work, and she never drank in the daytime. "I drank only at night," she said, or "on the weekends, sitting around the pool, I'd have a Bloody Mary." Maybe the drinking was "contained," she thought, and a martini or two "would then make everything alright." Instead of dealing with problems head-on, Mary would "just shelve them aside and anesthetize."

And while she may have turned to alcohol to soothe issues with motherhood or marriage, Mary did not deem herself a less worthy parent or spouse due to her drinking. "I don't think I was a bad wife or a bad mother, not because of alcoholism in any way," she told Larry King years after her son's death. "[But] I wish that I could be Richard's mother today because I know so much more. I'm not so career-driven as I was and I think that's what I feel bad about in terms of motherhood…that I wasn't there for him."

Either way, there was much to address, and much to recover from. The Ford Center provided space, a safety net, and an opportunity, as it had for so many celebrities before – among them Elizabeth Taylor, Liza Minnelli, Tony Curtis, and Johnny Cash.

Betty Ford and Mary had been friends since before the former First Lady of the White House made a rare TV guest appearance on an episode of *The Mary Tyler Moore Show* called "The Seminar" (January 10, 1976). Here, Mary Richards and Lou Grant travel to Washington, D.C. for a seminar, where he tries to impress Mary with a list of public figures and dignitaries that he calls friends, including Betty Ford.

When Mary and crew flew to D.C. to rehearse the scene with Mrs. Ford, they were shocked to find her tipsy, disoriented, and barely able to remember her few lines. One of was simply "Hello, Mary? This is Betty Ford." To which an incredulous Mary Richards responds, "Hi Betty. This is Mary…Queen of Scots."

Two years later, Ford, who said Mary was "terrific, talented and a joy to work with," acknowledged her alcoholism, sought treatment, and founded the Ford Center.

In the end, Mary and Ford formed a mutual respect. Both were ready to address many personal issues, warts and all. In *After All*, Mary publicly acknowledged her alcoholism and subsequent rehab at the Ford facility.

Apparently a tabloid reporter had caught a glimpse of her exiting the building. That's when she decided to announce her struggle to the world preemptively. She once revealed in the *National Ledger* that her marriage to Robert Levine was affected by her dependence on alcohol. "We would have insane arguments over dinner about things I couldn't remember the next day. Alcoholism brings to the fore hostilities and resentment; you can't have a marriage like that," she said. But at Levine's prompting, she then checked into the Ford rehab center and joined Alcoholics Anonymous.

Mary always tried to be as honest as possible in any predicament; her situation at the Ford Center proved liberating. She learned it was okay to have blemishes, physical or otherwise, and began to live life on her own terms. "It's essential that I make my own decisions," she asserted. Even if that later meant the decision to undergo plastic surgery to conceal whatever facial flaws she thought she had.

For the longest time, she would share only her most uplifting moments with her friends. She did not want to burden them with the "dreary parts" of her life, and believed it was unfair to present herself as an individual with issues; that doing so would deprive her friends of the "chance to be human." But she finally broke from that shell; she began to examine herself honestly, "rather than just smiling through life, denying emotions." She did not want to continue to close herself off, "pretending, acting things out, having acquaintances instead of friends." It may have sounded trite, but as she said, "I'm finding out who I am."

Certainly, Levine played a supporting role in that personal discovery, as well as her recuperation after complications from diabetes. Through the decades, the bond between Mary and Robert remained strong. Dr. Mark Atkinson, who had worked with her via the Juvenile Diabetes Research Foundation, told *Closer Magazine*, that Levine was Mary's dedicated husband and primary caregiver. "With his background in medicine," Atkinson said, Levine "understands" Mary's physical challenges, specifically diabetes, but including alcoholism, and labeled their marriage as solid. "They've laughed together, cried together, gotten disappointed together," Atkinson observed. "They've just been the perfect couple."

Levine cared enough to ensure that Mary sought the help she desperately needed; alcoholism plus diabetes is a deadly mix. By the time Mary entered the Ford facility, she was injecting herself with insulin three to four times a day, adhering to a strict diet and exercise program, and had thus far managed to sideline any severe side of the disease such as blindness, heart disease, or kidney failure.

Mary and Levine, married just ten months, presented a noble, unified front. She was "not what you would call an alcoholic," he said. And he agreed with her doctors: Drinking was dangerous for Mary, even if the kind of drinking that she did was mostly "social drinking."

Either way, Mary checked into the Ford facility because she was experiencing more frequent hypoglycemic episodes, which worsened while working on two TV movies simultaneously:

Heartsounds, filmed in Toronto, though set in New York, was a real-life story in which she played Martha Weinman Lear, married to James Garner's Dr. Harold Lear, a dying physician. In the more light-hearted *Finnegan Begin Again*, filmed in Richmond, Virginia, she portrayed school teacher Liz DeHaan, whose dissatisfying relationship with Sam Waterston's Paul Broadbent leads her to form an uneasy bond with Robert

Preston's Mike Finnegan, during the time that he cares for his memory-challenged wife Margaret (Sylvia Sidney).

According to David Davis, *Heartsounds* was filmed in Toronto because it was less expensive to do so. But while filming, there was a fire in the hotel as Mary lay asleep in her room. Garner tried to wake her by pounding on her door during an evacuation. "She forgot to pack her flat shoes," Davis said, "and was wearing high-heels as he aided her down several flights of stairs to safety. She credited him with saving her life, and admitted she was drinking vodka every night during that period."

Upon returning to their luxury high-rise Central Park apartment in the real New York City, Mary and Levine made an intense two-week study of her blood chemistry. He recommended that she stop drinking alcohol, which had altered her blood chemistry. It's not that she was drinking more but, as Levine deciphered, the disease became progressive and "more difficult to treat."

Although it was rumored that she entered the Ford Center on two different instances, as she later told Larry King, it was only once. But when admitted for the first four weeks, Mary tried to escape one evening after a conflict with one of the counselors. That night she packed her bags in the solitude of her room, and slipped out to the lawn. Although the Ford facility was not a prison, Mary "kind of convinced" herself that it was, and "hid behind a palm tree with fear." She likened the moment to a scene in *Birdman of Alcatraz*, the 1962 film starring Burt Lancaster as a man held in permanent isolation. She called a taxi, went to a hotel, and called the Ford Center to let them know she was safe. The next morning, Betty Ford herself called Mary where she was staying and requested that she return to the facility so they could talk. "And that saved my life," Mary said.

By the time she and Betty had finished their conversation in person, Mary was on her knees, begging to be admitted back into the center. She and other clients were taught how to examine themselves honestly, to remove the denial of alcoholism or any form of substance abuse or addiction. They would begin with group sessions and productive feedback from peers, and continued with private counseling and grief therapy if dealing with the loss of a loved one, as was Mary's case regarding Richie. In each case, the lectures and Alcoholic Anonymous meetings allowed a feeling of closure on some level. Such encounters were held on a daily and nightly basis, and she continued that schedule on her own for the next few years.

After that, Mary periodically attended A.A. meetings, but realized that some who struggle with alcoholism, even those who have been dry for decades, attend such regular sessions for life. "There are different forms of alcoholism," she said, and various degrees of involvement with the A.A.'s structured meeting format. For her, an occasional visit worked best because as she observed, "I'm married to a doctor who probably should have been a psychiatrist."

Levine gave Mary a great deal of help at home. After departing the Ford Center, she claimed to have no desire to drink, not even in a group with others who did so. "I don't even think about it," she said, but then joked, "I desire drugs!"

That doesn't sound exactly healthy, productive, or politically correct today, and it probably didn't then. But she felt that she was doing the best she could with the situation at hand. Before she entered the Ford Center, social drinking for Mary translated as one or two cocktails after work. Or as Levine once said, it was "expected behavior in her social and professional circles," whereas Ford provided "a supportive environment for abstinence...to gain some strength and understanding that it's okay to say no to alcohol."

Loyal friend Beverly Sanders also once described Mary as a social drinker "with no trapping of alcoholism," but acknowledged that her excessive appetite for sweets, drinking, and smoking had taken its toll. Mary had "less tolerance" and became "tired faster," Sanders said. "Diabetics may look fine but feel disgruntled and unhappy because their blood sugar is low."

Somehow Mary's energy remained high. As the chairperson and face for Juvenile Diabetes Research Foundation (JDRF), she was making frequent trips to Washington. She lobbied Congress to seek funding for the National Institute of Health that finances the research which, as she later told Carlos Ferrer, helped to "...cure this miserable situation."

"We're 100% behind her and proud to have her as a spokesperson," JDRF communication director Karen Schneider declared to *People* in 1984. According to what Levine told the periodical, Mary's struggles with diabetes and alcohol were not exacerbated by any other substance-abuse concerns, as one report had maintained. "It's fabricated. They made it up," he asserted of this early fake news. An ABC executive who monitored Mary on the *Heartsounds* set said, "There was no temperament, no tardiness...no difference from one day to another. There was none of this in Mary."

And while David Davis said "Mary did threaten to quit when her scenes were cut for time," rain or shine, her husband was by her side. He would rearrange his schedule on a regular basis to fly on the weekends to Toronto where she filmed *Heartsounds*, and to Richmond, Virginia for *Finnegan Begin Again*.

A few years after Mary exited the Betty Ford Center, she told TV host Eileen Prose that the experience freed her and taught her a new way of dealing with life and relating to people. She learned the true meaning of self-respect, which in turn enhanced her self-esteem. "This business about 'being nice to myself' comes from that experience," she asserted.

But her definition of an alcoholic remained elusive. "It is very tricky to pin down," she said. As a diabetic she admitted to having a more sensitive reaction to alcoholism than most. "I never drank in the daytime. I never allowed it to affect my work, but it was affecting me, and I was still finding it difficult to stop. So, being one who relies on other people and suggestions and advice when wisely put I went to the Betty Ford clinic and [was] so glad I did."

She was at peace with that decision, and content with her choice to once more play against type in *Heartsounds*. Her character Martha Lear, though light years away from Mary Richards, shared traits similar with Mary's own stage of middle age and medical concerns. With a teleplay by Fay Kanin, based on the 1984 book by Martha Weinman Lear, *Heartsounds* was about Lear's husband Hal (cousin to legendary TV mogul Norman Lear, the film's executive producer), who struggled in the final five years of his life after suffering a massive heart attack in 1973.

New York Times writer John J. O'Connor reviewed the film:

> In many respects, Martha [Moore] and Hal [Garner] are not your average couple. He was a successful doctor, a urologist, in Hartford, before coming to New York to set up an experimental program in sex therapy at a major hospital. He was divorced and had two children when he married Martha in the early 1960s. She is about 10 years younger than Hal and has worked in various editorial and freelance writing capacities for publications [that include The New York Times]. His first heart attack occurs when she is working on an assignment in Italy. An editor suggests that she keep a written record of the entire experience. When friends discover she is taking voluminous notes, it isn't difficult to conclude that there must be a book lurking somewhere down the road.
>
> On its most immediate level, [the movie is] "a love story about two people completely attached to each other...When the heart attack strikes, it quickly becomes apparent that Hal and Martha are not the sort of people to go quietly into just any good night...With his own medical background, Hal is

> capable of diagnosing his own symptoms and second-guessing the various experts around him. Martha's background in journalism has trained her to do the appropriate research and pose the uncomfortable questions. His will to live is formidable. Her desire to have him live is just about unrelenting. Together, they can hardly be ignored.
>
> In purely dramatic terms, Heartsounds [directed by Glenn Jordon] begins to sag about two-thirds of the way through as the ending becomes apparent and the story settles into a succession of inevitable crises. Nevertheless, the film packs something of the wallop of a powerful and unblinking documentary. With superb performances from Miss Moore and Mr. Garner, the highs as well as the lows of the couple's love story survive beautifully intact. And the unusual view of a profession that too often is handled with surgical gloves is refreshingly provocative.

In 1985, one year after *Heartsounds* aired on ABC, HBO screened *Finnegan Begin Again*, which O'Connor and the *New York Times* described as "decidedly uneven, but the heart is there, thumping away almost miraculously in the wonderfully warm performances."

The protagonists were Mary as Liz DeHaan and Preston as Mike Finnegan, the writer twenty years her senior who cares for Margaret (Sylvia Sidney), his wife stricken with Alzheimer's.

The film's title stemmed from an old Irish tune that Preston sings on screen as Finnegan with these lyrics: "There was a man named Michael Finnegan. He had whiskers on his chin-igan. The wind came up and blew them in-igan. Poor old Michael Finnegan."

According to *Mary Magazine* editor David Davis, the *Finnegan* script was penned by high-school English teacher Walter Lockwood, who submitted his screenplay directly to Mary. "She loved the script so much she immediately purchased the rights to it and planned to have it produced as a feature film in 1983." But following the unsuccessful box office receipts of *Six Weeks*, Mary had a hard time getting it green-lit for the big screen. That's when HBO, Home Box Office, stepped up to produce the project under its "HBO Premiere Films" banner.

Finnegan Begin Again, directed by Joan Micklin Silver, became the network's highest-rated movie, and the darling of TV critics, cable and otherwise. Both Mary and Preston were nominated for Cable ACE awards in 1985, before cable programming became eligible for traditional Emmy recognition. Even Silver, whose credits include acclaimed features like *Hester Street* (1975) and *Crossing Delancey* (1988), had nothing but high praise for her two leading actors. "I feel that they both have their characters so strongly, that a typhoon could come through here and they would still react as Mike and Liz."

On working with Preston for the first time, Mary gushed, "...he's a real huggy-bear kind of person. I'm mad for him." Preston said of Mary, "She's that hearty woman with great humor, and very easy to pretend to fall in love with."

Finnegan became the first of four projects Mary worked on with another beloved male co-star: actor Sam Waterston, with whom she also appeared in the feature *Just Between Friends* (1986), and two TV projects: *Gore Vidal's Lincoln* (1987), and *Stolen Babies* (1993). In one *Finnegan* scene with Waterston that involved a muddy, open gravesite, Mary was to have remained as *TV Guide* put it, "high and dry while one object of her character's affections (Preston) had it out with his rival (Waterston) for those same affections." The original set-up had Waterston leaping into the murky sludge. But during rehearsal, Mary made a playful suggestion: What if she took a dive, as well, in attempting to rescue Waterston?

Her idea was embraced by the film's creative team, but not without a measure of caution on her part. "Please," she said to all in earshot, "...let's try and get it in one take." At which point, Mary plunged right over Waterston's shoulder, and did a pratfall right in the middle of the muck.

In addition to veteran Sylvia Sidney, who had a lengthy and distinguished career prior to this film, supporting actors in *Finnegan* include David Huddleston, who played a newspaper editor, and who had previously played a mortician in a fifth-season episode of *The Mary Tyler Moore Show* ("What Are Friends For," November 16, 1974). Ironically, in *Finnegan*, his singular on-screen moment with Mary takes place in a funeral parlor.

Although the movie was filmed entirely on location in Richmond, Virginia, it was supposed to give the illusion of "Anytown, USA." Mock signs were raised on the exterior of the *Richmond Times Dispatch* newspaper that instead read "Morning Times Dispatch," representing the fictional newspaper that employed Finnegan. Famed saxophonist David Sanborn composed and performed the music for the film, which HBO-Cannon Video released on VHS in 1986. However, like many of Mary's TV-movies and theatrical films, *Finnegan* has yet to be released on DVD or Blu-ray.

ACT VI

Many Mary Returns

Mary participated in many on-screen reunions with the
casts of the *Dick Van Dyke* and *Mary Tyler Moore* shows,
while she also ventured into other TV lands – whether in
a starring or guest-starring capacity. Here, she appears
at the TV Land Awards in 2003. [Credit: David Van
Deusen/The Walnut Times. All rights reserved.]

Chapter

19

In the early part of 1984, *The Mary Tyler Moore Show* reruns were still going strong but, as Mary told the *New York Times*, she and Robert Levine were not regular watchers. "We get up too early," she said, "...although once we did come home after a party, tuned in for one episode, and wound up watching...three."

Despite its still-massive public popularity, Mary's legendary sitcom had become a mild distraction. She had long moved on, not only to other roles in front of the camera, but behind the scenes, and sometimes the curtain. From December 2, 1983 to April 6, 1985, Mary returned to Broadway as one of the producers of *Noises Off*, a comedy written by Michael Frayn, and directed by Michael Blakemore. It featured, among others, Victor Garber and Dorothy Loudon. MTM Enterprises produced the play in tandem with Michael Codron, Jonathan Farkas, Robert Fryer, Jerome Minskoff, James M. Nederlander, and the John F. Kennedy Center for the Performing Arts.

Noises Off earned Mary nominations for both a Tony and a Drama Desk Award. It received raves from critics, one of whom said the show was "almost more fun than we deserve, or can handle in an evening's play-going. The term 'hilarious' must have been coined in the expectation that something on the order of this farce-within-a-farce would eventually come along to justify it. In three acts of outrageous slapstick comedy, Frayn repeatedly appears in danger of letting things get out of hand, and then blithely goes ahead and lets them, to our astonishment and delight."

The success of *Noises Off* led to other live productions for Mary as producer, including *The Octette Bridge Club* and *Joe Egg*.

Octette, written by P.J. Barry and directed by Tom Moore (no relation), was about eight sisters of Irish descent in Providence, Rhode Island, who meet on alternate Friday nights to play bridge and gossip. Co-produced by MTM, Kenneth Waissman, and Lou Kramer, the play featured Gisela Caldwell, Peggy Cass, Lois De Banzie, and others for a brief run of 24 performances at the Music Box Theatre from March 5 to March 23, 1985.

Egg was a revival of the 1967 play, *A Day in the Death of Joe Egg* by English playwright Peter Nichols. Moore's edition ran for 93 performances at the Longacre Theatre from March 27 to June 12, 1985, and was directed by Arvin Brown. Co-produced with Emanuel Azenberg, Roger Berlind, Ivan Bloch, and the Shubert Organization, headed by chairman Gerald Schoenfeld and president Bernard B. Jacobs, *Joe Egg* earned Moore a Tony for Best Reproduction of a Play or Musical.

The success of *Egg* resulted in her next Broadway-bound victory with *Benefactors*, an original play by Michael Frayn, and directed by Michael Blakemore. It ran for 217 performances from December 22, 1985 through June 29, 1986, and garnered nominations for both a Tony and a Drama Desk Award. MTM co-produced it with Nederlander, Fryer, Codron, and Douglas Urbanski in association with CBS Productions.

During *Joe Egg's* run, Mary, at 48 years old, returned to CBS on TV in the fall of 1985 in a half-hour format with a sitcom called *Mary*, the same title used for her first one-hour variety series in 1979. In this new 30-minute *Mary*, she played Mary Brenner, who works at a seedy tabloid newspaper called *The Chicago Eagle*. The sitcom, its first two episodes directed by Danny DeVito (of TV *Taxi* fame), was funny, hip, and featured a standout supporting cast including James Farentino as her editor, with whom her character shared a mutual attraction and conflict of ethics; a pre-*Married With Children* Katey Sagal as a tough fellow desk-mate that seemed to be a combination of both Murray Slaughter and Rhoda Morgenstern from the original *MTM Show*; John Astin (*The Addams Family*) as an idiosyncratic theatre critic; David Byrd as a dumbfounded copy editor; and Carlene Watkins and James Tolkan as Mary's best friend and next-door neighbors, who were expediently engaged.

Shades of her *Dick Van Dyke* and *Mary Tyler Moore* characters were woven into Mary's new Brenner incarnation. This development was inescapable mostly because her small-screen weekly roles reflected facets of Mary's own personality. "Through the years, I've developed an experiential veneer that I can lay on this new lady," Mary told the *New York Times*. "Probably 75 percent of what Laura Petrie was and what Mary Richards was and what this new character will be is me."

In making *Mary*, the actress temporarily moved back to Los Angeles, away from husband Robert Levine and their fairly new life together in her beloved New York. Mary was willing to take such drastic measures after reawakening to the joys of performing humor in HBO's *Finnegan Begin Again* the previous year. "I had missed comedy and how long I'd been away from it," she said. "It was really an emotional experience for me. If I could have done two comedy feature films a year, I would have preferred it." But since such vehicles did not present themselves, *Mary*, the show, "seemed to be the forum in which to do it," even if Mary, the actress, was unable to pinpoint exactly what it was about comedy that appealed to her. "We'd have to do an analysis of my childhood," she told the *Times* with a smile, reiterating: "I'm not an innately funny person. I find it an almost overbearing responsibility when I think about having to be funny. I like simply standing next to the funny person," she said in a whimsical bit of self-deprecation.

She did note, however, the importance of solemnity, pacing, and pausing when it came to playing it for laughs. "Most comedians, when given a dramatic role, can knock your socks off. They have to find not only the truth of a situation in comedy, but have to embellish it and call into play a sense of timing."

In a perfect world, Mary would choose to appear in "one wonderful" motion picture per year, as well as a television show, and even a live stage production as well. "I'd love to have a blend," she said, "and never get too far from comedy. But you can't control those things."

But like most of her TV productions, Mary controlled *Mary*. She had dominion over all, from writing and dialogue to stories or directors. But as *New York Times* reporter Thomas O'Connor observed, Mary ruled "more by charm and suggestion than fiat, deferring to the new show's producers and directors," just as she had done on her original *Mary Tyler Moore* sitcom a few years before.

With yet another comparison to a certain fiery red-headed comedienne, one longtime MTM Enterprises executive said, "Mary's not Lucille Ball. She doesn't get involved with the lights and the props and every aspect of production." Although Mary maintained an office at MTM Enterprises in Studio City, she allegedly still did not dabble with the business aspects of MTM Enterprises. And although, too, she still served on the company's Board of Directors, the group reportedly met just twice in 15 years by the time of the new *Mary's* debut.

Mary said that her new show's executive producers and head writers, Ken Levine (no relation to Robert) and David Isaacs, who together wrote for *M*A*S*H* and the first year of *Cheers*, were proposed by Arthur Price, MTM's president for several years, and Mary's manager. She had agreed to do the series after several days of meeting with Levine and Isaacs in Manhattan. "We talked about what kind of job [she could] have," Mary said of Brenner. "They went away and two months later came back with the premise."

Despite her new sitcom's many obvious similarities to the *Mary Tyler Moore* show, including the Midwestern newsroom setting, Mary said any trappings related to her original sitcom were discarded. "Ken and David were very much aware, as I was," she said, "…that this one was going to be looked at with a giant magnifying glass, and there were going to be the inevitable comparisons."

Interestingly, Levine and Isaacs, both in their mid-thirties while working on *Mary*, had submitted scripts-on-spec to the original *Mary Tyler Moore* show. "All rejected," Levine lamented, assuredly as were countless other teleplays by additional writers. But now, Levine and Isaacs were in command, with a handle on *Mary's* new sitcom. "The audience has certain expectations of how they want to see Mary," Levine said. "You can't have Mary as a prison guard or a Nazi hunter or running a diner in some backwater. We wanted to give the show a sense of the '80s, just as the other show had a sense of the '70s."

Part of that refresh was giving Brenner an edgier, more independent spirit than Mary Richards. Brenner "knows how to cope," Levine said.

But both he and Mary agreed that the new series would mirror the continuous evolution of the feminist struggle, but arising from characters and situations as naturally as possible. "That was the case with the old show," Mary said. "We never set out to make a statement about a single woman's sense of dignity. It just sort of happened."

Of her return to the sitcom world, Mary opined, "If I were to think, 'Is this smart?' or 'Will they accept me?' I'd probably never work again."

Mary certainly wasn't desperate for cash and never would be, especially at this point. MTM Enterprises was still going strong with prime-time programming such as *Newhart, Hill Street Blues, Remington Steele*, and *St. Elsewhere*. The latter three aired on NBC, by then overseen by chairman Grant Tinker, Mary's friendly ex. And even before the *Mary Tyler Moore Show* had ended, Mary's financial future was assured; CBS had contracted with her for the long haul with new TV agreements, one of which became the present show, *Mary*.

In the process, the new show served as a platform and first acting job for some, like Katey Sagal. She was the daughter of iconic director Boris

Sagal who directed, among other things, the ABC miniseries *Rich Man, Poor Man*; *The Omega Man* feature film, and Elizabeth Montgomery in *A Case of Rape*. "I love Mary," said Katey of performing on the new sitcom. "What a way to start out, working with Mary. She taught me so much in subtle ways. I think she's a genius, her comedy timing is just incredible."

Michael Stern attended the taping of the *Mary* pilot and noticed the similarities to her first series. Not only did Sagal play "the Rhoda-type character," but "James Farentino played the Lou Grant type character," Stern pointed out. But these new characters were "tougher," with more of an edge; and Mary Brenner was not as cheerful as Mary Richards.

But off-camera, Stern said, "Mary still interacted with the audience between takes, just as she had done on her first series. She may have been a little nervous because it was the pilot episode, but she was fantastic with the studio audience. She knew that was an important thing to do…to make that behind-the-scenes connection."

It was an audience interaction also utilized by Valerie Harper while filming *Rhoda*, by Lucille Ball during each of her sitcoms (*I Love Lucy*, *The Lucy Show*, *Here's Lucy*, *Life With Lucy*), and certainly one that Carol Burnett used at the tapings of her much-loved variety series. Burnett, in fact, had learned the technique from Garry Moore (no relation to Mary) when she was a member of his TV variety-show repertory. But the Garry Moore and Burnett shows were not fictional sitcoms like *The Mary Tyler Moore Show* or *Rhoda*. The audience-interaction sequences were not presented on the air.

Pop-culture blogger Jackson Upperco offered his pertinent and thorough thoughts on the newest *Mary* in a post from 2013 titled "Moore Tries Again – A Look at *Mary* (1985-1986, CBS)." He begins with some creative background:

> Ken Levine, one of the creators of the series, who also wrote for Cheers and Frasier, among others, has an excellent blog in which he's dedicated a few posts to his experience working on this series. The original concept was to have Mary play the managing editor with James Farentino as her ex-husband, who is forced to work under her. CBS decided that audiences wouldn't accept Mary as the boss, so the pilot was rewritten to have Mary play a writer who loses her job as fashion editor at Women's Digest magazine and ends up finding work at a tabloid after the magazine folds.

They knew going in that the new format of the series was too similar to her earlier sitcom, but CBS had insisted upon it. They got a deal for 13 episodes, and after an extraordinarily well-received pilot, the order was upped to 18. But when the show failed to receive the ratings that Moore had anticipated (the kind she got the decade prior), creative clashes between producers and star were sparked.

Finally, though a renewal looked likely, Levine and his writing partner, David Isaacs, decided that they would not return following the 13th episode. Frustrated, Moore decided not to continue as well. So, though the show lasted only 13 episodes, it wasn't canceled. In fact, it did pretty well in the ratings (at least, in the beginning).

Here's what worked:

The idea of putting Mary in a sleazier environment, forcing her to be bolder and harsher; essentially, whenever she acted differently from Mary Richards, it was exciting
Farentino had an interesting chemistry with Moore, and though it seemed a little too reminiscent of Sam and Diane, it was a much fresher approach than Mary Richards had shared with Lou Grant
The quirky and well-designed Ed LaSalle, played by John Astin, who always gave some laughs and seemed to inspire the most original stories
And Katey Sagal, the show's MVP, who, in her first television role, is the funniest of the series and as a character and an actress, worked the best with Moore

Here's what didn't work:

Premise does feel too much like Moore's earlier and better series, and it's impossible not to make comparisons between the two
Not a lot of great story ideas, especially as time went on; aside from Astin's, none of the characters seemed to spark any really creative or memorable plots
Mary's neighbors were not funny: they were dull and sometimes annoying, and it's understandable why they were used less and less as the series continued

> The show loses steam after its fourth episode, and both the writing and Mary seem to be going through the motions, while all the recurring players fight an uphill battle.

That last point is what struck me the most interesting about this series. The first four episodes are fairly original and funny, but after that, I did not find a single installment to be as good as it should have been. Judging from what Levine has said, this could be the direct result of backstage strife, or, perhaps, the already tired premise just couldn't sustain itself any longer.

Upperco's opinions match those of the home audience as well. The new version was deemed too edgy for the audience and its stars' own taste. The new fake-take on *Mary* had potential, but suffered from poor reviews, mediocre ratings, and internal strife; the real Mary asked CBS to end the show. She was not pleased with its creative direction. She felt her character was surrounded by "negative quipsters," and the show in general did not focus on the characters' relationships. "That was my forte," she said, "…the kind of comedy that I enjoy doing…and I think the audience wants to see. As much as we had conversations with the writers and producers, they did not seem willing to make those accommodations. So, I just decided that it was better not to keep trying with it and take it off the air."

The original concept for this second coming of *Mary* was later utilized for the 1996-1997 CBS sitcom *Ink*, starring Ted Danson, and Mary Steenburgen, Danson's wife. It was created by Diane English, who ignited *Murphy Brown*, which Mary at times resented because of its similarity to *The Mary Tyler Moore Show*.

Meanwhile, Danson and Christine Lahti would become Mary's co-stars in 1986 for her return to the big screen with *Just Between Friends*, written and directed by *Mary Tyler Moore* co-creator and co-producer Allan Burns. Here, she played Holly Davis, a happy housewife and mother of two married to Danson's Chip Davis, who monitors earthquakes at a seismology center in California with his newly divorced friend (Harry Crandall, played by Sam Waterston). Holly soon discovers that Chip is having an affair with Lahti's Sandy Dunlap, a new friend she meets at an exercise class.

The reviews were mixed. *The Morning Call*'s Paul Willistein opened his review by calling the film an "*Ordinary People* mess around…a story by adults for adults," which "features excellent performances." He also wrote, "*Just Between Friends* is in the style of *Terms of Endearment*…It has laughter and it has tears – and it's thought provoking." He praised

Mary's performance and that of the cast as "excellent." "They make each other – and the movie – look good," he said. "The cinematography and the score, the latter featuring jazzman Earl Klugh, are also above average," despite "a couple of nasty words" in the script.

New York Times critic Vincent Canby labeled Burns "a clumsy director of his own material that's as heart-warming as an approaching headache," but he was much kinder to Mary. "Though *Just Between Friends* is a star vehicle it does no service to its star. She's been photographed and dressed in a way that makes her appear noticeably older than her screen husband, which is not one of the non-problems the film tackles, and so painfully thin that her false eyelashes look heavy."

"In *Ordinary People*," Canby continued, Mary "…gave a beautifully controlled performance as a dry, bitter woman. It was new territory for her. Audiences responded to her responding to it. *Just Between Friends* puts her back in the Mary-Janes she wears on television, and they look silly."

Burns had originally envisioned Holly Davis as a latter-day Mary Richards who had chosen marriage and children instead of a career. The movie was filmed under the working title of *Something in Common*, which was changed to *Just Between Us* and then to *Just Between Friends* to avoid confusion with another movie released around that time called *Nothing in Common*, starring Tom Hanks and Jackie Gleason. Martin Scorsese was slated to direct *Just* but withdrew due to a scheduling conflict, so in stepped Burns, who had only directed one other movie: 1984's *Just the Way You Are*, starring Kristy McNichol, which was plagued with behind-the-scenes issues. That movie also underwent a title change (it was filmed as *I Won't Dance*), while Susan Sarandon was originally cast as Sandy Dunlap in *Just Between Friends*, but had to bow out due to pregnancy, and was replaced with Lahti.

Rumors swirled in the press that Mary and Lahti were not getting along. But that wasn't true. "Mary was great to work with," said Lahti. "But one day we decided to play a trick on the press, and we pretended to have a huge fight on the set," which ended with Lahti calling Mary a "slut-burger."

Some other interesting tidbits about the show's cast:

Mary's good friend Beverly Sanders had two lines in the movie as one of the women in Helga's aerobics class. Mary had worked with Sam Waterston on *Finnegan Begin Again* (1985). Mary shared the same birthday with Danson, though she was born 1936 and he in 1947. He agreed to do the movie in order to "make out" with Mary, his teenage crush from *The Dick Van Dyke Show*.

The film's musical score was composed by Patrick Williams, who also wrote the music for *The Mary Tyler Moore Show*, which debuted when Mary was 30 years old. By the time she did *Just Between Friends* she was nearly 50, even though her character was supposed to be approximately 40 with two teenage children.

A scene where Holly plays tennis with Sandy and can't get a ball over the net was deleted from the film. Incidentally, it was the last movie produced by MTM Enterprises before the company was sold to Television South, a British broadcasting company, netting Mary $113 million in cash and stock.

Orion Pictures, which released the movie, folded in 1999 and was now owned by MGM, which supervised the DVD release of *Friends*.

The same year *Just Between Friends* made its big-screen premiere, Mary appeared on the premiere episode of the PBS children's TV show *Shalom Sesame*, which also featured guest-star Alan Alda, her future co-star in the 1996 feature film *Flirting with Disaster*. She guested on *Shalom Sesame* twice more.

Shalom Sesame was an American version of 1983's *Rechov SumSum* (רחוב סומסום), the Israeli rendition of America's famed PBS series *Sesame Street*. According to Wikipedia, *Shalom Sesame* was produced in 1986 and 1990 for public-television stations in the United States, and was geared toward introducing Israel and Judaism to children that are not necessarily fluent in the Hebrew language, since *Rechov SumSum* is completely done in Hebrew. In what turned out to be a charming, if brief *Shalom* segment, Mary learns a few words in Hebrew from a little girl named Maya.

That same year documented Mary's half-century birthday, and aging seemed ever on her mind. "When I turned 50," she said, "I was practically stopping people in the street to say, 'Can you believe I'm 50? This is what it looks like, and it's not bad, is it?'" she once exclaimed with a hearty laugh. "I was never considered beautiful even in my youth. It might have been different if I was, say, a fashion model. I have always put the emphasis on what comes from inside me."

"The older I get, the wiser I get, the more knowledge I have," she added. "As you get older, you learn to put things in perspective. Not everything is life or death, not everything is so important you have to put yourself through a wringer to get it. I hope to do more movies, and I may write more books, but right now I am just enjoying my life."

That same year, Mary shared more eloquent words when she was inducted into the Television Academy Hall of Fame. The award was presented by Ed Asner, Valerie Harper, Ted Knight, Cloris Leachman, Gavin MacLeod, and James Farentino. Mary said:

If I have achieved any degree of success in television, it is in great part because I've been fortunate enough to have been surrounded by the finest artists and craftspeople. As you can tell from the people you saw on this stage tonight and the others in the film clips, both in front of and behind the cameras, they are the best. My deepest thanks to Carl Reiner for a scholarship to the University of Comedy that was called The Dick Van Dyke Show, where among other things, I learned at the master's foot how to get a laugh with a straight line. To Grant Tinker for introducing Jim to Allan and convincing them that they should become Brooks and Burns. To Jay Sandrich, who sets the clock for comedy timing. To my dear friend Arthur Price, whose wisdom and guidance so lovingly given over the years has become my solid foundation for everything I do in this business. And finally, the audience, who recognized some kindred spirits in the characters that I have played and took them, and me, into their hearts. Along with my gratitude to the Television Academy, you also have my promise...that I will continue to try to do...whatever it is you thought I did to deserve this! Thank you.

Chapter

20

On January 8, 1987, Mary returned to the stage. She premiered at the Music Box Theatre in New York with actress Lynn Redgrave in A.R. Gurney, Jr.'s new play, *Sweet Sue*, which co-starred John K. Linton and Barry Tubb, both of whom performed in the nude. With this production, Mary returned to humor – and Broadway. According to *New York Times* theatre critic Mel Gussow, Mary's "comic timing, perfected during her years on television, suits [her portrayal of] Susan well."

In *Sweet*, Mary and Redgrave portrayed the same female character, split in two – as Sue and Sue Too, respectively. Similarly, Linton and Tub played Jake and Jake Too. A middle-aged divorcée, Sue becomes infatuated with her son's college roommate, who's staying in her home for the summer.

Gussow observed, "The questions raised is, will she or won't he? Stripped of its clone-like pretentions, *Sweet Sue* courts comparison with a problem play of another era, Robert Anderson's *Tea and Sympathy*. In that drama, a schoolmaster's ladylike wife sleeps with a young student. *Sweet Sue* is something of a reversal; it is the older woman who is in search of a romantic experience. At that end of the twinned rite of passage, one almost expects the young man to whisper, Anderson-style, 'Years from now…when you talk about this…and you will…be kind'…it is the playwright who is less kind to his characters. Susan and her shadow, Susan Too, are duplicate halves of a single dull woman; this is a very limited partnership."

Mary addressed the play's comedic and dramatic elements with TV journalist Eileen Prose:

> It's a very interesting thing the way A.R. Gurney writes
> it…in that when you read it on the page, it comes

across basically as wonderful, riveting drama. Then you get up and you place your stamp on it, and [it] becomes comedy as well. It's wonderful. And I'm not crediting myself. I mean this just happens. He has obviously laid it out in such a way that he wants the actor's input and it just becomes a wonderful, recognizable exaggeration of truth. As Gurney puts it this is not a case of ego and alter ego. In other words, I don't play the Good Susan and Lynn [doesn't play] the evil, conniving one. It's not that at all. We are each of the complete character of Sue. But they are different aspects, just as Picasso painted the same, painting the two aspects of the one woman. That's what Gurney has done with these characters in the play. [Sue] is an illustrator... basically an artist who has so followed the rules and regulations of life that she never was able to freely give up herself until she meets this kid and goes through the mating dance of infatuation over a summer...which eventually helps her to find herself...to free herself. And he also makes some changes in life.

Prose wondered if there were any parallels between *Sweet Sue's* premise and Mary's real-life situation with Robert Levine, her younger husband of four years. Mary admitted she had to break a few rules to formalize that relationship but asserted that age, within reason, did not make a difference. Their similarities, in background, thinking, and approach to living, were more important to Mary than chronological age.

When first connecting with Levine, Mary was lonely, but her needs with men were different than when she was younger. She said Levine was not a father figure for her in any sense, and that they made decisions together. She found herself grown up; standing firm, and professing to him things like, "These are the areas in which I have strong feelings, and if you can allow that...if you can live with that...then let's do that together."

Mary cared for Levine because "he loves me." He laughed at all of the things that made her smile and, as she said, "We take very seriously the same things in our world." She called him "a fine doctor," respecting his dedication to his profession. He was able to read a script and point out things to her that, she said, "I probably wouldn't have discovered for another week or two...he is very smart...and so embracing and so always there for me."

Mary felt the same appreciation for Lynn Redgrave from a professional standpoint while performing in *Sweet Sue*. "It is wonderful to work with her. It's not only fun, but it is safe and secure, because I can rely on her. I know she cares about me, and she will be there to support me as I need her in a scene. I just feel safe and supportive as I do [with] a few close friends."

This sweetness and light contrasts sharply with later statements Mary made about Redgrave in *After All*. The play's producer suggested that the two women spend the day together before rehearsals began, to get acquainted. "We went walking all around the city, talking, window-shopping, eating and we really bonded and became fast good friends," Mary recalled.

It seemed a harmless experiment, if not ultimately very productive. But Mary believed it was important for an actor to feel safe when working, even if that was a "rare" development. "Most of the time you're out there [performing], basically on your own, and only to a small degree can you rely on your fellow performer. It has happened to me quite often in my work that I've been surrounded by friends. So, I'm the lucky one once again."

When Prose asked about Mary's earlier Broadway ventures, Mary replied, "But you know what? I *have* flopped on Broadway," in reference to her experience in 1968 with *Breakfast at Tiffany's*. "The world does not come to an end," she said, when failure rears its ugly head; "[it's] not all that important."

In wake of *Sweet Sue*'s success, she delivered a shattering TV-movie performance as the mentally unstable Mary Todd in NBC's two-part historical miniseries *Gore Vidal's Lincoln*, which debuted March 27, 1988, and co-starred Sam Waterston as Abraham Lincoln. American historian Harold Holzer reviewed the film and interviewed its female lead for the *New York Times*. He praised her extensive research for the project. For example, in one scene, Mary wore a snug brown wig and a swirling, hoop-skirted dress for the celebration of Lincoln's re-election at a telegraph office. Holzer felt that Victorian propriety would most likely prevent the real Mrs. Lincoln from attending.

In Mary's eyes, Mrs. Lincoln was an enigma, "…an educated woman in an age when women weren't supposed to be educated, obsessed with spending in a European tradition that royalty must impress their subjects. She also slipped into insanity. Yet, I am convinced that [Todd] was important to Lincoln – an integral part of his life and a great influence on him. When I first read the script, all I asked was to see more of my character."

According to Holzer, Mary got her wish. "But, occasionally, the resulting overemphasis may misrepresent history. In one scene, Mr. and Mrs. Lincoln are shown together attending the funeral of their 11-year-old son. In reality, [Todd] was too grief-stricken to attend and stayed home."

Sam Waterston, who played President Lincoln, defended the artistic license of having Mrs. Lincoln mourn at her son's gravesite. "Well, if you showed it that way, you would need a scene that explained that in those days women didn't always go to funerals, then another scene to show how Mary felt. Here we can show everything at once.''

Writer Ernest Kinoy agreed. In adapting his teleplay from the novel by Gore Vidal, he said, the network "insisted on a funeral. So we gave them one.''

But Holzer claimed the most potentially confusing result of Mary's eagerness to enlarge her role stemmed from the finale with lines verbatim from Vidal's novel, things like the President "…willed his own murder as a form of atonement for the great and terrible thing he had done for giving so bloody and absolute a rebirth to the nation."

In the book, such sentiments were spoken by Lincoln's private secretary. When Mary as the President's widow voiced them instead, Holzer said she demonstrated "a fatalism and historical perspective hardly possible in her state of hysteria and self-pity following her husband's murder. It was in just such a state that the real Mary would confide to a friend a few days after the tragedy, 'In my crushing sorrow, I have found myself almost doubting the goodness of God.' To suggest that the First Lady instead rationalized Lincoln's death as an act of ultimate sacrifice for the Union not only misconstrues the 'messiah' message voiced from thousands of pulpits the Sunday after the assassination but ascribes them to perhaps their least likely proponent."

In portraying a woman who had to endure the deaths of three of her sons, Mary called upon her own personal tragedy. "I lost a son and I have first-hand experience with that indescribable pain. Every actor has to use everything he or she has been through in order to portray a character."

During a conversation with *Redbook*'s Kathy Henderson that same year, Mary no longer blamed God for any tragedy in her life. There "is no answer," she said. "In living through the worst, you become acutely aware of how easily the worst can happen – when you least expect it – and there's nothing you can do about it…I think my experiences have made me fatalistic in a good sense. I don't ask God, 'Why me?' anymore. I'm all right now. I can look back at the happy times, but I can also look back at the unhappy ones and say, 'That's all right.'…I'm happier now than I've ever been."

A writer for *Savvy* magazine observed, "Despite the light-years she'd advanced the cause of women, Mary still felt it necessary to define herself in…[nurturing] maternal terms. And TV heroines today define themselves…with Mary."

In a subsequent interview with journalist Steven M.L. Aronson and *Architectural Digest*, Mary called Mary Todd Lincoln "...the most fascinating woman I have ever read about." She also talked about "all the stuff" she amassed in preparation for *Lincoln*, keepsakes held dear in the library of the country estate she and Levine purchased in upstate New York.

On screen, Mary was dedicated to perfecting her performance, including mastering Todd's Kentucky accent, studying with a dialect coach. Sam Waterston told *Entertainment Tonight* on the *Lincoln* set: "I've always had a good time working with her. I think this is the boldest thing she's done that I've done with her, and I think it's wonderful...wonderfully courageous."

Lincoln received seven Emmy nominations, including those for Ruby Dee and Mary, who lost to Jessica Tandy for *Foxfire*. Lamont Johnson won for his direction. On her costumes, Mary told *Hollywood Insider* on the *Lincoln* set: "Thank God we don't wear these anymore. Everything is gusseted and corseted very tightly. Women of that era were smaller. I don't mean that they were thinner, because nobody can be thinner than I am, but they were shorter. So they had to piece together existing costumes or make from scratch new clothes for me."

In promoting *Lincoln*, Mary appeared on *Live with Regis and Kathie Lee* and explained Todd's wild spending sprees. "During a time when there wasn't enough money to pay for the soldiers' uniforms, she was re-carpeting the White House and spending money on drapery and kid gloves. In her mind she thought, if you show the people that their leaders have silks and satins and brooches, they would feel confident. She really believed that."

Mary's ancestral military history was there for motivation if she wanted to use it: Her paternal great-grandfather Lieutenant Lewis Tilghman Moore was a Confederate soldier; Mary's father, George Tyler Moore, owned a signed pardon from Andrew Johnson; and the house once owned by Mary's great-grandfather was now the Stonewall Jackson's Headquarters Museum in Winchester, Virginia.

Her more recent history played a role in *Lincoln*, literally, when Robert Levine appeared as an extra during the inauguration sequence.

But trivia aside, *Lincoln* became another dramatic departure for Mary's acting resume. Few people knew how parts of Mary's personal life resonated with the character of Mary Todd Lincoln.

Chapter

21

In the fall of 1988, Mary and CBS reteamed once more with *Annie McGuire*, another attempt at the half-hour comedy format. *McGuire* aired 8:30 PM on Wednesday nights before *The Van Dyke Show*, a third 30-minute CBS sitcom starring Dick Van Dyke. The two programs were promoted as a semi-reunion of sorts for the legendary stars. The network, the critics, and the audience were excited about the development and the possibilities. But enthusiasm soon waned for the show, which was originally titled *The Mary Tyler Moore Program*, and listed simply as *Mary Tyler Moore* in early print ads and in the *TV Guide* Fall Preview issue. It was later changed to *Annie's World*, and then *Annie Block* before becoming *Annie McGuire*.

In discussing the show's leading role with the *New York Times*, Mary envisioned Annie McGuire as to the first weekly TV character that she played "who is, occasionally, going to have some stains on her clothes. She will take a nap every now and again, screw something up in the house, make a really bad decision with her child and has a sexual vitality that needs to be paid attention to."

The show co-starred Denis Arndt as Mary's husband Nick McGuire; Eileen Heckart, who played Mary's Aunt Flo on *The Mary Tyler Moore Show*, as her mother Emma Block; John Randolph as her father-in-law, and future Oscar-winner Adrien Brody as one of her children. It was a contemporary one-camera dramedy, filmed in the style pioneered by Jim Brooks and Allan Burns' *Room 222* in 1969 and, to a lesser extent, on the less-popular *Hooperman* and *Buffalo Bill* shows from the 1980s. In effect, the 30-minute *McGuire* was filmed like a movie with exterior and interior sets, but without "a studio audience." The 1988 new *Van Dyke Show*, which co-starred Dick's son Barry Van Dyke, was a farcical sitcom videotaped with multiple cameras in front of that live audience. *McGuire's* scripts were superior and sophisticated, while *Van Dyke's* stories were infantile and old-fashioned. Mary herself complained that Van Dyke's show served as a poor lead-in to her more thoroughly modern and non-silly *Annie*. According to one interview about Van Dyke's new program, Mary was so displeased with its presentation, she wondered incredulously, "What is he doing?!" Even Van Dyke himself later called his then-new series, "Sad."

In the end, *Annie McGuire* and *The Van Dyke Show* failed to recapture the magic or the ratings of the original *Mary Tyler Moore* or *Dick Van Dyke* sitcoms, and both were gone by the spring of 1989. But it wasn't for lack of trying, even though *Annie*, by early winter of 1988, ranked 65 out of 72 in the Nielsen ratings. "If I go down, at least I will go down with my head held high," she told the *Christian Science Monitor* on November 23, 1988.

The television audience was not that wild about *Annie*, but the *Monitor's* Arthur Unger wrote, "The new MTM show [was] embraced by practically all the nation's television critics, even though many argued that the program was airing too early in the evening."

Unger echoed Mary's grievances about the less-than-worthy lead-in provided by Dick's relatively dated entry. "The early time slot may be the reason viewership has been so low: the series needs the kind of sophisticated, mature adult audience that usually isn't watching at that hour. Matters are made even worse by the fact that the lead-in program...is the slapsticky *Van Dyke Show*, which got even lower ratings."

"*Annie McGuire* is hard to categorize," Unger continued. "On the surface, it might seem just another variation on several previous MTM series. But this time, Moore, as Annie, plays a woman of approximately her own age, rather than a much younger person; she is not always perky and adept at problem-solving; she has her character flaws. Her unusual relationship with her left-wing mother is lovingly antagonistic, the one with her right-wing-father-in-law, shaky. Her relationships with her new husband, his children, and her own child are fraught with all the usual difficulties, which she fails to resolve just about as often as she succeeds. Story lines range from totally realistic to gently fantastic: One concerned her unwilling involvement in caring for the homeless, another [episode involved] her try at coping emotionally with past infidelities of her new husband."

Howard Rosenberg of the *Los Angeles Times*:

> After reviewing a new series, it's sometimes difficult finding the time or inclination to return for a second or third look. I plead guilty to that concerning some of the

[new shows that debuted in the fall of 1988]. One I have seen regularly, and one that surely deserves preservation is Annie McGuire, the series that returns Mary Tyler Moore as a career woman with a new husband, a feisty mother and a father-in-law.

Executive producers Elliot Shoenman and Paul Wolf have given America a witty, urbane, laugh-trackless half-hour of fresh characters and dialogue. [A recent] episode, in which Annie and her husband endured socializing with an insufferable couple for business reasons was often roaringly funny and comedy that anyone could relate to.

The characters are delightfully written and the supporting cast, including Eileen Heckart...and John Randolph, are all stars. And of course there is Moore herself, performing with confidence while doing all those special things – the timing, the exclamations, the little looks – that define her comedy. Yes, please read lips here – she finally has another series WORTHY OF HER TALENTS!

One never knows what looks for a series put on hiatus [which was Annie's designation on December 14, 1988 when Rosenberg offered his perspective], whether that lapse is really a reprieve [it wasn't] or actually a disguised postponement of cancellation [it was].

Annie McGuire surely merits the former, if for no other reason than that CBS put it in an immediate hole by pairing it with The Van Dyke Show, a weak lead-in that would inevitably emphasize Moore's past sitcom glories – and not giving it a 9 or 9:30 berth.

In speaking with Unger about *Annie* for *The Christian Science Monitor*, Mary said, "I believe in this show so much." She wanted "to do everything possible to give it its chance." Of all the series with which she was connected, *McGuire* most reflected her input. "I never really got involved in any production aspect of *The Dick Van Dyke Show* or any of the *Mary Tyler Moore* shows," she claimed, even though that wasn't entirely true. She had exercised considerable input with her twin attempts at the weekly variety show format in the fall of 1978, though not as much in the *Mary* sitcom from the 1985-1986 season. But this time around, she thought, "I want to do something different. I decided to be an integral part of it."

Mary agreed that the early time period was counter-productive to *Annie's* potential success, but she didn't blame the network because "the first episode we showed them was not anything like the subtle adult show we do now." The entire show was subsequently recast and rebooted. Mary, along with Rosenberg, had envisioned it in the 9:00 o'clock hour on Monday nights, sandwiched between *Newhart*, an MTM Enterprises show, and *Designing Women*. "That would be just dandy," she chirped.

When Unger wondered if *Annie* was "reaching for more contemporary relevance," Mary rejected that suggestion. "What we are going for is intelligence," which she believed encompassed "all aspects of comedy, some of it real, some of it totally frivolous." But she did not want the show to be confused with the dramadies of the previous year including *Hooperman* simply because *Annie* did not employ a laugh track. "I just want to give audiences credit to know when something is funny. Then, if they choose not to laugh, so be it."

In comparing the role of Annie to Laura Petrie or Mary Richards, Mary said, "She's a very different character…much more creative, less organized, not at all as wetly rigid as the other ladies….Annie is a [biological] mother…[and] a woman taking on the mothering of two stepchildren, and a working woman, fitting many aspects of life into her day. And she doesn't always succeed. She's not a perfect mother, not perfect at her job. She feels the pressure of not being able to let her own child go now that he has a stepfather. Annie is closer to the real me, if for no other reason than we have grown together. Annie is a woman in her late 40s. I am 50; so I can identify with her much more than I can [now] with Mary Richards, who was in her 30s and Laura Petrie in her 20s."

In Mary's eyes, *Annie McGuire* was not a feminist series, but a "sensitive show. Unless you are an anti-feminist person, you have to agree that everybody deserves a fair shake. Annie has a career and a home, and she does both. That's what the show is all about…real life, not feminism."

Verisimilitude was important for Mary to incorporate into Annie's fabricated life. For example, in one scene from the show, Annie was supposed to make breakfast for her children before dashing off to catch the ferry from Bayonne to Manhattan. But Mary refuted that. "These children are perfectly capable of fixing breakfast for themselves…That's something Annie might do on a Saturday as a special treat, but we are not going to paint an unrealistic picture here…I don't want Annie to become Harriet Nelson."

"We didn't do the bacon-and-eggs bit," decided Mary, who was proud of Annie's relationships with her husband (as played by Arndt) and her mother (Heckart). "They are the most comfortable and yet exciting scenes I have ever played, alive with electricity and honest speech patterns that let us overlap naturally, just as real people do."

Aside from hoping *Annie McGuire* would become a hit, Mary wanted the show to inspire people to say, "Hey, I never thought of that!" or "Wow, what an interesting reaction Annie had!" She wanted to "turn people's heads a little bit" and "make them smile."

"It may not work," she said, "[and]...it may not prove to be commercial."

Unfortunately, these comments proved true for *Annie McGuire*. But even before it was cancelled, Mary refused to consider the possibility of retiring from series television. "I couldn't even begin to [address] that right now," she told Unger. But she was certain of one thing: As opposed to the earlier portion of her life and career, Mary found her middle years "a lot more inviting, interesting, stimulating.

With the cancellation of *Annie McGuire*, arrived the demise of MTM Enterprises, almost simultaneously. A little history, courtesy of Wikipedia:

For several years MTM Enterprises, with CBS, co-owned the CBS Studio Center in Studio City, California, where a majority of their programs were filmed and videotaped. Most of them aired on CBS. In 1986, MTM acquired Jim Victory Television, which distributed the majority of its programming in the syndication market (except *The Mary Tyler Moore Show* and *The Bob Newhart Show*, both of which were originally distributed by Viacom Enterprises). Victory was later reincorporated as MTM Television Distribution, which was folded into 20th Television after News Corporation purchased MTM. Grant Tinker oversaw MTM's operation until leaving the company in 1981, when he became chairman of NBC. Lawyers backing NBC's then-owner RCA convinced him to sell his remaining shares of MTM. Tinker later regretted leaving MTM, believing that the company started to decline without him.

In 1988, MTM was purchased for $320 million by TVS Entertainment, a United Kingdom broadcaster and independent station for the South and Southeast of England. After TVS relinquished its broadcast access to Meridian Broadcasting, several American companies (and to some extent, Meridian) were interested in attaining it, including Pat Robertson's International Family Entertainment (IFE), which made an initial bid. A few shareholders, such as Julian Tregar, declined the offer from IFE. In November, TCW Capital made an offer, but withdrew it some weeks later after reviewing the books at TVS. Robertson's company increased its offer to £45.3M, but continued to be opposed by Tregar, who blocked the agreement on a technicality, alleging that the bid was too low. IFE finally increased the offer to assuage the remaining shareholders, and on January 23, 1993 their bid of £56.5M was finally accepted, and completed on February 1, 1993 (four weeks following Meridian's initial offer).

Four years later, IFE along with MTM were sold to News Corporation's 20th Century Fox and became Fox Family Worldwide, a joint venture of News Corporation and Saban Entertainment. Its library assets were folded into 20th Century Fox Television even after Fox Family Worldwide was purchased by the Walt Disney Company in 2001. The last shows to be produced by MTM were the UPN Network's *Good News*, a.k.a. *The Good News*, about a young African-American pastor (played by David Ramsey) who lived in Compton, California; and NBC's popular *The Pretender*, starring Michael T. Weiss. *News* was cancelled in 1998 when MTM shut down, while *The Pretender* continued until 2000, as 20th Century Fox Television had taken over the series in 1997 before MTM was dissolved.

MTM Enterprises also included a country-music record label, MTM Records, distributed by Capitol Records, in operation from 1984 to 1988. It was headed by Howard Stark (who died in 2017), and Tommy West (originally of the music duo Cashman and West), who had worked together at ABC Records.

Reporter Nate Rau of *USA Today* once labeled MTM Records, home to artists such as Holly Dunn, Judy Rodman, and Becky Hobbs, "a pivotal chapter in Nashville music history." It "paved the way, and in some ways served as the blueprint, for upstart independent country labels." MTM Records also ignited the career of music superstar Trisha Yearwood, who entered the industry through an internship there.

Rau wrote that "MTM was shuttered despite its growing success for behind-the-scenes business reasons related to its parent company."

After nearly twenty years of remarkable success, MTM Enterprises was sold in 1988, a development signified in the closing credits of *St. Elsewhere*'s final episode when Mimsy the MTM kitten appeared within her logo on life support, with an EKG monitor going to flat-line. It was a poignant visual end to a vibrant company that was headlined by a vibrant individual.

In what seemed to be a liberating move of creative and personal self-expression, Mary hosted an episode of the irreverent late-night variety show, *Saturday Night Live*, which aired on April 2, 1989. With Elvis Costello as her musical guest, Mary held nothing back in her opening monologue, the host's tradition for the show, which is always closely monitored by both fans and foes of SNL:

It's so great, so great to be here. I'm a huge fan of Saturday Night Live and I am thrilled that Elvis Costello is here! And yet, it's a little embarrassing for me tonight because, as you may have read, a group representing the American family has urged that the show be boycotted because, apparently, the show did a 'comedy' sketch some weeks ago in which they used a bad word...28 times. I didn't see the show, but apparently, that bad word was...penis.

All right, 'nuff said.

So you see it's a little awkward for me tonight because throughout my career, I've been associated with the best in family entertainment. But I come from the school of show business that says when you give your word, you'll do something, you do it. Since I agreed to host the show in January, well here I am......28 times. How can you say...well, I guess they had their reasons.

I guess I just don't get political satire. But I promise that the bad word will be not used tonight. Not that I'm a prude, or anything. Far from it. I just believe that there's a time and a place for everything, right? The time for family entertainment is when the entire family is gathered around the television set, no matter what the time, day or night. The time for the other thing is when you're in your bedroom, with your married partner, the door bolted, watching a porno film on the VCR.

Not that I have ever watched a porno film, but if I did, that's the way I would do it, wouldn't you? I guess I am a little old-fashioned.

Anyway, don't let anything I've said concern you in the least. I'm just glad I got that off my mind. Now, I can concentrate on doing a great show. Elvis Costello's penis is here tonight. So stick around. We'll be right back!

In his book, *Sweethearts of '60s TV*, Ronald L. Smith says Mary closed the 1980s with a various measure of triumphs and missteps. That SNL monologue might have been a little bit of both. But each new character she brought to the screen, either for television or movie houses, was immediately compared to Laura Petrie or Mary Richards. She found it challenging to recreate, at least on a weekly basis, the kind of appeal she delivered her two previous hit shows. She was at that "awkward age between *thirtysomething* and *Golden Girls*, a time of life that has resisted sitcom humor." Forty- and fifty-something sitcom stars Smith continued, "…seemed to be stuck playing a single parent with problematic teens."

That certainly was the case for Valerie Harper, and her *Valerie* sitcom from the 1980s, over which she struggled to maintain control. She ultimately exited the show, which became *Valerie's Family* when her character was killed off, and then finally, *The Hogan Family*, when she was replaced altogether by Sandy Duncan. Mary had warned Valerie about not featuring precocious, scene-stealing young actors in any new series, which is what Jason Bateman embodied as Harper's eldest TV son on *Valerie*.

Mary made certain such was not the case with any of her own shows. *Annie McGuire*, for instance, featured less-than-charismatic child performers. By the same token, and as Smith observed, Mary wasn't "obsessed with proving she's a great dramatic actress, or necessarily becoming Number 1 in sitcoms again."

Like the rest of the world, she just wanted to work, and was willing to take risks in doing so. She learned to relax, and was in a position to pick and choose her work. It was all part of her new self-realization. "I've broken out of a shell," she said. She was happily married to Robert Levine, and was "relatively healthy."

"I have enough money to keep me supplied and to contribute to other people's well-being," she said. "I'm pretty well off in every sense."

Chapter

22

Mary's rebooted free spirit was evident in 1990, when she attended the televised *WWE WrestleMania VI* held in Canada, the first to be held outside of the United States. The event took place at the SkyDome in Toronto. Attendance was 67,678, then a record for the facility. Also at the function were WWE Hall of Famer and future multi-time world champions Edge and Christian, as were Steve Allen, Hollywood columnist Rona Barrett, and a very young Stephen Amell. Amell, later of TV's *Arrow* superhero series, would go on to compete in a match at SummerSlam in 2015.

While seated, Mary was approached by a WrestleMania announcer, who wondered if she was enjoying herself. "I'm having a wonderful time," she said. "It's terrific. It's the best of athletics and theatre. I've never seen anything so exciting." She played along as the announcer quizzed her about contemporary players and performers, some of whom she couldn't name. But as usual, charm and humor carried her through. "She may be Mary Tyler Moore," TV host Sean Mooney said, "but she will always been Mary Richards to me." Perhaps it's best that the camera did not catch Mary's reaction. For years she'd been trying to make the public think of her as *anything* but Mary Richards.

About one month later, in the first week of May 1990, near Mother's Day, Mary was a guest speaker at a luncheon-fashion show in Garden City, Long Island to raise funds for the North Shore Child and Family Guidance Center. Besides supporting the center, she was there for her mother-in-law, Marion Levine, of Port Washington, the executive director of the center which to this day still helps individuals and families cope with various issues and challenges. In talking with the *New York Times* reporter who covered the event, Mary called Mrs. Levine "the glue that holds together both the center and the family." The fundraiser was attended by 300 women.

According to *Times* reporter Diane Ketcham, "The sparkling, caring Mary you see on the screen is the Mary you meet in person," and Mrs. Levine agreed. "She is a very generous person. She's become an integral part of the family."

Mary spoke glowingly of her mother-in-law as well – though, as Ketcham observed, both women admitted their relationship took some adjusting. "With my reserved English background I was suddenly involved with a loving, verbal family who don't hold anything back," Mary said. "This was a Jewish family. Robert's the middle son and they didn't count on him marrying a non-Jew, past the age of wanting children and a celebrity to boot. It was Marion who got us past the personal hurdles. She's like a best friend."

"You have different expectations of what will happen to your child," the elder Mrs. Levine relayed. "This was a big surprise to us. Mary's my peer. How do you relate as a mother to someone who is your peer? She's become a very good friend."

Robert Levine, meanwhile, said his wife and mother got along just fine. "A mother-and-daughter-in-law relationship is about being friends. Age has nothing to do with that."

A few months later, Mary appeared in two TV movies that premiered the same winter month.

The Last Best Year, aired on ABC November 4, 1990, and also starred Bernadette Peters. *Thanksgiving Day*, co-starring Tony Curtis and Sonny Bono, screened on NBC November 19, 1990.

Year, originally titled *The Last Best Year of My Life*, was written and produced by David Rintels and based on the experiences of his psychotherapist wife Victoria Riskin, who also served as the film's producer. Mary played Wendy Haller, a psychologist who lost her father to a stroke when she was a child. This part of her past comes back to haunt her when a new patient, Jane Murray, a single career woman played by Peters, comes to her for help when almost simultaneously she loses her married lover and is diagnosed with liver cancer. Many who heard of the project before its airing leapt to the conclusion that the film would be a comedy because Mary and Peters were involved with the production. Riskin told one reporter, "Some people may think…this movie is going to be a laugh a minute. But they're brilliant dramatic actresses. From the beginning there was a real supportive exchange between them. You always worry when two very strong actresses come on the set, how it's going to go. But it went very well."

As it happened, working on *Year* ignited a lifelong friendship and respect shared between the two women. Mary explained: "This is really Bernadette's film. I've always admired her as an actress. She's a singer of songs who can also act them better than anyone I have ever seen. I always wanted to know the soul behind the voice. Oh, that soul would take a poet to describe." Likewise, Peters said of Mary, "Because we had a rehearsal period where we talked about ourselves and the characters, we got to know each...and trust each other. She came from a Catholic background, as I did. She would tell me, 'You know, great things happen after 40, like the hair doesn't grow as much on your legs.' We'd go to the ladies room and discuss things like that."

On *Cinapse.com*, Frank Calvillo called *The Last Year* an "obscure 1990 TV-movie [that] accidentally turns out to be a tribute to a TV icon." He explored Mary's career in comparison to Peters:

"There's no question whatsoever that Mary Tyler Moore and Bernadette Peters both earned the title of legend after lengthy and acclaimed careers. While the former became a television pioneer and icon thanks to a pair of revolutionary long-running sitcoms, the latter ascended the heights of Broadway to become the first lady of American musical theater. Yet for some reason, the film world never knew quite what to do with either actress. Moore snagged an Oscar nomination for her incredible work in *Ordinary People,* and Peters charmed her way through the otherwise forgettable film version of *Pennies from Heaven*. The two found more success in the land of made-for-TV movies, where both actresses were allowed to shine. And as evidenced by the dramatic 1990 offering *The Last Best Year*, shine they both did."

Calvillo concluded: "*The Last Best Year* does what very few other movie-of-the-week fare of the time did, which is to go against typecasting. The film is outside the wheelhouse of both actresses, yet the pair admirably step up to the plate, and the result is outstanding. Even more impressive is the fact that two such incredibly different acting styles can come together so harmoniously. Moore exudes vulnerability and strength, at times spontaneously, wonderfully playing off of Peters as she excellently taps into Jane's mixture of fear and regret."

John Leonard offered his review of the film for *New York* magazine. "Neither [actress] has ever been better at doing what they do best, which is to make you love them as much as we would want to be loved ourselves," he wrote. A pessimist at heart, Leonard acknowledged having "a tear in the eye and a lump in the throat" while viewing the movie. He was hesitant to accept Mary as anything other than a cheerful young woman who tossed "her hat in the air." She "adds another anguished glaze to the very different picture we got of her in *Ordinary People* and as

Mary Todd Lincoln," and decided that her "terrific smile" that "used to be a gift must now be earned."

On the opposite coast, Howard Rosenberg of the *Los Angeles Times* called *Year* "…a heartfelt drama…[a] sweet, gentle and inevitably teary story of a symbiotic bond established by these two women brought together by tragedy, each gaining strength from the other as the dying Jane seeks to put her life in order and Wendy seeks the resolve to confront her own demons."

Unfortunately, Mary's other teledrama, *Thanksgiving Day* (later known as *The Good Family* when repeated on the Lifetime network) was not so well-received. In his review for the *Baltimore Evening Sun*, Michael Hill wrote:

> Thanksgiving Day is like a nice, shiny luxury car, equipped with all the options, that just happens to be missing its spark plugs. No matter how comfortable the seats, how fine the finish, the thing still won't start up and take you anywhere. Ultimately, it's just a very expensive piece of junk.
>
> So NBC's Thanksgiving Day has Mary Tyler Moore as appealing as ever, Tony Curtis crazier than ever, a promising arena in black comedy, an interesting idea in a wacky, dysfunctional family trying to make it through the holidays, but, despite all that, it never gets up and running. It just lies there like week-old stuffing.
>
> The film…opens with the fowl holiday once again upon the Schloss family, which is headed by Tony Curtis, kingpin of the famed Schloss glove company, who has invited his best customer to Thanksgiving dinner.
>
> Also showing up for the meal are ne'er-do-well son Randy, played by Chicago radio personality Jonathon Brandmeier, who's working too hard here, and off-at-college daughter Barbara, played by Curtis' attractive and personable real daughter, Kelly. If the Schloss family is lucky, shut-in son Michael (Andy Hirsch) might tear himself away from the TV long enough to take in the meal.
>
> The funny part is that best customer and wife don't like turkey, so Paula Schloss, Mary Tyler Moore looking and acting as fine as you can remember, and longtime Schloss servant Richard (Cal Gibson) are supposed to

get some roast beef on the table. They forget. The pressure's too much for dear old Dad and he keels over while slicing the big bird.

Things just get wackier as Randy, who's got a couple of kids and an endless line of bimbo girlfriends, proceeds to gamble away the family fortune, Barbara announces that she is gay and introduces everyone to her obnoxious lover, and Ned Monk, the richest guy in town (Detroit) played by Joe Bologna, makes a play for his old sweetheart Paula.

All along are various quirks and foibles, funny stuff at funerals, silly stuff at the club, slapstick on the golf course. But it all just sits there. It's like watching a stand-up comedian who seems to be a nice guy doing material that really isn't that bad but who just can't connect with the audience. It makes you uncomfortable. You want to turn your head away.

Eventually, Thanksgiving Day diagnoses its own ills. In its last half hour, it finally starts moving, but it's no longer the luxury car, it's more of a regular family sedan.

By that point, the Schloss clan has lost its fortune and the boys have joined in a catfish-raising venture. You find yourself touched by this, rooting for them. And you realize that what Thanksgiving Day failed to do in the beginning was make you care about these characters before turning them into comic foils.

If somehow the structure had been reversed, if you had gotten to know these people before the script started poking fun at them, Thanksgiving Day could have had you cruising along, hitting the black comedy as if it were some unexpected and hilarious pothole.

Trying to build the movie in the opposite direction is much more difficult, requiring comedy that is so funny you can't help but laugh. And this Thanksgiving Day needs several more helpings before it gets that funny."

A more festive occasion arrived February 18, 1991, when CBS aired *Mary Tyler Moore: The 20th Anniversary Show*. It was the first of what became several re-gathering specials, tributes, and nods not just to her legendary sitcom and its stars, but also to the original *Van Dyke Show* and stars of that series from the 1960s. According to the A.C. Nielsen Company, the anniversary special, 90 minutes in length, was ranked the eleventh most-watched television show that week. Clips from the original *MTM Show* were interspersed with new recollections from Mary and her fellow stars, including Ed Asner, Valerie Harper, Cloris Leachman, Gavin MacLeod, Betty White, and Georgia Engel. Mary called the special "a bittersweet experience" due to the absence of Ted Knight, who had passed away in 1986.

When CBS had first approached Mary with the concept, she was apprehensive. "Doing a reunion show has always been something I've been afraid of because that series was such a gem, I didn't want to risk doing anything that would tarnish the memory of it." But she was "extremely pleased" with the special, which was produced by Jack Haley, Jr., writer, producer and director of *That's Entertainment I* and *II*, *That's Dancin'*, and many other clip-tributes to Hollywood icons such as Cary Grant, Vincent Minelli (Liza's father), and the 50th Anniversary of *The Wizard of Oz* (which starred Liza's mother Judy Garland as Dorothy opposite Haley's father as the Tin Man).

Haley, Jr. hired Laurie Jacobson as a co-producer and writer for the *Anniversary* special, which they had only two months to complete. Jacobson detailed the experience in the June 1992 issue of *Hollywood Then & Now* magazine, with an article that was subsequently republished in the premiere issue of David Davis' *Mary Magazine*. Here are some excerpts:

> Phase One:
>
> We didn't start with a completely blank page. There were a few guidelines. We knew that Mary would host the show. Other cast members might join her, but none of them had been asked and there was every possibility that the work schedule of seven actors would conflict. So, we needed to come up with a variety of scenarios that could fly with one actor or half a dozen. Of course we would use clips from the series to fill the one-hour format, which meant – after commercials, station breaks and host material – we'd have just thirty-four minutes for clips. We knew before we started that we'd run long [the special was originally planned as one hour then expanded to 90 minutes]. There was too much great material. As Jack Haley said, in the seven seasons of Mary Tyler Moore lay "an embarrassment of riches!"

Next, we watched the shows, all 168 episodes, carefully logging each one scene by scene, noting anything that might stand out as special. Themes began to emerge: Mary's lousy parties, her dates, Murray vs. Sue Ann, Ted's malaprops, Mr. Grant's office, Rhoda vs. Phyllis – there were dozens. During the next month, December 1990, we built these themes into segments which we viewed over and over, paring them down, filling them in; creating new categories out of old. We also wrestled with a concept for the show. It might turn out to be a reunion, but since we weren't sure, we couldn't call it that. We thought about bringing them back as their characters to the show [and addressing] what had happened to them, but the death of Ted Knight made that awkward. Mary didn't want the special to take itself too seriously.

Allan Burns, Jim Brooks and Ed. Weinberger, the producers of the [original] series felt the same way. We decided on a 'celebration,' wrote a rough script for the entire troupe and prayed they'd show up."

Another 30 Minutes:

January brought good news. The clip segments were so good, CBS was giving us another thirty minutes [ten would go for clips]. And we were getting a positive response from the actors. Everyone was a resounding yes. Jack volunteered his house as the shoot location, so we met Mary and her husband there one afternoon a week before the shoot. Mary, who is 52, looked radiant and fresh and carried herself with tremendous grace. Her dancer's training was still very much in evidence. Dr. Robert Levine, a 38 year-old cardiologist, was very attentive to her and concerned about every aspect of the production.

Mary loved Jack's living room, the huge stone fireplace and long languorous couch. She seemed immediately comfortable in the surroundings and with the production and writing staff. We invited her to view the clips.

Mary proved to be the greatest audience. The segments sent her on an emotional roller coaster. She surprised us with her modesty and the compliments flowed from her lips. She loved the script. It was funny and hit all the points she wanted covered. She loved the clips. All her favorite scenes were there and everyone got their fair shake. She even asked if the show didn't favor her too much. We couldn't wait to see the emotional fireworks when the cast was finally together.

Day One:

The first day of the two-day shoot was a light one. Only Mary, Gavin Macleod and Georgia Engel were working.

Jack's living room had been "feminized": pillows, flowers; an oil painting in pastel shades. It looked warm and inviting despite the load of equipment, lights and wires just out of the camera range. Mary's trademark 'M' was hung on the stone fireplace by the property master, Sal, a chunky guy whose low-riding pants always revealed the top of his butt.

Mary's hair and make-up men fussed over her, arranging her dress, final touches to her hair. Then she went before the camera for two quick CBS promotions. The first was for George Burns' 95th birthday: "Happy Birthday, George. We all love you." She sat on the edge of the hearth, looked straight into the camera and read the phrase three times in a row, three completely different ways with only a beat in between. Bam! On the next one: "What are you doing on Monday night?"

Again, three widely different readings and we were through. She was absolute professionalism – and damn, she was good. Mary went to her "dressing room," – Jack's bedroom – to change for the show. Sal tried to adjust the "M," but instead knocked it to the stone hearth where it broke into four pieces.

This was the "M" Mary had treasured all these years. Her assistant had hand-carried it across the country. Not only that, several years before Mary donated it to a charity auction and her husband bought it back for her for $10,000. We stared at the pieces in shock. Sal ran to glue it together and Jack made the difficult decision to not inform Mary until the end of the shoot. Moments later Mary was warmly greeting Georgia

Engel and Gavin MacLeod who played Georgette and Murray. There was much hugging and kissing before the trio was dressed and read for the set.

A Breeze:

The shoot was a breeze. We shot "singles" of Mary and two-shots of Gavin and Georgia and "three shots" of all of them. For several two and three shots I just sat out of camera range to read lines for Betty White and Valerie Harper. "You know," I said to Gavin and Georgia, "I don't even feel nervous. I feel like I'm with old friends."

"We are your old friends," Georgia cooed sincerely. She flew in from New York, where she now makes her home and where she has returned to her first love, the stage. Gavin lives in the San Fernando Valley and is kept busy launching Princess cruises around the country, in between theatre engagements.

MacLeod stuck around after the shoot and shared stories with another producer and me. He'd been friends with the late Ted Knight, WJM's bumbling anchorman, Ted Baxter, since the late '50s. "It's a shame no one will ever know what a brilliant dramatic actor Ted was. He was one of the kindest people I ever knew."

Gavin told us anecdotes about the series. "The show that I got the most mail on was an episode where Murray thought he was in love with Mary. I got so many letters from men who told me there was a woman in their office they felt the same way about. It was amazing....When the series ended, I got huge amounts of mail from little old ladies who loved Murray and who thought I'd never work again." Gavin's follow-up series, The Love Boat, did better in the ratings than Mary ever did, and made him lots of money.

"The episode when I had to lift Betty and land her on top of a wedding cake – oh that was something I wish I could do over again. I overshot the cake just a few inches and landed Betty's tailbone on the edge of the table. I knew it hurt, I heard it! But she didn't flinch and she held that cake under her with her legs and sheer will. She is so brilliant...I think she's one of the most beautiful women around." Not that Gavin is looking. He is blissfully happy in his second marriage and he delights in his children and grandchildren. Gavin MacLeod has discovered what is really important for him in this life, and he treasures every minute.

The first day had come off without a hitch - except the "M." I was happy to have had some quality times with the actors. Tomorrow would be much different. We had one day and the majority of the show ahead of us.

Day Two:

I got to Jack's at 9:00 AM. The actors had arrived more than an hour earlier for make-up and hair. When all seven remaining cast members were gathered together again for the first time in thirteen years, all hell broke loose. They laughed. They teased each other. ("Gee, isn't it funny," joked Valerie Harper, "that both the guys' hair turned white and none of ours did?") They hugged endlessly. You could cut the warmth with a knife.

Inside Jack's house his master bedroom and bath had been transformed into dressing rooms for Mary and Valerie. An office was assigned to Gavin and Ed Asner. The guest bed and bath were for Georgia, Betty and Cloris Leachman. Cloris is very high-key and this morning was no exception. She had fallen back somewhat into her character from the show, Phyllis Lindstrom – a neurotic, self-centered woman who was always competing with Rhoda for Mary's affection. Cloris pretended to be very hurt that Valerie got to share Mary's dressing room.

With a mischievous grin, she pulled Valerie's name off the door and replaced it with her own. They were all running back and forth to each others' rooms like little kids at a slumber party. This was going to be fun. With all seven grouped on the couch before the cameras, the jokes and laughter flowed. As Mary introduced them, each had an aside for her. Ed griped that Mary always had to be taller than he was. Betty, saccharine-sweet, offered to let down the hem of Mary's above-the-knee dress. Later, during a scene in which Valerie pointed out that Mary Richards was the first television character to show it was okay to be over thirty, single and female, Betty ad-libbed, "Lassie, there was Lassie."

The people just out of camera range had a difficult time suppressing their laughter. There were about thirty crew members, several execs from MTM and CBS, about a dozen people from Haley's office, Mary's assistants and a crew from Entertainment Tonight who were trying to interview the actors whenever they could get one of them alone.

Jack's House:

Jack's house is at the top of a cul-de-sac. Parked just outside the front door was an enormous catering truck and a table of breakfast foods. Valet parkers reigned at the hilltop, trying to organize a sea of cars while placating fussy neighbors. By 1 PM, the area was set with tables and chairs for us to have lunch.

We broke to eat around 2 PM. The cast had another surprise waiting for them. Their former director, Jay Sandrich and producers Jim Brooks, Allan Burns and Ed. Weinberger were anxiously waiting to greet their old pals. The warmth and affection these people had for each other was so deep that many of us felt we were intruding. Suffice it to say, Jack's house was a heavenly place to be that day.

Time magazine interrupted the proceedings for a group photo of this incredible reunion. The whole gang – actors, producers, directors – piled into the library where a backdrop and lighting had been set up for hours. The photographer asked for the group to pose with the "M."

In a few moments, everybody's favorite prop man, Sal, carried it in. He had glued it, but he hadn't touched up the paint. Mary took one look at it and began to cry. One could hardly blame her. Seven years on the show, thirteen years at home and not a scratch. One day with us and blammo. She returned moments later, apologized for her outburst and smiled broadly for the photographer. As we'd all observed earlier, "Damn - she was good."

Before lunch, we showed the segment that led into the clip tribute to Ted Knight, who died in 1986. It had been an emotional experience. They laughed because he was so funny. Then they cried because they miss him. But the big tear-jerker we saved for the last group shot of the day. The last scene from the final episode was about to play. MTM and CBS execs alike had cried when we played it for them. We all had. We knew the cast would be deeply moved. To capture their honest reactions, we could only show it once. We set up three cameras to catch every single angle and let it roll.

Once again, they relived the farewell of the WJM news team. From Lou Grant's "I treasure you people," to Mary's eyes brimmed full. On screen, the cast moved into a group hug – something that happened simultaneously during rehearsal.

Then, to the tune of "It's a Long Way to Tipperary," they file out of the newsroom for the last time. When Mary takes her last look before switching off the lights, you could've heard a pin drop on the set. Tears literally poured down Gavin's face. Betty and Georgia clung to each other. Valerie and Mary held hands while Mary tried valiantly to fight back her tears. As the scene ended, Ed stood up, "Seven magnificent years." He hugged her, and just as in that rehearsal years earlier, the group spontaneously comforted one another in a group hug.

There wasn't a dry eye in the place.

All but Mary and Ed were through for the day. All the photographers and TV crews were gone. After twelve hours, the house had quieted down to the bare bones crew. Mary and Ed were incredible. They did everything in one take. We wrapped the shoot about 7:30 PM.

We had several more screenings for MTM and Brooks and Weinberger before the February 8th airdate. We met our deadline in plenty of time and somehow managed to please everyone with the show. For me that was the nicest compliment we could receive.

A short time after the series closed up shop at MTM studios, they put up a plaque outside Stage 2 [where Roseanne then reigned]. It says, "On this stage, a company of loving and talented friends created a television classic, The Mary Tyler Moore Show, 1970-1977."

It's still there and they are darned proud of it.

Chapter

23

With *Mary Tyler Moore: The 20th Anniversary Show* behind her, something her followers had long waited to see, Mary continued on with her life and career. It was nicely documented for the June 1991 issue of *Architectural Digest* magazine, of all places.

In that interview, Mary talked about the upstate New York country home that she and Robert Levine had purchased, far away from Hollywood's glitter and glare. "We began by being sensible. What we were looking for was an apartment in Manhattan with a terrace. And that became an impossible quest. We were just never able to find anything that was right – the right size, the right neighborhood, and [one] that would accept dogs…And here we are. There's not even a movie house in this town."

In another article that Mary wrote for *Architectural Digest* some years later, she talked about how she and Levine initially had "no idea" what they were looking for in a home. That is, until they found what she later called "a beautiful Cotswolds-style cottage" in Dutchess County, New York. It was surrounded by 21 acres of horse trails and meadows that eventually expanded to 30, then 150 acres.

The house was originally constructed as a hunting lodge in the 1950s. Mary found this ironic, because she was such an animal lover and "so anti-hunting." The first renovation the Levines made was to demolish the stands where hunters used to hide in the trees. Over the years, the couple added fieldstone to the façade and rearranged some of the interior, but as Mary said, they "tried to preserve the old-fashioned feel."

They still retained their apartment in New York, but they journeyed to their country home for weekends, and grabbed "great chunks of time whenever we can," she said. They filled the home with warm colors and rustic, comfortable décor that seemed to fit their sensibilities. "It's not what you would call elegant," she said, "but it's very cozy and personalized."

The home's entry hall was one of Mary's favorite spots. It was designed as a hexagon with cranberry walls and wood flooring salvaged from an old barn. The paintings were family heirlooms of her ancestors. The somber-looking bearded man was John Moore, the family member who Mary claimed had stowed away on a tea ship in 1735 as a child. And the sword that rested on the opposite wall was swung by Lewis Tilghman Moore, a good friend of Stonewall Jackson during the Civil War.

But what Mary called "the real key" to her country life with Levine was the animals. Over the years they had various horses, some of which were rescued, a golden retriever, and a miniature Schnauzer who went everywhere with the couple, even slept with them. The estate had four ponds and a stream, where Mary loved to hear the little frogs that gathered there and sang. "All the wild animals seem to know that they can come here and be protected," she said. In the winter, Mary and Levine would bring truckloads of hay to feed the deer. And she wasn't surprised when a guest once counted 85 of them on their lawn.

Levine thought that when they finally had horses of their own, Mary's need to collect animal decorations would dissipate. But it didn't. Her love for animals was still reflected in the décor and artwork displayed throughout the house. "It's important to surround yourself with things that you love in your home," Mary told writer Steven M.L. Aronson. For her, having animals around "just puts things in perspective. They remind me of what really matters in life."

Moving to the country worked out better for Mary than she had ever dreamed. She seemed at rest there, conducting her talk with Aronson who said she utilized a "clear, confident voice that Andy Warhol said could make her 'the biggest thing in politics since Reagan.'"

Mary's eyes, Aronson also explained, shone when she flashed "the spectacular smile," which John Leonard once defined as "a cross between a cannibal and a piano." Aronson called her country estate "a compound of long roofs, sloping up and wide lawns sloping gently down – so bright they, too, seem to be shining – to a pool of ponds spilling one into the other."

Apparently, country living was something Mary had longed for but never knew she desired. She said the rural setting allowed her the chance to entertain in a relaxed way, to do things she had not formally trained herself to do, "...like fiddle with flowers...to finally know the difference between an annual and a perennial. To be able to go into the vegetable garden and fool around a little bit. And the horses...being able to ride them – my mare is pregnant, she's going to foal soon, she's going to put her babe on the ground, as they say – to be a part of that."

She enjoyed activities that had short-term results which were visible and rewarding, as opposed to working in a weekly TV series. "Because...that...is kind of in the abstract," she said, "... you do it and you don't see it for about six weeks, and then you see it and it's gone. And you really don't get paid money that you hold in your hand, and it's all done through computers. You never really see the fruits of your labor, I think, in the kind of business I'm in. But having a [country home] changes all that. Three falls ago I planted three hundred and twenty-five daffodil bulbs, and that spring I saw three hundred and twenty-five of those suckers come up."

In short: Mary felt in touch with nature. She talked not only to the animals, but to the trees. As far as she was concerned, they all talked back. "It's a very calming effect," she confided to Aronson, "...very calming."

The acquisition and renovation of the country home took approximately three years, during which time the Levines lived on cots in the main house, and in the caretaker's cottage when the main house was being worked on. "Just like Gypsies we moved back and forth whenever we needed to be out of the way," Mary said. "This place at times looked like a war zone. It was all very complicated. You don't do anything that looks as relaxed and informal as this without a lot of organization, you know. But at least it now has a little of everything you could ever want."

This new residence was her third with Levine, and her eighteenth house, thus far, but she promised, "*This* is it. This is my sign-off."

This internal interaction with her surroundings had always been part of her. Mary explained in her second memoir, *Growing Up Again*, that among her favorite playthings as a child was a dollhouse that spoke to her with an adult's voice. She believed her desire to own various residences might have somehow been tied to her longing to redecorate what she called "that magical little house." Of course, the dollhouse was missing an exterior wall. "Every film set consists of the same three-wall configuration," she observed, "...maybe that's why I've always felt comfortable on a set."

In October 1991, five months after her interview with *Architectural Digest*, Mary played co-host (with Carol Burnett and Marlo Thomas in separate segments) on the TV special, *Funny Women of Television*. Jack

Haley, Jr., the special's executive producer, said that the NBC show showcased "breakthrough" series like *The Mary Tyler Moore Show*.

Although she did not make any new TV show or film in 1991, Mary continued to advocate for animals throughout that year and on into 1992. Then, on May 9 of 1992, she regrouped with Dick Van Dyke, Carl Reiner, Rose Marie, and Morey Amsterdam for "Comic Relief 1992," a live-stage event. The cast of *The Dick Van Dyke Show* received a five-minute standing ovation. Although Mary and Marie did not always get along on the *Van Dyke* set back in the day, by 1992 they had long buried the hatchet. And when Amsterdam died a few years later (in 1996), both women were devastated. Marie had known Amsterdam since she was 9 years old, and Mary always had a soft spot in her heart and a great deal of respect for the diminutive performer. "He was a human joke machine," she said. "You could name any subject and within two seconds he could make a joke. And a damn good joke, too. I came to *The Dick Van Dyke Show* as a complete comedy novice and I owe him my gratitude for the know-how I have today."

On September 22, 1992, the entire Hollywood community had the chance to extend their gratitude to Mary for the entire world to see when she finally received her star on the Hollywood Walk of Fame. "In the future, should I have any doubts," she mused at the ceremony that day, with regard to her validity as a star, "I can always come down here and remind myself that I was not a figment of my own imagination."

Of course, Mary's know-how wasn't limited to comedy. Her talents were as diverse as her interests. In February of 1993, she attended the annual Hill's Science Diet Winners' Circle Awards banquet in New York. The following March she was one of the chairs at an A.S.P.C.A. charity event, and a short time later donated her own sable coat as auction item for the annual P.E.T.A. Awards, which honored celebrities who altered their thinking about wearing fur.

Busy as ever, Mary participated in several other events. On March 20, 1993, she was honored at the Museum of Television and Radio's 10th Annual Television Festival which took place at the Paley Center in Beverly Hills. This particular ceremony, subtitled, *An Evening with Mary Tyler Moore*, acknowledged Mary for her portrayal of women in television. Those attending this festivity were, among others, her former co-star Valerie Harper, and entertainment historian Daniel Wachtenheim.

According to Wachtenheim, Mary, while at the podium, addressed her career including her two favorite episodes of *The Mary Tyler Moore Show*: "Put on a Happy Face" (February 24, 1973), and "Support Your Local Mother" (October 24, 1970).

In "Happy," while Rhoda's life is on the upswing, Mary has seen better days. She awakens with a hair bump, and everything goes downhill from there, while she does her best to prep for that evening's Teddy Awards. She can't seem to win anything that night, except the Teddy. She never finds the right dress, and attends the event with a cold and dateless. She loses a slipper and her false eyelashes and, once at the podium to give her acceptance speech, she blurts out, "I usually look so much better than this."

In "Local," Ida Morgenstern, Rhoda's mother, makes her first appearance, but her daughter refuses to see her. Ida is simply too much for Rhoda's patience. It's then Mary who invites Ida to stay at her apartment, and soon understands all too well Rhoda's issues with her mother.

"The evening at the Paley Center," Wachtenheim said, "...was devoted to Mary because one year earlier they had saluted *The Mary Tyler Moore Show*, and the entire cast was present, except for Mary whose father had passed away. So, Mary was paid tribute the following year. She impressed me as a very elegant, lovely, accomplished businesswoman. She was very professional, and extremely intelligent. Not as soft or gentle as you would think, she was a firm, tough cookie, and a true team player. I met her after the show for a brief moment. And I had met her another time at the Thalians Ball when they saluted her. She was signing autographs, and it was clear that her eyesight was compromised. She asked [those seeking her signature] to place their pictures in front of her so she could sign them, and she did sign each and every one of them. She was very lovely to her fans."

In April, Mary joined Academy officials and Dick Clark, John Chancellor, Phil Donahue, and Bob Newhart, at the groundbreaking for an East Coast home of the TV Academy Hall of Fame. This was at the Disney-MGM Studios Theme Park in Orlando, Florida.

Around this time, reruns of *The Mary Tyler Moore Show* on Nick at Nite had expanded to double airings beginning at 10 P.M. The network was also winning viewers over with reruns of *The Dick Van Dyke Show*. Its star, then 70 years young, was named Nick at Nite's on-air "chairman," appearing in promotional spots about "preserving our television heritage."

In March of 1993, Van Dyke hosted a 3-hour special about the series that featured his five personal favorite episodes. Other stars from the series were on hand: Larry Mathews and *Van Dyke Show* bit players Kathleen Freeman and Frank Adamo who, as previously noted, doubled as Van Dyke's personal assistant during the sitcom's original run, and Mary's personal assistant on *The Mary Tyler Moore Show*.

Unfortunately, Mary did not appear on-screen for the Nick at Nite special, but at least delivered her voice off-camera, exclaiming at one point, "Oh, Rob!"

Come March 25, 1993, her fans hailed Mary when she finally returned to work in the Lifetime TV-movie *Stolen Babies*, for which she won an Emmy (her seventh), this time for portraying Georgia Tann, a real-life cruel and corrupt adoption official who lived during the 1930s and 1940s. When Mary originally signed to play this part, the movie was called *Stolen Children*, but this was changed after the producers learned there was a documentary with the same name.

Viewers loved Mary's acceptance speech at the Emmy ceremony that year. She stepped up to the podium and said, "Sorry, Ed," to Ed Asner – now she had earned as many Emmys as him. In retrospect, it might be considered a foreshadowing of when Mary and Asner would co-star in the 1997 TV-movie, *Payback*, for which he served as producer, instead of Mary supervising the project through MTM Enterprises.

But for now, Mary enjoyed a wave of *Stolen* publicity, including the usual talk-show appearances (*Larry King Live*; *Prime Time Live*; *CBS This Morning*; *Late Night with David Letterman*) for a movie that one *New York* magazine critic called "intelligent and provocative."

In her interview with Carlos Ferrer, Mary explained the way that her character Georgia Tann had tricked and convinced poor, indigent couples to give up their babies to a wealthy home. She was amazed that "people bought that," and that "The parents of these babies thought, 'Oh, this is the most wonderful thing I could do for this child because I'm poor and who knows what [their future will be for this child]. They would give their babies to this awful woman," who would then market these children to "movie stars and other wealthy people. She was quite notorious."

Mary felt especially honored to win the Emmy for interpreting Tann. This wasn't about the dramatic challenge of playing "…such a fascinating and [dreadful] human being," she said, but because doing so allowed her to flex her acting chops past her comfort zone. On the *Stolen Babies* set, Mary was not surrounded by actors who became like family. "That's not to deny the impact of the other actors in *Stolen Babies*," she cautioned, "…but I'm usually at my best when I'm feeling confident. And they gave me confidence," as opposed to merely being a comforting acting company.

In addition to her role in *Stolen Babies*, which became Lifetime's then-highest-rated TV movie, Mary's 1993 TV appearances included: the *14th Annual Cable Ace Awards* (as a presenter); the *45th Annual Prime-Time Emmy Awards* (as a presenter and a winner); the TV talk show *Aspel*

& Company; segments of *CBS This Morning*; and *Late Night with David Letterman*.

In February of 1994, Mary bit her lip and attended a breakfast celebrating the 40th anniversary of Truman Capote's signing with Random House for his first novella, *Breakfast at Tiffany's*. Putting aside memories of her ill-fated Broadway edition of the novella in 1967, Mary joined Patricia Neal and others in commemorating the creation of the Truman Capote Literary Trust. In March 1994, she appeared in the ABC TV special, *PEOPLE's 20th Birthday*, which celebrated that magazine's two decades of publication. That same month, she took in a performance of a new Broadway musical edition of *Cyrano*, starring Robert Guillaume (of TV's *Soap* and *Benson*), and visited backstage. On March 6, she taped *The American Comedy Awards*, during which she presented Dick Van Dyke with a lifetime achievement award. The special eventually aired on ABC on May 23.

A singular performance-in-character transpired a few months later. In a small but chipper voiceover cameo named for her mother, Mary portrayed a call-in character named Marjorie on "Frasier's Day Off," the first-season episode of NBC's long-running *Frasier* sitcom that aired May 12, 1994. The comedy, featuring Kelsey Grammer as the harried radio psychologist he introduced on *Cheers*, was known for its celebrity voice guests. On her "Day Off" segment, Mary's vocals are heard when Frasier requires a much-needed break from the office, made evident upon showing up for work delirious and somewhat drug-overdosed. Besides Mary, other celebrity callers for *Frasier* included: Patricia Hearst, Steve Lawrence, Eydie Gormé, Tommy Hilfiger, Garry Trudeau, and Steve Young. Mary's Marjorie dialogue from her episode goes something like this, loopy Frasier and all:

> **Frasier:** "Hello! You're on the crane with Frasier Air!"
>
> **Marjorie:** "Hi, Dr. Crane. This is Marjorie. You see, I'm...I'm having a problem with my boss. He doesn't seem to respect me, and I don't have the courage to confront him."
>
> **Frasier:** "Okay, okay, Marjorie. Well, let's...let's see. Let's do a little role-playing, okay? Look, I'll be your boss, you be yourself, you be Marjorie...and uh...come on in and talk to me in a very forceful way. Tell me what you think, and you just might be surprised by what happens!"

Marjorie: "Well, okay... 'Listen, Mr. Ross. I've worked for this company for six years and I've never missed a day. But you've constantly promoted people less qualified than I am and I don't think that's fair.'"

Frasier: "Well, Marjorie, I must say I admire your forthrightness and uh...I wish more of my employees came and spoke to me with an open mind. You know, you're going to get that promotion!"

Marjorie: "Hey, that was great!"

Frasier [excited]: "Yeah! Wasn't it? Wasn't it? Okay, it's my turn! I'm Marjorie and you're the boss now! Come on! Come on...!"

(Frasier's brother Niles, as played by David Hyde Pierce, arrives with security and together they hustle the delusional Frasier away.)

On May 23, 1994, Mary appeared in *The Dick Van Dyke Show Remembered*, a one-hour CBS-TV special hosted by Charles Kuralt. She and Van Dyke, along with Rose Marie, Morey Amsterdam, Larry Mathews, Ann Guilbert, Carl Reiner, and Sheldon Leonard, recalled their experiences and favorite scenes from the show. One of the highlights of the special, which was a ratings success, was a montage featuring Mary's "Oh, Rob!" squeal.

While participating in live events and periodic TV specials, Mary was considering another weekly series. This time it was a one-hour drama in which she would have played a divorce lawyer with a tendency to fall in love with her clients. But the concept went nowhere, eventually morphing into what became *New York News*, which debuted approximately 18 months later.

Also in 1994, Mary had hosted an Emmy-watching party at the Russian Tea Room in Manhattan. She co-hosted with Carol Burnett and Lily Tomlin the NBC special, *The Funny Woman of Television: A Museum of Television and Radio Tribute*.

Mary's physical health and fitness had always been a priority, but by this time such aspects of her life had become a premium – and she was determined to profit from them. She completed a three-part *Everywoman's Workout* video series that was released in October 1994. She had earlier joked that she would be the only actress who went to "her grave not having done an exercise video." But her personal trainer Laure Redmond was impressed by Mary's ability to inspire Redmond's other clients. Because Mary believed there was "a whole lot of audience out there that doesn't identify with a 23-year-old instructor," she then partnered with Redmond to move forward on the trio of videos.

Consequently, the triad of videos titled *Aerobics*, *Body Sculpting*, and *Power Stride* were presented by the GoodTimes Entertainment company, which was responsible for Cindy Crawford's successful video series. The first two videos in Mary's series were 30 minutes of aerobics based on her personal workout routine. The third video features Mary in the park demonstrating how everyday movements can be a part of anyone's exercise regimen. "I have a dancer's body," she said, "and we know so much now about dance through the president's council of fitness, and sports and medicine [President's Council on Fitness, Sports, and Nutrition]. Studies show that you really don't have to do more than 30 minutes [of dance or any form of exercise] to keep in shape. I hope people will find someone with whom they can identify and get out there and do it."

Mary donated all the profits from *Everywoman's Workout*, which was aimed at women 35 and older, to the Juvenile Diabetes Foundation. Even during this venture, her parents' influence weighed on her mind. "Dancing established the habit of exercise for me," she once stated. "My mother was tall and thin, perfectly proportioned, sort of like an aged Barbie Doll. My father is like Ken," she added with a laugh, and twinkled eyes. "I'm lucky to have inherited that. But anybody can lose that [genetic edge] if they just sit back and watch television."

That last statement seems ironic, considering that her success and fortune came from people "sitting back watching television." And during this era before commercial video release of TV shows, those broadcasts were the only way she could be seen in the first place.

As with any of her new endeavors, Mary hit the ground – and the press – running, appearing on TV talk shows like *Late Night with Conan O'Brien*, *Larry King Live*, and *Sally Jessy Raphael*. On *Raphael* she addressed her life and career and took questions from the audience. Ed Asner, Carl Reiner, and Larry Mathews were seen in taped messages, while Gavin MacLeod surprised her in the studio.

When Raphael asked MacLeod to name his favorite episode of *Mary Tyler Moore*, he mentioned "Murray in Love" (October 4, 1975), in which Murray on his 40th birthday wakes up feeling in love with Mary Richards. "It was a very emotional week for me," MacLeod told Mary, Sally, and the audience, "…because you'd have to be deaf, dumb and blind not to be in love with Mary Tyler Moore. So, I was feeling a lot during the filming of that episode."

On October 29 of that year, Mary joined other leading laugh-makers when she was honored at The Second Annual Comedy Hall of Fame Television Show. Clips from almost all of her films were screened, as were classic scenes from her long-running sitcom. She was introduced by Dick Van Dyke, who described her as "bright, charming, uplifting, generous and nice?...Never...She's the nicest." In accepting the award, Mary said, "I've been blessed with an abundance of creative individuals around me." She mentioned Carl Reiner, Allan Burns and Jim Brooks, and Grant Tinker, whom she thanked "for giving up a career as a tennis bum" to navigate her professional decisions through "the shark-infested waters" of the entertainment industry. She joked to her colleagues, the studio audience, the viewers at home, and anyone watching around the world: "More often than not, you've given me the finger of approval – I mean the thumb pointed in an upward direction."

Then, in November 1994, during Mary's appearance on *Conan O'Brien* in November 1994, Ed Asner made some of his own feelings clear. In a taped segment, the actor confessed to being in love with her and still was. Although Mary Richards and Asner's Lou Grant did briefly get romantic in "Lou Dates Mary," a seventh-season episode of *The Mary Tyler Moore Show* (March 12, 1977), after seeing the clip from Asner on *O'Brien*, Mary laughed and said "There was no dating" between the two, "...but we did go out after lunch and get an ice cream cone at Baskin-Robbins very often." She then closed the segment by sharing an off-color joke about her neighbor catching her 11-year-old daughter with her hand in a young boy's lap.

But according to an article in *Vanity Fair*, Mary and Asner did date, shortly after she divorced Grant Tinker. "We'll call it a momentary lapse of judgment on her part," Asner had joked. "But I was quite honored." Of the date itself, he said, "We were just too close for comfort so I retreated into my comedic self and let the boys have at her."

The topics were less romantic, although not any less provocative, during Mary's October appearance on *Larry King Live*, as she discussed her book, *After All*, which was almost completed. "It's not a memoir," she said. "I didn't have that kind of life. But what I did have was a lot of long-term associations with some very bright and interesting people. I also wrote about some of the personal experiences I've been through in my life, and my thoughts and reactions." She was proud of the fact that she wrote the book by herself. "I hold that pencil without any help," she said.

In one interview, Mary made it clear that she did not hire a ghostwriter. She maintained that she would not have done the book had she not written it by herself. She had begun the project by composing a few essays that she submitted to her agent, who encouraged her to move forward with a full-length tome. "The hardest part of writing a book was making myself sit down and do it," she said. "But I never came up out of the chair without feeling I had accomplished some wonderful stuff."

Penning *After All* was also cathartic for her. "As I wrote, attitudes I thought I had, feelings I thought I had, no longer existed," she said. "I didn't know I had changed until I was forced to look at myself while I was writing. So it was very enlightening for me."

Besides her round of talk-show guest spots in late 1994, Mary made personal appearances at a few live events during that period. She greeted Bob Newhart at his Friar's Roast in New York City on October 11.

Around this time, Mary spoke with *For Women Only* magazine about her 11-year marriage with Robert Levine. They were compared to *The Odd Couple*: She was neat-minded Felix to his sloppy Oscar. "He leaves a trail from one end of the apartment to the other," she joked. "We're constantly trying to adapt for each other." And Levine was still keeping tabs on her health, while Mary remained as diligent as possible with her vegetarian diet. Once a month, she allowed herself an omelet when her cholesterol level was "well below reasonable."

Her active lifestyle contributed to her health, and she was cheerfully settled by now in her country estate with Levine. The couple took seven-mile walks, rode horses, and worked out in their fully equipped gym. She felt secure in their relationship. "He's very honest about the way I look," she said. "He'll go, 'Are you getting another wrinkle there?' And I'm constantly pointing out the growing bald spot on the back of his head."

Mary was happy if not at peace. "I'm not sure about that," she said, "because as happy as I am, I'm also aware of the temporal aspects of life and how quickly things can change. I'm certainly not sitting back, hugging myself and saying, 'Ah, little Mary, happy at last,' because it may not last," she said. "I've learned to live in the moment."

Chapter

24

In January 1995, Mary was Chairperson for the Juvenile Diabetes Foundation. She was at the center of the annual charity event, the Carousel of Hope Ball in Beverly Hills. The gala was attended by people like the Duchess of York, Jay Leno, Barbra Streisand, Shirley MacLaine, Sylvester Stallone, Joan Collins, and Faye Dunaway. The evening resulted in over one million dollars in donations for the JDF. Mary, adorned in an attractive red gown with a matching sequined jacket, commented, "This is the only purely research-oriented organization working toward a cure for diabetes."

That same month, on a smaller scale, she turned to the animal-rights arena. She joined a line of celebrities who banded together to demand the release of Spike, a 65-year-old, 12 ½-pound Maine lobster in a viewing tank in Malibu, at the famed Gladstone's restaurant on Pacific Coast Highway. In an open letter, Mary wrote that while she did not pretend "to know precisely how Spike feels living in a small tank," she was certain he would prefer his native waters. She then offered $1000 to spring Spike, who had a free plane ticket waiting (his final disposition is unknown).

On February 9, 1995, the Museum of Television and Radio in New York presented the live event titled *A Salute to Mary Tyler Moore*, with Ed Asner, Gavin MacLeod, and Betty White on hand to help Mary celebrate 30-plus years on TV. Several classic clips were screened, and audience members were able to ask questions. Also that month: Mary appeared at another charity activity for diabetes, this time a basketball game sponsored by the JDF. She brought her nephew Jason, via her marriage to Robert Levine, and was joined by Spike Lee and other celebrities.

Sometime after that, Mary and Levine attended the annual Westminster Kennel Club Dog Show in Manhattan, accompanied by Dash, their golden retriever, and Dudley, their French hound. She had appeared at the previous year's event, and exclaimed, "There's only one other person I know who's happier to be around dogs than I, and that's Betty White and she made me the way I am!"

In her book, *Betty White's Pet Love*, first published in 1983, White writes, "I don't see much of Mary Tyler Levine these days. I remember sitting with her in the hospital when my husband was dying and Mary said to me, 'Where did it all go wrong for us?'"

In 1995, everything seemed to be going right for both women. After attending that year's edition of the Westminster affair, Mary reunited with the multi-talented Dudley Moore, her co-star from *Six Weeks*, for a celebrity function in New York City. The multi-talented actor/comedian/musician had just released his album, *Songs Without Words*, just as Mary began to develop a one-woman show in which she was to have played Eleanor Roosevelt.

In March 1995, Mary was interviewed for cover stories for *Ladies' Home Journal Beauty* and *A&E Monthly*, and attended the annual Women in Film luncheon in New York City (also attended by Brenda Vaccaro, Angela Lansbury, Carol Burnett, and Susan Sarandon, among others). That same month, she and Levine attended an AMFAR benefit in New York to raise money for AIDS research, and participated in "Walk for the Cure," an annual event hosted by the JDF. It garnered over $50,000 for diabetes research. At a fundraising ball related to the latter event, Mary gave a speech about the progress of the research.

By late spring of 1995, she completed and submitted her manuscript for *After All* to Putnam Publishing, which released the book the following Christmas. In between that time, three new books with several references to Mary were published: *Tinker in Television*, an autobiography by Grant Tinker; *Saturday Night Live: The First 20 Years* by Michael Cader; and Vince Waldron's *The Official Dick Van Dyke Show Book*.

In *Tinker in Television*, her second husband narrated how loving and attentive a mother Mary was to her son Richie (with Richard Meeker). Tinker also cited examples of her innate business instincts regarding the television industry.

The *Saturday Night Live* tome presented an illustrated history of that groundbreaking show on which Mary made a few appearances. The book included a lengthy quote from *SNL* regular Mary Gross naming Mary Richards as her favorite impersonation (opposite Julia Louis-Dreyfus as

Rhoda). Gross also addressed the squabble surrounding a skit in which she was asked to play Mary Tyler Moore giving a speech about her marriage to the younger Robert Levine: "I was not at all comfortable with this piece. I thought it was unkind, and I didn't see any reason to satirize her marriage to a younger person. I thought, if she's found happiness, why should we make fun of it? Men do it all the time…I was told that we really needed this piece…for technical purposes…So we did do it." Gross later learned that Mary had seen the segment, was upset about it, and took up the issue with Tinker, who at that time was head of entertainment at the network. To Mary's chagrin, Tinker allowed the piece to air. This was a contrast to his behavior years before, when he prevented Mary's interview with Rona Barrett from being screened shortly after Richie Meeker's death following the release of *Ordinary People*.

Nora Dunn, another former *SNL* regular, had a completely different experience with Mary. Of all those who guest-hosted the show, her favorite was Mary, who had played the third Sweeney sister in the fictional musical/eccentric sibling skit Dunn had regularly performed with Jan Hooks. For Dunn, rehearsing that number with Mary and musical director Marc Shaiman was "the most fun I ever had on the show. I can't ever remember having a better time." And when *The Sweeney Sisters* opened the Emmys telecast in 1988, Nunn got to sing to Mary. But it wasn't just any ordinary song that she sang: Dunn performed "Love Is All Around," the theme to *The Mary Tyler Moore Show* that was composed by Sonny Curtis. Curtis, a former member of Buddy Holly & the Crickets, was also responsible for classic rock tunes like "I Fought the Law." When Dunn sang "Love Is All Around," cameras caught Mary as she giggled in the audience.

Waldron's book, meanwhile, perfectly captured the essence of *The Dick Van Dyke Show*, and Mary's participation in that series, with many revealing comments.

In 1995, thirty years after the airing of *Van Dyke's* final original season, Mary continued to make TV movies like *Stolen Memories: Secrets from the Rose Garden* for the Family Channel. Nick at Nite readied to screen MTM Enterprises' litany of shows including *Rhoda*, *Phyllis*, *Lou Grant*, *The Betty White Show*, and *WKRP in Cincinnati*. MTM Classic Video released all seven seasons of *The Mary Tyler Moore Show* on videocassette.

On May 16, clips of the *MTM Show* were included on Brett Butler's ABC special *TV Laughs at Life*, an hour-long program that chronicled sitcoms' takes on weddings, births, and other milestones of life. Also included were clips from *I Love Lucy*, *Roseanne*, *All in the Family*, *Cheers*, *Home Improvement*, and *The Golden Girls*.

Three days later, Mary hosted CBS's *Ed Sullivan's All-Star Comedy Special*, a slick retrospective that included clips of high-end celebrities and stars in the making, including Joan Rivers, Carol Burnett, Jackie Mason, George Carlin, and Phyllis Diller.

In the fall of 1995, Mary, with a new face and a short, bright-red haircut, starred in an all-new darker scripted series called *New York News*, which was loosely based on a 1994 feature film. *The Paper* starred Glenn Close and Michael Keaton (a former regular on both of Mary's failed variety TV shows). That title was almost utilized for the series, which filmed in Manhattan, near where Mary lived. Here, she portrayed the fiery-red-haired, high-strung tabloid-like newspaper Editor-in-Chief Louise "The Dragon" Felcott, presented as a kind of combination of Mary Richards and Lou Grant.

News, which *Entertainment Weekly* called "gritty," co-starred Gregory Harrison (*Trapper John, M.D.*, CBS, 1979-1986) as an ace reporter, along with Madeline (*Blazing Saddles*) Kahn (who succumbed to cancer four years later at 57) as the paper's high-maintenance gossip columnist. Mary's first major scene as Felcott takes place in a dismal bathroom, where viewers catch a glimpse of her feet peeking out from underneath a stall door. As the show's executive producer Ian Sander once assessed, it was a startling image to viewers expecting a Mary Richards-like character from Mary. "But very quickly we come to realize that she is Louise Felcott. There is that cooler, colder side of her that she's willing to explore."

Mary reveled in playing a darker version of herself. "I never thought I'd say this," she said about playing Felcott, "…But it's so *easy*. I get to go in two, three times a week and drop these great lines of dialogue and then go home."

She was granted that luxury due to the expansive size of the cast. As was becoming standard procedure for TV shows at the time, a one-hour drama like *News* featured a large ensemble of actors. Mary is even billed last in the opening credits as: "with Mary Tyler Moore," and not "starring." But the reviews were not kind. In November 1995, one *Chicago Tribune* TV columnist suggested reruns of the original *Mary Tyler Moore Show* instead of viewing the *News*, which the critic called a "less good" television series.

Jeff Jarvis, of *TV Guide*, did not fault Mary; in fact, he wanted to see more of her. "The show's biggest mistake is not making more of the new Mary Tyler Moore," he wrote. He also did not blame Mary for eventually wanting to leave the show. "In her too-few scenes," Jarvis wrote, "the new, harder Mary is fun to watch, accompanied by *uh-oh* music," and Felcott's "ass saving this sinking ship from the sandy bottom" dialogue. "And it's about time somebody let Mary talk like a grown-up. But sadly, Mary just stomps around acting tough; she's not part of the big stories. A real New York tab would know how to treat a real star like her. *New York News* doesn't."

Unruffled by such decidedly *mixed* reviews, Mary was dedicated to promoting the *News*, which she did with a September appearance on CBS's *Late Night with David Letterman*, who had been a regular on the short-lived 1978 *Mary* variety series. When she walked on stage, Letterman said she looked like a million bucks, to which Mary replied, "David, you say that to all your guests!" "I do not," he returned. At which point, she rolled a series of clips displaying Letterman saying that to at least three other guests and a dog.

While she had once worried that her *Mary* sitcom was too snippy for her taste (and asked CBS to put it out of its misery), there were no such concerns or requests about *New York News*. She took things one step further and told Letterman's audience that she planned to frequently say "ass" on *New York News*, after which she delivered a few F-bombs for a bewildered Letterman and viewers everywhere. "I know that David has this woman-on-a-pedestal image of me," she joked to *Entertainment Weekly* afterwards, "...so it's fun to put him on the spot. He reminds me of my father."

George Tyler Moore most likely did not approve of his daughter's fresh mouth, or her rebooted face. Not only had Mary changed her hair color and style for her new show, but as she continued to tell *Entertainment Weekly*, "I lost the baby fat, and with the help of a cosmetic surgeon, I've pulled up some of the slack. I like to think of [the surgery] as staying fit. And if it can keep my face up where it belongs, then I will go to a doctor and get his assistance."

But that wasn't baby fat on her sixty-year-old face; it was her own genetic design. Altering her natural looks certainly didn't help *New York News*, which became an increasingly uncomfortable experience. As she told the *New York Times*, "I'm very frustrated with the lack of development of my character. I wanted [her] to be doing something other than being tough, and hard-edged and mean."

Claiming the show's production team had ignored her suggestions, Mary aired her grievances to the press, which infuriated Ian Sander, the producer. "I feel like the little kid in the class who stands up and screams, 'I gotta pee!' and everyone looks at her, not realizing that she's had her hand up for a *long time*!"

Mary's creative frustration may have been tied to insecurities about her appearance. She simply did not look the same anymore. To her credit, she admitted as much in *After All*, published in tandem with the debut of *News*. She ultimately regretted her first major facelift and subsequent surgeries, but could not resist trying to fix things. Her discomfort with the *News* role may have had more to do with a lack of self-esteem off-screen. Somehow, Mary did not understand that she was so beloved by her fans that any appearance of natural aging would not put them off. They simply enjoyed her work, which she continued to promote around the clock and around the dial, specifically in two new television appearances

First, Mary was profiled and interviewed on the set of *New York News* for *E!'s Look at Hollywood's Most Powerful Women*, which aired in October, hosted by actress Sela Ward (of NBC's *Sisters* drama). The special also chronicled Sharon Stone, Roseanne, and Oprah Winfrey, who had long admired Mary.

Secondly, on December 6, 1995, Mary served as host for TV's *17th Annual Cable Ace Awards*. Stargazer Michael Stern was there for this show's rehearsal, and was jolted by the way Mary looked. "She was backstage," he recalled. "I was like, "Oh – Bonnie Franklin is here?" But it wasn't Franklin, the strawberry-blonde star of *One Day at a Time*, another legendary CBS sitcom. It was Mary, who Stern observed with her new short, red hair, and freckles that were usually camouflaged by Hollywood make-up.

Although Stern caught a glimpse of Mary during the show's rehearsal, he said, "She did not look like Mary Tyler Moore until the actual taping of the awards show."

If Mary ever "not looked like" Mary Tyler Moore, it was for a provocative "TV Hall of Fame" photo layout in *Vanity Fair* for the magazine's December 1995 issue in which she posed with Dick Van Dyke. In yet another shocking display of yes, "spunk," she and Van Dyke were outfitted in black leather S&M wardrobe for the shoot. Wearing a laced-up corset-vest, Van Dyke glances bemusedly over his shoulder towards Mary, who's straddling him brandishing a riding crop.

But Mary had no idea going in that such subversion of their images were intended. As she explained that month on *The Tonight Show with Jay Leno*, the image was captured by renowned photographer Annie Liebowitz, whom both she and Van Dyke trusted implicitly. "Hi Dick...Hi Mary," Liebowitz apparently told them. "The costumes are over there."

"We didn't even think about the implications," Mary relayed to Leno.

She told *Newsweek*, "It was really hard work getting into that rubber suit...a lot of pulling and stretching and sticking to the rubber, and use of baby powder. It's not as much fun as it looks." When asked if this was the path that Rob and Laura's marriage might have taken in the then-1990s, Mary replied, "I rather doubt it. I think it would have been a much more circumspect, New Rochelle kind of thing."

Another of Mary's photo layouts was published in the December 23rd issue of *TV Guide*, and was much less erotic and revealing. The cover story theme was the varied hair styles of television stars. In a section titled, "Mare's Hair," the actress addressed the gamut of her different tresses over the years:

As Laura on *The Dick Van Dyke Show*: "It was so hard to achieve that flip…We had to back-comb it and use so much hair spray that you could have hung clothes on it. It was part of my womanly duty to submit to all the indignity and suffering to become beautiful."

Her major *Mary Tyler Moore Show* misstep: "That long fall I wore the first year!"

The spiky, ginger-toned look that she sported on the *New York News*: "Back in the days when I was more self-conscious I never cut my hair because I'd be afraid that somebody would get upset. Now that I've matured and live my life more for myself, I love experimenting. I like my red hair; I look like a little clown."

She wasn't the only one to feel that way. Joan Rivers appeared on the Howard Stern radio show and said that Mary looked like "the Joker" from the *Batman* franchise. Deeply hurt by the remark, Mary allegedly stopped speaking to Rivers, with whom she was once good friends. But she continued making other promotional appearances, one of which took place December 1, 1995 on *The Tonight Show with Jay Leno*, when she was confronted with yet another reference to a villain from the *Batman* universe. Referring to her skin-tight polka-dot leotard, Leno remarked how similar he thought she looked to the Riddler.

Batman comparisons aside, Mary's expanded exposure in the press did little to save *New York News*, which she eventually quit. But she had abandoned a drowning ship. After one season, the *News* sank into the realm of low ratings. It was cancelled mostly because it was compounded with a tough time slot: 9:00 Thursday night opposite NBC's super *Seinfeld*, still going strong in its sixth of nine seasons. "It's a joke," Mary had at first quipped before she jumped ship, "…because *Seinfeld* is the best show on TV. But hopefully, it will be a good enough show that the network will move us and back us up."

Mary was one of *Seinfeld's* biggest fans, and after its star decided to end the show in 1998, she was one of those first in line to see him perform his stand-up act on Broadway. While his TV show was still on the air, Mary watched it religiously, a mortal sin during her days on *New York*

News. And while her series never switched time slots, Mary continued to keep busy with more promotional TV appearances for *After All*.

In chatting with talk-show host Larry King, she described how writing the book became a cathartic, if sometimes challenging process that contributed to her self-worth. These concerns had plagued her repeatedly, since her childhood performances in her family's living room. Insecurities, she told King, are what drive those in the entertainment field. Even authors are part of "show business."

For her, composing *After All* "…was on a couple of occasions, quite painful," an experience that once brought tears to her eyes while on a plane trip. She recalled, "I had to keep my face toward the window for some minutes." But mostly it was just a "fascinating process," which she likened to sessions with a therapist. "You bring up feelings that you think you know, feelings that I thought I retained from childhood that have long since changed and evolved into and become something else. I learned that I have forgiven myself for a lot of failings I have and I've forgiven those who I blamed for those failings and [there was] a lot of evolution and healing."

She was surprised at the book's bestseller success. "I never expect anything I do to turn out well." With a morbid reference, she added, "If I had murdered someone, I probably would not have written the book. If I had been deliberately deceptive or unkind I probably wouldn't have written it." In writing and sharing her story, Mary tried to be as honest as she could. She gave just as much of herself to that book as to any endeavor; creative or otherwise. Her sturdy stock, with a strict and unyielding heritage, was in check.

"A good portion of what we are is genetic," she told King. "I really do believe that we are not born into this world [with] clean slates, upon which our parents write. I think we are predisposed as I was born predisposed to diabetes. I might not have developed it and [been] presented with it but I did and the same is probably true of my addiction to alcohol. Maybe the circumstances are what tipped me over the edge." She once more noted pride in her solo production of the book. There was not a co-writer or an "as told to" assistant, she said. "This was me," she said, "deciding what aspects of my life were going to be in there and how I used my stories to help the reader define 'me.'"

When King wondered if she had left out anything too embarrassing or painful to share Mary at first replied with a smile. "Oh, sure," she said, "…lots of stuff." But then she backtracked. "No. I didn't leave out anything," she assured him, beyond what the traditional editing process required. She listened to her editor, Laura Yorke with Putnam Publishing. Mary always trusted those friends, colleagues, and professionals in her inner circle. She likened the editing of *After All* to when Carl Reiner supervised the *Van Dyke* series or when Jim Brooks and Allen Burns did the same for the *Mary Tyler Moore Show*. "They were always so responsive and so secure about themselves. And I learned that lesson from them." So, when the time arrived for working with Yorke on *After All*, she was "willing and very familiar with the process."

Mary made more promotional appearances for her book, including a spot on NBC's *The Today Show*. Bryant Gumbel asked about her son, her divorces, and alcoholism. When the segment was over, she said, "I feel much better now."

That may have been an offhand comparison of the interview with therapy, but her life was indeed under constant examination. She was not "just any" celebrity; the public expected her to be as open, cheerful, and guileless as the roles which built her stardom. She had learned the appearance of standing firm, even if in reality she may have been wobbling from an assortment of heartaches. We knew as much about Mary as she would allow or wanted us to know. When a situation became too difficult, she would periodically shut down or walk away. It seems a curious mix of self-hatred and self-love. It may have been the lingering residue of childhood sexual abuse.

On *Live with Regis and Kathie Lee*, she talked about her molestation by a family friend when she six, which she had addressed in one of the most personal sections of *After All*. Mary wrote about the way her mother reacted to the incident. Marjorie Moore told her the abuse never took place. Both of Mary's parents were prone to deny what they didn't like, a reflection of early twentieth-century pressure to conform, perhaps. Marjorie Moore was unable to confront her own alcoholism in particular. So, why wouldn't she ignore other traumas? That kind of denial, as far as Mary was concerned, was more abusive from a psychological standpoint than the sexual assault she fell victim to.

But Mary didn't want *After All* to be classified as a depressing memoir. There were many uplifting and wonderful moments in her life and career that she wanted to share.

On December 13, CBS aired *People Yearbook '95*, an hour-long TV special that featured a segment on Mary and the book, excerpts of which first appeared in the October issue of *People*. She was shown at her home in upstate New York with her dogs and horses. Host Paula Zahn, like Oprah Winfrey and others, told her how Mary Richards had inspired her to follow a career in television journalism.

Jane Pauley, whose parents' first names were Mary and Dick (nod of irony to Moore and Van Dyke), once said her successful career was a direct result of Mary Richards. The ratings success of the original *Mary*

Tyler Moore Show during its first run on CBS Saturday nights in the 1970s increased Pauley's visibility on the CBS affiliate in Indianapolis where she anchored the 11:00 News. She was then offered a position to anchor *The Today Show* on NBC. In 2018, Pauley was profiled in the *Los Angeles Times*, which pointed out how she had in turn influenced millions of women who saw themselves in her – especially once she married *Doonesbury* cartoonist Garry Trudeau, started a family, and cycled through a series of unfortunate hairstyles in the 1980s. Her pregnancies in 1983 and 1986 helped to boost *Today*'s ratings and removed the puritanical stigma surrounding expectant moms on TV.

But it wasn't only female journalists who were inspired by Mary or Mary Richards.

Singer Joan Jett once acknowledged her admiration for Mary and her famed sitcom. "The show was important because Mary was living her life as a strong, single woman," said Jett, whose rock version of "Love Is All Around" was utilized on the *Mary and Rhoda* TV-movie reunion in 2000. Jett had begun performing her rendition of the theme in concerts because she "figured there were probably a lot of fans who grew up watching the show." In 1996, ESPN had asked Jett to record the song to promote women's college basketball. The song had also appeared in the album, *Fit to be Tied – Great Hits by Joan Jett & the Blackhearts*.

Actress-comedienne Carol Burnett once told Nora Ephron, "If there is an after-life, I want to come back and be Mary. I think she's just wonderful."

Comedienne Sandra Bernhard had described herself as "a Mary Tyler Moore freak!" She recalled, "When they use to run her shows at 3:00 in the morning in New York, I would wake up just to sing the theme song."

Echoing Milton Berle's previously stated sentiment on Mary, fellow comedienne Paula Poundstone at one point suggested, "If everyone watched at least one episode of *The Mary Tyler Moore Show* every day, the world would be a better place."

Comedienne-turned-talk-show host Rosie O'Donnell claimed the MTM sitcom had a "big influence" on her life and profession. "It really helped me understand what I wanted to do in my career," she said.

Years before becoming Regis Philbin's co-host, Kathie Lee Gifford began her career as an actress in a pilot produced by MTM Enterprises which featured non-stop musical numbers. After the taping completed, Lee was touched when Mary approached the cast and said that, even though she was unsure if this new show was going to air (it did not), she thought they were all "great." "That really encouraged…and inspired me to go on," said Lee.

Another Lee, actress Lee Grant, starred in the short-lived sitcom *Fay* (NBC, 1975-1976) which, like the short-lived sitcom, *Diana* (NBC, 1973-1974), starring Diana Rigg of *The Avengers*, was heavily influenced by *The Mary Tyler Moore Show*. Although *Fay* starred Grant as a divorcée with a daughter (played by a young Helen Hunt, who later found stardom via TV's *Mad About You*), the show borrowed significantly from the *MTMS*, right down to the set. "Mary really changed the way women are portrayed on television," said Grant, who called her predecessor "television's first trailblazer."

Other thespians like Polly Bergen also thought highly of Mary. "I admire Mary because she is a severe diabetic," Bergen said, "...yet she has accomplished so much."

Dana Hill, the young actress best known for her role as Audrey Griswold in the 1985 movie *National Lampoon's European Vacation*, was a big fan of Mary's. Hill, who died in 1996 at age 34 after a long battle with diabetes, had starred in the short-lived CBS sitcom *The Two of Us* with Peter Cook and Mimi Kennedy.

Mary had personally befriended the animal-loving actress Tippi Hedren, best known for her performance in the 1963 Alfred Hitchcock film, *The Birds*. Hedren resided in a cottage on the grounds of the Shambala Preserve near Acton, California, a nonprofit center for big-cat care. She was surrounded by lions, tigers, leopards, cougars, and elephants. Each animal had been confined to cages, and were set free to roam in Hedren's African-type setting. When Mary went to visit Hedren at the preserve in 1997, she had the chance to feed one of the elephants an entire watermelon. Hedren, then 69, was also the driving force behind a bill to amend the Animal Welfare Act, which addresses the killing of exotic animals.

Meanwhile Mary found herself sometimes mistaken for other famous women, including Carol Burnett, Marlo Thomas, and Michele Lee.

Ironically, both Mary and this other Lee had received critical acclaim for portraying mentally challenged women in made-for-cable movies. Mary had starred in the 1996 Family Channel's *Stolen Memories: Secrets from the Rose Garden*, and Lee had starred in and produced the 1997 Lifetime movie, *Color Me Perfect*, in which she played a mentally challenged woman whose IQ was restored through a miraculous brain treatment.

In 1969, Lee starred with Van Dyke in the feature film, *The Comic*.

And while Mary had once auditioned to play the TV daughter of Danny Thomas, real-life father to Marlo, she was often mistaken for Burnett, including one day when she went shopping for shoes in Manhattan. When the shoe she desired was unavailable, the store's salesman, who had been fawning over Mary, placed a special order so as not to upset her. Two weeks later, the shoes arrived with a note attached, starting with "Dear Miss Burnett..."

On December 17, 1995, Mary's life and career up until that point was the subject of A&E's *Biography* series which utilized clips, photos, and interviews with Mary, Ed Asner, Carl Reiner, Betty White, Grant Tinker, and Dick Van Dyke. And while *New York News* may have by now joined Mary's lengthy line of failed weekly TV shows, her "Mary Richards" role topped the list of "All-Time Favorite TV Characters" in polls conducted by *Biography*, *TV Guide*, and *Entertainment Weekly* magazines.

Other cast members of the *Mary Tyler Moore* and *Dick Van Dyke* shows remained at the top of their game. Van Dyke's *Diagnosis: Murder* medical-crime-drama was enjoying a new life on CBS; Ann Morgan Guilbert had a semi-regular role on *The Nanny*, and in movies like *Grumpier Old Men*; and Morey Amsterdam and Rose Marie guest-starred on the NBC sitcom *Caroline in the City* for an episode that aired February 1, 1996.

In "Caroline and the Watch," Amsterdam and Marie played married writers who sell an antique desk to cartoonist Caroline, played by Lea Thompson, Mary's co-star from 1994's *Stolen Babies* Lifetime TV-movie, and her colorist Richard (Malcom Gets).

Many in the press, at home, and within the industry had referred to the *Caroline* sitcom as *The Mary Tyler Moore Show* of the '90s. Comments like this were also made about *Suddenly Susan* starring Brooke Shields, and even Téa Leoni's show *The Naked Truth*, in which Mary guest-starred. Before these comparisons were made, Lauren Tewes, in her likable supporting performance as cruise director Julie McCoy to Gavin MacLeod's Captain Stubing on *The Love Boat*, had been called "the next Mary Tyler Moore." Back in the mid-'80s, even NBC's short-lived *Family Ties* spin-off, *Sara*, starring a pre-movie-star Geena Davis, was compared to the *MTMS*. "[But] we've been desperately trying not to do that show," said *Sara* executive producer Gary David Goldberg.

"Who knows how these trends happen?" observed Fox Group president John Matoian in 1996. "It does seem to come in groups on all networks." And sometimes those trends are not so subtle.

On NBC's *Suddenly Susan*, Shields played a newly single literary agent. In one scene from the pilot, Susan watches *The Mary Tyler Moore Show*, and tosses her remote in the air – only to have it fall and hit her on the head. "Susan and Mary both have strength and a slightly endearing awkwardness," said Shields.

Around the same time, ABC aired two Mary-like shows. *Life's Work* starred stand-up comedienne Lisa Ann Walter as an assistant state's attorney attempting to balance love and work. In *Townies*, Molly Ringwald played a small-town New England girl. "There are similarities between my character and Mary," Ringwald acknowledged. "I'm the glue that keeps everyone else together."

Meanwhile, Fox TV was considering a series starring then-recent *NYPD Blue* veteran Gail O'Grady, who played a marketing executive with a hectic romantic and professional life.

No doubt about it: The networks seemed to want another Mary, even as Mary wanted another Mary. The sole exception was ABC's *Roseanne*. This blue-collar sitcom with the sometimes blue language had managed to break the popularity rules of every generation as the first sitcom with female lead that fared well in the 1990s since the demise of *The Mary Tyler Moore Show*. It was resurrected more than twenty years later with remarkable success, until Barr's loose lips (and racist Tweets) sank her own ship.

Today the reigning queen of daytime TV talk shows, Ellen DeGeneres did not fare so well in 1990s sitcom land with *Ellen*. Though once considered the female answer to *Seinfeld*, it was never a super-hit. The closing years of CBS's *Murphy Brown* which, like *Roseanne*, was rebooted decades later, had never attained the popularity of its earliest seasons. And as hard as NBC's *Caroline in the City* tried to be hip and cool, its success was less than lukewarm after leaving the ideal "Must-See" time slot following *Seinfeld* on Thursday nights.

Two years before, then NBC entertainment president Warren Littlefield had an objective: a situation comedy with a female lead. "Step one was *Caroline in the City*," he said. "But that wasn't the be-all and end-all of that goal." At the time, reruns of *The Mary Tyler Moore Show* were airing on Nick at Nite, where it became one of that network's most popular retro shows. Additionally, a female-led series pleased those on Madison Avenue which catered to the core female consumers in the home-viewing audience.

Brooke Shields felt it was "definitely a heavy responsibility" to even be considered the new Mary. "I have big shoes to fill," she said, "literally and figuratively." Comedienne Lisa Ann Walter, of *Life's Work*, however, had an alternative perspective. "My feeling about it is everybody wants to be the new Mary, but the world is made up of Rhodas. I certainly wouldn't mind being America's sweetheart, but I don't think I could ever wear hip huggers the way our Mary did, not on these child-bearing hips."

Each of the series may have had its own charm, but what could live up to the nostalgic gold mined by the members of the WJM news team? As Bob Newhart once said, "*The Mary Tyler Moore Show* was the best-cast show in the history of television." At the end of 1995 and beyond, there was and remained only one Mary Tyler Moore.

Chapter

25

While many actresses might have been content with a TV track record like hers, Mary continued to play un-Mary-like characters. Her most recent was the mentally impaired Jessica from the TV-movie *Stolen Memories: Secrets from the Rose Garden*, which aired on CBS January 7, 1996. Filmed in Wilmington, North Carolina, *Stolen Memories* was produced by Lavin Entertainment Group, headed by actress Linda Lavin, of classic TV's *Alice*. Lavin also starred in the film which was co-produced by Jack Lorenz, the Family Channel, and MTM Entertainment, Mary's new production company (MTM Enterprises had long been disbanded).

Written by Tim Cagney, and directed by Bob Clark (*Porky's*, *A Christmas Story*), *Stolen Memories* shared one word in its the title with Mary's 1993 Lifetime TV film *Stolen Babies*, for which she won that seventh Emmy. CBS inserted the "Stolen" reference hoping to lure viewers for the telemovie, originally called *The Rose Garden* (based on the novella of the same name). Lavin personally phoned Mary and requested her to be in the film. "I think this is one of the best things I've ever done," Mary later told Larry King, but a few critics disagreed.

Variety's Carole Horst said *Memories* was "lushly filmed on location in North Carolina," and that it showcased "formidable" talent from Lavin, Shirley Knight, Paul Winfield, Allison Mack (*Smallville*), and newcomer Nathan Watt. "But its weakest link is the 'child-woman'" played by Mary, "...the most challenging role in the film."

To summarize the plot: It's 1956 and a disgruntled 12-year-old Freddie (Watt) is sent south for the summer to learn of his heritage from three eccentric aunts: Earline (Lavin), Sally Ann (Knight), and the mentally challenged Jessie (Mary). Jessie has a troubled past and a child's mind. Their old house and small town eventually win Freddie over, especially Jessie, with whom he forms a solid bond, and whose flashbacks provide insight into her disabled present, revealing a long-buried truth involving prejudice and murder.

The audiences, Horst suggested, should be leery of any television film with a significant star portraying a mentally challenged adult: "Will the performer be actorly grandstanding, embarrassing both to the viewer and performer? Or will it be credible, convincing and poignant? Moore is none of these, but she turns in her best, and there's too much talent on-screen and off to detract from the overall piece. First-time scripter Tim Cagney does a fine job layering subtext and capturing relationships; his use of locations as symbols – especially the climactic carnival scene – is somewhat obvious but adds texture to the plot. But it's Lavin…and Knight who draw, with conviction and intelligence, the strongest roles. Watt also carries his role with conviction."

"*Memories*," Horst concluded, "…uncovers some awful truths and provides satisfying epiphanies for the characters; it teaches some lovely lessons in a charming way and, as the Family Channel mandates, celebrates the power of family."

Tom Shales of *The Washington Post* had some unflattering words for *Memories*. "Yes, it's happening again: Tireless Mary is stretching. She's proving her versatility. She's doing some Serious Acting. She's barking up the wrong tree. She's embarrassing herself with a bad performance in a rather strange, if fitfully affecting, TV movie…Whether Moore is embarked on a campaign to alter and expand her TV image, or perversely to besmirch it, remains debatable… She seems to be tired of being the Mary Tyler Moore many of us know and love, but we're not tired of knowing and loving her."

The film's script, and Mary's perception of it as "a relationship story," is what attracted her to portraying Jessie. She wanted to appear in the movie because, as she once said, "I like to go to work scared. I don't like to go to work anymore knowing what I'm going to do. I enjoy playing roles that challenge me."

It was a sentiment she shared in one way or the other with additional roles beyond Laura Petrie and Mary Richards. But to prepare for playing Jessie, her husband Robert arranged through a medical associate for Mary to share some time with a woman who was as similarly challenged as Jessie. "I was able to observe her, yet also be reminded by the neurologist that everyone reacts [to a brain disorder] differently," she continued. "So I could pretty much design the character I'm playing, which is essentially a six-year-old child. I get to experiment, within the plot guidelines, with no restrictions, because a six-year-old doesn't set restrictions for herself."

Mary also had some fun while making *Memories*, particularly with good friend Linda Lavin. In 1979, the song-and-dance actress had made a guest appearance on *The Mary Tyler Moore Hour*, one of Mary's short-lived variety shows. But Lavin had not performed with her in a drama before *Memories*. In the scorching heat of Wilmington, the two ladies got along famously with a lot of laughs on the side.

"Mary and I love to shop," recalled Lavin in the *Post*. After completing a hospital scene, she was still in her johnny medical garb, and Mary was outfitted in Jessie's little print dress. They decided to visit a dress shop in Burgaw, a small town near Wilmington that as Lavin described it, "looks like it's locked in the '50s." When they entered the shop, Lavin told the owner, "I hasten to explain to you that I have not just escaped from a hospital! We're making a movie."

The owner nodded in concession, until Mary interjected, "She says that to everybody. And she also tells them she's in the movies."

"So now I really do look like someone who's escaped from an asylum," Lavin laughed, "and Mary was making sure people believed it!"

The same year *Stolen Memories* aired on the small screen, Mary took another step away from her stereotype, this time on the big screen, as Ben Stiller's neurotic adoptive mother Pearl in *Flirting with Disaster*. The movie also starred Téa Leoni, Alan Alda, George Segal, and Lily Tomlin. It was written and directed by David O. Russell, who previously helmed hits like *Spanking the Monkey*, and wrote the Oscar-winning hit *Silver Linings Playbook*, and the Oscar-nominated *American Hustle*.

According to *Mary Magazine* editor David Davis, Russell wanted Mary to star opposite Dick Van Dyke as Stiller's drug-dealing birthparents. Mary read the script, and deemed that scenario amusing, but not enough of a challenge for her acting abilities. "She thought it was too cheap and easy," Davis said. "So, she told the director she would rather play Pearl," a role Russell had envisioned for either Madeline Kahn or Anne Bancroft. But Mary wasn't going for it. "Now, why would you want to do that?" she said. A short time later, Mary showed up at audition in what Davis described as a "cleavage-bearing, slinky, sexy gown," and won over Russell, who subsequently cast Tomlin and Alda as the drug-dealing birthparents instead.

Mary "cranked up" her energy, aggression, and speech pattern, and convinced Russell that she would be Pearl. "It took him three or four weeks to make up his mind," she said. "It reminded me a little bit of the time I went through with Robert Redford when he cast me in *Ordinary People*." While working with Mary, Russell struggled with having stars in his eyes and then awakening the next day and asking himself "What the hell am I doing?"

It was then he invited Mary to his apartment to get busy working on developing her interpretation of Pearl. He was immediately impressed with the research Mary had already completed, as well her disposition. "She was so great with our baby," Russell remembered.

"That part of it never changes," Mary said of the audition process. "The insecurity, hoping and praying, and then you finally get the [role]. You think, now what'll I do? I don't really know what I'm doing here."

Mary, however, had been performing for decades. She was simply relishing the temporary insecurities that any actor or any individual might feel when starting a new job. She just liked "to give audiences surprises."

Exhibit B-Cup: baring her chest in *Disaster*:

For some reason, Mary's Pearl decides to advise her daughter-in-law, played by Roseanne Arquette, about the benefits of a support bra. *Venice Magazine* called the scene "possibly the film's funniest," in which Mary showcases "her comic genius when it comes to timing and sheer physicality." "Of course," the magazine added, "moviegoers shouldn't miss the end credits where, again, Moore displays some never-before-seen, outrageous, almost fiendish talents."

A team player, Mary displayed her support for fellow *Disaster* cast members like Arquette and Leoni. The former registered on film more than Mary ever expected. While making the movie, she saw Arquette creating "a very natural, low key character," and then upon seeing the finished film, Mary viewed "another dimension, another magical thing happening."

Those were important words for Arquette to hear. When she first began working with Mary and the rest of the film's cast, she was somewhat overwhelmed. "It was hard not to be intimidated by them," she said in *Venice*, "...because they were in my house [on TV] all the time growing up."

Mary had deemed Leoni "the next Lucille Ball." Upon hearing that endorsement, the younger actress said: "I have a bit of interest in pratfalls. Mary was very sweet and kind and always laughed. And she has a great, robust laugh. When I first met her I was flustered and nervous. This is a woman I idolized, but she put me at ease immediately. But I never could get used to calling her Mary, or Mare; she's Mary Tyler Moore for God's sake."

Either way, it all came together on screen. The film opened nationwide to mixed reviews and box-office receipts. In effect, the *Disaster* film was anything but. Leoni and Arquette's roles worked, and so did Mary's parts. And Mary was excited about the film. It was her first feature since *Just Between Friends* (1986), and she hit the publicity trail running, as usual.

In a shiny silver warm-up suit, Mary made a glittery appearance on the *Late Show with David Letterman*. She talked about teaching *Disaster* co-star Tomlin how to belch on cue, which the former *Laugh-In*-turned-movie star was apparently having trouble accomplishing. In a perhaps prearranged line of questioning, Letterman asked about that rumored nude scene in *Flirting*. She said the press had blown the whole thing out or proportion; all she did in the movie was simply lift her sweater to reveal her brassiere. But when Letterman asked the audience if they'd like to see Mary nude in *Flirting* or any movie, they responded with thunderous applause.

The topic, so to speak, breasted again a short time later when Mary appeared on Charles Grodin's CNBC prime-time talk show. After showing a clip of what had now become her infamous cleavage scene, Grodin said, "Didn't you lift up your top and show your breasts on Letterman?" To which Mary replied, "No! That was Drew Barrymore; people get us confused all the time."

In April 1996, *Entertainment Weekly* said *Disaster* was "far from uplifting...But it may end up doing wonders for the bra business." Mary told the periodical that the bra she wore in the film "covers more than what I wear to the beach. But that's as close as I'll come to a nude scene."

She continued to address her appearance in general for an interview with *Venice Magazine*, which was also published that month. Upon first watching *Ordinary People*, she thought she "wasn't pretty enough," and that it was easier to "get away with so much more on the small screen...back in the days when it was still important [to] look young." "I was right on the edge there," she said.

In choosing a more liberating view, she then proclaimed, "Hey, look at me. I'm 40 and isn't it wonderful? I look pretty good, don't I – and even better at 50?" And she was anticipating turning 60, which she referred to as an even "more amazing milestone."

On the one hand, Mary was pleasantly surprised at how "pretty" she looked in *Flirting with Disaster*, which she thought was going to be filmed with "soft-edged photography" as "a bonus" to somehow protect or enhance her appearance. On the other hand, her appearance was no longer "important" or "intrinsic" to her self-worth. She was fit, eating healthy, and proud that she had stopped smoking and drinking. "I'm kind of a perfect person," she said.

That last remark was intended as a joke, and she would attempt such humor again, as when reuniting with the *MTM Show* cast for the *Oprah* show in 2008. She wrote about the experience in *Growing Up Again*. "I guess I can live with my perfection," she joked.

In either case, Mary's words were betrayed by her actions. She sounded less self-deprecating than confused. Her smile appeared to mask a measure of pain, while her plastic surgery was like a mask that protected her from displaying true emotions. Instead of adding to her self-esteem, her plastic surgeries seemed to provoke dependence on them. Her penchant for cigarettes and alcohol may have subsided, but she almost seemed addicted to facelifts, as if such procedures somehow shielded her from others and intimacy. Mary, and countless others, in and out of the entertainment industry, seemed to utilize humor as a coping mechanism. In the end, she said divorcing Grant Tinker was the initial impetus for her attaining "a new face."

But did Mary also select that first surgery because she didn't feel "pretty" enough in *Ordinary People*? And what good did that initial procedure do, if afterwards she still had doubts about her appearance in *Flirting with Disaster*? The title of that movie could have easily been a metaphor for her life at the time, while she may have also been flirting with self-deception.

Whatever insecurities she may have fostered, Mary soldiered on, through the good and badlands of Hollywood press and publicity. She was there at the Paris Theatre in Las Vegas for the premiere of *Flirting with Disaster*, which was hosted by Miramax to benefit the Juvenile Diabetes Foundation. For a second consecutive year, *Star Magazine* voted her Best-Dressed Woman on a list that also included Whoopi Goldberg (from ABC's *The View*), Leeza Gibbons (*Entertainment Tonight*), and Loni Anderson (best-known from *WKRP in Cincinnati*, from MTM Enterprises).

Mary also made tabloid and TV news headlines for a less positive development: the shocking admission that she helped her cancer-stricken brother commit suicide, which she had addressed in her book. Every news outlet ran a piece on the revelation, some even including interviews with her. She was not holding back, it seemed, not when it came to having her voice heard or getting her book sold. Always a hard worker, Mary had also learned how cathartic it was to write, share, and then have her life revealed as honestly as possible in *After All*.

More promotion for that book surfaced in February 1996, when Mary guest-starred on two episodes of ABC's *Ellen* sitcom starring Ellen DeGeneres: for a scripted performance in "Lobster Diary," airing February 21, followed one week later by a cameo in the show's opening credits when she teaches Ellen how to toss her hat in the air.

But it's the "Lobster" tale that proved most significant and close to Mary's heart. It was based on a real-life incident – discussed in the previous chapter – when Mary donated money to save a lobster in 1994.

Here, Mary, playing herself, presents Ellen with an award for kidnapping a 65-year-old lobster from a seafood restaurant which was about to raffle it off as dinner for a winning patron. "The issue here is not saving lobsters," Mary told *Ellen* producers before she agreed to appear on the segment. "The real issue is the way in which they're killed. There are scientific studies about their nervous systems, their pain reflex. They mate for life and actually hold each other's claws while mating. To throw any living creature into a pot of boiling water is so inhumane. I gather it's hard to kill a lobster, but I'm sure there are other ways than scalding it, which takes five minutes."

By now, Mary was "incrementally" involved in the way of animal rights and issues after her move to upstate New York. "The more time I spend in the country and being around cows and lambs who are our neighbors, the more I said to myself, 'How is their eye any less complicated than my own?' It got to the point where I could no longer eat meat," she once recalled, "…it just kind of choked going down."

In the spring of 1996, Mary did not skip a beat in lending three of her Arnold Scaasi original dresses for a retrospective of the designer's work held by the New York Historical Society. She had previously donated another Scaasi – a $112,000 sable coat – to animal rights advocates at PETA, the People for the Ethical Treatment of Animals. The group decorated the coat with animal traps, electronic devices, and various other macabre fur-processing paraphernalia, displaying it outside the retrospective's opening-night soiree. But Scaasi was unfazed. As far as he was concerned, animal rights were old news, as irrelevant as platform heels. "Fur is an issue which is no longer in women's minds," he claimed. "PETA people wear leather shoes and eat meat."

Such a statement must have infuriated Mary. She had lent her voice and public persona to PETA to battle against what she and the animal-activist group believed to be many injustices; namely, cruelty to pregnant mares on "urine farms." According to *Mary Magazine*, at the time, PETA claimed more than 80,000 mares were impregnated each year and held nearly motionless for six months in order to collect their urine to make Premarin, an estrogen drug therapy used to alleviate menopause symptoms and help protect against the onset of osteoporosis.

Mary, who had narrated a video for PETA previously, was "appalled" upon learning how Premarin was manufactured. She sought to increase awareness of the availability of plant-based drugs. Wyeth-Ayerst, the Canadian company that had manufactured Premarin for more than five decades, claimed to regularly investigate claims of abuse on these farms. "It is in our best interest for these animals to be treated well," a spokesman had said.

At this time, Mary needed a piece of bone removed from her baby toe. But trouper that she was, it did not prevent her from participating in various activities that spring, while on be-flowered crutches, including an ASPCA event in New York City, or being named "Queen of Brooklyn" at that "Welcome Back to Brooklyn Festival." "I hope to enjoy a fruitful reign as queen," she said, "...though I'd prefer to be a king. That word seems more regal, somehow. I hope I do well by my subjects, if not by making them laugh, at least by making them thrive and prosper." Those celebrity "subjects" attending the ceremony included actors Harvey Keitel and Daniel Benzali, drummer Max Roach, and radio deejay Cousin Brucie Morrow.

Also that spring of 1996, Mary made a personal appearance for a book signing at the Mall of America in Minneapolis, the largest mall in the world, where she celebrated the paperback release of *After All*. The hardcover edition had by then become a *New York Times* bestseller, and was selected as #9 on the list of 10 best titles of the year by *Entertainment Weekly*. The paperback event featured a special "cameo" by a woman from Mary's past named Hazel Frederick. Decades prior, Frederick, now 88 years old, had been shopping in downtown Minneapolis, adorned in a green coat with fur collar and matching scarf, while Mary's camera crew was filming her legendary show's now-famed "hat-tossing" opening credit sequence. "It was her day off and she went down to Dayton's [department store]," Frederick's granddaughter Carol Berg told CBS News in 1996. "She saw the crowd and was curious...walked up and there she was," in the middle of it all.

Frederick was captured on-screen for all time with a quizzical, near-horrified expression. As reported by CBS News, her identity remained a mystery to nearly everyone until another fateful day, nearly thirty years later, when Mary invited her on stage during that book signing and introduced her to 5,000 people as "my co-star." Frederick's photo was on the cover of the local newspaper and, as Mary signed copies of her books, Hazel signed copies of the newspaper.

Frederick never earned a nickel from either "performance," but after the once-anonymous woman died at age 91, her family said the notoriety she attained was priceless. Frederick's grimace years before had a simple explanation. When she saw a stranger run into the street and throw a hat into the air, she was simply concerned for Mary's safety, which only endeared her to the actress. "I just thought she was so funny," Mary later said while shaking her head in bemused disbelief of it all.

The summer of 1996 was joyful for Mary in other ways. She began planning the festivities for the July 20th wedding in her home in Millbrook, New York of her good friend Bernadette Peters. The actress, now 48, was marrying the much younger financial advisor Michael Wittenberg, 34. Although Wittenberg would die tragically in a helicopter crash just a few years later (in 2008), his wedding ceremony with Peters was filled with beauty; attended by 200 guests at the Levines' sprawling 30-acre country estate (which later expanded to 150 acres). The celebration was a cherished memory for Mary and Peters, who was deeply grateful to the Levines for literally and so very generously opening their home.

According to what a wedding guest told *People* magazine, "Mary wanted everything to be perfect." She had a beautiful tree on her property decorated with flowers and tulle. She placed down a lengthy white satin runway from her home to the tree, and ordered arrangements of white, yellow and pink roses that were floated in the pool. "Mary glowed as brightly as the bride," the guest said.

A florist who visited Mary's home noticed how protective she was of her animals on the grounds including a golden retriever, a Petit Basset Griffon Vendéen, and a goat. When the florist exited the premises, Mary said, "Please be careful when you back up. My little friends are all around."

Mary's book signing for *After All* at the Merritt Bookstore in Millbrook also proved how much she was adored by her neighbors. The store's owner said, "Six hundred people showed up. Mary was a real trouper. Her arm really began to ache after a while, but she insisted on signing all the books."

Her arm hurt temporarily, but she was healthier and more vibrant than she had been in years. This was in large part due to her husband's care, including a special "cocktail" of vitamins and nutrients that he had prepared for her. That mix included a then-new super antioxidant called Glutathione Forte, which was created just for diabetics, as well as significant doses of vitamins B and C, plus others. "She's one of the strongest women I've ever known," Robert Levine said of his wife's overall state of well-being.

"I enjoy my life now," Mary added. "It's a good life."

As her good life became a "cocktail" of triumphs and struggles, Mary retained an active lifestyle. Shortly after hosting Peters' wedding, Mary and Levine traveled to France and attended the 49th annual Cannes Film Festival. Upon their return to the States, Mary made a guest appearance on *Larry King Live*, where she discussed her roles as Laura Petrie and Mary Richards, and topics like her unconventional marriage to Levine. That's when things got a little dicey. On King's insistence of potential marital woe due to her age gap with Levine, Mary snapped, "What does it matter?!" Fortunately, the conversation became somewhat less toxic when she began addressing her passion for animals.

The following September, Mary joined Broadway legend Tommy Tune, fashion designer Donna Karan, and other distinguished guests at a Manhattan rooftop party held at multi-talented Joel Grey's apartment. It was all to celebrate the release of Bernadette Peters' new CD, *I'll Be Your Baby Tonight*. With a toast, Mary thanked Peters for her friendship, saying, "She has brought a presence into my life. I'm not a person with a lot of friends, and Bernadette has become one of my best."

One month later, she appeared on *The Rosie O'Donnell Show*, where the hostess, a lifelong devotee of all things classic television, showed Mary her school composition book of that series. O'Donnell had also at some point prepared 200 trivia questions about the adventures of Mary Richards, each neatly typed on three-by-five index cards, during a "Mary Tyler War" between O'Donnell and *MTM Show* trivia expert Davenia McFadden. But it was Mary who challenged Rosie with the query, "What kind of car did Mary Richards get for her graduation?" Rosie guessed the correct color – brown – but was stumped for the make of the car – a Hudson.

A few days after that, Mary met with Becton Dickinson and Co. President Charles F. Baer and Becton Dickinson Diabetes Interdisciplinary Research Program Principle Investigator J. Denis McGarry, Ph. D., professor of internal medicine and biochemistry at the University of Texas Southwestern Medical Center. They reviewed a presentation of genetically engineered cells that can act as surrogates for normal insulin-producing tissue, which is destroyed in diabetic patients.

Ten days following, Mary shared some smiles at the Copacabana with Stewart Lane and Tony Stevens at the Stage Directors and Choreographer's Foundation annual gala.

Come November, another daytime chat show appearance was set on *Live! With Regis & Kathie Lee*, with Barbara Walters subbing for Lee. Mary looked radiant and brought photos of the anniversary gift she received from her husband: two tiger cubs they rented for two hours of play time. When Walters wondered why, Mary replied, "Because he loves wild cats...he's crazy mad for them."

Meanwhile, home viewers continued to be crazy for Mary's classic TV shows. On December 15, Nick at Nite aired its annual Christmas-themed lineup, which included holiday episodes of *The Dick Van Dyke Show* and *The Mary Tyler Moore Show*. Around this time, Mary was honored at the annual "Women in Film" luncheon, along with O'Donnell and multi-award-winning Rita Moreno. That same month, she appeared on *The Tonight Show starring Jay Leno*, where she talked about that now-benchmark book-signing for the paperback edition of *After All* at the Mall of America. She also talked about members of the younger generation who encounter her sitcom for the first time. "They actually recognize me," she said. "I've changed a lot." She then playfully responded openly to Leno's question regarding her plastic surgery. "We don't call it plastic surgery, Jay. We call it cosmetic procedures!"

Unfortunately, there was no such laughter when a few months later she reunited with Ed Asner for the ABC TV-movie drama *Payback*. The movie aired February 10, 1997, but filmed in the fall of 1996 in and around Portland, Oregon. In *Payback*, loosely based on a true story, Mary played Kathryn Stanfill, a working mother who witnesses a brutal incident of police violence. She becomes the target of a rogue cop's vengeance after she reports the crime to Jack Patkanis, an internal affairs investigator portrayed by Asner.

Also appearing in this film was Denis Arndt, who had played Mary's husband in *Annie McGuire*. This time, he's a college professor who is set up by the crooked police officer, accused of sexually molesting one of his students. Beverly Sanders, Mary's good friend, performs as Kathryn's business partner at the restaurant, while, the rogue cop is played by Fredric Lane, who had appeared in *Ordinary People*, if not in any scenes with Mary. Asner's daughter Kate Asner appears as a restaurant employee.

A psychological thriller, *Payback* was a departure for Mary, and she was on her game, even if nearly forfeiting her performance. Asner was thrilled that she agreed to do the movie, and at first praised her performance.

After seeing her performance in *Lincoln*, Asner had sought to develop a dramatic film in which he would star with Mary. That became *Payback*. Even though he and Mary clashed behind the scenes, Asner remained loyal, and never forgot their roots. "Mary's show put me on the map," he said, and he felt fortunate to have spent those seven years with such a "spectacular lady." In an interview with *Entertainment Weekly*, Asner called her "one of the best dramatic actresses around," citing her work in *Lincoln* as well as *Ordinary People*.

But Mary once admitted that, without the proper snacks to keep up her blood-sugar level, "Sometimes I can get cranky."

Apparently, this behavior dated back to her days on *The Mary Tyler Moore Show*. "It wasn't that Mary's wants were met," Asner also told *TV Guide* that same year. "It's that they were anticipated. I mean, writers, Grant [Tinker], they were all right there on the set all the time so any time she had a problem, it was taken care of."

"In a sense," Mary said on the *Payback* set, "we haven't changed. We're still squabbling but we're also very deferential, and because Ed's a damn fine actor I would never argue with him – except when it affects a scene," she added with a laugh.

The situation, minus the comedy, definitely seemed to return while making *Payback*. There was a lot of drama behind the scenes of this dramatic film. Mary frequently questioned lines, and even blocking and lighting styles. Before shooting a diner scene, she held lengthy conferences with Asner and director Ken Cameron. "I think this is going to slow down to a screeching halt," she grumbled. "You've got to get him moving in this scene," she told Cameron in reference to Asner. "And please, could I be photographed on this side?" she asked, motioning her face towards the light. "It's always been that way, if I have a choice."

Mary acknowledged that she was tough. "I do explode sometimes. But I like to think that I do so for a reason."

Her discontent continued. Before the movie's debut, she viewed a rough cut and was displeased with how her Stanfill role was developed in connection with Asner's Patkanis. She wasn't afraid to voice her concerns publicly. In an interview with *The New York Times* on December 7, 1996, Mary said, "I'm very disappointed with what they did to my character. It doesn't use me to the full extent they promised. It does no honor to the past relationship between Ed and I."

Apparently, Mary had agreed to do the movie only if her character was fleshed out, with the rapport between Stanfill and Patkanis emphasized. Her request was similar to other post-Mary Richards roles. "I wanted to play a woman with some bite and some flaws," she said. Several script revisions later, Mary finally agreed to appear in *Payback* as a woman who now possessed "a lot of guilt about her son," she said.

The character's emotional parallels to Mary's son Richie, now gone 17 years at *Payback's* filming, did not go unnoticed, by Mary or anyone else associated with the movie. "I've told my story for years to various analysts," she said with tears in her eyes behind the scenes of *Payback*. "My son, if he had lived, would be a year younger than my husband." And if others were still questioning the age-appropriateness of Mary's relationship with Robert Levine, Mary was not. She continued to affirm her love and dedication to the third marriage in her life. "For the first time, I really believe I have found my life partner," she said, once more crediting Levine with her sobriety and increasing assertiveness. "Robert grew up in a family where emotions were welcomed. I began to see through his eyes aspects of myself that I didn't know were there – this rigidity, this expectation of perfection that I had for myself and others."

But that perfectionism made a temporary return on the *Payback* set. Even after the movie's script was extensively revised and new footage filmed, Mary claimed those alterations were removed by executive producer Kenneth Kaufman. "I made some suggestions as to how it might be changed, but he refused to change anything," she said. "Before we went into production, we talked about preserving the special aura that Ed and I have. But now, I'm just a stereotypical hand-wringing mother."

Kaufman, a TV-movie veteran, was stunned by Mary's criticism and refused to comment; nor did anyone else at the network. It was Asner's production company that first pitched the film and, while making the movie, he enjoyed the process. Later Asner said he was "shocked and saddened" by her remarks. "I hope it's just a momentary feeling that Mary's having," he said. "I hope it's not something she stays with, because she's wrong."

With the passage of time, Asner better understood the bigger picture. "She was suffering the ravages of diabetes," he later said, while the topic of plastic surgery once more came into the forefront. "She didn't like the way she looked and chose to, for want of a better expression, pick on the director and producer," he added. Due to her adversarial position, he described the work environment on *Playback* as "tense…whereas before," on *The Mary Tyler Moore Show*, Mary "had been a total delight" to work with.

Mary's *Payback* discourse in public mimicked the creative displeasure she felt toward the *New York News* series a few years before. Her issues with that TV production may have also been spurred by personal discomfort with her appearance, which had changed drastically from her days on *Mary Tyler Moore* through her work in *Six Weeks*, the last screen appearance that featured the face she was born with.

Some medical studies have suggested that elective plastic surgery is detrimental to those stricken with diabetes. Had Mary been more content with her original features, she may have lived longer than her 80 years. Asner felt that Mary might not have appreciated a longer term on Earth. "I think she was suffering most of the time," he said. "She was never in a lot of pain on the *Mary* show, none that I noticed anyway. But I did see her once have an insulin overload or pain event. I'm not sure which it was. But she became hysterical and fortunately was taken care of."

Asner said Mary was "…not a happy person, due to more than her share of grief from failed marriages, suicides, and having drunks for parents." Still, that faults and frailties do not define or lesson anyone's self worth, but rather "contributes to and shapes who we are."

As 1996 came to a close, Mary and Robert Levine were still dividing their time between their New York apartment and their massive rustic retreat in the Millbrook area of New York. Friends, neighbors, and residents of Millbrook were charmed by how the couple's affection for one another had remained.

Dorothy King lived two houses away from the Levines. As she recalled in a letter to *Mary Magazine*, Mary and her husband spent "many of their weekends [in Millbrook] and I have seen them pass by on their horses. She's always friendly and smiles and waves. Her husband is a doll and they really seem happy."

Another source said the Levines had frequented the Millbrook Café. During these visits, Dr. Levine was always concerned that she ate properly, to not aggravate her diabetes; he always inquired as to how exactly her meals were prepared. Mary loved carrot cake and when she ordered it, Robert would shake his head, and make certain she would not overindulge in the treat.

Millbrook residents said Mary was as nice as her famous TV counterparts. "She doesn't look or [behave] like a star around here," said a resident of the town. "She never wears make-up and she dresses casually. And she's always doing nice things for the community." As an example, Mary used to take ballet lessons at a local dance studio, which she one day noticed was lacking mirrors for the children's class. When she learned that the studio simply could not afford the expense, Mary donated the money. "Little girls need mirrors if they are going to learn ballet," she said.

Mary had also by then become a significant supporter of community events in the town, and was active in their substance abuse programs as well. She was on the board of directors of the Conservation of Human Resources, a local service for alcohol and drug-addicted people and their families. She even did what she could for those who worked for her, including her housekeeper in New York City for whom she hosted a dinner party. She was always concerned for her employees and made certain that they were catering to their health.

This remained true, even when she acknowledged at least periodically sneaking in a few sugary treats, which is never a fully healthy choice for a diabetic. Mary once addressed it with her trademark wit.

The day after her 60th birthday, on December 30, 1996, Mary appeared on *The Late Show with David Letterman*, and told a funny story about hiding M&M's and Good 'n' Plenty candies on a recent airline flight with her husband. As the couple left the plane, Levine turned to her and asked calmly, "Mary, what is that stuck to your pants?" As it turned out, Mary had two Good 'n' Plenty candies "…plastered to my ass!"

That night, Letterman presented her with a cow for her special birthday which marked the six remarkable decades of her life and career. The honors accumulated when, also in 1996, *TV Guide* ranked her #5 of their "50 Greatest TV Stars of All Time" special collector's issue list. The tally included first choice Lucille Ball and others like Carol Burnett, Johnny Carson, James Garner, Jackie Gleason, Dinah Shore, and Roseanne Barr.

Although Ed Asner did not make that list (and should have!), he was busy taping a cameo TV appearance on the season premiere of the *Roseanne* sitcom. A dream sequence featured Barr as Mary Richards and John Goodman as Lou Grant. This all happened the same year that Mary had lent her voice to Buena Vista's animated holiday/family movie *How The Toys Saved Christmas*, in which she played a character named Granny Rose. According to author Marc Shapiro, her participation in this film "would be an ironic twist on Moore's attempt to shake her Mary Richards image that she would do a voiceover in an extremely G-rated feature."

While making *The Mary Tyler Moore Show*, which she once described in *Entertainment Weekly* as "that early stage" of her life, Mary had been "perfectly happy" playing herself. But now, with *How The Toys Saved Christmas* she said, "I've changed so much."

Also around this time, a more tangible change was taking place: Mary had replaced Dyan Cannon as Catherine Wilde, Téa Leoni's mother and George Segal's wife in the first of four episodes of NBC's second season pick-up of ABC's first-year series *The Naked Truth*, produced by A-listers Bernie Brillstein and Brad Grey. The new *Naked* was somewhat of a reunion for Mary, Segal, and Leoni, who starred together in *Flirting with Disaster*.

In the new *Truth*, Leoni, a photographer in the original concept, now portrayed an advice columnist for a tabloid newspaper headed by editor George Wendt (*Cheers*). It's a concept that also harkened back to Mary's CBS days on *New York News*, if only slightly. It received generally positive reviews and a prime spot on Thursday night's "Must-See-TV" schedule after *Seinfeld* and before *ER*.

Whereas *New York News* on CBS also once screened opposite *Seinfeld* on NBC, *The Naked Truth* was now following that sitcom "about nothing." But to tell the *Truth*, the strategic relocation failed to help anything about *Naked*. According to the real *New York Daily News*, *Naked Truth* got demolished in the ratings, and was taken off the market. In the end, Leoni said about the *Truth*: "The first year was fun; the second was trying; and the third was like some horrible ex-boyfriend."

Truth's demise was also a disappointment for Mary because, as she had once observed, the show taped before a live audience like *The Mary*

Tyler Moore Show, and was "an answer to a dream. It was wonderful being with an audience again. This is exactly what I want to do."

Chapter

26

In early 1997, during her return to weekly television with *The Naked Truth*, Mary purchased the historic Conrad Shindler House on German Street in Shepherdstown, West Virginia to serve as the home of the center for the Study of the Civil War. The building was formally presented to the Shepherd College foundation in 1995. The center had been renamed the "George Tyler Moore Center for the Study of the Civil War" in honor of her father. Both she and her dad had always had an abiding interest in the Civil War, and were descendants of Conrad Shindler, a coppersmith and farmer who lived in the house in the early 1880s.

By this time, too, Mary was busy promoting her new, if low-budget, movie *Keys to Tulsa*, which was actually filmed in 1995, and released briefly on the big screen in early 1997 before Polygram distributed it on video. She had a small but key supporting role in *Tulsa* as Cynthia Boudreau, a less-than-sophisticated if wealthy woman from Arkansas who refuses to help her son, played by Eric Stoltz, during several brushes with the law. This movie was the fourth time Mary portrayed a character with a Southern accent, following her performances in Gore Vidal's *Lincoln*, *Stolen Babies*, and *Stolen Memories: Secrets from the Rose Garden*.

When shooting *Stolen Memories* on location in Wilmington, North Carolina, Mary wanted to study the accents of local citizens. "Dialects are gone," she said, "...not only in Wilmington, but everywhere...New York, Texas. Television has done that. We listen to TV and we drop the warm, funny speech patterns that have made us different."

Mary Magazine editor David Davis reviewed Mary's unique performance in *Tulsa*: "She obviously had a great time playing Cynthia

Boudreau…[She] has a very funny scene toward the end of the movie where she is humiliated at her engagement party by her younger son getting drunk and falling into the table, with her following, and Stoltz's date [played by Joanna Going] dancing with her breasts falling out of her low-cut dress. Mary does a dead-on Southern accent and is a strong presence in this otherwise dreary movie. James Coburn [as Harmon Shaw] and James Spader [as Ronnie Stover] round out the cast, but Mary is by far the best thing in this film, which" was, as Mary herself once described as a movie about "sex, drugs and violence and, in the end, there's a tornado."

But that climactic scene "must have ended up on the cutting-room floor," Davis said, because the version he screened, "had no trace of a twister."

During an interview with *Entertainment Tonight* on the *Tulsa* set, Mary complained of a lack of appealing characters to play. "It's not so much that I've been selective," she said. "So I don't do [films] as often as I'd like to." She was still doing "the things that aging actresses are supposed to do," such as gardening, and while she was also "experimenting with life as it was meant to be led."

A symbol of Mary's impact on pop culture was seen in *Romy & Michelle's High School Reunion*, another big-screen release from 1997. Lisa Kudrow and Mira Sorvino provide what Davis called "a wonderfully funny running joke" between the two: Which is the more attractive ("The Mary") and who's the dumpier sidekick ("The Rhoda")?

A similar reference occurs in Janeane Garofalo's movie from that year, *The Matchmaker*, in which Mary is name-checked. Garofalo plays a political aide on assignment in Ireland during a matchmaking festival. In one scene, a man tells her, "You're so Mary Tyler Moore." To which she responds, "Yeah. I'm so Mary Tyler Moore."

Also in 1997, Mary Richards was satirized on *Mad TV*, Fox's popular late-night sketch-comedy series. In the skit, which was praised by *TV Guide*, Mary Richards admits to her WJM-TV newsroom cohorts that she is a lesbian, and that her lover is a tie-dyed and caftan-wrapped Rhoda. Both the writers and the actors provide wicked fun – especially Mary Scheer as Mary.

Added to this late-night mix was *Saturday Night Live* regular Victoria Jackson's performance in a Care-Free gum commercial which paid homage to the opening credit sequence of *The Mary Tyler Moore Show*. While adorned in a long, dark wig, Jackson closes the commercial by tossing a stick of gum in the air, mimicking Mary Richards' famed hat toss.

In February of 1997, however, Mary had to throw in the towel as host for the Directors Guild of America Awards (DGA) in New York. She was unable to fulfill her duties because of temporarily blurred vision, a complication of diabetes. But Mary made it clear to the press that she was not losing her sight. Such reports, she said, had been haunting her for months. She noted, "Even my father phoned me and said, 'I know you play brave and don't tell me things, but are you blind?'" The rumor started when she developed "a bleed," a condition common for diabetics called "Diabetic retinopathy," that occurs when blood vessels nourishing the retina weaken, and blood leaking into the eye from the weakened capillaries dims a person's vision. "It either rectifies itself or can be corrected with laser treatments," Mary said.

Observed one representative of the DGA: "Only blindness would keep Mary Tyler Moore from us tonight." Consequently, *CBS This Morning* co-anchor Paula Zahn, who also happened to be Mary's neighbor, subbed as host that night. A few days later, Mary's health issue was resolved, and she was back at the top of her game – in more ways than one.

Around this time, Mary had apparently had grown one half of an inch. "I'm getting taller," she said. "What I don't understand is that almost all my life I measured 5' 7 ¼", and now I measure 5' 7 ¾.'" But she was not adding density to her frame. "I still weigh a trim 122 pounds," she maintained.

In March 1997, Mary scheduled an appearance on *The Tonight Show with Jay Leno*, looking healthy, once more putting to rest rumors that she had gone blind. She also discussed her passion for animal causes, which Leno teased her about. Mary said she wouldn't even swat a mosquito, and instead would blow them off her arm. But when Leno wondered what she would do if she had ants crawling everywhere in her kitchen, she said, "I'll call the maid."

In April 1997, Mary made a surprise visit on *The Oprah Winfrey Show*, whose host was overwhelmed, visibly moved and in shock. Upon seeing her idol, Oprah screamed, "Oh my God!" It was a reaction rarely seen from the usually collected talk-show queen. Mary's entrance was part of a special event that was organized by Winfrey's staff during a tribute to her favorite celebrity women. Gushing tears and sweating up a storm from the excitement, Winfrey told Mary: "You have no idea what you mean to me. You were my inspiration!"

"Oh," Mary said with a smile, "...I think I do."

Winfrey added, "There were those of us who only had the television for our inspiration and you were one of those women who was a light. I wanted to work in Minneapolis with you!" But Mary said that she was the one in awe of Winfrey, specifically due to the talk-show queen's charitable work for illiteracy. She went on to talk about possibly traveling to Chicago to participate in Winfrey's "Unique Lives and Experiences" seminars. She also talked about how much she enjoyed working on *The Naked Truth*.

This very special episode of *The Oprah Winfrey Show* had also included Winfrey's perfectly mimicked rendition of the opening credits sequence to *The Mary Tyler Moore Show* in which she inserted herself for Mary in frame after replicated frame. [About two years later, a similarly satiric rendering of the same sequence was performed by Ann Marie Johnson as Mary Richards in an African-American re-do comedy take-off called *Mary Tyler Mo* for the skit-based prime-time TV show *In Living Color*.]

On June 25, 1997, Mary was a presenter at the *51st Annual Tony Awards*, which aired on CBS. Dressed in a stunning long black gown, she presented the award for Best Revival of a Play to *A Doll's House*.

Still looking radiant, in late July she made another appearance on *The Late Show with David Letterman*, where she discussed her rural life on her New York estate. She also talked about the time Dick Cavett pointed a telescope at Woody Allen's apartment on Thanksgiving Day and they watched him on his sofa munching a turkey leg.

After that, Mary chatted about the new children's book-on-tape she did for *Completely Yours*, a mini-album of children's stories. Her voice is heard in a segment regarding adoption. *A Mother for Choco* is about a little bird lost in the forest, who asks various animals "Are you my mother?" Mary played a mothering bear who takes a bird home to meet her children. Ed Asner, Bea Arthur, and Lily Tomlin also lent their voices to the project. All proceeds went to the Westwood Children's Center for foster parenting.

Poundstone, too, promoted the book series with an appearance on *The Rosie O'Donnell Show*, where she talked about spending a week at Mary's home with two of her foster children. During the segment, O'Donnell ran a clip of Mary telling Paula, "Make sure you dust in the corners."

This was a riff on Mary's reputation for having a just-so appearance. She was consistently neat as a whistle, with each article and crease of clothing always immaculate, finely tailored, and pressed. It was one facet of her life over which she could maintain absolute control.

Although she had long been sober, relatively free from alcohol abuse, and on a strict, nutritious diet, Mary would still periodically sneak a sweet snack. She needed her strength to stay busy, active, and current in the public eye. She did things like travel to Haverford, Pennsylvania for a fundraising book-signing at a public school; or attended the Hall of Fame Awards Induction of Grant Tinker

September 1997 was a busy month for Mary, who presented Barbra Streisand with the Emmy for her television special, *Barbra: The Concert*, at the *47th Annual Emmy Awards*. The special co-host that night, Cybil Shepherd, had introduced Mary by saying, "Between us, this actress and I have won a total of seven Emmys. I've won none and she's won seven."

On September 12, Mary appeared with people like Matthew Broderick at an ASPCA event in Manhattan, three days before she taped a segment of the *Mike and Maty* TV show on which a 5-year-old boy named Luke interviewed celebrities as they arrived for the Emmys. When Mary passed by, the boy didn't know who she was. She tried to list her TV credits, but they failed to hit a chord with Luke. And when he afterwards told her that he hoped she would win an award that night, she said, "No. I'm just presenting an award. I wasn't nominated."

The following October, CBS reran *The Dick Van Dyke Show Remembered* clips special, while Mary made a brief appearance in a "No Butts" video which addressed kicking her three-pack-a-day cigarette habit in 1985. She talked about how diabetic retinopathy had forced her to quit smoking, while the video also gave a few glimpses of Mary in her daily exercise routine.

In November 1997, Mary and her husband took in the movie premiere *The Bridges of Madison County*, and participated in the JDF's Walk-for-the-Cure. It was then Mary peered down to the ground, noticed a penny, and picked it up for luck. It went into the pocket of her sheer jacket.

Come 1998, Mary lent her support and her voice to another philanthropic project, this time directly involving Rosie O'Donnell and her For All Kids Foundations which distributes funds to children's charities. Mary made a generous donation to the organization, and agreed to utilize her vocal skills for the animated HBO special *Kids Are Punny 2*, based on O'Donnell's best-selling book, compiled of puns, jokes, and stories sent in by her talk show's young audience. Jackie Mason, John Leguizamo, and *That Girl's* Marlo Thomas, Mary's TV-single-girl-persona predecessor, among others, also participated in the special.

The following summer, Mary worked once more with HBO by hosting that network's documentary *Three Cats From Miami and Other Pet Practitioners*. This special, Mary told entertainment journalist Nancy Matsumoto, "has such a good, strong message about what animals can give us."

In one segment of the special, Mary asks, "Did you ever think you'd see a stingray leap out of its pond and give a kiss on the face?" It's that actual vision that motivates a young boy with cerebral palsy to rise from his wheelchair. Another segment features a horse named Frosty which provides physical therapy for children with Down syndrome.

Mary herself had been dealing with her emotional connections with animals. She had just put to sleep her 13-year-old golden retriever Dash, and spent the past few months coping with that loss and the effect it had on her family including Dash's 11-year-old "brother" Dudley, a French basset hound. "Dudley has definitely been laconic since we had to put Dash down," she told *The New York Post*. "He kind of removes himself from activities and I'm making a special effort to take him outside with me. I know we will have another dog, but first we have to get through the grieving process for Dash."

The uplifting HBO special celebrated the innate healing gifts of animals as varied as canines, pigs, and fish. Taped in Atlanta, Georgia, the show was sponsored by the Delta Society, which had pioneered the field of animal-assisted therapy, in which animals rehabilitate, comfort, and assist people in need. Mary, impressed by the Society's efforts, said she was a "huge believer in the gift animals have to offer," and sent the Society a sizable donation. Delta's president called to thank her, and asked if she would consider hosting their awards show. "I'd love to," she said. "I love the fact that all animals are what they advertise themselves to be. There are no surprises, which is not true of humans, is it?"

Mary's concern for animals was shown again on October 3, 1998, when she was named the Dog Walkers Chairperson at Woofstock '98, the American Society for the Prevention of Cruelty to Animals' 8th Annual Dog Walk. The event, which included nearly 2000 dogs and their owners, raised money for homeless and abandoned animals and helped the shelter program run by the Society in New York City.

Mary later paid a visit to New York's beleaguered Center for Animal Care and Control on E. 11th Street, where she was outraged by the cramped, filthy conditions at the Center's shelter. She, her husband, and Bernadette Peters made a 40-minute in-person appeal to New York Mayor Rudolph Giuliani. Their objective was to transform the plagued facility, and bring it exposure and funding. The system was under fire from animal advocates for exorbitant pet euthanasia, inferior management, and limited financing. Horrified by what she called the Center's "standard of living conditions and dying conditions," Mary said, "Dogs and cats in the shelter are stacked into tiny cages on dirty wards. They sleep, eat and go to the bathroom in the same place. Few are bathed or exercised. It's terrible."

At the time, the agency operated five shelters, and killed about 40,000 pets annually approximately two days after they arrived on the premises.

Very few were actually adopted. In her meeting with Giuliani, Mary offered to initiate a private funding drive. "I began to see this as a do-able thing, making life better for the animals," she said, describing Giuliani as "very receptive" to her input. Her objective was to save pets' lives by increasing adoptions and giving owners incentives to spay and neuter their animals. According to Bruce Teitelbaum, Giuliani's chief of staff, "She had some suggestions about how to improve the system. The mayor said, 'They sound like reasonable ideas. Let's sit down and analyze them.'"

Once she conquered New York, Mary dispatched a researcher to visit shelters in San Francisco and Las Vegas, which had less killings and made adoptions a priority. The optimum standard she envisioned for New York's animals was already in place at Pet Orphans Fund, a top-notch shelter in Los Angeles. There, dogs waiting for adoption were housed in sanitary, comfortable private rooms with sofas and even individual television sets.

Mary continued to use her public persona for good toward the year's end. She crusaded for abused women in the week-long Marshall's Women in Comedy Festival, which began November 11. On the first night of what was billed as the world's first all-female comedy festival, she hosted a gala at Carnegie Hall, starring Paula Poundstone and Rita Rudner. The festivities, sponsored by Marshall's clothing store chain, benefited Victim Services and the Center for Children and Families, both of which assisted battered women and children. Judy Gold, Kathy Griffith, and Mary's friend and *The View* co-host Joy Behar were among the comedians who performed in theaters and clubs during the week-long festival. There were also celebrations held at the Friars Club and the Museum of Television and Radio, during which film clips were screened of other iconic TV funny ladies. To promote the event, Mary appeared on *The View* with Behar, Poundstone, and Rudner. But she clashed with meat-eater Star Jones, then a co-host on the female-geared chat show. On the topic of what and what not to eat, Mary continued to urge everyone to think twice about eating anything "with a face."

That December, Mary didn't have to think even for a moment about attending the first White Rose Awards Gala in New York, where guests such as Bette Midler, Kathie Lee Gifford, Whoopi Goldberg, and Katie Couric bid significant dollars at an auction to support Rosie O'Donnell's charities. "Everybody better be on their cautionary stance," warned Mary as she entered New York's Marriot Marquis. "Rosie will shame you."

In January 1999, Mary supported another female comedian by attending the Broadway opening of Sandra Bernhard's one-woman show *I'm Still Here, Damn It!* which was also seen by the likes (and dislikes?)

of John Waters, Michael Douglas, Naomi Campbell, and Liza Minnelli. At a party thrown in Bernhard's honor after the show, Mary arrived with a bouquet of flowers for its star. Bernhard for years had what might be called an "infatuation" with Mary. While growing up, she religiously watched and loved *The Dick Van Dyke Show* and *The Mary Tyler Moore Show*. Bernhard was delighted when she discovered that Mary was also a fan of hers, and had also attended Bernhard's other one-woman show *Without You, I'm Nothing*. When Bernhard published her memoir *Confessions of a Pretty Lady* in 1988, Mary's endorsement appeared on the back flap. "It's the sometimes shocking, always funny stream-of-consciousness of a very funny lady," she wrote.

Approximately eight weeks after taking in Bernhard's *Damn* show, Mary, outfitted in a slinky negligee, performed in a live comedy skit with Katie Couric during a Drama League Gala honoring O'Donnell. Journalists Liz Smith and Diane Sawyer and the casts of a Broadway revival of *Cabaret* and several other live stage productions also participated in the event. That same month, Mary reunited with her former *MTM Show* co-stars Valerie Harper, Georgia Engel, Betty White, and Ed Asner at the 14th Annual TV Academy Hall of Fame Awards.

Come April 23, Mary and Gene Wilder performed in the A.R. Gurney play *Love Letters* for a one-night-only performance at C.W. Post University in Long Island, which benefitted the North Shore Child and Family Guidance Center Association. Many female/male celebrity duos had performed the play, including former *Dallas* co-stars Linda Gray and Larry Hagman, and significant-others-turned-married-couple Elizabeth Montgomery and Robert Foxworth. The play chronicles the diverse, often tragic lives of Andrew Makepeace Ladd III and Melissa Gardner, as told through the romantic notes they shared with one another over time.

Also in April, Mary was interviewed on the E! network's *Celebrity Profile* segment on Dick Van Dyke, along with his brother Jerry, Rose Marie, and Carl Reiner. They all agreed that Dick was hard to know and very private, even more so than Mary, who had recently commented about her former co-star in *People* magazine. "With the white hair, those blue eyes and those white teeth," she said, "...he's a knock-out."

Mary delivered yet another colorful performance in May with a guest-voice-appearance, this time for the Fox TV series, *King of the Hill*. She played Reverend Karen Stroop, whose church is scorched due to unexpected circumstances.

Come June 22, 1999, Mary took a much more serious tone when testifying before Congress on Capitol Hill along with 100 diabetic kids, ages 2-17, from across America. An accompanying event was hosted by Strom Thurmond. Mary's friend Larry King, a Type 2 diabetic, was an honoree, and Tony Bennett performed a song composed just for that day titled, "Promise to Remember Me." Mary explained to *Countdown Magazine*: "I was afraid if I testified for more diabetes research funding, they'd take a look at me and say, 'Wait a minute; you look strong and healthy, you have a lot of energy, we don't see the problem here,' but the kids sitting down and talking about what it's like living with this disease…it's very hard to remove to the memory of a child from your frontal lobe."

Two children from each state lobbied their congressmen for more funding for the National Institutes of Health. "She has done so much to raise public awareness of the seriousness of diabetes," said John J. McDonough, the JDF International Chairman of the Board. "She's been very up front about it and she's been outspoken in several ways."

In her speech, Mary talked about her recent surgery to correct the severe diabetic-related eye issue that left her temporarily visually impaired. She told her story in a forthright manner, described the range of complications that result from diabetes, and all the challenges the disease creates for those stricken with it. As always, her candor complemented JDF's aggressive pursuit of research to improve care and chances of a cure.

"We run it like a business," McDonough said of JDF, which by that time had donated $290 million to research. "From the bed to the bedside," he said, was a common mantra, as laboratory advances bettered the lives of patients, with Mary as the prime example. Or as Mary put it with that Southern twang she many times employed in character on-screen, "I'm a just-right busy person."

She was also at times a controversial figure, as with one headline-making move in 1999. At one of the many charities events Mary attended that year, she refused to pose with Daytime Emmy winner Susan Lucci because the *All My Children* star's gown was adorned with a fur-lined trim. Upon making this observation, Mary swiftly exited the event. She never condoned killing animals for fur, used for comfort or fashion.

To help drive the point home, Mary had recently complained about a classic image of herself wearing a fur coat on the cover of the Columbia House video release of *The Mary Tyler Moore Show*. Subsequently, she hurried a letter to the powers that be, requesting to have the image replaced with a fur-less photo. According to a Columbia House representative, the photograph in question had been provided by MTM Enterprises. Its spokesperson, Tony Thomopoulos said, "Unfortunately, I can't change what's already out there." But he did promise that all future promo campaigns would not include images with fur.

In October of that year, Mary's face, or at least half of it, appeared on the cover of *TV Guide's* "Fifty Greatest Characters Ever!" issue which featured Mary Richards as #21 on the list. The magazine noted, "When she would throw her hat up in the air....well there went our hearts."

That same month, Mary was profiled on the MSNBC series *Headliners & Legends* with Matt Lauer. Among the highlights of the show were rare clips of Mary from the NBC archives and rare photos from her Aunt Bertie's scrapbook.

That same year, on her 63rd birthday, Mary appeared on CNN's *Larry King Live* with Dick Van Dyke. They discussed their mutual admiration and desire to reunite for a command performance, possibly in a revival of the award-winning play, *The Gin Game*, about two seniors who meet in a retirement home for a game of gin rummy.

On November 21, 1999, Mary made a guest appearance on Bravo TV's *Inside the Actors Studio* hosted by James Lipton. She discussed her life and took questions from the audience, and Lipton was impressed with her candor. "No subject was taboo," he said. At the end of the interview, the audience of film students joined Mary on stage for a rousing rendition of "Love Is All Around," Sonny Curtis's *Mary Tyler Moore* theme.

To close the millennium in grand style, Mary and Robert Levine celebrated New Year's Eve at the White House with President Bill Clinton and First Lady Hillary Clinton, Elizabeth Taylor, and rock star Bono, who performed.

But the real news was that she would soon reunite on screen with another very familiar former TV co-star.

ACT VII

Back for Moore

Mary continued to reconnect with the cast members of the
Dick Van Dyke and *Mary Tyler Moore* sitcoms in one form or another.
Here, she poses on the set of *The Dick Van Dyke Show Revisited* in
2004. [Credit: David Van Deusen/*The Walnut Times*.
]

Chapter

27

Mary kicked off the new millennium with *Mary and Rhoda*, a semi-reunion TV-movie of *The Mary Tyler Moore Show*, co-starring Valerie Harper in an updated story about their famed characters' lives with contrasting daughters. Premiering on ABC February 7, 2000, *Mary and Rhoda* had been in development since early 1998, when Mary announced she would be returning to weekly TV, but not on CBS. This time, it was ABC, which ordered 13 episodes of a sitcom that would feature Mary Richards and Rhoda Morgenstern in their late 50s living in New York City, each with a 20-year-old daughter. In a gimmicky "ironic twist," Mary named her daughter Rhoda, and Rhoda named her daughter Mary. Moore had first pitched this concept to CBS-affiliated Fox Television, which by that time owned MTM Enterprises.

According to *Variety*, Mary made the surprising decision to seek the help of Tom Fontana, the creative mind behind NBC's gritty *Homicide: Life on the Street* and HBO's prison drama *Oz*. Stunned by Mary's request, Fontana said, "it was either the best idea I'd ever heard or the worst, but I was the worst possible person to do it. Unless [Moore] wanted [Mary Richards] to have been a heroin addict for the last 20 years – that I could do."

Fortunately, the Fontana-CBS-Fox potential alliance fell through when ABC committed to the project.

Mary had long vowed never to do another sitcom, nor reprise the character of Mary Richards, but she was doing both via the creation of *Mary and Rhoda*. The idea had been generated when Moore and Har had appeared together on *The Rosie O'Donnell Show* in late 1997. After they exited the studio, they said almost simultaneously that they should work together. Mary had sought to bring back some of the storytelling style of her original series. She felt that quality was severely lacking on TV sitcoms of the time. "They seem [today] to write a series of jokes and then try to add a story," she said, "and I want to get back to writing a story, and then adding the jokes."

By January 1998, scripts for the *Mary and Rhoda* half-hour sitcom were still being fleshed out, but one of them suggested Mary as the head of a television newsroom that hearkened back to the WJM newsroom from her original series. The new show, with a pilot script by Jeff Lowell (*Spin City*), was to be filmed in New York, which was home to both Moore and Harper, who lived with her second-husband Tony Cacciotti, and their 15-year-old daughter Cristina. Years after Harper's divorce from Richard Schaal in 1978, and after *Rhoda* was cancelled in 1979, Harper had met Cacciotti upon hiring him as a physical trainer. The two began dating, and he eventually became her manager and one of the producers on the *Valerie* series that ended for her in 1985. They married two years later, and Harper went on to star in two other sitcoms: *City*, in 1989, and *The Office* in 1994.

Had the potential new *Mary and Rhoda* sitcom gone to series, it would have been Harper's seventh series, and Mary's eighth. She agreed to do it only if it was filmed in New York, relatively close to her country estate.

At one point, Cloris Leachman, who by 1999, had appeared as a regular in approximately seven series, including the *Ellen* sitcom (in which Mary made a guest appearance), had approached Mary about including the Phyllis Lindstrom character in the new *Mary and Rhoda* project. But Mary rejected that idea. When Leachman wondered why, Mary just smiled and walked away, as she often did when confronted by questions or concerns that she simply did not feel like answering.

While Leachman and Phyllis were not invited to the *Mary and Rhoda* party, there was some chatter of Ed Asner returning to his *MTM Show* roots with a 2-hour TV-movie based on his Lou Grant character, from an idea suggested by Gene Reynolds (of TV's *M*A*S*H*). Although there had been creative tension between Mary and Asner while making *Payback*, that apparently became water under the bridge. Two years later, he was even considering making an appearance on the *Mary and Rhoda* sitcom. "I hope the show comes off. Both of them are consummate performers," he said of Mary and Harper. "A network would be crazy not to do it."

But ABC's sanity was temporary. The *Mary and Rhoda* half-hour sitcom, performed in front of an audience, never saw the light of day, or prime time. According to *Mary Magazine* editor David Davis, the project was not shelved but postponed. "ABC became dissatisfied with the first script. New writers were brought in…new scripts were written, and rejected. Finally, ABC decided to give up on the project and cancel the show before it ever got made." "This was one of those cases where the stars just didn't line up correctly," said ABC's Jamie Tarses on the day he announced the cancelation.

One year later, however, the *Mary and Rhoda* one-shot two-hour TV-movie (without an audience) made it to the ABC airwaves as a "backdoor" pilot for a new series. Harper said the network "probably felt a movie was a less costly alternative to a full-fledged series."

In the new film, Mary Richards' offspring was not named Rhoda, but rather Rose Cronin (played by Joie Lenz, today known as Bethany Joy Lenz), a New York University dropout pursuing a career in stand-up comedy. She is more like the mother-earthy Rhoda, while Rhoda's polished progeny, now named Meredith Rousseau (and played by Marisa Ryan), is a premed student at Barnard College who is more refined like Mary Richards.

The teleplay was penned by Katie Ford, then 34, who commenced her career as a stand-up comedienne when she was just 14. Previously, Ford had written for shows like *Family Ties*. "There was one initial phone call from Mary," she recalled. "We came from the same place about where we wanted to approach [the movie]. Her instincts are unbelievable. She gave me a lot of confidence and made me want to do it well for her because she had such a great eye."

The new *Mary and Rhoda* movie attempted to distance itself from *The Mary Tyler Moore Show*. "We were trying to move away from that, not to be [dismissive], because it's important to see who they'd be now," said the film's Emmy-winning director Barnet Kellman, whose credits include *Murphy Brown* and *Mad About You* (both of which would be rebooted in the 21st Century).

In the refreshed *Mary and Rhoda*, Mary Richards was now the recent widow of Congressman Steven Cronin, whose faulty investments left her in dire economic straits, forcing her to seek employment after eight years of retirement. She eventually finds a position as a segment producer at a local news show hosted by Cecile Andrews, portrayed by Christine Ebersole (from the 1986 edition of Harper's *Valerie* sitcom). Mary accuses her young supervisor, Jonah Seimeier (Elon Gold) of hiring her to avoid being accused of age discrimination. She also takes issue with him regarding the content of the news; she feels it has become more "tabloid-ish" and exploitative since her days at WJM.

Meanwhile, Rhoda has returned to Manhattan after divorcing her philandering French husband. She has a tendency to be condescending toward her ex-spouse, who was close to Meredith, which causes some friction between mother and daughter. No longer designing costumes or dressing windows, Rhoda is an assistant to a fashion photographer, and has aspirations of her own in that industry. "The old Rhoda was waiting for a man to stamp her valid," Harper said. "She has grown much more confident over the years in that she's unwilling to stay in a marriage that is not a good one. She still has the same spirit, still has the New York accent. She had her baby in her late 30s so she's pretty well formed-up. Rhoda is suffering a bit of empty nest [syndrome]. She's coming home; she wants to be near her daughter, who's seeking her own life, so that's delicate. She likes to be needed, wants to be loved."

Mary and writer Ford had developed the *Mary and Rhoda* premise together. From the onset, Ford envisioned the film as a drama because, she thought, "...that's the only way to explain the 20 years we haven't seen and the only way the comedy will work for me. As a drama, it's just easier to do." According to Ford, the two-hour format gave Mary and Rhoda breathing room to reestablish themselves as new people in fresh lives. "I give credit to anyone who attempted it as a series. I don't think I could have done that in a half-hour."

But that may have been why *Mary and Rhoda* failed. They should have stuck to the *original program*. The initial idea of making a new *M&R* series as a half-hour sitcom was solid; it held true to the initial *Mary Tyler Moore Show* mythology and format that was beloved for years. To come along decades later and alter that increasingly cherished conception and perception, for all intents and no purpose, was artistic suicide. The reason the 2018 *Roseanne* initially succeeded was exactly why the *Mary and Rhoda* movie did not. The new *Roseanne* picked up right where the original *Roseanne* left off. It was simply a continuation of the first series with the same sets, the same cast, and presented in the same manner (shot in front of a live audience). The same process was applied to the *Murphy Brown* re-do, but sadly *not* with *Mary and Rhoda*. Ford's and Mary's instincts, this time, were completely off the mark.

Mary also missed her mark, literally, one day while filming an exterior scene for the movie. Apparently, she had tripped on some rolled-up carpeting on location, and subsequently broke a bone in her wrist. She ended up on her hands and knees "spread-eagled," she joked, "...and they got it on film! They hired a stuntwoman to do this, but they're using my take. I'd like some recognition from the stuntmen association for this."

But Mary would never again have to worry about tripping through any incarnation of *Mary and Rhoda*. This backdoor pilot never made it through the front door as a series, and ultimately neither Mary nor Harper lost any sleep over the decision. "Love Them, Not the Movie," aptly read the *TV Guide* movie review headline by Matt Roush. Even *Mary Tyler Moore Show* director Jay Sandrich called the film "a terrible idea," but cited miscasting as the reason why. "Mary can't play Mary Richards anymore. But Valerie could. Valerie should have played Mary."

That was a strange remark, especially in comparison to what Marisa Ryan said about playing Rhoda's offspring Meredith. "She's trying to be on her own…[to] get out of Rhoda's grasp [and] deal with the divorce. Actually, she's more like Mary, more studious, focused, more of a go-getter. She has the humor, but she's more straight-laced than Rhoda."

Sandrich's thoughts, meanwhile, were more rudimentary; he was implying that Mary simply did not look the part anymore. Both her extensive plastic surgery and her frail health contributed to her literal and figurative weak performance on the show. The warm character traits of Mary Richards were oddly missing from Mary's new rendition, whereas Harper's performance as Rhoda was not bizarre but still audience-accessible.

What a wasted opportunity was *Mary and Rhoda*. The magic was gone, stifled, and buried. The new idea was far removed from the concept of the original series; the actresses and their characters were placed in a foreign environment. As a result, the audience was confused and confounded. A punk-rocking version of "Love Is All Around" by Joan Jett was a noble attempt to set a modern pace, but in the end the entire presentation fell flat. The following review in *Variety*, published February 6, 2000, said it all:

> Rhoda you haven't changed a bit. The sarcasm, the wishy-washiness, the inner-turmoil surrounding a mother-daughter relationship – it's still boiling over and inviting as ever. Mary, you're a whole lot harder to write for, and attempting to put a few scars on the smile that turned everyone on is a tricky proposition.
>
> The grand return of Mary Richards and Rhoda Morgenstern lacks the zing of The Mary Tyler Moore Show, taking obvious routes one moment, heading into slapstick the next and then negotiating curves in the plot that are just plain baffling.
>
> Taking characters from a great sitcom and moving them into this feel-good drama is a tough task, one that the script isn't up to. There' are too many unsympathetic characters, among them the leading

ladies' two daughters, to recapture the magic of the classic MTM. Fans of the great sitcom will certainly ask, "Where's the humor?"

Mary and Rhoda are single, and both have returned to New York, though neither has spoken to the other for years. Mary, now Richards-Cronin, has been in Italy since the death five months earlier of her congressman husband. Upon her return, she immediately learns her daughter Rose (Joie Lenz) has moved in with a boyfriend. At least she's still enrolled at NYU.

Rhoda's daughter Meredith (Marisa Ryan) is less than thrilled to see mom at the doorstep. Meredith – get it? the daughters are Mare and Ro – is confused why Rhoda, after wandering around Europe in search of personal answers after her divorce, would wind up in Gotham. It's a perfect place, she says, to jump-start her passion for art and photography.

Naturally, Mary and Rhoda attempt to find each other, and when they do, all is forgiven and whatever one needs, the other can deliver. Rhoda needs a place to stay; Mary has an extra room. Mary fears being alone; Rhoda is still a chatterbox and a shoulder to lean on. Both are concerned they're not on equal footing financially and, surprise, Mary's husband spent all the money during his last campaign. Mary needs a job. She's 60 – a fact she harps on – and it has been eight years since she last worked for ABC News.

Taking a job at a station that's the evil antithesis of WJM, Mary gets devious after working on a story about a white teen gang member who has committed murder. Vain anchorwoman Cecile Andrews (Ebersole) wants to stay in the good graces of impatient station head Jonah Seimeier (Gold) and gives her news report a dishonest twist. Mary recuts the seg and switches tapes, which wins over her colleagues and patrons at a bar who watch the news with her.

Valerie Harper, who mugs her way through a job as a photographer's assistant, brings Rhoda to life with no baggage. Her depiction is pure and comfortable.

Over the years, she has lost none of her spunk, and her bitterness toward her ex flows without exaggeration. Her relationship with her daughter is at a great stage of imbalance, a reflection of the manner in which she and 'mom' Nancy Walker went toe-to-toe during the 1970s. It's a well-executed version of a woman not wanting to repeat her mother's mistakes.

Mary is more multi-dimensional – or at least that's what this telepic tries to say – and it's harder to get a grip on who she truly has become. Sure she still can't throw a party, but this now threatens the family unit. She appears to have lost her sense of humor, and when she has to face the caustic people behind the nightly news, she suddenly puts on a brave face and decides to do things her way. Calmly and determined.

That would be acceptable were the script not forcing odd awkward situations upon her.

Side issues are labored, and the supporting cast is limited to one-dimensional characterizations which shortchanges Lenz and Ryan. Were this a series, as had been planned, its ability to have a life beyond an initial 13 episodes would have been doubtful.

The doubts that *Mary and Rhoda* would ever become a weekly series were exacerbated by creative and personal conflicts between Mary and Valerie. Bill Persky disclosed: "Valerie felt that Mary was not properly appreciative of her. So, there was a rift there; one I think they resolved."

The same year that *Mary and Rhoda* premiered and died on ABC, Mary gave birth to *Labor Pains*, which was originally intended for theatrical release, but instead went direct to video. *Mary Magazine* editor David Davis labeled *Pains* a "breezy comedy," in which Mary played Esther Raymond, whose daughter Sarah (Kyra Sedgwick) cloaks her pregnancy from everyone except her best friend (Lela Rochon) until the day she goes into labor. Rob Morrow, of CBS-TV's *Northern Exposure* and later of that network's *Numb3rs* drama, co-starred as Sarah's ex-boyfriend who discovers he is the father of her baby, while another veteran actress, Elizabeth Ashley, portrays Murrow's wealthy mother.

In March 2000, Mary was featured in the latest issue of *Modern Maturity* magazine in which she and thirteen other celebrities gave advice to the President. Mary's suggestion was this: "Bring scientific advances from the animal lab to the patient's bedside."

By June of 2000, Mary performed opposite Elliott Gould in *Good as Gold*, yet another TV-movie/backdoor pilot. Written by and starring Elon

Gold, who played her son (after playing her boss on *Mary and Rhoda*), *Good as Gold* unfortunately never aired.

Off-screen but live on stage in Los Angeles, Mary joined Dick Van Dyke, Carol Burnett, Jason Alexander, and Kelsey Grammer for *Television Night at the Hollywood Bowl*, a benefit concert featuring TV stars singing various theme songs. Mary and Van Dyke performed "Love Is All Around." Perhaps predictably, she tried to alter the lyrics of "The Ballad of Davy Crocket" from "killed him a bear when he was only 3" to "saved him a bear."

Around this time, the Watkins Glen, New York sector of the Farm Sanctuary, a rescue, education and advocacy nonprofit, informed Mary that they were in desperate need of legislation to protect farm animals. Consequently, she narrated an educational video that was sent to politicians requesting to make those changes. She said it was also sent to the Agricultural Department "begging them for humane treatment while they make their dollars…to come face to face with a sheep, cow, pig, or goat and to look into their eyes is to see the depth of their souls…whether it's fear and terror in the eyes of an animal traveling to slaughter, or the joy and trust in the eyes of an animal safe and comfortable at a place like Farm Sanctuary. Animals look to us for compassion and protection, and it is our duty to relieve their suffering."

On October 7, 2000, Mary was honored at the 45th Annual Thalians Ball, named for Thalia, the Greek goddess of comedy. Previous honorees have included Carol Burnett, Ann Margaret, Liza Minnelli, Shirley MacLaine, Lucille Ball, Whoopi Goldberg, and Sally Field.

The event took place at the Century Plaza Hotel, where Mary was presented with that year's "Ms. Wonderful" award for her work for juvenile diabetes, animal-rights causes, and her illustrious career. The black-tie crowd of about 1,000 gathered to raise funds for the charity.

Some of the celebrities featured that night live on stage included Lorna Luft (daughter of Judy Garland and Sidney Luft), who performed two songs; dancers from *A Chorus Line*; the '60s pop group the Turtles, who sang "Love Is All Around"; and comic Paula Poundstone, who stunned those attending with her act, which included "F…Mary Tyler Moore" references (recited all in good fun, of course). Also attending were Phyllis Diller, Buddy Hackett, Dick Van Patten, Rip Taylor, Steve Allen (in what became the last public appearance before his demise on October 30 at age 78), Ruth Buzzi, Jo Anne Worley, Red Buttons, Ed Asner, Rose Marie, Betty White, and Dick Van Dyke. The latter was joined on stage by Mary in a musical melody of "Well, Did You Evah," "With You on My Arm," "Put It There, Pal," and "Our Love Is Here to Stay." At one point, musical lyrics once again became an issue for Mary, this time because she could not remember them. She was reduced to giggles, and forced to begin again, while Van Dyke just laughed. "Network heads made us sleep in adjoining beds," Mary sang. "Today, we'd be rolling in the hay."

Upon exiting the stage, Mary appeared overwhelmed by the 3-hour tribute to her career. "In truth," she said, "I can't believe they were talking about me or that the woman was me. It's a very odd out-of-body kind of experience."

Mary continued to keep busy with appearances like those on *The View*, where she promoted another edition of *The Great American Meatout*, which was taking place in Washington, D.C. For many years before and after that night, the *Meatout* had enjoyed broad public support from educators, health providers, manufacturers and retailers of meatless foods, public-interest advocates, writers, mass media, public officials, and famous entertainers like Mary. She was joined at the 2000 event by Casey Kasem, Peter Falk, Rue McClanahan, and more stars. Thousands of people from across America and other countries organized educational events ranging from simple information tables and exhibits to elaborate receptions, cooking demonstrations, and festivals. They encouraged people to "kick the meat habit," at least for a day, and explore a more wholesome, less violent diet. As was the case during her last appearance on *The View*, Mary clashed with Star Jones about vegetarianism.

A few weeks after she hashed it out with Jones, Mary continued her save-the-animals campaign with ASPCA president and CEO Larry Hawk, urging fellow New Yorkers to "just say no" to carriage horses. The two joined forces at a news conference on the steps of City Hall to call for a boycott of carriage-horse rides until working conditions improved. "Forget your visions of romance and nostalgia," said Hawk. "Current city law allows these animals to work and live in deplorable conditions." Mary, who by now owned nine horses on her Dutchess County farm, called the rides "a charming and romantic idyll in the park" for everyone but the animals. The horses worked long hours in sweltering heat and icy weather, pulled heavy carriages through noisy crowded streets, lived in firetrap stables, and never got a day off to graze in an outdoor field.

The law had been revised in 1993, when the City Council increased hours of operation and permitted the carriages in more midtown areas. After being blocked by Mayor David Dinkins, the rules were put into effect by Mayor Rudolph Giuliani when he was elected in 1994. In the proposed legislation the horses' workday would have been shortened to eight hours, one less than now; stalls would have to be larger, with fans and automatic sprinklers; and blanketing of the horses would be required in freezing weather.

Mary had not ridden a city horse-drawn carriage since appearing in a scene with Dudley Moore in her 1982 feature film *Six Weeks*. "If I had known what those horses were going through, I would have balked," she said. "I would not have participated in that." Hawk added, "New York in the year 2000 is no place for horses."

To help pay for the changes, the ASPCA proposed raising the cost of one ride from $34.00 to $45.00. But Gloria McGill, an operator of Chateau Stables and a trustee of the New York City Horse and Carriage Association, took umbrage with the suggestion. "Not again!" she said. "I can't see where we can create any more laws...I have a whole book of rules we have to follow."

According to recent New York mandates, the conditions for carriage horses have since improved, validating Mary's earnest charitable efforts. She may have put the cart before the horse at times, but she also put her money where her mouth was, and contributed millions of dollars to worthwhile causes over the years. And around the same time she advocated for those carriage-horse rights, Mary hosted a live online chat on philanthropy in general.

Chapter

28

In January 2001, Mary was honored at the Avon Women of Enterprise Awards, where she made a moving speech to the all-women audience, with a reference to the death of her son Richie. "I feel his absence every day of my life," she said.

A few weeks later, she was inducted into the Museum of Television and Radio in New York with a tribute of clips. During a question-and-answer session, Mortimer Levitt, who founded the Custom Shop Clothiers and was a patron of the arts until his death (at age 98 in 2005), rose and commented on Mary's slightly spiked hairstyle. "I see you didn't have time to have your hair done today," he said. The evening's chair, Barbara Walters, hostess Mary Hart, and the audience gasped. But Mary, with a gracious smile firmly in place, just laughed it off.

On March 20, 2001, Mary once more became the celebrity sponsor of the next "Great American Meatout." Alongside fellow actors Kevin Kline, Jonathan Lipnicki, and former astronaut Jim Lovell (commander of Apollo 13), she again testified before Congress in support of increased funding for diabetes research and embryonic stem-cell research, which she called "truly life affirming." Joining Mary and her celebrity comrades in the hearing room were about 200 children with diabetes and their families, representing the Juvenile Diabetes Research Foundation Children's Congress.

In late 2001, Mary returned to acting, traveling to Vancouver to begin work on *Cheats*, a teen movie comedy that was eventually released November 1, 2002. The film was about four high-school misfits, played by Matthew Lawrence (younger brother to Joey), Elden Henson, Martin Starr, and Trevor Fehrman, who cheat their way through school but lose each other's friendship in the process. Mary played Mrs. Stark, the high-school principal who suspects the group of cheating, but can never seem to catch them. Her character had some skeletons in her closet, and Mary liked that. During an interview with *Entertainment Tonight*, her not-so-lighter side emerged when she said, "I love playing characters with a dark side." This was more than evident with her TV-movie, *Like Mother, Like Son: The Strange Story of Sante and Kenny Kimes*. This real-life-inspired tale was directed by Arthur Allan Seidelman, and written by Paul Eric Myers, from Adrian Havill's book. The film co-stars Robert Forster, Gabriel Olds, and Jean Stapleton, and premiered on May 21, 2001.

With a promise that echoed her words from decades before about the TV special *Mary's Incredible Dream*, Mary told entertainment journalist Ericka Sóuter, "You will see an all new Mary in this movie. I wear very low-cut dresses and the type of undergarments Julia Roberts wore in [the 2000 feature film] *Erin Brockovich*."

Mary had envisioned Roberts portraying her in a potential Mary Tyler Moore biopic ("She's got that mouth, among other wonderful things."), and was mesmerized by the theatrical challenges of portraying Sante. She pursued the part aggressively. Mary called CBS and said, "I want to play the role," which was something she would "never" do. As she once observed, "It's not my nature to set things in motion. Not even at MTM [Enterprises]. That's one part of me that I wish I could change, but, so far, it hasn't happened. I don't have any initiative. I wait for things to come my way."

Not even if a potential new series like, as a *TV Guide* reporter suggested, *Murder, She Wrote* came along? "No," Mary replied. "It's a charming show, but charming is not what I'm about. If I did TV again, I'd want something with a bit more bite and humor."

A different time, she said, "I know I am fondly thought of as a personality, but I am an actress. I enjoy creating something that is truly unlike me."

Like Mother, Like Son at least had that kind of bite. Some would be shocked, not amused, to see Mary play Sante, a barely dressed sociopath who schemes with her son (Olds) to kill New York high-roller Irene Silverman (Stapleton). "This [kind of story] fascinates me," Mary said to Sóuter. "It makes you wonder about people you know."

According to Laura Fries of *Variety*, however, there was nothing wonderful about *Like Mother, Like Son*, which she reviewed a few days before it aired:

> The ghost of Mary Richards has forever been laid to rest. Mary Tyler Moore, who in a calculated effort to take roles to dispel her goody two shoes image, has gone from the woman who could turn the world on with

a smile to the woman who can creep you out with just one look. Moore stars in this low-rent psychological drama based on the true story of Sante Kimes, a marginally successful con artist, who with her son Kenny, was convicted of the murder of a Manhattan socialite.

Director Arthur Allan Seidelman provides an unremarkable account of a story that at best should have been played out as a small-screen version of The Grifters or at least a campy Sunday night diversion. The telepic doesn't come close to either option. Instead, the tale is recounted unimaginatively through a series of unconvincing flashbacks full of equally unconvincing wigs and costumes to take us up to the murder of poor clueless Irene Silverman [Stapleton] in 1998.

It turns out that Sante, whom one judge refers to as 'a sociopath of unremitting malevolence,' believes she deserves whatever she wants, having struggled through a horrible childhood and a string of abusive men. She's the type of small-time swindler who has a quick comeback for any inquiry or accusation and has deluded herself into believing her own lies.

Her oldest son, Ken [Olds], is quick to tire of his mother's behavior and refuses to participate in her various schemes and shoplifting adventures. The younger [version of] Kenny [Alex Breden] is eager for his mother's approval and enjoys her 'games.'

Sante actually lands a big fish in wealthy businessman Ken 'Pappa' Kimes [Forster], who despite her unrepentant behavior, marries her and treats her sons as his own. But apparently wealth and family stability aren't enough for Sante. The law finally catches up with her and she is sent to prison for four years. The domestic bliss she comes home to is quickly shattered when 'Pappa' dies and leaves them penniless, so Sante and Kenny head to the Big Apple and big- time scams.

Moore does plenty of peacocking as Sante, and although plenty scary, it's hardly a convincing performance. Gabriel Olds, as the adult Kenny waffles

> in a no-man's land somewhere between American Psycho and Joe Preppy, never really displaying the same taste for crime as his mother.
>
> Stapleton and Forster have the most thankless of roles, simple pawns in Sante's game who don't even warrant enough screen time for much sympathy. Writer Paul Eric Meyers obviously tries to save the sympathy for Kenny, giving him wistful scenes where he tells the matronly Irene, 'You seem like you would have made a nice mother.' But that's about as far as the character development goes. Production is as low rent as the criminals portrayed here with technical credits meeting the bare minimum.

According to her interview with the *Philadelphia Enquirer* on May 13, 2001, when Mary first learned that CBS was interested in developing this movie, she did something she had never done before. "I initiated it," she said. "I knew I wanted to play this part." So she contacted her agent, who informed the network that Mary was very much interested in the film, for which she also became an executive producer.

"It was just an instinctive, gut reaction that I knew I wanted to do this," Mary said, "...probably born out of the strong feeling that there is no [perceived] villainy in the minds of people who do these terrible things. They firmly believe that they did what they had to do, and that justice is on their side, as twisted as that may seem."

Such a perspective was reinforced for Mary when she viewed Sante's interview on CNN's *Larry King Live*. "I came away from that almost feeling that she was set up, that she hadn't committed murder or been involved in all these crimes. That's how strong her conviction was."

"What I wanted to do," she added, "...and what I think we managed to do was show the sociopath personality. This isn't about arching an eyebrow or yelling 'bitch' or 'bastard.' This is a deep look inside the woman and how she got to be the way she is."

Mary took her role in the film so seriously that she visited a few days with a psychiatrist, a colleague of her husband Robert Levine, who taught her about the sociopathic mindset. She went to Riker's Island and spent the day talking to people who had known Sante. Mary found it fascinating that everybody loved this woman, from the guards to her fellow prisoners. They all described her as a pleasant individual; one of the inmates even called her "Mom." Mary wanted to "use that to show that someone can be sinister, though she's not able to see it...that [Sante] was a human being with doubts and fears."

"She was even a caring person," Mary said. "There was a side of her that hated herself; that thought she wasn't good enough, pretty enough or smart enough. She was paranoid and thought the whole world was against her. She was a sick person – very sick – but I wouldn't call her evil."

Some of these words seem to echo more of Mary's less-than-worthy feelings about herself: "she wasn't good enough, pretty enough or smart enough...the whole world was against her." In childhood, she could never live up to her father's demands; she never felt nurtured by her mother; she was sexually abused by her neighbor. Later, she would not find marital bliss like Laura Petrie until after two failed marriages; she had no knack for motherhood like Laura did. Some might say that she never recaptured the success of Mary Richards

Of Mary's performance as Sante, who died in prison at 79 in 2014, director Seidelman said, "She has an uncanny understanding of someone who can set a goal and go after it at all costs. This is a successful lady who has dealt on a private level with a lot of tragedy in her life. Yet she has moved forward in a very determined manner. She is able to take the kind of focus, the intense pursuit of a goal, and use it to understand the negative use of that kind of energy."

After filming was completed on *Like Mother, Like Son*, Mary had a revelation. "That people can be so loving and so mothering to you," she said, "but they are really serving themselves; that might be the message" of the movie. "People like Sante will use you, and you will be stunned when you find out you have been used."

In the film, Sante smiles through life, using ploys and deceptions to get what she wants. She does not think twice about stealing a mink coat or participating in shopping sprees with her son. The only difference is that she is married to Forster's character, a wealthy man who plays into her life games, even though he doesn't comprehend her behavior.

Meanwhile, *Like Mother, Like Son* marked the first time Mary performed with Stapleton, though not extensively. "I have only two brief scenes with Jean," Mary said. "But they were wonderful. Before we began filming, I sent her a card that said, 'I apologize already for what I have to do to you.' She got a big kick out of it.'"

Less familiar to Mary was Olds, whom she called "extraordinary." "He comes across as a very complex person, someone you really want to know more about. He just grips you, and without very much dialogue, he's able to capture your imagination."

Beyond her co-star experiences, the strange twists of TV fate in the life and career similarities between Mary and *Bewitched* star Elizabeth Montgomery continued to take shape with *Like Mother, Like Son*.

Many fans of Mary were shocked by this film, just as Montgomery fans had been unsettled by their favorite *Bewitched* actress in the 1991 CBS TV-movie, *Sins of the Mother*. Montgomery portrayed the evil Ruth Coe opposite Dale Midkiff as her troubled son Kevin Coe. Two years later, Montgomery took a similar diabolical lead in the 1993 CBS TV-movie, *The Black Widow Murders: The Blanche Taylor Moore Story*, in which Montgomery portrayed yet another evil mother – this time to David Clennon. To top it all off, literally, the dark hair and style of Mary's in *Like Mother, Like Son* seemed replicated by Montgomery in *Sins of the Mother*. All three films, including Montgomery's *Black Widow Murders* were, sadly, based on true stories.

Mary and Montgomery also seemed to entertain parallel lives off-screen. As a child, Mary had performed in the family living room with her cousin Gail; Montgomery with her cousin Amanda would do the same. Later, Mary would marry young, divorce, and then wed twice more, first to an older man, Grant Tinker, before finally falling in love and staying the longest with a younger man, Dr. Robert Levine, many years her junior.

The trajectory of Montgomery's married life had eerie echoes. She first married the same-aged New York high-roller Fred Cammann who wanted a stay-at-home wife, and that union ended in divorce. Next were her failed marriages to actor Gig Young, and *Bewitched* director/producer William Asher, both much older than Montgomery, who eventually found lasting love with actor Robert Foxworth, ten years her junior.

Mary had spent a lifetime in trying to please her demanding father. Montgomery did the same with regard to her overbearing dad Robert Montgomery, an actor, which made things worse when her career, by way of *Bewitched*, became more successful than his. And while Montgomery had never publically admitted to any issue with alcohol, there were many signs that suggested such an inference, none the least of which was her early death at age 62 due to colon cancer. This ailment has been documented by certain medical studies as the result of alcoholism.

In a more positive analogy between Mary and Montgomery, former CBS-turned-Screen Gems executive Harry Ackerman, who co-created *Bewitched*, believed there was a nonthreatening likability and quality shared by Mary and Elizabeth. "They both exude a wholesome sex appeal," he said. "Women don't resent them and men can have their daydreams."

In comparing Mary to other top TV female icons, Barbara Walters once observed, "...aside from Lucille Ball and Carol Burnett, very few women had ever become long-running television clowns," even though Mary never classified herself that way. But during the heyday of *The*

Mary Tyler Moore Show, she did say, "The public has trouble accepting women as both funny and feminine. On my show I'm surrounded by Ed Asner, Ted Knight and Gavin MacLeod. They get the laughs and I get the straight lines. So I supposed the public doesn't think of me as such a funny lady."

It certainly was no laughing matter when, later in 2001, due to a foot injury and subsequent infection brought on by diabetes, Mary was forced to bow out of the starring role in the Broadway comedy *Buffalo Gal* by A.R. Gurney (*Love Letters*, *Sweet Sue*), one of her favorite writers. According to *Playbill*, Mary was to have portrayed a famous actress who returns to her hometown of Buffalo, New York to star in a production of *The Cherry Orchard* by Anton Chekhov. The character, named Amanda, is then unexpectedly confronted with the sale of her grandmother's house, a development *Playbill* described as "shades of Chekhov," and the reemerged romantic interest of her former high-school boyfriend.

Mary was replaced by fellow actress Mariette Hartley, known for countless television appearances including a guest spot on *The Rockford Files* starring James Garner, Mary's co-star from the *Heartsounds* TV-movie. Hartley became best-known to TV watchers for her witty repartee with Garner in a series of popular commercials for Polaroid cameras. With Hartley now in place in *Buffalo Gal*, the production previewed from June 13 to June 24 at the Williamstown Theatre Festival, and then officially opened at the Nikos Stage, the smaller of the two available venues.

The play would have been a nice fit for Mary on several levels, allowing her the chance to once more do comedy in front of a live audience, if not on television. And it would have granted her an opportunity to literally play into nostalgia. Both she and all of those associated with *Buffalo Gal* were disappointed that she couldn't participate in any manner with the production. "We are saddened that Mary Tyler Moore will not be joining us....this summer," said festival producer Michael Ritchie. "But her health needs to be her first concern."

Meanwhile, Mary's eternal co-star Valerie Harper was busy touring the country to promote her book, *Today, I Am a Ma'am*, a humorous look at aging. (The title was a reference to the *Mary Tyler Moore* episode, "Today I Am a Ma'am," in which Mary and Rhoda invite their dates back to Mary's apartment.) Harper had also recently replaced Linda Lavin, Mary's TV co-star from *Stolen Memories: Secrets from the Rose Garden*, in the hit Broadway play, *Tale of the Allergist's Wife*, co-starring Mary lookalike Michelle Lee and Tony Roberts.

The following fall, however, the world became a much more somber place due to the terrorist attacks of September 11, 2001. Shortly after,

Mary attended a celebrity-laden event at which she and her husband had a serious discussion with *The View* co-host Joy Behar and her husband. "We were talking about what if there was another terrorist attack," Behar recalled years later to journalist Emily Strohm. "A lot of people were suffering from asthma from the fallout of the attack and we were scared."

Within 24 hours, Mary had delivered two gas masks to Behar's home. "That was the kind of person that she was," Behar remembered. "She listened to what you said, took it in and then tried to help you with it. That was a sweet thing she did, and really, I liked her a lot. Some people send flowers, she sends gas masks."

Also in 2001, Mary adopted her dog Shana, following the passing of her beloved French hound Dudley the year before. And while the close of 2001 and early part of 2002 would bring more tears, with the loss of various dear friends and colleagues to Mary, there was at least some laughter in the rain.

In November, she was a presenter at the Emmy Awards, where she handed the statuette to Patricia Heaton, star of *Everybody Loves Raymond*, one of Mary's favorite contemporary sitcoms. She also introduced a clip tribute honoring the 50th Anniversary of *I Love Lucy*, which Mary called "the best situation comedy of all time."

All seemed merry, too, when Mary reunited with Cloris Leachman on December 17th for a holiday episode of *The Ellen Show* titled "Ellen's First Christmess." Here, Mary played Ellen's Aunt Mary Tathum, a globe-trotting reporter in Chicago, who comes to Clark for the joyful season. The segment also featured a cameo from Ed Asner as a Santa Claus in a mall.

Meanwhile, the end of 2001 delivered two relatively uplifting milestones for Mary: On November 24, 2001, she and Robert Levine celebrated their 18th anniversary, which meant they were now married longer than her 17-year-union to second spouse Grant Tinker; and December 29 was Mary's 65th birthday.

Two days later, however, Mary's friend and colleague, actress Eileen Heckart, succumbed to cancer at age 74 at her home in Norwalk, California. Heckart had played Mary's Aunt Flo on *The Mary Tyler Moore Show* and her mother in the 1988 CBS sitcom *Annie McGuire*. Heckart first caught the public's eye on Broadway as the love-starved Rosemary Sidney in *Picnic*. The next year she created the stage role of Mrs. Daigle in "The Bad Seed," and repeated that part in the 1956 film version, for which she garnered an Academy Award nomination. She eventually won an Oscar for her supporting role in the 1972 feature film *Butterflies Are Free* starring Goldie Hawn and Edward Albert. Heckart had been battling cancer for three years. Her son Mark Yankee said.

"She was one of the great ladies of stage, TV and movies and an all-around wonderful woman."

In a letter to the *New York Times*, dated, June 18, 2000, Mary's friend Dick Cavett wrote in defense of Heckart, who he felt was slighted that year at the televised Tony Awards ceremony.

> To the Editor:
>
> How is it possible that the Tony Awards could commit such an egregious affront to one of our leading actresses?
>
> I refer to the great Eileen Heckart who – the announcer's voice informed us – had been given an "Excellence" award. But when and where? They could not find room for this great artist of the theater in a scant 180 minutes of air time? And yet there was plenty of time for . . . (you fill in the blanks.)
>
> Or is there some category beyond "excellence" that Miss Heckart must yet strive for before she is actually permitted to be seen?
>
> How dumb.
>
> Dick Cavett

A few months after Heckart died, two male celebrity icons and acquaintances of Mary passed away on the same day – March 27, 2002. Milton Berle, Mary's fan and friend, died at age 94. Fortunately, they had the opportunity to work together in 1991 when she hosted the Showtime TV special *Just for Laughs*. The other male celebrity loss for Mary, however, was more personal and tragic. Unlike Berle, who had lived a long and fruitful life, Dudley Moore, Mary's co-star from 1982's *Six Weeks*, died at only age 67, the result of pneumonia, following various serious illnesses.

Five weeks after the demise of Dudley and Berle, make-up artist Kevyn Aucoin succumbed to a brain tumor on May 7, 2002 in New York. He had featured Mary with two elaborate photos in his book, *Face Forward*, which was published by Little, Brown in 1999. Model Carré Otis said, "He was an artist who could take a face and transform it into someone else," which he did with Mary, as well as other stars such as Calista Flockhart and Audrey Hepburn. They, along with Cher and additional female and male icons, attended a party for the book's release that was hosted by *InStyle* magazine. Mary told *People* magazine, "Not only does [Kevyn] make the most of beautiful faces, he's also fun to be with." In his book, Aucoin wrote of Mary, "Her resilience and triumph in the face of seemingly insurmountable adversity makes her a hero to everyone who knows her, and I am at the top of her list of her admirers."

The rest of 2002 was relatively more uplifting for Mary. As David Davis documented in *Mary Magazine* in February of that year, she was honored with a lifetime achievement award for her dedication to the welfare of animals. With the assistance of two "madcap Mutts" in Manhattan at the Pierre Hotel, where Mary had wed Robert Levine, the American Society for the Prevention of Cruelty to Animals (ASPCA) presented the accolade. At the annual Humane Awards ceremony, the ASPCA also paid tribute to many remarkable canine and human heroes of the September 11, 2001 rescue effort.

Mary was now the chairwoman of the Farm Animal's Sanctuary's Sentient Being campaign, what David Davis refers to as her latest "pet project." It hoped to move laws forward that would protect the conditions of animals who are slaughtered for food. "Every little step is an achievement because some soul will be enlightened and will have an epiphany, as I did," Mary said. "I think people trust me...they rely on me and they know I'm not a flake." Although her initial reaction to the Humane Award was, "I'm not old enough!"

No matter her age, Mary was always there for ASPCA, as when they requested her aid in the drive to make New York City a "No-Kill" city; she was "delighted" with the prospect. "The city kills 40,000 dogs and cats every year," she said. "That is an accurate number." She was undertaking the no-kill shelter project, as well as encouraging everyone to get their dogs and cats from shelters, as opposed to purchasing their pets from pet stores. "There are too many who need you already for you to waste their lives," she said. "And spaying and neutering of all cats and dogs, that's the other thing very high on my list. It has to come from many fronts in order for us to reach the no-kill state. You need enough people working on it and you have enough fund-raising events so that the money is there to back the things that you need to do. Like the traveling, maybe, that has to be undertaken. Not for me, because I always pay my own way. But for other people who are not as fortunate as I who need to travel and need those expenses paid. We need a lot of help."

ASPCA had sought the help of and respectfully acknowledged the generous contributions of other parties, including members of the New York City Police Department, the Federal Emergency Management Agency, and Port Authority Search and Rescue Teams, along with pet therapy organizations, veterinarians and volunteers.

Port Authority Canine Unit Officer David Lim and his dog Sprig, a black Labrador retriever, accepted an award on behalf of Sirius, Lim's former canine partner, whose life was lost at Ground Zero. "None of us are guaranteed a tomorrow," said Dr. Larry Hawk, ASPCA's president and CEO, whose sister Kathy was a flight attendant for United Airlines and who perished during the attacks on the World Trade Center. "Don't delay in making a bigger difference," he said. "As you start making that difference and making this world a better [place] for animals and all living creatures, please remember that laughter and smiles are the biggest antidote for fear."

Mary nodded that day, but may have felt conflicted about being recognized around the same time by the City of Hope, which had been a target of animal-rights groups due to its animal research. For Mary, that was "a horrendous no win situation." What she had been working for was to make "a switch from the bench to the bedside." The time had arrived, she said, to "translate our knowledge into activities that involve people and not animals. There has been among the scientists in the world a huge shift to that. We can't get away from that altogether. But the circumstances have been improved. Scientists are much more aware of the sensitivity of animals and what they need to do to make them as comfortable as possible while they're working with them. I wouldn't be doing what I do if they weren't making an effort."

She had a "rich animal life," which by then included two dogs, both rescued from shelters. One was a Miniature Schnauzer that Mary was lucky enough to get at only 8 weeks old; the other was a golden retriever who found his way to her home when he was 6 months old. By then, too, she had two goats at her country estate, along with eleven horses, six of which were rescued. She also had two "cop" horses from the mounted police, who retired the animals at age 4 and 5 due to physical issues and aging. Mary said they were "just out to pasture" and had "nothing but a good time, eating their heads off, romping and frolicking and just doing all good horsy things." She also had 5 horses that she and her husband Robert Levine rode, "and they intermingle, too. They're just not kept separately."

The Schnauzer, at 2½ years old, was named Shana, as in Shana Meydela, because her husband was Jewish. When they acquired Shana, Mary said to Levine, "This is a German dog. What are we going to tell your family?" He said, "Well, let's think. Maybe we can name her something Jewish." And that's when they came up with the name "Shana Meydela," which is Yiddish for "pretty girl."

Mary's golden retriever, 3½, was named Shadow. "He came with that name," she said. "I take no responsibility for that. It's a good name since he shadows Shana. They are the best of friends. They roughhouse together. You can't believe that somebody isn't going to have a broken leg. They are on top of each other all the time. But the Golden is so tender and careful around her. He can scare her with his feet pounding on either side of her without having to actually touch her. And she loves it. She can't get enough rough treatment."

Mary, however, didn't house any cats, despite the MTM Enterprises logo featuring that famous kitten. Mary confessed, "I don't understand cats." She had to have an animal that responded to her enthusiastically, and cats she said, "...take their sweet time. I know they are that way naturally, and it's up to me to be patient with them or to not deal with them, and I've chosen the latter," she laughed.

She admitted to not having the kind of personality that could warm up to felines. "I am not secure enough that I can walk in the front door and have a cat stare at me and say, 'Oh, it's you again.' I need the approbation that comes from dogs."

Mary had her own way of describing those who have pets in their lives. She was fond of the term "guardian," as opposed to "master" or "owner." Having a pet, she said, was "an honor that is bestowed on some of us and we need to treat it that way."

She thought it was helpful to point out the increasing number of affordable daycare centers for dogs in particular. "Very often successful people will say they can't have a dog because they work every day," Mary observed. Now, dog daycare centers offer pick-up and delivery services, and have their canine participants play with each other all day long. "You can have your dog obedience-trained during the day," she said, "...they can even go swimming. The point is that for a small fee you can have your dog leading a pretty damn nice life. There are so many wealthy people who work every day who just don't think they can do it, but it adds so much to their lives."

Animal lives or human lives? In Mary's opinion, the answer was probably both. She said, "Animals can give you so much in terms of a warm, full, rich feeling about yourself and your life. When you sit down with an animal or just watch it playing off on its own with another animal, you are inspired. And that stays with you...and gives you more to go on than you ever had before."

Chapter

29

In the early spring of 2002, Mary returned to the public eye when she was featured in the clips special, *CBS: 50 Years from Television City*, hosted by Carol Burnett. Around the same time, TLC, then known as The Learning Channel, produced and aired specials on four TV productions from MTM Enterprises: *The Mary Tyler Moore Show*, *The Bob Newhart Show*, *Hill Street Blues*, and *L.A. Law*.

The all-famous (and sometime notorious) May "sweeps" period followed, with several television reunions and retrospectives about classic TV shows. Viewers were treated to everything from tributes to *M*A*S*H*, *The Honeymooners*, *I Love Lucy*, *American Bandstand*, and Gilda Radner, to *The Cosby Show* and *Laverne & Shirley*.

On May 8, 2002, TV Land erected a bronze statue capturing her Mary Richards signature hat-toss at the Minneapolis, Minnesota intersection where that scene from her famous sitcom was originally filmed. To this day, fans visit the corner. Larry Jones, then TV Land general manager, presided over the ceremony. "We hope this statue will remind passers-by of the freedom and optimism that Mary has come to represent."

On hand for the festivities, Mary recalled in one interview why the hat-toss was originally incorporated into the opening credit sequence: The beret was a Christmas gift from an aunt, and *Mary Tyler Moore* co-creator Jim Brooks suggested she bring it with her for the Minneapolis location shoot, where it would reach freezing temperatures. Brooks instructed Mary to run into the middle of the street, and throw her hat in the air, like she was "really glad to be there!" "It's the seminal moment of the show," Mary said. "It not only speaks to Mary Richards' feelings, but to my feelings as well. The show represented my hopes and dreams, and I wondered if my abilities were honed enough to carry my own show."

The 8-feet-tall statue was temporarily housed in the Meet Minneapolis visitor center while the Nicollet Mall was under construction. When Mary first heard about the sculpture, she joked, "I hope it's vertical and not horizontal!" After shown a rendering of the statue, Mary's only complaint was that her hands looked too big. Gwendolyn Gillen, the artist that designed the statue (and who ironically died two days after Moore), made them smaller, and Mary was pleased with the result. "I think it's wonderful. I'm so proud of it. I never thought I'd have a statue. And I'm not even riding a horse, although wouldn't that have been fun? I think it makes people happy to think about that moment because they've all had that moment of exuberance in their life."

On the morning of the unveiling, Mary arrived at 7:15 AM, greeting over 2,500 fans at 7th Street, and Nicollet Mall with her trademark phrases, "Ohhhhhh, Rob!" and "Mr. Graaaant." She signed copies of *After All*, and even scribbled on a ticket stub from the previous night's Minnesota Twins game at which she threw the first pitch, an accomplishment she was still excited about.

Thousands of tams were handed out to fans, who tossed them in the air simultaneously as the familiar Sonny Curtis theme song, "Love Is All Around," played in the background. When the statue was unveiled, Mary gasped in mock horror and quipped, "I think it's been in the sun too long." She tossed her tam in the air several times for the press and was interviewed by Diane Sawyer, Bryant Gumbel, and Paula Zahn. The crowd yelled out things like, "Where's Rhoda?" "Dance for Us!" and "We love you!"

Upon hearing the ninth "We love you!" Mary said, "I know!"

This wasn't the first statue sponsored by TV Land's Landmarks project. A bronze image of Jackie Gleason's "Ralph Kramden" character from TV's *The Honeymooners* was erected the previous year at Port Authority in New York. This also wasn't the first time that Mary was immortalized in bronze. After her 1986 induction in the Television Academy Hall of Fame, a bust of her image was erected outside the Television Academy Arts & Sciences buildings in Los Angeles and Orlando. Still, this new statue in Minneapolis symbolized something different. It was in the middle of a busy city – Mary Richards' city. And it was in the center of everyday life, a sign that Mary Richards (and Mary) was a part of American culture. Her image wasn't secluded in an area dedicated to TV or entertainment. It was a public display of exuberance, just as in those filmed moments.

Echoing Mary's assessment of what the statue represents, sculptress Gillen said at the 2002 dedication: "She helped break the stereotype of womanhood that our generation grew up believing was our destiny. She was the light breeze that blew through our minds and left us with the feeling that we could do anything we wanted to do."

Mary continued to celebrate her original sitcom, sometimes with two different specials on two different networks on the same night, as was the case on May 13, 2002. On CBS, she hosted *The Mary Tyler Moore Reunion*, another clips special in the vein of *Mary Tyler Moore: The 20th Anniversary Show* ten years before. The same night, ABC featured her on *TV Guide's 50 Best Shows of All Time: A 50th Anniversary Celebration.*

The *TV Guide* special also featured performers like Roseanne, Kelsey Grammer, and Ted Danson, Mary's co-star from *Just Between Friends*. The CBS special presented the actress conducting one-on-one interviews with her famous former sitcom co-stars including Ed Asner, Valerie Harper, Cloris Leachman, Gavin MacLeod, Georgia Engel, and Betty White. Those conversations, Mary said, were "about how we felt when we did scenes, how we felt about each other, and when someone would get out of line. It didn't occur to us that there was any other way to do a reunion special than to sit on a couch and cue the clips."

The idea for the 2002 reunion was generated by Gary Smith, the show's producer and director, who addressed Mary's concerns before she could even express them. She thought the public had grown weary of "the old way" of doing reunion specials, "...or would be if we were to try it again." Mary was impressed with a then-recent *Carol Burnett Show* reunion special, which she thought was done "beautifully." "People seem to want to see something that's a little different," she said.

As mentioned elsewhere, there was a measure of rivalry between actors Asner, MacLeod, and Knight (who died of lung cancer in 1986) on the original *MTM Show*. But their male camaraderie was also strong. Mary and the entire cast missed Knight dearly with every reunion, on or off-camera. "He was such a good guy," she said. "Every time we see each other we talk about how it seems only halfway right without him."

The show's female cast, meanwhile, including Harper, Leachman, Engel, and White, were "very supportive of each other," Mary said. "It was a decision on the part of executive producers Jim Brooks and Allan Burns that we didn't want anybody who was difficult to get along with, no matter how talented they were. We wanted people who were going to be supportive of the rest of the cast. And we were not disappointed."

Mary recalled that she kept an even temper because she "had to set an example for the rest. I never really felt free to give in to my emotions. I was the mother. And we were truly one close family."

Near the close of the special, the results of an online poll revealed the all-time favorite episode of the show as "Chuckles Bites the Dust" (October 25, 1975). Mary named her personal favorite: "The one when everything goes wrong for Mary and she had to go to the Teddy Awards to accept an award looking really awful – with a false eyelash" ("Put on a Happy Face" – February 24, 1973).

The sole somber aspect of the special was the absence of Knight. "He was such a good guy," Mary said. "We talk about how important he was, not only to the show but also to us. I was waiting for the Laurence Olivier role that surely was going to come Ted's way, but he was taken too soon. The man had such breadth, depth, and imagination. He cared very much about his work."

But there was a point in the show's second year, when Knight sought to be written out of the series. "He was afraid he'd be forever typecast as a buffoon." It was then Allan Burns convinced Knight that it was impossible for anyone to confuse him with Ted Baxter, and the actor remained with the show until its final episode in 1977, winning smiles and accolades along the way. He also went on to star in movies like 1980's *Caddyshack*, and in his own sitcom *Too Close for Comfort*, which later changed to *The Ted Knight Show*.

In all, Mary wasn't surprised by the high ratings of reunion specials like hers, and others, such as the one for *The Carol Burnett Show*. It all had to do with the audience's general desire for "the way it was. It's an important part of us that is comforting to hang onto now."

To promote the new special Mary made the talk-show circuit such as spots on *Late Night with David Letterman* and *The Rosie O'Donnell Show*, where fellow guest Penny Marshall told her, "I should have been on the *Mary Tyler Moore Reunion*. I was on that show a lot." She was not wrong. Marshall played a bar patron in the fourth season, and was Mary's neighbor Paula Kovacs in the sixth year, before moving on to her starring role opposite Cindy Williams on *Laverne & Shirley*.

On June 2, 2002, Mary was a presenter at the 56th Annual Tony Awards. As in the previous seven years, the awards telecast aired on PBS for the first hour, and CBS for the final two hours. She proudly announced *"Thoroughly Modern Millie!"* as the Tony Award winner for best musical. Mary, of course, had starred opposite Julie Andrews and Carol Channing in the 1967 Universal film on which the new *Millie* stage show was based, while Sutton Foster played Millie in the revival.

A few days after the Tony telecast, Mary was one of the celebrities who shared their favorite love stories on the CBS special, *AFI's 100 Years...100 Passions*. This was the American Film Institute's look at the top romantic films ever made, as selected by a panel of 1800 film-industry notables. Harrison Ford, Faye Dunaway, Janet Jackson, and Kathleen Turner were among the other celebrities who participated, as well as the late Neil Simon, with whom Mary would later publicly bicker about her performance in his *Rose's Dilemma* in December 2003.

As the summer of 2002 continued, Mary co-hosted with Bernadette Peters another edition of Broadway Barks, with other celebs like David Hasselhoff, and daytime TV's *Passions* star Josh Ryan Evans attending. Performers included Brooke Shields, who won solid reviews for her starring role in a revival of *Cabaret*, and who was fresh off of her TV sitcom, *Suddenly Susan* (NBC, 1996-2000) which had been compared many times to *The Mary Tyler Moore Show.*

In late 2002, Mary decided to reunite with Dick Van Dyke in the PBS television special edition of the play, *The Gin Game*, which did not air until May 4, 2003.

The Gin Game became the first time in over twenty years that the former classic TV lovebirds worked together. They seemed to revel in the unsavory language of the new characters they now portrayed: senior nursing home residents Fonsia Dorsey, played by Mary, and Weller Martin, played by Van Dyke, who interacted during a series of gin-rummy card games.

Thirty years before, Van Dyke had enjoyed what he believed was a premium rendition of *The Gin Game* starring Hume Cronyn and Jessica Tandy. "You can't get better than that," he thought. Van Dyke so thoroughly enjoyed the play that in a later conversation with Mary, he said, "Someday we're going to be old enough do that, and I'd like to do it." To which she replied, "I'd like to take a crack at that, too." Van Dyke later talked to her again and said, "Mary, we're old enough now," and she agreed. "We were trying to sell it, for some reason," recalled Van Dyke. "I don't know whether it was because it's dated material, or Mary and I are dated, or what. Finally, PBS said why don't we go ahead and do it."

"Dick had always wanted to do *The Gin Game* and, after many years of cajoling, he finally convinced Mary to do the play with him," observed David Van Deusen, editor of *The Dick Van Dyke Show* newsletter *The Walnut Times* (named in honor of the *Van Dyke* 1963 episode, "It May Look Like a Walnut"). "Their characters were a stark departure from what fans had become accustomed to, but I think the performances of both were very convincing and genuinely appreciated by fans – all despite the fact that much of the foul language that came out of their mouths was probably offensive to many…and probably not something routinely heard on PBS. I know that Dick had to overdub some of his lines to allow the show to play in certain areas of the country."

Mary and Dick's *Gin Game* became part of KCET/Hollywood's acclaimed drama series *PBS Hollywood Presents*. It was directed by

Arvin Brown, and began production July 29, 2002. Based on the Pulitzer-winning play by D.L. Coburn, who adapted his work for this new TV edition, *The Gin Game* was described in a PBS press release as "a powerfully bittersweet comedy."

"Though Weller is the much more seasoned player," the press release detailed, "Fonsia consistently beats him and the more they play, the more frustrated Weller becomes. As the games progress, their ailments, misfortunes and losses are exposed in funny, honest and increasingly heated moments. What begins as a tentative friendship quickly turns into a battle of wills, but their need for companionship keeps the game going until all their cards are on the table." Pat Mitchell, then president and CEO of PBS, said this was "a significant event in television history. Dick Van Dyke and Mary Tyler Moore are two of America's most beloved television icons and we are thrilled to reunite them in a production that will showcase their legendary chemistry in ways we've never seen before."

Mary Mazur, executive producer of *PBS Hollywood Presents*, added, "*The Gin Game* is a superbly crafted play about winning and losing – about friendship, loneliness and loss. Dick and Mary are masters at both comedy and drama, which makes them the perfect pair for the production."

Airing on May 4, 2003, *The Gin Game* was a unique vehicle for Mary and Van Dyke as senior citizens who come to terms over a game of cards. Now seniors themselves, Mary, in her mid-60s, and Van Dyke, in his mid-70s, acted their age in this *Game*. But to many eyes she appeared older and less healthy than he did. Loyal watchers of *The Dick Van Dyke Show* compared their appearance to a classic episode ("The Brave and the Backache" – February 12, 1964), in which a physically compromised Rob and Laura at one point both bend over due to temporary back ailments, and joke with one another in elderly voices.

"This play could be viewed from an existential point of view," recalled Coburn. "I thought that for a long time. But the play is rather simple and straightforward. I'm very pleased that people will view this wonderful production with Dick and Mary and simply enjoy it, without thinking of it in terms of existentialism. But comedy is a wonderful way to give expression to the deeper things that we ponder."

Coburn had added a dance sequence for a previous production of *The Gin Game* which was performed by Julie Harris and Charles Durning. With Mary and Van Dyke now in the *Game*, director Arvin Brown thought utilizing the dance sequence would be "irresistible – because they're both fabulous dancers." "As they dance together," he observed, "I have the camera on a crane, and we rise up slowly with them. The camera expresses their sense of being lifted. In the next moment, a hand-held camera is directly on their faces, moving in a circular way with them as they dance. Those kinds of decisions you can make with the camera are life-enhancing for the piece."

"Mary found wonderful ways to try to entice Dick on to the floor with her," Brown continued, "because his character is reluctant to dance. Dick and Mary very carefully sidestepped any question of coming together and suddenly dazzling us with fancy footwork. It's a lovely moment to watch them do it, but it's a Fonsia-Weller moment."

According to Brown, Mary and Van Dyke did not behave "like legends for one second. They certainly know the position they occupy in the American psyche. They were coming back together again for the first time since [1969, and *Dick Van Dyke and the Other Woman*], and people were thrilled with the idea of this. I think they were genuinely touched by people's interest in the project."

Mary and Van Dyke had reunited several times on-screen between *Dick Van Dyke and the Other Woman* and *The Gin Game* – her variety special, for one – but *The Gin Game* was the first time in a long while that they performed as equal co-stars in any lengthy production. Their combined fan base had long waited to see them in a more formal production, especially on television. Both stars, especially Mary, knew that the stakes and expectations were high.

Mary and Van Dyke shared on *PBS.org* their thoughts in detail about appearing in this special program. Mary's comments, in particular, can be taken as applying to her own life. Some of the insights seemed to address if not flat-out describe her personal experiences. Portions of her *Gin Game* assessment are as follows:

> The characters are so beautifully drawn. They are complete characters, true to themselves. There's not one moment in this play where I say to myself, as an actress, "I wish this moment would pass." Such moments do exist in most everything you do [such as "I don't understand this line, etc...but] not so in The Gin Game. Every moment may be challenging [or] scary, but it's enjoyable.

> Fonsia is a woman who is thoroughly...clinically depressed. She wanted everything to be perfect and she imposed unreachable goals on her husband and on her son and much of her family. As a result, when she reaches 71 [years of age], she's in retirement...[and] has no one left in her life. Nobody comes to visit her.

There was a lot that appealed to me about Fonsia. I love strong women and they can be misguided...self-serving...or...rigid, and this woman is rigid. But she meets Weller Martin and there's a ray of hope. This man has a sense of humor and he makes her laugh...forget how little [time] she has left and for how...few days....It's heartbreaking to watch them both have the potential to enrich themselves and lose it.

The big surprise that I loved about Fonsia was that she appeared to be in the beginning very much a victim – a victim of a family that was no longer paying attention to her. She was at an old-age home where she didn't have any real options in life. She seemed to be very frail, very fragile. And it evolves, through her seeing [Weller's] manipulation of her in these gin games, which my character keeps winning. A resentment builds, and through that resentment a lot of anger and hostility that she tried to keep quiet during the early part of her life came out, and gripped him by the throat in her very angry hands.

You see the potential of a couple who certainly had some attraction to each other...who could have been good for each other, could have a life together or nearby, and see it dissipate. Not only dissipate but be beaten to death. So, it's a very sad piece, but it is also inspirational...[a viewer can] see how easy it is to let go of something that could be good, to let [their] own determination and habit and ways of living that are self-serving get in the way of something good.

Weller is angry on the surface because Fonsia's winning all the games. But as [the story] evolves and he begins to divulge things about himself then he gets angry at himself. And that emerges and takes over his character. She is seemingly more innocent in the beginning, and she seems to be just delighted that she's winning these games. But as she sees his hostility emerge she then gives vent to her memories of her life and where she had failed. And she can't quite forgive herself so she takes it out on him.

Fonsia certainly is a very religious person and was raised to be a lady and...to always read the Bible and be fluent in it and call upon the Lord in the most embracing terms that one can, [and] never take the Lord's name in vain. And Weller is just the opposite. He's gone berserk. I have a feeling that he was probably like that even when he was young, before he started getting so inverted as a human being.

This is heady...good stuff. It's timeless because it's truthful about...the human nature of people who have [led this kind of life]. It's recognizable. You see it. You see parts of yourself in these characters.

The play is about the head games that people get into even in old age, sometimes especially in old age. It's only then that you can feel free enough to recall the reality, the brutality of what you did in your life. It's not about, "Oh my arthritis...or my whatever." It's about the psychological dissipation, and the psychological hope that is out there.

Weller represents a lot of what her ex, now deceased husband was...that maniacal determination to win...the use of foul language. All of those things really oppressed Fonsia. And she sees it in him and so, in the strange way that we folk do, we tend to gravitate toward what we know, even though it's awful, even though it's bad for us and we hate it...you tend to want to go back to that. Child abusers produce child abusers, alcoholics beget alcoholics.

The play is about wasted opportunity....a seemingly hopeless situation that presents...the possibility of a happy ending. And in seeking it, how our pasts take us over and prevent that happy ending from occurring.

I love the fact that it deals with older people and how insoluble it seems, dealing with deteriorating health and encroaching age. If you're very lucky you can stay in your own home with nursing care, but for the most part, people have to go into institutional care, and there's no way that can be anything but bleak.

It's one of the most challenging roles of my life. And the fact that I am doing with Dick enabled me to take it on because I knew I would feel supported and I would be comfortable and I would be working with somebody who was going to bring a great deal to it. It's just so much fun. When we're not on camera playing these characters tearing at each other's souls, we have so much fun reminiscing and talking about mutual friends and so on.

It's a lot of dialogue to memorize. And for us in this project, where we are locked at a table for a good portion of it, playing cards, which had to be dealt and drawn and taken, and gin that has to come at a certain point. And Dick can do sleight-of-hand like a pro. He can make cards flip and disappear, but shuffling was something he had to really work at. It was a tremendous challenge because it's hard enough to memorize a two-character play to begin with but when you add all of that to it it's a steep mountain that I found that I was climbing every morning.

I think we've done it: getting up extra early, studying the lines, letting them digest, buoying Dick's spirits because he's used to doing comedy and this is kind of oppressive in certain ways. I think we've done a really good job.

[Playwright D.L.] Coburn was there with us for three days, three, four days of rehearsal and the first two or three days of shooting. And it was great. The best thing he did for me was come over and squeeze my arm and grin from ear to ear after I would do a scene and I knew I had pleased him, and you can't ask for more than that.

Arvin Brown was the best director. He knows when to push and when to withdraw and how to get us going at our peak production. He made me feel so up to the role. I came into it feeling this is a heady piece of work I have to do, and I want it to be really great. He allowed me to do that. And he modulated us. He brought out the best of our abilities and helped us find some moments that I didn't know were out there.

I was talking with Dick about the difference between doing comedy and drama. Drama is slower and comedy is fast [with the right] timing [and] pace. In comedy, if there's dead air, you want to cover it and get going...onto the next line. And in drama, you really

have to believe in yourself enough to know that space
is not necessarily dead air. That's an opportunity to
find another color.

It would take a different kind of mechanics to do this for the stage. We have the luxury of tape. We were only given ten days of rehearsal to put this together and 12 days of taping. As a result, we are not perfect in the roles when we're performing but because of the magic of tape, we can go back and do it again and again and again until it's right. You don't have that luxury on stage. But what you do have on stage is three months of rehearsal. So that it is a part of your being and you don't even think about it anymore.

Mary's chemistry with Van Dyke remained solid. For example, during one tense moment in playing *Gin*, Van Dyke's character refers to Mary's as a bitch. Upon completing the scene, Mary turned to Van Dyke and joked out-of-character, literally, "You've been wanting to call me that for years."

In another interplay, Fonsia gives Weller an unladylike rap in the chops, which one reporter compared to a scene from *Who's Afraid of Virginia Woolf?* "It really is!" Mary laughed in agreement. "That slap was so loud I shocked myself. Are you OK, Dick?" she said to Van Dyke by her side. "Has the welt gone down?"

"Don't let her kid you," Van Dyke smiled as he bounced Mary's joke back at her. "She's been waiting over 40 years to do that!"

While such playful interaction perfectly defined their chemistry, Mary found it challenging to pinpoint exactly why she and Van Dyke worked so well together. "I don't know how to explain it," she told the *Los Angeles Times*. "We are just Dick and Mary."

Chapter

30

Mary followed up her *Gin Game* with Dick Van Dyke by playing with Burt Reynolds in a holiday TV-movie called *Miss Lettie and Me*, which aired December 8, 2002 on TNT as a Johnson & Johnson Spotlight Presentation. Although Mary and Reynolds "sound like a dream team," wrote critic Laura Fries in *Variety*, "...the two veterans aren't utilized to their full potential." And while "the pic has its moments," Fries called it "as fluffy and sterile as its sponsor's cotton swabs."

Entertainment Weekly described *Lettie* as a "listless love story," and gave it a "C-"grade, while *Star Magazine* called Mary's performance "exceptional."

Based on the short story "Poor Little Innocent Lambs" by Katherine Paterson (*Jacob Have I Loved*), *Miss Lettie and Me* was filmed in Griffin, Georgia by the Polson Company in association with Viacom Productions and Magna Global Entertainment. Co-producer Dalene Young (*Little Darlings, Jonathan: The Boy Nobody Wanted*) penned the teleplay, which was directed by Ian Barry (*The Doctor Blake Mysteries, Early Edition, Farscape*).

Mary played sixty-something Lettie Anderson, a rancorous woman who isolates herself for years as the head of her family's farm, which she operates with the assistance of her longtime employee Isaiah Griffin (played by Charlie Robinson), and her former lover Samuel Madison (Reynolds). She feels aimless and left behind by relatives who have taken her for granted, including her orphaned niece Alison (portrayed by Jennifer Crumbly Bonder). But Lettie is ultimately inspired by Alison's young daughter Travis (Holliston Coleman), who becomes the "Me" in the title.

"If you love predictability," Anita Gates observed in *The New York Times*, "you'll be crazy about *Miss Lettie and Me*. Travis thinks small-town life is appalling until she learns good country values...There's a sentimental speech about the changing seasons, a heartwarming Christmas pageant and a little lamb that goes to school one day. As for Lettie's bitterness, it comes from bringing up her orphaned niece, Allison (Travis's mom), and what thanks did she get?"

"Moore comes alive towards the latter part of the film," concluded *Variety*'s Fries, "...especially when verbally sparring with Robinson. Most of the film however, rests on the shoulders of young Coleman as Travis. Although extremely earnest and amazingly cute, it's too much for the young girl. In fact, Coleman may actually be too cute for her own good."

Mary may have flinched upon reading the comment. After all, such statements had once been made concerning her own looks and talents.

But work continued to beckon. In the summer of 2003 Mary flew to Nova Scotia for the TV-movie *Blessings*, which aired the following October 1. This time, she co-starred with China Chow, Kathleen Quinlan (*The Abduction of St. Anne*, the mystic 1975 ABC TV-movie), and father-and-son Ralph Waite (*The Waltons*) and Liam Waite. In a story reminiscent of *Miss Lettie and Me*, Mary portrayed Lydia Blessing, yet another bitter recluse. This time she is an heiress who develops a strong bond with her live-in handyman (Liam) while they care for an abandoned newborn.

Mary read the *Blessings* script before casting took place and was immediately interested in the role, if with some initial apprehension about playing what was an elderly character. "For my age," she told CBS News, "mid-60s to...82 it is a stretch. But I thought I could handle it, especially after doing *The Gin Game* with Dick Van Dyke where I played a woman in her early 80s. I was just so challenged and fascinated by this script, which takes you through some emotional things and some funny things. But primarily it doesn't tie up every little frayed ending into a neat little bow and it leaves you gasping."

Mary evidently had forgotten that the Fonsia character in *Gin Game* was "only" 73. It was a sad truth that Mary looked older in real life. She knew this, but who would want to admit it? Meanwhile, critic Ann Donahue of *Variety* was not so subtle with her review of *Blessings*:

> CBS Sunday Movie *Blessings* is so intent on tear-jerking that it does everything short of coming to your

house and kicking your puppy. Based on Anna Quindlen's bestselling novel, [this film] should have a built-in fan base, but it's hard to imagine the uninitiated sticking around for two hours of unrelenting emotional crises and death.

Eighty-year-old heiress Lydia Blessing (Mary Tyler Moore, made up to look incredibly wizened) is sole mistress of her huge estate, Blessings. She employs a young, tart-tongued housekeeper, Jennifer (China Chow), and is on the lookout for a groundskeeper, having fired the last one for not putting away his work gloves and making weak coffee.

Conveniently, Skip Cuddy (Liam Waite) has just been released from jail for his unwitting participation in a convenience store holdup. He accepts the job after [a cute meeting] with Lydia in a Wal-Mart parking lot. Their attempt at peaceful bucolic living comes abruptly to an end when a teenage couple drops off their newborn daughter on the steps of the garage where Skip lives on the property.

In a recipe for disaster, the trio opts to keep quiet about the baby's arrival. They settle into an uneasy routine on the estate, always keeping an eye out for intruders and family members who would snatch the child, Faith, into the foster care system if they knew she existed.

Moore, as ever, does a bang-up job, portraying Lydia as a woman who has always relied on her wealth and status to overcompensate for naiveté. The presence of the tot brings up unpleasant memories for Lydia of her younger days on the estate, setting up a series of flashbacks.

These look period-appropriate and give more texture to Lydia's brittleness – as portrayed by Janaya Stephens, she really had a big problem picking the right guys – but unfortunately, the repercussions are teased out as a "twist" that's really quite obvious and discovered only when the action returns to the present day.

> The pace is akin to that of a legit performance, which is always hard to pull off successfully on television. There are many scenes of the characters standing around and talking, alternating with scenes of them sitting around and talking. It's not the most dynamic staging, and the lack of action makes the lessons of the story much more overt than they should be.

As one mishap after another befalls the clan at Blessings, subtlety goes out the window. All that's missing are framed posters with inspirational sayings like: "Be careful what you wish for" and "Be thankful for what you already have" hanging in the background.

Mary should have kept such maudlin advice in mind two months later, in December 2003, when she walked out of the Neil Simon play, *Rose's Dilemma*, citing issues with the playwright. Reportedly, Simon kept reworking the dialogue, which he expected her to learn immediately. "Things started out okay," David Davis observed, "but quickly disintegrated when Mary couldn't keep up with all the last-minute rewrites. They tried to accommodate her by having her read a letter in a scene, instead of having to memorize its content. But she still struggled with what became perpetual changes. So, she wore an earpiece, and instructed her assistant, Terry Sims, to read her the script."

When Simon got word of this development, "…he was furious," Davis said. "He said this threw off the rhythm of the play. So, during a dress rehearsal, Simon had his wife [actress-singer/dancer Elaine Joyce] hand-deliver a note to Mary in her dressing room which read, 'Learn your lines or get out of my play.'" Mary became furious, rushed out the door while still wearing her wig, and immediately left the building and the play. And although Mary allegedly later made light of the situation, Mara Buxbaum, her then-representative from PMK Public Relations, at first released a statement saying, "Mary is devastated. She's been working tirelessly for months and feels pushed out of this production."

Mary was eventually replaced by actress Patricia Hodges, whom Simon had hailed as "perfect for the role." But without Mary's name on the marquee, the play bombed, closing two months later following poor reviews. "Apparently," Davis said, "it was a wobbly production all along, in part because Simon was in the midst of kidney dialysis and not in the best of spirits."

On March 12, 2003, spirits were higher when Mary and the cast of *The Dick Van Dyke Show* were honored with "The Legend Award" at the televised *TV Land Awards*. While at the podium, Rose Marie, caught up in the moment, encouraged a newly scripted episode of the beloved series, exclaiming, "Yes – we'll do it!"

Mary, for one, had never shown interest in reprising Laura for any TV-reunion movie. She responded to Marie, and the audience, with a defiant, "No, we won't!"

However, it was only one year later when she, Marie, and fellow *Van Dyke* cast-mates regrouped for the 159th episode of *The Dick Van Dyke Show Revisited*. It aired May 11, 2004, and was introduced by life-long *Van Dyke/Tyler Moore* shows fan Ray Romano. Romano's own sitcom, *Everybody Loves Raymond*, also happened to be one of Mary's favorite shows. In fact, a few years before, in 2000, she participated in a CBS special that commemorated *Raymond*'s 100th episode. So, with Romano now hosting *Revisited*, the mutual admiration society was complete. And this special stood apart from the previous *Van Dyke* reunion from 1994 titled *The Dick Van Dyke Show Remembered*, when the cast celebrated, documentary-style, the original series.

The *Revisited* special revived the remaining *Van Dyke* characters within a story. In *Revisited* Rob and Laura Petrie have moved to Manhattan, where he's retired and she's fulfilling a lifelong dream of owning and operating a dance studio. His former boss, the self-serving TV variety show host Alan Brady (Carl Reiner, who penned the script), calls Rob out of retirement to write Alan's eulogy ahead of time, so he can control what it will say.

This innovative, if slightly morbid, tale included appearances by Marie's Sally, now married to long-time boyfriend Herman Glimsher (the returning Bill Idelson, who had written many *Van Dyke* episodes); Millie Helper (Anne Guilbert, who by then had dropped "Morgan" from her stage name), the Petrie's former neighbor (and Laura's best friend); Rob's brother Stacy (Jerry Van Dyke, Dick's real-life sibling), and Larry Mathews as the adult Ritchie, now the proud owner of his parents' original New Rochelle homestead.

Acknowledgements were made of original cast members and their roles: Jerry Paris as Millie's wisecracking dentist-husband Dr. Jerry Helper (and Rob's best friend); Richard Deacon as the put-upon Mel Cooley, producer and harried brother-in-law to *The Alan Brady Show*'s star; and on-and-off-screen "human joke machine" Morey Amsterdam as Buddy Sorrell.

At the invitation of Reiner, David Van Deusen "had the privilege to 'hang out' on the set and observe the behind-the-scenes happenings along with a handful of family members and a few other invited guests. During breaks in the shooting, it was evident that the cast was truly in the moment and appreciating what they had been so blessed to be a part of some 45 or so years before."

Van Deusen went on, "Most noteworthy was the interaction of Rose Marie and Mary, who seemed to really enjoy each other's company. As we have come to find out in *Wait for Your Laugh*, the film biography on Rose Marie's life and career, Rose and Mary's relationship was a bit strained from time to time during the run of *The Dick Van Dyke Show*. But this was not the case during the filming of *The Dick Van Dyke Show Revisited*, as I think that each of them came to realize and treasure each other's friendship."

From Van Deusen's perspective, "*The Dick Van Dyke Show Revisited* was a unique and marvelous production for many reasons. It afforded both new and old generations of fans to find out what had become of Rob, Laura, Buddy, Sally, Alan, and even Ritchie – not to mention Millie and Herman - and to see the Petries living 'in color.' What a treat!"

Revisited was indeed a noble, though in some ways awkward effort. Beyond the odd premise, Romano's involvement seemed forced and unnecessary. And how believable is it that Ritchie Petrie would restock his childhood home with furniture identical to his 1960s boyhood? While the sense of nostalgia was appreciated, the Petries having a marooned-in-time living room was not.

In like manner, Mary also seemed out of place. She was called "Laura," but she could just as easily pass as an updated version of Mary Richards.

A similar situation had occurred some years before when Robert Young as Jim Anderson regrouped with his TV *Father Knows Best* cast-mates for the first of two 1977 reunion movies of that family series which originally ran from 1954 to 1960 on CBS and NBC. By the time the initial *Best* reunion aired on May 15, 1977, Young was also known for his starring role in *Marcus Welby, M.D.*, a one-hour medical drama which screened on ABC from 1969 to 1975. In the first *Father* redo, *The Father Knows Best Reunion*, he seems more like Dr. Welby than Jim Anderson, his *Father* role. Both Anderson and Welby are paternal figures, but different characters, and Young did not fully rediscover his *Best* voice until the second *Knows* reunion, *Father Knows Best: Home for Christmas*, which aired December 18, 1977.

It's a worthy comparison to Mary's remix of Laura/Mary on *Van Dyke Revisited*. Consider the comments of *Father Knows Best* actor Billy Gray who played Young's on-screen son, Jim, "Bud" Anderson, Jr. in both the original *Father* series and its subsequent reunions. Gray recently remembered *Home's* first day of rehearsal when Young, who struggled with depression and alcohol throughout his life, remained locked in his dressing room, refusing to be on the *Best* set. "It was a strange thing to see," Gray said.

Nothing quite like this happened on *Revisited*'s initial rehearsal day, but Mary too had struggled with depression and alcoholism. This may have contributed to an inability to find Laura's voice, even though Larry Mathews doesn't see it that way. As far as he's concerned, Mary was back in fine form as his TV mom, and very different from her Mary Richards role. "When we did the *Revisited* special," he observed, "I saw her only as Laura Petrie," adding that she was "thrilled" to be there. "She was very embracing of the entire thing, and she loved it."

According to Mathews, he and Mary shared "some quality time together," during which she sent some much-appreciated compliments his way, after he finished rehearsing one of his scenes in the Petries' living room. Here, Ritchie talks on the phone with Reiner's Alan Brady who, like Rob and Laura, now lives in Manhattan. Reiner was not on-set. Mathews performed alone, carefully measuring the timing of the scene, which contained exposition that helped to set up the premise.

When the director yelled "cut," Mary made her approach to Mathews.

"I've been meaning to tell you something," she said, "...you are amazing."

"Thank you, Mary," he replied. "I try to do the best I can."

"No, no," she insisted. "You're not hearing me. You're brilliant. One of the hardest things for an actor to do is a timed scene on the phone when there is no other actor to interact with, and you did it perfectly. I just want you to know how proud I am of you...as an actor...but more so of the adult you have become, and all that you have accomplished in your field."

Mathews periodically performs on-screen or does voiceovers for animated TV shows like *Family Guy*, but has been working for years behind-the-scenes in the industry, inspired by *Van Dyke Show* director John Rich. Today, he is the Vice President of Sales for CCI Digital, a post-production house based in Burbank, California. While performing on *Revisited*, he worked for Matchframe Video, which served as the special's post-production company. When hearing Mary's praise, he was "...stunned and taken aback." "She gave me a hug," he said, "...just as my Mom walked up to me."

Mary turned to Mrs. Mazzeo (Mathews' real last name), and reiterated her accolades. "You know, Mrs. Mazzeo. Your son is a wonderful human being. He's done great things with his life, and you should be very proud of him. I know I am."

Overwhelmed by Mary's words, Mathews was inspired. Due to her dedicated involvement in various charities for animals and diabetes, he suggested having the *Revisited* cast sign a few copies of the script, which could be auctioned off at one of her charity events. Mary loved the idea and worked on gathering the scripts with Mathews and her husband Robert Levine, whom he remembered as "a very nice man. I really liked him a lot. He was always very unassuming, approachable and down-to-earth. And he was a rock and supportive force for Mary in all their years together. It was clear that they were a great couple. He truly loved her, she loved him, and they loved each other."

Mutual appreciation was also apparent on the *Revisited* set between Mary and Rose Marie. Mathews recalled the interactions between these two strong-willed women as nothing but pleasant, without the conflict that transpired when they worked on the original *Van Dyke* series or at the TV Land Awards. "They actually had a couple of heart-to-heart talks where they kind of just put everything aside," Mathews recalled, "...and they exchanged hugs and moved beyond it all. First and foremost, they were professionals who respected one another in that way. It was a good thing for both of them to make their peace." As he saw it, civility should be evident in any work environment. "What people in our business tend to forget about is this: If you're a star...someone with a real presence, no matter your personal feelings, your level of professionalism will shine through and override everything else. It has to. You can't be emotional. You just have to let things go because there is a lot of microscopes."

Mathews' perspective on Mary's level of power at MTM Enterprises or during any stage of her career echoed Ed Asner's previous statements. "Mary was a pro," Mathews said. "But I think she, as a business woman having to run her company, was a little different in her interactions with certain people at times. She was tough. She really was. I never saw how tough, but I know people who did notice it, and they would say, she could be a ball-buster at times."

"Grant Tinker may have run the day to day operations of MTM," Mathews continued, "but Mary had an influence over what products they took on, who they worked with, and other aspects of the company. She was a smart person and he was, too, and I doubt anyone could ever have their name on a business like she did and not have some kind of hand in it. She was savvy enough to the point where she didn't always let people know just how much power she had."

But while working on *Revisited*, Mary's diabetes was starting to take its toll. "She was very frail, and thin," Mathews observed. "She would have trouble remembering her lines, and would have to go back and concentrate on delivering them and just getting them out there."

Sadly, Rose Marie was having similar struggles. The show was scheduled to have two tapings, in front of a live audience, just like the original series. But after the first week of rehearsal, plans changed when iner realized that both Mary and Marie were struggling with their lines.

"So," Mathews said, "...we shot it like a regular single camera show at that point. Everyone else was fine. Dick was fine. Jerry was fine. And Annie was great," he said in reference to Ann Guilbert, who passed away in 2016, while Van Dyke's brother died two years later.

Guilbert died, Mathews said, "...because she smoked too damn much," a habit the character actress shared with Mary and Van Dyke, who would do cigarette commercials during the original series. "But she got along very well with Mary. They were always friendly and had a good time...Everyone got along." The camaraderie carried over onto the screen, and turned *Revisited* into a hit in the ratings, enough so that the special was repeated several times on both TV Land and CBS (where it was later paired with a clips-reunion special of *The Carol Burnett Show*).

While the critics were none too kind towards *Revisited* (Billy Goodykoontz of *The Arizona Republic* suggested, "Next time, just show old *Van Dyke* clips"), for Mathews the experience was "amazing. It was like time had stood still and forty-something years later we picked right up where we left off," he said. "It was wonderful." As a keepsake of the event, Mathews retained a photo with him, Mary, the Van Dyke brothers, Marie, Guilbert, and Reiner on the set. "Only three of us are alive now."

Chapter

31

The same year *The Dick Van Dyke Show Revisited* debuted, Mary played a strange ex-socialite named Aunt Lulu in the December holiday CBS TV-movie *Snow Wonder*, based on a short story by Connie Willis, adapted to script by Rodney Patrick Vaccaro, and directed by Peter Werner. Besides Mary, the cast included Jennifer Esposito, Camryn Manheim, Poppy Montgomery, Jason Priestley, and Eric Szmanda, among others. According to the network's press release, *Snow Wonder*, filmed in New Orleans in July of 2005, was about a suspiciously magical Christmas Eve snowstorm that brings small miracles into the lives of people around the country. Five otherwise-distinct stories were connected by the odd blizzard, which affects the characters' lives in profound ways.

But as reviewed by Brian Lowry in *Variety* magazine, *Snow Wonder* was "the sort of schmaltz that has served CBS in good stead the last few holiday seasons. Not all of the disconnected stories deliver the heartwarming goods, but pic flits between them amiably enough, and the oversized cast allows multiple performers to parachute in for what must have been a few days' work. Gentle as a dusting of snow and equally insubstantial, telepic is at the least a weightless alternative to the antics on *Desperate Housewives*...

"The remaining plots are highlighted by Mary Tyler Moore's appearance as the eccentric aunt of a young man (Szmanda)...and there is one clever bit, as Moore's Aunt Lula has a history of being known as 'the unidentified woman from her fleeting liaisons with famous men.'"

A character with such contrast to Mary's expected "niceness" may have been the reason she was attracted to this very un-Mary-Richards-type role in the first place.

After completing *Snow Wonder*, Mary went on a one-year hiatus.

In late January 2006, at 69 years old, she returned to work as a Mary Richards-like character named Christine St. George for a three-episode arc of the FOX-TV sitcom *That '70s Show*. St. George was a 1970s career woman employed at a TV station in the Upper Midwest. (Sound familiar?) While Richards was "ladylike and wholesome and welcoming," said Mary to *USA Today*, "this [role] is just the opposite. Christine St. George is a very self-centered woman, a tad psychotic."

The first day on the *'70s* set, Mary found a large "Welcome Back, Mary!" banner waiting for her on the show's soundstage which, as fate would have it, was the same place where *The Mary Tyler Moore Show* was filmed. The plaque on the soundstage wall, commemorating Mary's original sitcom, was still there. But the sets and the acting space, were not the same, of course; new audience bleachers were constructed. Sitcoms were now being shot differently, with an additional camera. And Mary was amazed at the technological advances made in areas such as editing. But despite it all, she said, there was "an aura."

That '70s Show's creative team played with the concepts of Mary's past incarnation. St. George placed a single rose on her desk, as Richards did. Gavin MacLeod made a guest appearance in one episode in which St. George fires him because he's frequently penning tales about Minnesota.

In one scene, series regular (and future film star) Mila Kunis as Jackie Burkhart asks St. George what she thinks of a hat. St. George replies, "I'll show you what I think of it," and as Mary recalled, "I hurled it to the sky with such venom."

"She will try anything," said Kunis about working with Mary. "She's very gung-ho."

The atmosphere, however, may have become too comfortable for actress Debra Jo Rupp, who played *'70s* mother Kitty Forman. While attending college, Rupp had enjoyed watching *The Mary Tyler Moore Show*. Years later, when she found herself on the same set with Mary, Rupp became a little tongue-tied at certain moments. At one point, Rupp needed to ask Mary about a scene, and referred to her as "Mare," as would Rhoda, Murray or Ted Baxter might have on the *MTM Show*. Rupp was mortified, and told Mary, "Oh, my God. That's too intimate."

But Mary was unfazed. She enjoyed working on a weekly sitcom again, and that's all that mattered. "It's the sound of laughter," she said. "That's what I miss more than anything."

A short time later, Mary reiterated to Carlos Ferrer how much she enjoyed performing on the *'70s Show*, and returning to the familiar filming technique and surroundings. "*That '70s Show*...was the first multi-camera [sitcom] I've done in a long time, and...I love it. I forgot how much I love it." She embraced her reprise to weekly TV, performing in front of a live audience, the multi-camera format, and being on the set of any television show or movie where even a single camera was mostly utilized. Either format worked for her because she was so excited to work.

Before her *Mary Tyler Moore* sitcom, of course, *The Dick Van Dyke Show* utilized the multi-camera approach. It was a Desilu Studio practice originated in 1951 for *I Love Lucy* on CBS. In those days, a total of 300 people in the studio audience was the standard size for a sitcom. Mary said, that's "all you need to get the reaction you want in a comedy, and it's best that [the show in question] be a comedy."

The multi-camera or film technique allowed for the luxury of "stopping tape," or film, should there be any flubs in dialogue or technical difficulties. In such a case, especially when making a television series in front of a live audience, "You're nervous, you want to please that group of people, but...you can back up a few words and cover that nasty little mistake and go on," Mary maintained. In doing so, she decided, the TV or movie process becomes "a perfect, perfect world." She said that she loved performing in big-screen features "more than anything...because you have the luxury of time...a slightly larger budget," than with any television show or TV movie when the funding is usually calculated "down to the penny."

On August 3, 2006, the *New York Post* reported that Mary pocketed $6.6 million for the sale of her co-op apartment that she owned for decades in the famed San Remo. Mary apparently gifted the apartment to her mother-in-law several years before moving to an apartment at 927 Fifth Avenue, which she had sold in 2005 for $18 million.

The six-room apartment on the 21st floor of the Central Park West building had two bedrooms, two baths, a maid's room, and a formal dining room. It also had a partial park view and a full view of the Manhattan skyline. Mary, who had registered her main address in Millbrook, New York, sold the apartment to socialite art dealer Solange Landau, according to public records.

Certainly cost was not the issue for Oprah Winfrey when, on May 29, 2008, the talk-show-maven-turned-"Queen of All Media" invited the entire *Mary Tyler Moore* cast to her set, which was transformed into an exact replica of Mary Richards' living room and the fictional WJM-TV newsroom. Mary was overwhelmed with the results, as were her former co-stars Ed Asner, Valerie Harper, Gavin MacLeod, Cloris Leachman, Georgia Engel, and Betty White.

That day, Winfrey once more professed her love for *The Mary Tyler Moore Show* and its star. "The show was a light in my life and Mary was a trailblazer for my generation. She's the reason I wanted my own production company. It's the reason there is a HARPO [Winfrey's media company] because that was the inspiration."

Oprah show production designer Tara Denise explained on *Oprah.com* how it all transpired. She and her crew went to extensive lengths to recreate the *Moore* show's two main visual centerpieces. "When I first heard we were going to do the *Mary Tyler Moore* set, I was just ecstatic," Denise said. "It's history. I really think it's a show that we all admired, and so we really wanted to give it the best representation and show it as close as we could get it."

Before any construction – or re-construction – of the sets took place, the crew began viewing DVDs of the original show. "We just started watching them over and over again," relayed single-name scenic designer Dustin. "We found out how tall [Mary] actually was, and we scaled all the drawings based on her height." The *Oprah* show's art director then shopped thrift stores, antique shops, "…just about everywhere," even eBay, seeking items that would match the original *Tyler Moore Show* sets.

But as Mary would later point out in her second memoir, *Growing Up Again*, several challenges surfaced during the *Oprah* recreation of her famous sitcom sets. One was more serious than the other.

While searching her memory for *MTM Show* anecdotes to share on *Oprah*, Mary recalled stumbling her way to what she thought was her old dressing room. Upon opening what she thought was her dressing-room door Mary caught a full Monty of Asner stepping out of his shower. That's right. It was his dressing room, not Mary's. As Asner tried to reach for a towel, Mary tipped over a floor lamp while backing up in a fluster. It was the kind of experience that needed to be immediately addressed or "not at all," Mary wrote.

They both opted for "not at all," until Mary eventually documented it in *Growing Up Again*, when she felt compelled to compare notes and address Asner's "rave reviews of his enormous talent through the years"; how such gifts "should not be limited to what you see on screen."

Flash-forward, so to speak, to behind-the-scenes of Oprah's rebooted *MTM Show* sets, as Mary was being guided through before taping by Oprah's assistant director (A.D.). He informed her that the floor level of the remade WJM-TV set was ten inches lower than the original. It all had something to do with the piping on the Oprah soundstage. Although Oprah's A.D. apologized for the discrepancy, Mary was grateful to him for giving her a heads-up about the glitch. With her vision issues then increasing, she told him, "Imagine what disaster could befall your most earnest Mary."

Shortly thereafter, however, Mary could have used that A.D.'s guidance when she tripped and fell over her dog Spanky, and broke her kneecap. And though mostly immobile in recovery, at least Mary was able to complete the manuscript for *Growing Up Again*, which was published in September 2008.

While promoting *Growing*, she granted an interview to entertainment journalists Marilyn Beck and Stacy Jenel Smith for *The National Ledger*. Beck and Smith touted her "terrific turn" as Joyce, Brooke Shields' mother on the NBC TV series *Lipstick Jungle*, while Mary hoped for additional chances to take that turn again. "If I have my druthers," she said, "There will be more. I love the fact that my character is well-rounded and has depth." Mary "adored" working with Shields, who she called "…just wonderful. I love her talent and her great sense of humor."

She told Beck and Smith that diabetes had left her not only with diminished eyesight, but periodically feeling "down in the dumps…not knowing which way to turn." That's when she turned to her Catholic upbringing for comfort, even though she later began to question her religion's tenets. "I couldn't live with them," she said. "I knew, for example, I would be using birth control."   But during her various challenges and tragedies over the years, she received "strength from God's presence in my life. Time is a great healer."

In 2009, Mary, now 72, appeared in her final feature film, *Against the Current*, a title which she might have felt applied in several ways to her own life. Directed and written by Peter Callahan, *Current* starred Joseph Fiennes as a man who attempts to supersede his tragic past by swimming the 150-mile length of the lower Hudson River. Mary has a small but substantial part as mother to Liz Clark, played by Elizabeth Reaser, who also stars along with Justin Kirk, Michelle Trachtenberg, and Pell James.

When he first reviewed the film for *Variety*, Justin Chang described it as "a long, slow trip down the Hudson River for a grief-stricken swimmer as well as the audience…A waterlogged spin on the road-trip movie that banally confronts the question of whether taking one's own life can ever be justified…[A film that]…could drift idly through theaters before docking at cable and homevid stations."   Nevertheless, Chang felt that "Mary Tyler Moore's colorful cameo as Liz's mom has the disruptive impact of a pebble hurled into still water."

Kirk Honeycutt of *The Associated Press/The Hollywood Reporter* wrote:

"Outfitting his river movie *Against the Current* with comedy, sadness and wit, writer-director Peter Callahan plunges into the Hudson for a downstream swim through emotional currents that run stronger and more treacherously than the river's. Callahan has written a smart movie, and his casting might be even smarter. Then comes the film's supreme comic interlude as the trio stops for the night at Liz's mother's exquisite Hudson Valley domicile. Mary Tyler Moore as Liz's society-matron mother and Michelle Trachtenberg as her 20-year-old hottie sister have everyone's heads spinning. Gossip, opinions, snide and cutting remarks flow over the dinner table; it must be an aphrodisiac, though, given what happens next."

Growing Up Again focused on Mary's life as a type-1 diabetic, and the proceeds were donated to the Juvenile Diabetes Research Foundation, of which she was the international chairman. As she told *Parade* magazine at the time, "I've had the fame and the joy of getting laughter – those are gifts. Now, I want others to learn how I fell down and picked myself up" – both literally and figuratively.

By then, Mary seemed to have a measure of peace. She professed to not having a drink since 1984. She had been married to Robert Levine for 25 years. Still, the loss of her son Richie haunted her. When *Parade* reporter Kevin Sessums wondered if she had forgiven herself for not being…"a good mother?" she quietly finished his question. "No, I haven't. I still feel as if I weren't a good enough mother. I didn't break any rules. I didn't cause my son any pain. But I did bring to my life some of my father, who was very controlling and very remote. I was working a lot. I wasn't there enough."

However, she still yearned to work. "I love it," she said. "But when one looks at what happened to television, there are so few shows that interest me." Mary betrayed her political leanings when she admitted to watching "a lot of Fox News. I like Charles Krauthammer and Bill O'Reilly," even though she still did not consider herself what Sessums called "a right-winger." "Maybe more of a libertarian centrist," she temporized.

If one-time presidential candidate John McCain had asked her to campaign for him, she would have, despite the majority of the Republican Party's stance against stem-cell research. She had long advocated this branch of science, alongside other celebrities like Michael J. Fox, who was diagnosed with Parkinson's disease in 1991, and Christopher Reeve, who broke his neck in a horrific horse-riding accident in 1995 and was subsequently paralyzed. It was Mary and Reeve who on, July 15, 2001, co-authored an editorial for the *Los Angeles Times* about the importance of stem-cell research which might lead to the cure for diabetes and several

ills.   By this time, Reeve had become the Chairman of the Christopher
Reeve Paralysis Foundation.

> Although President Bush has been in office barely six
> months, he will soon be facing a decision that will
> determine a large part of his presidential legacy. In the
> next few weeks, he will decide whether to allow federal
> funding for research using human embryonic stem
> cells. If he decides against federal support, his legacy
> will be a missed opportunity to make a difference by
> bringing new hope and better lives to 100 million
> Americans facing incurable diseases and life-
> threatening medical conditions, just like the two of us.
> Stem cells could lead to dramatic new treatments or
> even cures for Alzheimer's, cancer, Parkinson's,
> diabetes, heart disease and spinal cord injuries.
> Millions of patients and their families were overjoyed at
> this news. But that joy turned to concern when stem
> cell research became ensnared in controversy.
>
> Some, but by no means all, right-to-life activists oppose
> federal funding of stem cell research involving fertilized
> eggs because they believe it is immoral. We respect
> their concern. However, as people who work every day
> with men, women and children facing incurable
> conditions, we believe this is not an issue that should
> be caught up in the abortion debate.
>
> In making an ethical judgment about this promising
> research, a critical fact is that, under National
> Institutes of Health guidelines, the stem cells that
> could help most to promote new cures and treatments
> would be obtained from excess frozen fertilized eggs.
> These are eggs left over after a couple completes the
> infertility treatment called in vitro fertilization, or IVF. In
> fact, about 100,000 of them are now sitting frozen in
> IVF clinics, destined to be destroyed or remain frozen
> forever. The better, moral choice is to donate them to
> research; the way people donate organs, to help
> millions of Americans have a better life.
>
> It's important to remember that without federal funding
> there will be no federal oversight of stem cell research.
> Instead, stem cell research will be left to individuals
> and private companies that can use fertilized eggs,

free from federal regulations that prevent violations of ethical standards.

Recent newspaper stories have described research advances using adult stem cells or stem cells from fat tissue, which some have tried to use to bolster their arguments against research using stem cells harvested from fertilized eggs. But 80 Nobel Prize winners recently wrote to President Bush to say it is much too early to tell whether adult stem cells have the same potential as their embryonic counterparts. The studies behind the news reports also make it clear that scientists don't yet have conclusive proof that fat tissue really does contain stem cells.

As President Bush considers his options, he will find that many pro-life members of his party, including Sen. Orrin Hatch (R-Utah), Sen. Strom Thurmond (R-S.C.), former Sen. Connie Mack (R-Fla.), former Speaker of the House Newt Gingrich (R-Ga.) and many others strongly support federal funding for stem cell research. So does the American public. In fact, a poll released this spring by the Coalition for the Advancement of Medical Research found that, after hearing both sides, public support for research using stem cells from excess fertilized eggs is overwhelming – 70%.

Moreover, this support includes surprisingly strong backing from Catholics (72%), fundamentalist Christians (63%) and abortion opponents (57%). The poll shows that stem cell research does not divide Americans along pro-life or pro-choice lines, but unites them in support of medical progress to save lives.

All forms of stem cell research could lead to the kinds of medical advances that one day will be compared to the development of penicillin, the polio vaccine and AIDS drugs. President Bush has a historic opportunity to make this his legacy. Millions of families facing incurable diseases and devastating medical conditions hope President Bush will seize this opportunity and not let it slip away.

When Sessums wondered how she reconciled this stance with her Catholic upbringing, Mary replied:

"Certainly George Bush felt he had an obligation to his religion to say he was afraid of it. But no fetus is involved. It's much the same as a family who loses a child. Isn't it a good thing to be able to give those organs to help someone?"

Sessums switched to a more lighthearted subject, a trio of male co-stars from her career: Elvis Presley, whose romantic interest she had once rejected; Robert Redford, a former heartthrob from a distance who became her favorite director for close-ups; and the very liberal Ed Asner. While each of them was definitely in her past, Sessums still wondered, which was her type?

"I think maybe Elvis, because he went so against the grain," she said. "The only leading man I ever had a crush on was James Garner," – in contrast to the time Mary admitted to an innocent mutual romantic admiration between her and Dick Van Dyke. And during her separation from Grant Tinker, "Frank Sinatra did come on to me once," she added. "Ol' Blue Eyes" had an assistant phone her to ask if she would take a call from him.

"Please, by all means," was Mary's response.

Two days later, she heard nothing. But then she and Tinker went out for dinner to discuss a potential reconciliation. Not two feet away from them sat Sinatra. "He came over to say hello," Mary recalled. "I never heard from him after that." As she went on to reveal, "The only other man who ever looked at me the way Frank did was, and don't take this the wrong way – Pope John Paul II. Both men seemed to look into my soul and instantly know me."

Sessums then ended the interview with one more question. "Quick," he said to her. "Fill in the blank: Mary Tyler Moore is…"

"Trustworthy," she replied. "Honest."

"Her laughter," Sessums observed, "…that lovely lightness," then filled the room right before she concluded with a grin, "Unless I'm lying."

Chapter

32

At 74 years old, Mary reunited again with Dick Van Dyke for a special edition of *The Rachael Ray Show* that aired May 2011. In similar fashion to Oprah Winfrey's treatment of the *MTM* series in 2008, Ray recreated the living-room set of *The Dick Van Dyke Show*.

But by then Mary was struggling with increasing health issues. She had been forced to give up her favorite hobbies, such as ballet and horseback riding. The thief of diabetes had begun to steal her eyesight; she started to experience memory loss, and was periodically bedridden, though fortunately her loving husband Robert Levine was never far from her side.

According to a report in *The Los Angeles Times* on March 13, 2011, Mary was scheduled for surgery at an undisclosed hospital to remove a benign tumor called a meningioma. Physicians had been monitoring the growth for quite some time; it wasn't considered life-threatening, and she was expected to make a full recovery. Dr. Neil A. Martin, chair of neurosurgery at UCLA's Ronald Reagan Medical Center, said meningiomas account for slightly more than a quarter of all brain tumors; they grow out of the meninges, the membranes that surround the brain and spinal cord. Technically, meningiomas are not classified as brain tumors, as they do not form in brain tissue, but originate next to the bone of the skull in the dura or arachnoid tissues. From there they grow inward, placing pressure on the brain. When they expand to about 1/2 to 4 inches in size, significant pressure on the brain develops, which in turn may cause neurological symptoms. Although most common in older women like Mary, meningiomas may strike at any age.

Although about 5% turn cancerous, most are generally benign, slow-developing tumors that may require little treatment beyond close observation.

Surgery is delicate at any age for anyone, healthy or unhealthy, male or female, let alone brain surgery for someone like the senior, frail Mary. Her health challenges were measured and exacerbated by her history of alcoholism and diabetes. Another factor to be considered was her history of cosmetic surgeries, which now came back into the fore.

According to an article in *Globe Magazine*, dated February 26, 1991, Mary was ignoring the advice of physicians and friends who were concerned that she was over-doing it with plastic surgery. Another article, about ten years later, in *Celebrity Focus* magazine, suggested that she was once on some kind of unofficial cosmetic-surgery blacklist. The warning to surgeons was to refrain from performing any procedures on her because, as one doctor stated it, "She doesn't know when to stop. I've been told not to touch her."

However, the highly regarded William M. Narva, M.D., never heard of any such list. Dr. Narva spent most of his 35-year Navy career in the Washington, D.C., area. A 1956 medical school graduate of Yale University, Narva enlisted as an ensign in the medical corps; accepted the dermatology training offered by the Navy; completed an internship at Bethesda; and began his residency at a naval hospital in San Diego. After a five-year tour at a naval hospital in Oakland he was named chief of dermatology at the National Naval Medical Center in Bethesda, Maryland. He treated President Lyndon B. Johnson, and every president up to George H.W. Bush. He then became staff medical officer for the chief of naval operations, director of the Naval Reserve Division at the Bureau of Medicine and Surgery, and vice president of the Uniformed Services University of the Health Sciences (USU). Five years after a promotion to rear admiral in 1982, Narva was appointed attending physician to the U.S. Congress, which included members of the Supreme Court.

The long-retired but revered Dr. Narva became a physician, confidant, and friend not only to political dignitaries, but to A-list Hollywood stars such as celebrity couple Frank and Barbara Sinatra. Narva holds an intriguing perspective on the matter of Mary, diabetes, surgery – plastic or otherwise – and her cardiologist husband. From his perspective, any diabetic should be strong enough to have plastic surgery if their sugar levels and all vital signs are healthy enough and properly controlled. "With good plastic surgery," he said, "…you're not damaging anything. It's almost, most of the time, bloodless. So, if you are closely monitored, surgery should not be an issue."

Of course, many of us might agree with Shakespeare's Falstaff that "Caution is preferable to rash bravery." To be sure, it takes a certain combination of self-esteem, wealth, and insecurity to consider surgical intervention to your looks. But with regard to Dr. Narva and his

former patients, any and all surgical procedures were considered on an individual basis. If any of his patients were diabetic, and their condition was "out of control," he would not have recommended any surgery, cosmetic or otherwise. "And I don't think Mary Tyler Moore's diabetes was ever out of control," he admitted. "And she was married to a cardiologist," who was dedicated to caring for her and monitoring her health.

Nightclub comedienne Totie Fields was not so lucky. As documented in the *New York Times*, Fields, a diabetic and overweight, died "of an apparent heart attack" on August 2, 1978. She had struggled to resume her career after the amputation of her left leg in 1976, following cosmetic breast and eye surgery, and two previous heart attacks. Her leg was amputated at Columbia Presbyterian Hospital, reportedly due to phlebitis, and she was later fitted with an artificial limb. In April of 1978, Fields filed a lawsuit seeking $2 million in damages from seven physicians and St. Joseph's Hospital in Stamford, Connecticut, where she had gone for cosmetic eyelid surgery and developed phlebitis. The lawsuit was never resolved.

In Fields', Mary's, or anybody's case, Dr. Narva said, "Plastic surgeons are exquisitely careful about who they operate on because they are fully aware that [the majority of their work] is *elective* surgery. The last thing they want to do is have a patient like Mary Tyler Moore, and not be absolutely certain that there are no additional medical complications. The real sophistication in being a good plastic surgeon rests with asking, 'Why is this patient getting this surgery? Do they have a realistic understanding of what to expect?' Because if you have a patient who is irrational, you're going to wind up with someone who's going to say to you, after you fixed her nose, 'Oh, that's not the nose you promised me.' Patients can be meshuggeneh" [the Yiddish term for 'insane'].

"The real art in being a good plastic surgeon is picking a rational patient," he said, "…making sure the patient will not get you into trouble; and that your patient is reasonable about what you're trying to accomplish. The rest is the art work of the plastic surgeon. Most of those [plastic surgeons] that I've met were very sophisticated and careful about the selection of their patients, especially if they had a [celebrity] potential patient like Mary Tyler Moore. If you screw up, the world's going to know about it.

"Usually, a good plastic surgeon sits down with their patient and says, 'Tell me what you want done and tell me why you want it done.' And when they're able to, they take you in front of a screen. They take a picture. They can manipulate the picture and say, 'Hey, this is the kind of nose you want, this is the kind of nose I can make you,' and you get the blood-work to make sure they can withstand the anesthesia. The anesthesiologist would also be consulted. So, you can't *hide* anything because before you put the patient under anesthesia, they have to complete all kinds of lab work to see that there is no contraindication to their potential surgical procedure. An anesthetic would place the patient to sleep for a few hours. It's all carefully worked out. So, just the fact that a patient is diabetic doesn't preclude them from getting surgery. If you know it's there you can monitor them, she'll be exquisitely, closely monitored.

"A plastic surgeon is a good surgeon. They are trained as a surgeon before they become a plastic surgeon. They fully understand what happens to tissue. They understand the fluctuations of diabetes. They fully understand body chemistries, would not move forward with any surgery if it was deemed potentially hazardous."

As to whether Mary's brain surgery in 2011 at age 75 was a factor in her death, Narva observed:

"The prognosis has to do with the type of brain 'tumor.' There are many brain tumors that are *considered benign*. One of my good friends was a *neurologist* with me at the Navy Hospital in Bethesda who developed a brain tumor that he diagnosed himself. By the time they removed his tumor, they had almost extracted half of the hemisphere that was his brain. Fortunately, there are two sides to the brain: a dominant side and a non-dominant side. He had the entire non-dominant side removed and he was able to continue his life and practice like nothing had happened. So, he worked with half a brain."

Mary was diagnosed and treated for a benign meningioma. In his assessment, Narva said, "This would require yearly examinations even if asymptomatic to assert that there was no recurrence or an additional site might appear."

To her credit, and as mentioned elsewhere, Mary over the years admitted to some regret with her choices for various cosmetic procedures. But now, in 2011, it wasn't elective: The meningioma tumor had to be removed.

The brain surgery was a success, but her physical and mental capacities were never the same again. She worked very little, stayed out of the public eye, and catered more to her four-legged friends. In a conversation with *People* magazine in 2012, she said, "I'm constantly laughing at my pets. I feel more comfortable with animals than I do with people, if you want to know."

Also that year, she told an interviewer about her pit bull Spanky, "He has, as with some dogs that have been written about, the ability to sense when things are off in their owners, their masters, whatever we're calling them in this day and age. He can tell when my blood sugar is dipping low."

Around the same time, Mary observed, "I've been a diabetic for about 35 years now, and I'm one of the very lucky few who has managed to live that long without having major problems. I do have problems with my eyes, one eye in particular, and when I fall, I generally break a bone." That had happened twice by then.

When able to work, Mary moved forward and gave it her all, if dipping a few more times into the past to do so. From 2011 to 2013, she made two guest-star appearances on TV Land's hit nostalgia-and-girl-geared sitcom *Hot in Cleveland*, which starred former *Mary Tyler Moore* regular Betty White, along with other past sitcom staples Valerie Bertinelli (*One Day at a Time*), Jane Leeves (*Frasier*), and Wendie Malick (*Just Shoot Me*). Joining Mary for her second episode with White were remaining female *MTMS* alumni Valerie Harper, Cloris Leachman, and Georgia Engel.

The episode, which aired September 4, 2013, was called "Love Is All Around," the title of the pilot for *The Mary Tyler Moore Show*. It even referenced that sitcom's famed musical theme. Here, Elka (White) and Mamie Sue (Engel) opt to reunite their bowling team, called GLOB: the Gorgeous Ladies of Bowling, which includes Diane (Mary), Peg (Leachman), and Angie (Harper). These once-friends had lost contact decades before when egos clashed following a winning season. As journalist Kimberly Nordyke observed in *The Hollywood Reporter*, this re-gathering, which transpired on the CBS Radford Street lot in Studio City, California, where *Hot* was produced, was filtered with "mostly laughter – and only a few tears."

For Mary, reconnecting with her former *Moore* castmates was always "a special occasion," as she resided in New York, and they mostly lived in Los Angeles. Now one of those special occasions arrived in *Cleveland*, allowing Mary and friends and colleagues to pick up right where they left off, as if it was 1970 all over again.

"Even though we are playing different people [on *Hot in Cleveland*]," she observed at another time, "...we are still ourselves, and no matter where you put us, we will continue to be ourselves and interact as only you can when you've been together for a long, long time."

Mary cried when asked which was her favorite *Hot* scene with Harper. She noted that each reunion moment, on-screen or off, was significant. "We look into each other's eyes and would be comforting and uplifting for each other."

According to Harper, while taping the episode, Mary frequently and generously instructed the writers to save the humorous lines for Harper. Mary believed such words were better-suited to her friend. All previous resentments had dissolved.

Overall, Mary was melancholy about the experience. It saddened her that she, and the cast and crew of her original series were unable to regroup as much as they would have liked to. "It makes me feel, well, why don't I have this in my current life? Where are all these friends and buddies and co-workers and people who love each other? Why aren't they around?"

Mary recalled how the MTM writers had explored issues that had never been addressed before, with Harper noting how the MTM scripts were measures above the rest. "They never went over the line," she decided, and Mary agreed.

Michael Stern had attended the *Mary Tyler-Cleveland* combination taping, and the experience was quite different from when he was present for the filming of the 1970s *MTMS* and 1985 revised *Mary* sitcoms. By the time Mary taped what became her second and last episode of *Hot in Cleveland* (and ultimately her final fictional performance on screen), she was as Stern recalled, "...very sick."

Stern, who attended hundreds of show tapings over a forty-plus-year span, experienced a unique observation during the *Tyler* cast reunion on *Cleveland*. Not only did Mary receive a standing ovation when introduced to the audience, but so did Harper, Leachman, Engel, and White. Apart from reunion get-togethers, they were playing fictional characters together for the first time on-screen since the spring of 1977. The applause became so thunderous that the audience was instructed to "bring it down a few notches because it was disrupting the show's actual taping," remembered Stern. "I wish there was a behind-the-scenes DVD of just this episode because it would be an hour and a half of just applause. It was amazing. The audience was so lively and excited. They all wanted to be there to see Mary, Valerie, Cloris, Georgia again. It was like seeing old friends."

Others from the original *Tyler* show were also on the *Cleveland* set that day, including *Tyler* co-creator Jim Brooks, and director Jay Sandrich. Stern remembered that Sandrich summed up the experience as "bittersweet," in reference to Mary's poor health in particular. "It's great they are all here," he told Stern of the reunited cast. "But it's sad that they are all there."

"It's like some memories are better than the real thing," Stern decided. "However, being in that studio audience was so electrifying," particularly when for the moments when Harper in character as Angie, accidentally refers to Mary's character, Diane, as "Mare," which is how Rhoda referred Mary Richards on the original MTM show.

"Everyone laughed at that," Stern said, "...because it was just a force of habit. But they had to stop tape and re-cut the scene." Mary, physically frail throughout the taping, was seated, as if for protection, behind a large dining table with the cast during their scene. But according to Stern, "She never missed her lines. Maybe she was fed her lines with a hearing device. I'm not sure. But she never got out of that chair while on camera, and at the end of each scene, someone would escort her off and back on that set."

"At one point," he continued, "...she did stand up by herself and walked about maybe 8 feet towards the audience," reaching out to her beloved fans as Stern had observed her doing so during the taping of the *Tyler* show in 1975, and ten years later on the revised and short-lived *Mary* sitcom. "She thanked everyone for being there, just as she had before," Stern recounts. She was still the 'Mary Tyler Moore' you wanted her to be. But she was weak and it was heartbreaking to see. Just like Jay Sandrich had said. It was bittersweet."

After the episode completed taping, Stern was on that sound stage, "immediately," but Mary was the only one who swiftly disappeared. "We don't know where she went," Stern recalled. "She was gone."

Approximately one week earlier, on January 29, 2012, Van Dyke presented his best-loved co-star with a Life Achievement Award at the televised Screen Actors Guild Awards. Guild president Ken Howard, who starred in the acclaimed MTM-produced TV drama *The White Shadow* (CBS, 1978-1981), began the tribute by saying: "Mary Tyler Moore won our hearts as Laura Petrie and Mary Richards, and our respects as her production company became synonymous with quality television, our awe as she tackled difficult subject matter in film and on Broadway, and our admiration as she turned her public recognition into a catalyst to draw attention to critical and deeply personal health and social issues. She truly embodies the spirit behind SAG's Life Achievement Award, and we are honored to proclaim her as its 48th recipient."

While it proved poignant to have her friends and colleagues expressing their appreciation, it was Mary's own words that night that resounded. She decided to talk about applying for her SAG card when she was only 18. At the time, there were six other "Mary Moores," and it was suggested that she change her name if she wanted to succeed in Hollywood.

But even at 18, Mary knew she only ever wanted to be known as Mary. "Change my name? Oh, come on. No, I'm Mary. Mary Moore. Everyone is going to know my name," she said. For her, success would have been hollow if she had to forfeit her identity. Instead of selecting a new name, she added her middle name, Tyler, to her application. "I spoke it out loud. It sounded right," she said that night at the SAG Awards. "I wrote it out on the form, and it looked right. And it was right. SAG was happy. My father was happy. And tonight, after having the privilege of working among the most talented people imaginable, I too am happy after all," with that last phrase a wink and a nod to the *Mary Tyler Moore Show* theme's ending lyric.

It was a warm memory lingering in the present moment. Sure, she had looked healthier, but her spirits were up and, as Mary told *Screen Actors Magazine* at the time, she was "thrilled" to receive the award. "It's a bit like winning 'Miss Congeniality,'" she said. In short, Mary's smile was intact – the same smile that had encouraged and charmed for years; the toothy grin with the big heart behind it, signifying an upbeat attitude across the years.

Only a short time before, Mary had been just as spirited, though physically stronger, when one interviewer asked her to give advice to aspiring entertainment industry professionals. She suggested eliminating negative words and thoughts. "Just believe in yourself...and keep going and be prepared for the tough moments. Just follow your conviction and let it build all the time. But really want it. Because [the entertainment industry] is tough...you have to be strong."

Her indomitable drive to succeed might be uncommon, she said, but "...in a very healthy way...Anybody should be driven to work in a field that is satisfying to them...a field that gives something to other people...whether it's journalism or performing or nursing...medicine, whatever. You should be driven! Work is tremendously satisfying."

She promised to "Never!" retire, claiming optimism as her best trait. "I find that the muscles involved in smiling are easier to use than the ones involved in frowning. I'm a pretty up person." She was asked what she liked least about herself. "I'm...easily prone to be terribly depressed. Not manic. I'm easygoing. But I can worry a lot." She admitted that there's a price to pay for being pleasant, though "not an obvious one," she said. "You never really allow people to get very close to you. In being very nice, you're kind of keeping them at arm's length. You're never allowing them to see you blow up and really get furious…to see you at what you think is your worst."

ACT VIII

From Here To Eternity

**Mary's star on the Hollywood Walk of Fame. [Credit: Robert S.
Ray/Classic TV Preservation Society.]**

Chapter

33

In a conversation with Barbara Walters, Mary once claimed she did not have any close female friends. But that was not true in the case of fellow actors Beverly Sanders and Hope Lange. Doubtless, others were close too. She acknowledged being "very much attached to every single one of" the cast members from *The Mary Tyler Moore Show*, but never felt comfortable in burdening them with unhappy feelings. She would "go to a shrink instead," not for long-term Freudian analysis, but just to relieve a few unresolved thoughts. She liked the idea of saying, "Here's what I'm feeling. Here's what I'm doing. What do you think?" and then attaining answers.

Mary admitted to self-doubts and feeling inferior, academically. She was not actively involved in the business of living. Her life always seemed to zero in on performance. She was not boring, but never allowed herself to become overly excited about any prospect.

Her health was always a concern, but she would get into trouble discussing diabetes because the deadly disease, in most cases, can take years off people's lives. She always considered herself one of the lucky ones. She had to take injections with insulin. She learned how to do it. She was "so cavalier" about it by now. She could practically sit there and "do it without you even knowing I'm doing it." It became a part of her life; to maintain her blood-sugar level. A diabetic must eat properly and stay away from sugar and carbohydrates, and she "did that…most of the time."

Fame and fortune failed to bring Mary tranquility, but she figured such was the case with everyone. Success offered a certain satisfaction that she did her job well. But peace of mind stemmed from some hard-to-define area that might be more attainable with aging, maturity, and love. "Love of a person you live with," she said, "…reassurance from that person."

That was certainly true when it came to her remarkable relationship with Robert Levine, but Mary was restless when it came to work. She was energized by her craft. She had a purpose and she knew it. She never quit or retired, and only stopped working due to her increasingly poor physical state. But she never ceased pursuing or honing her vocation. As long as the scripts were "valid" and challenging, the directors were interesting, and the actors were fun to be with and good at what they did, she wanted to "keep on performing." She still wanted to "find a way to make people laugh…that's what's going to be important."

Aging was always on her mind. Like many, Mary believed maturing was easier on men, nowadays. She confessed to "a certain vanity and…resentment that men get better and better looking as they get older and that it doesn't happen with women." It especially applied in visual arts, but she tried to accept it without too much resentment. She considered herself a hard-working, professional, and dedicated individual who took seriously everything she did. But she was also a carefree spirit who looked for the funny side of life.

She once told Diane Sawyer, "Had I not become an actress…I probably would have been homeless. There wasn't…very much in life that I was prepared to do. But I was disciplined."

She was also very private and fiercely protective of herself and those closest to her. Whether the cause of her low-self-esteem was childhood sexual abuse, a demanding father, or a lax mother, the fact remained: She wasn't always easy to get along with. And she had copped to that fact in frank interviews and in her books.

Her personal and profession associations with those like her first husband Richard Meeker, her son Richie, Grant Tinker, Ed Asner, Lucille Ball, and Valerie Harper were at times strained. She was a busy, active woman. Complexities aside, she was still Mary Tyler Moore, famous for her smile and charitable ways even when she felt uncomfortable. She plodded along but with remarkable results each step of the way.

According to Karen Sharpe, "It's called paying back. And I believe in that…to use whatever fame you have to help others. That's the kind of motto that many of us in the industry have. It's just the way it is. You use your celebrity for something more important than just the work. And that's something I'm glad Mary did and that many do, and they are very quiet about it when they do it. There are many things that many celebrities do that no one knows about…as when stars pay for people's surgeries and when they support people below the line. Many stars have helped the less fortunate…many of whom they work with."

"We are a generous community," Sharpe said. "I've always thought show-people to be very generous…and that's part of what I love about the industry. We have the money and the clout to make good things happen."

Mary certainly fit in that category, and Sharpe and her director-husband Stanley Kramer thought she was a "brilliant" actress, especially after viewing her performance in *Ordinary People*. For them, Mary's instant identification to Laura Petrie or Mary Richards was a non-issue. "She was so identified with *The Dick Van Dyke Show*, which really made her, and then her own show, of course, which was great, too. And I was faithful to watching both of her series. But when you're an actor you're supposed to be able to do everything, even though you can get so identified with a particular role, character, voice and timber."

Stanley Kramer had cast Mary's beloved and very identifiable co-star Dick Van Dyke in the 1979 feature, *The Runner Stumbles*, which became Kramer's final film.

Runner has to do with a small-town priest, played by Van Dyke, who stands trial for murdering a nun, played by Kathleen Quinlan (Mary's co-star from 1993's *Stolen Babies* TV-movie), with whom he had secretly fallen in love. According to Sharpe, the role of the priest was intended for Oskar Werner, a handsome, brooding, blonde actor that Kramer had cast in his classic 1964 film *Ship of Fools*. But when Werner's son was traumatized and in a coma resulting from a skiing accident, he was forced to exit *Runner*. At which point, Sharpe suggested Albert Finney as a replacement, while her husband mentioned Van Dyke. But she was vehemently against that decision. "No," she protested, "…absolutely not!"

Sharpe believed Van Dyke was too associated with Rob Petrie to play a murderous priest. "No one will ever take him seriously in that role," she told her husband. "But then Stanley said the movie wouldn't be any fun to make without Dick Van Dyke."

Despite his wife's misgivings, and with her eventual blessing, Kramer cast Van Dyke who, according to Sharpe, "was wonderful in the role. Dick did a really good job. But the audience never accepted him in the part, and the critics were very harsh."

In the end, however, Sharpe was correct about Van Dyke being misperceived in the role. But that was not due to any lack of talent on his part; the audience simply did not accept him in the role of an adulterous, possibly killer cleric. Such a part was too far over the edge of Rob Petrie, as Mary's potential roles in *The Stepford Wives* or *Misery* might have been. But somehow, Mary playing the cold-hearted Beth Jarrett in *Ordinary People* was a different matter. Certainly, a mother in bitter mourning over the loss of her son is more sympathetic than a philandering priest. At the same time, Sharpe said, "Mary was not quite as etched as Dick. So, she was able to more seamlessly do the crossover into [mainstream] drama, which she did so magnificently. I was so proud of her and her career."

Sharpe empathized, to some extent, with Mary's battles with alcoholism and diabetes because Stanley Kramer suffered from diabetes and Parkinson's. "It was very tough for him in the last few years," Sharpe said.

Mary's deadly mix of alcoholism and diabetes as an adult may have been sparked by dark memories from growing up. Drinking for a diabetic "is very dangerous," said Sharpe, who was dedicated to her husband's career, "…though it depends on if you have high sugar or low sugar. When Sharpe first met Kramer, he, like Mary, was a chain smoker, who enjoyed steaks and red meat, "all of the things that I feel are very bad for you," Sharpe said. When Kramer proposed to Sharpe, she said yes on one condition: "It's me or the cigarettes."

"So, he gave up smoking just like that," she recalled. "And I took all the meat out of his diet. And I put him on a healthy diet. But he was very sweet. He didn't complain. He never complained about anything like that. In the thirty-five years that we were married he went with the flow of everything. He was very easy to get along with. Also, we ate home a lot. I'm not much for going out."

Unlike Mary, Sharpe never had plastic surgery, and she has been blessed with good health, physically and psychologically, with her self-worth intact. Although she is unsure if plastic surgery has any ill effect on diabetes, Sharpe does not sit in judgment one way or the other of anyone who seeks to go under the knife. "If people want to do plastic surgery," she said, "I think they should. I don't believe in it myself. I've never done it and I would never do it. I feel I've earned every wrinkle I have. I don't think I want to live forever. But I think it's good to look as nice as you can for your age, and people should be able to choose whatever they want to do. But everything has to be age-appropriate for me – and you have to be the best you can be – at any age."

Had Mary's conflicted youth more resembled Sharpe's more uplifting upbringing – had Mary's parents been more sensitive and caring – her physical and emotional health may not have suffered; she may not have developed diabetes or alcoholism.

According to a study in 2012 conducted by scientists at the National Institute on Alcohol Abuse and Alcoholism (NIAAA) and UNC's Bowles Center for Alcohol Studies, the link between alcoholism and anxiety disorders such as post-traumatic stress disorder (PTSD), which is many times the result of childhood sexual abuse, has well been established.

Heavy alcohol use increases the risk for traumatic events like car accidents and domestic violence. But that only partially explains the connection. The study suggested that heavy alcohol use rewires the brain's circuitry, making it harder for alcoholics to recover psychologically following a traumatic experience. And that was almost like a *Catch-22* experience for Mary.

Fortunately, she later found and married Dr. Robert Levine, who since the moment they met was dedicated to her every need, just as Sharpe had catered to Stanley Kramer. It is a blessing when somebody with such needs is joined by a compassionate, involved spouse. The female is not always the supportive one; the man is not always demanding.

But unlike Mary, Sharpe, though successful in her own right, was not the star of the family. That was her husband. The public stress level was not as high for Mrs. Stanley Kramer or for Levine, sometimes referred to as *Mr. Moore*. And the public's push for perfection was not as important to the lower-profile spouses. Thus, they were healthier in every capacity than their more significant-in-the-public-eye others.

But any measure of celebrity results in a more than average life; and Mary's life and career in particular was above average. Her complexities and conflicts as a human being were public domain, while they added to her artistry. As any actor, singer, dancer, director, producer, or writer will acknowledge, many private conflicts may be turned to aid their craft. Celebrities remain on guard in their private lives; and that's okay. It is a natural development, part of human nature. It is acceptable behavior, relatively speaking, in their above-average lives.

Many in Mary's inner circle had little choice but to figuratively tiptoe in her presence, even when even just reaching out to her, on a personal or professional basis.

David Van Deusen, editor and publisher of *The Walnut Times*, experienced through the years the highs and lows of interacting with Mary, which ultimately concluded on a happy note.

Although he always treated her with dignity and respect, in truth, Mary was his most challenging interview to acquire and schedule for *The Walnut Times*. The rest of *The Dick Van Dyke Show* cast was accessible and pleased to chat with Van Deusen after his initial request. But Mary "seemed evasive and was difficult to pin down," he said.

At one point, he nearly gave up attempting to contact her. After submitting countless requests without success, he finally told her publicist, "If Mary does not want to do an interview with me, please just tell me that and I won't continue asking."

Mary finally agreed to a conversation around 2000, to help promote the *Mary and Rhoda* TV-movie. At least that's what Van Deusen believed. "Our interview was just delightful and not rushed," he recalled. "Mary gave me all the time that I asked for and more. She provided photos for use with the article and graciously signed a couple of unique color photos from *The Dick Van Dyke Show* for me."

Van Deusen felt he was not the only one who had difficulties in engaging Mary. "My sense in reflection is that she was just a very private and guarded individual and that it took a great deal to earn her trust. I fully understood that she did not want to be taken advantage of due to her celebrity, and because of that, she had her boundaries. It's clear that she also had some very close friends and trusted relationships, too, like Bernadette Peters, Betty White, and Valerie Harper. These associations were evident in the public view and clearly very important to Mary."

On the set of *The Dick Van Dyke Show Revisited*, which Carl Reiner invited Van Deusen to visit, "Mary was very friendly with her former cast and crew members," he said. "But beyond them, I felt she was somewhat guarded and seemingly unapproachable. She often retreated to her dressing room during breaks in the shooting while others were more fully engaged with each other. I do not know why she did not interact more with others, but that was certainly her prerogative and choice, and I respect that. I can only surmise that fatigue and her ever-present health challenges were contributing factors."

Van Deusen had little or no direct contact with Mary from 2004 until 2011. But during this period, he continued to send her copies of *The Walnut Times*, as well as the annual *Walnut Times/Dick Van Dyke Show* holiday card. They saw one another again during a taping of *The Rachael Ray Show* in May 2011, when he was in the studio audience and she appeared on the show to surprise Dick Van Dyke, who was there to promote his biography *My Lucky Life In and Out of Show Business*. "When Mary made her surprise entrance," Van Deusen recalled, "it was apparent that her balance seemed off. Dick moved quickly across the set and accompanied her over to the interview couch. During a commercial break, Dick came out to the audience to talk with me and when he returned to the set, he told Mary that I was there. She called out to me to say hello and I waved, but she was unable to quickly locate me in the audience – I think a result of her failing eyesight due to the ravages of her years of diabetes. Only a few days after the show's airing Mary announced that she would be having brain surgery."

Mary's final live public appearance was at the 2012 Screen Actors Guild Awards when Van Dyke presented her with the Life Achievement Award. "Unlike the traditional presentation segment," Van Deusen said, "...when a tribute of clips is shown and then the honoree is announced and makes a grand entrance, Mary was escorted to the podium during the darkness so that she was there and ready when the montage ended to offer her remarks. Fans who saw the show would concur that her comments were brief and somewhat stilted. Dick did all he could to help support her and bring the presentation to a close with all the dignity and grace that Mary deserved. But everyone observed her startle when Dick leaned over and gave her a kiss, because, sadly, she couldn't see him coming due to her visual degradation."

Approximately three years later, Van Deusen began to prepare the final issue of *The Walnut Times*, which was scheduled for publication in January 2015. He contacted Mary, and other cast members of the *Van Dyke Show*, to see if she and they would like to offer any sentiments on the publication's closing. But Mary never replied.

Van Deusen's final touch-point with Mary arrived in October 2016. He was standing in the greeting-card aisle seeking a birthday card for a friend when he noticed a card with a kitten on the front cover. "I was immediately reminded of Mary and the closing logo of her show when the MTM kitten uttered its cute *meow*," he said.

Van Deusen purchased the card, which was blank on the inside. Later that evening, he sat down and wrote Mary a note to "wish her well and to let her know that her fans still appreciated her and the characters that she brought to life during her long-tenured career. Of course, I said, that my favorite was Laura Petrie. I dropped the card in the mail and based on previous past experience, I did not expect a reply."

A few days later, however, Van Deusen received what he described as "a very nice voicemail" from Robert Levine which said, "I just wanted to let you know that we received your card and wanted to thank you for it and to tell you that it brought a smile to Mary's face. I really do appreciate you thinking of her and for being so kind."

Treva Silverman, double Emmy-winner for her writing on *The Mary Tyler Moore Show*, summarized Mary's life and career in this way:

> When we were doing *The Mary Tyler Moore Show*, I didn't know much about her parents. Even though they went to the filmings, and she introduced them from the audience, it was hard to figure them out, except they seemed a little remote.
>
> When the tragedy of losing her only son happened, a friend of mine went to her place the moment he heard about it. He called me after he had been there and told me this: Her close friends and relatives had gathered, and were trying to comfort her. How do you

comfort someone who was going through what she was going through?

Her friends were giving her long, heartfelt hugs, sharing tears, holding her close. Then her mother and father arrived and stood at the door. They saw her across the room. "Hello, Mary," her father said and her mother nodded: "Mary." And that was it. Eventually they made their way over to her, but no hugs, no warmth, no anything remotely empathetic. It explained a lot to me. Growing up with parents like that.

Years later, many years later, she met Robert – whose essence was exactly the opposite: warm, giving, sweet, funny, unafraid to be emotional – it was obvious she felt treasured and was able to return that feeling. She had a kind of glow about her when she was with him and when she talked about him.

There was a wonderful French film called, *And Now My Love* [1974]...about a couple who don't meet until the end; they have to go through experiences that make them right for each other. That's how I perceive Mary. She had to learn and grow and gain her own sense of herself before she was ready to be with Robert. And by the time she did, she could give herself to him completely. Of all the prizes she won, that was, maybe, the biggest accomplishment of her life.

Chapter

34

On May 24, 2013, Mary, now 76 years old, fell while walking down the stairs in her Greenwich, Connecticut home. Her husband phoned 911, one in a series of recent calls made from the Levine residence to emergency services. Observed Dr. Michael Hunter, "She fell on a number of separate occasions in the years leading up to her death. Evidently, Mary was vulnerable to having a serious accident."

Hunter wondered if Mary's tumbles were the result of her alcoholism. But in June 2013, when she returned home from the hospital with a damaged hip on the mend, several incident reports failed to provide any such collaboration for this theory. "There's no mention of alcohol," Hunter said. "So, I can conclude Mary had not been drinking before she fell."

But there was indication that Mary had been careless with her diabetic condition, and that her addiction to alcohol had worsened in the years following her diagnosis. Reiterating previous observations from others, Hunter said, "Excessive alcohol can have dire consequences for a diabetic. Although the sugar in alcoholic drinks may temporarily raise the level of blood sugar, large amounts of alcohol inhibits the liver from releasing glucose. This increases the chances of low blood sugar leading to hypoglycemic shock."

On August 22, 2013, Mary once again required medical attention. She was conscious but had difficulty breathing. There was no indication from this report that Mary required hospital treatment but, according to Hunter, "Whatever the problem was, it was likely dealt with at the scene."

But her breathing difficulty may have been connected to yet another of Mary's harmful previous habits: smoking. "Smoking damages the lungs and can cause respiratory infections and breathing problems," Hunter said. "It also damages the body in other ways."

With Mary, it may have contributed to significant artery damage. Toward the end of her life, she acknowledged having poor circulation in her legs. She suffered from progressive obstruction to her arteries called peripheral artery disease, for which smoking is a leading cause. "Once chemicals from cigarette smoke enter the bloodstream," Hunter observed, "...they damage the blood vessels, and increase the risk of atherosclerosis," a disease in which a waxy plaque builds up in the arteries over time, restricting blood flow. "It's a major cause of heart disease and cardiac arrest," Hunter added. "But Mary was more vulnerable to the risks of smoking because of her diabetes."

Still, she continued to smoke after her diagnosis of diabetes. In his investigation of Mary's health history, Hunter learned she had surgery that resulted from diabetic retinopathy. Mary had once revealed, and as Hunter later restated, "This is where high blood sugar levels from diabetes cause damage to the tiny blood vessels in the retina of the eye. The damaged vessels leak fluid into the eye blurring vision and eventually are replaced by new, abnormal blood vessels which scar the retina and lead to blindness. Smoking triples the progression of diabetic retinopathy. But Mary's emerging health issues may have actually encouraged her to quit."

By the 1980s, Mary came to watch her diet more carefully than usual. She was taking the proper medication, and by degrees, she was exercising – good at any age. As she had with drinking, Mary had stopped smoking for thirty years before she died. "And over time," Hunter decided, "artery damage caused by smoking can heal."

He did not believe that smoking played a significant role in Mary's cardiac arrest. But even with the best management, "there are still serious complications that diabetics can develop over time." As well as poor circulation, Mary had nerve damage in her feet – called peripheral neuropathy. "This lack of sensation makes it harder to notice an injury to the foot," Hunter said. "And the restricted blood flow to the area affected by peripheral artery disease means the body is less effective at fighting an infection."

"It's a combination of factors that means a simple toe infection is at risk of becoming gangrenous," he continued. "It's estimated that every 30 seconds a leg is amputated due to diabetes." Mary herself once acknowledged, "I came close to losing my vision. I've almost had to have a toe amputation on two occasions, so it's every day another corner and you don't know what's around it."

Indeed. On January 18, 2014, Mary once more called 911 from her Connecticut home. But this time, it was not a medical emergency. This time, she reported Robert Levine to the police, claiming the couple had an argument and that he refused to leave. By the time the authorities arrived, she had calmed down. Her call was made in a state of panic and confusion. Marc Shapiro said, "Mary was suffering degrees of dementia besides her physical ailments, and would occasionally talk nonsensically because of her illness."

Dr. Hunter explained: "Dementia is a group of related symptoms associated with a decline in the brain's ability to function. It's often characterized by memory loss, and problems arise with mental sharpness. There are many causes of dementia, the most common being Alzheimer's disease. Aside from memory loss, people with dementia often suffer from a complication called dysphagia, which is a difficulty swallowing food." Essentially, they forget how to swallow. "And among patients with dysphagia, caused by dementia, the most common cause of death is aspiration pneumonia. It's also the most common cause of death in end-stage Alzheimer's disease. I believe Mary contracted her pneumonia because she was struggling to eat. It was then very difficult for her to fight infection."

In December 2014, for Mary's 78th birthday, her husband threw a party, and invited a few of her closest friends. But she was not feeling well. Her eyesight was failing and she was not able to walk. According to Treva Silverman, "Her vision was I think at that point legally blind. But it wasn't obvious because somebody, I think it was Robert, would stand in back of her and say, 'Oh, this is *so and so* coming up with her husband.' She really didn't want pity. She just wanted to be charming and gracious."

Throughout 2014, many of Mary's friends and colleagues had mentioned her heart and kidney issues, or that she was visually impaired. Dick Van Dyke told *The Wire*, "I don't see her often, but I talk to her a bunch. She hasn't been too well. She's really having a battle with it, I'm sorry to say." Betty White relayed to *Closer* magazine, "Her eyesight is what the big problem is right now. [It's] almost beyond the point [of being able to see]."

The last time Carl Reiner visited with Mary, she was nearly blind. "I walked up to her," Reiner relayed to *ABC News*. "I was *this close* to her but she didn't say anything. And I said, 'Hello, Mary. And she said, 'Oh, Carl.' She couldn't see me, but she heard my voice. We hugged, and that was the last time I saw her."

In these last few years, to put it simply, Mary was fighting for her life. Anything and everything that could be done to help her physically was being done. Her dedicated husband made certain that she received only the best medical care. But still, she felt the need for another kind of therapy: work. Consequently, Levine reached out to Bill Persky to help motivate Mary from a creative standpoint. Persky recalled:

"Robert said to me it would be great if she had some work. So, I sat with her from around 2014 to 2015 and I began writing a one-woman Broadway show for her called, *A Sit Down with Mary Tyler Moore*; one that would reflect all the important chairs of her careers...from *The Dick Van Dyke Show*...her office on *The Mary Tyler Moore Show*...the doctor's office where she found out about her illness...and the final was a director's chair where she would just talk with the audience. It was really going to be a great show. But unfortunately, we never got to the point. She became so fragile there was really no way she could have done it."

A Sit Down with Mary Tyler Moore was reminiscent of the skit Persky had composed for Mary's second TV special *How to Survive the '70s and Maybe Even Bump Into Happiness*. Both projects reflected the different portions of her life, for better or for worse. They were intended to reflect her successes as well as failures. But there was no doubt that she had ultimately attained stardom. "It took her time to get there," Persky observed. "She went through a lot of stages in her life, but she did so with a great sense of humor. She was a really fabulous person."

But as Marc Shapiro had noted in the Reelz Channel documentary, "Mary Tyler Moore in her later years was not the Mary Tyler Moore she had wanted to be. She had largely become a recluse. People weren't seeing her around like they used to."

In summary, by this time, Mary's Type 1 Diabetes accounted for several of the physical challenges she struggled with in her later years. Her falls were likely caused by failing eyesight and uncertainty walking. Her breathing issues were linked to her high blood-sugar levels. An increased risk of death from heart disease and stroke was further exacerbated by her past smoking, which ultimately damaged her arteries in some manner. And there was also the other life-threatening condition that was completely unrelated to her diabetes: her previously discussed brain meningioma.

Although it was non-cancerous, the tumor placed pressure on the brain that could cause herniation, what Dr. Hunter described as "a bulging of the brain's membrane." This could cause serious breathing, heart-rate, and blood-pressure issues, and lead to cardiac arrest.

Consequently, he assessed, by the time Mary was 80 years old, her diabetes would have "massively compromised her immune system. Combined with her poor circulation from her artery disease the infection proved too much for her. And her life support would have been switched off in the knowledge that she no longer had the strength to get better."

Hunter was left to wonder if the drinking of Marjorie Moore had later influenced the health of her daughter Mary. But without an autopsy, which Mary never had, he could not determine the physical effects of her mother's drinking on Mary's heart. But he could decipher "a clear connection to Mary's own relationship to alcohol."

"Regularly drinking too much alcohol causes high blood pressure," said Hunter, which is also detrimental to those who are diabetic. "Over time, this puts strain on the heart muscle and can lead to cardiovascular disease, which increases your risk of heart attack and stroke."

Overall, however, "the strength and stamina Mary showed in the face of her condition and to cope with the challenges of her illness until the age of 80," Hunter added, was "quite remarkable."

And although Mary's tumor-removal surgery in 2011 was successful, according to Hunter, there was "a significant chance" of the meningioma returning. He wondered if this was what ultimately what caused her death.

The recent demise of Grant Tinker would have added additional anxiety to Mary's life. She had many times referred to Tinker, her second husband and fondest colleague, in much the same way, before, during and after their failed marriage. When Tinker died November 28, 2016, Mary, in a statement to the press, said (as reproduced in *Variety*):

"I am deeply saddened that my former husband and professional mentor Grant Tinker has passed away. I'm forever grateful for and proud of what we achieved together with the creation of *The Mary Tyler Moore Show*, and founding of MTM Enterprises (an independent production company that created what remain some of the best TV shows ever made). Grant was a brilliant, driven executive who uniquely understood that the secret to great TV content was freedom for its creators and performing artists. This was manifest in his 'first be best and then be first' approach. He lived life to the fullest in his nearly 91 years and he left an indelible mark on the television industry and its audiences. My thoughts are with his four children, John, Mark, Michael and Jodie."

Seven weeks later, Valerie Harper tweeted, "I was kindly warned by Mary Tyler Moore's dear husband Dr. Robert Levine that she was in the very last stages of life."

Seven days later, on January 25, 2017, at 2:15 in the afternoon, Mary passed away at Greenwich Hospital in Connecticut from cardiopulmonary arrest, after being placed on a respirator the previous week. Her demise "was definitely peaceful," said her longtime assistant Terry Sims. She was surrounded by friends and, most importantly, her husband was at her side. "It was a beautiful marriage," said Bernadette Peters. "They cared about each other more than anything." Levine "took phenomenal care of Mary," added Sims. "He would never let anything happen to her."

Two days after Mary passed away, and as reported by *The Milwaukee Journal Sentinel*, Gwendolyn Gillen, the artist who created Mary's hat-tossing 8-foot bronze statue for Minneapolis' Nicollet Mall in 2002, died at 76. A gathering of Mary's fans had just visited the statue paying tribute to her and her "spunky" Mary Richards Minneapolis newswoman. The statue was still temporarily housed in the Meet Minneapolis visitor center while Nicollet Mall was under construction. "[Mary] helped break the stereotype of womanhood that our generation grew up believing was our destiny," Gillen had said when the statue was dedicated. "She was the light breeze that blew through our minds and left us with the feeling that we could do anything we wanted to."

TV Land had commissioned that statue from Gillen, who was selected from 21 applicants for the job; and now Mary's soul was commissioned to Heaven, as her closest family members, friends, and colleagues were preparing to laud her work and humanity on Earth with the same sentiment Gillen once shared.

Chapter

35

A few days after her death, Mary was laid to rest during a private ceremony at Oak Lawn Cemetery in Fairfield, Connecticut, close to the Greenwich residence she shared for over three decades with her now-widowed husband Robert Levine. Her gravesite was adorned with a statue of an angel and scores of flowers including white orchids and roses. A small number of fans gathered outside the front gate of the cemetery with signs that read, "I Love You," "Rest in Peace" and "Mary = Love!"

According to a report in Texas's *The Brownsville Herald*, only about 50 people attended the funeral and burial, including Levine, actress Bernadette Peters, and other close family members and friends including Bill Persky. "There was a large service for Mary later in Los Angeles," Persky recalled. "But in New York there weren't many people there, certainly not from the [entertainment] industry. Most of those attending were just family, her very close friends from New York, and doctors and those associated with various diabetes charities. The weather was freezing, and it was perfectly drab day for such a thing to happen. At the end, everyone there placed an individual rose on her casket."

When it was his turn to speak, Persky "…felt the need to say something," which was to vocalize the phrase, "Oh, Rob." And then, as he concluded, "…that was it."

The New York memorial service was attended by only a small group because, according to Gavin Macleod, it was scheduled so swiftly after Mary died, and many did not have time to plan and rearrange their schedules in order to be present. But the core of Mary Richards from *The Mary Tyler Moore Show* was finely represented in the most poignant of ways that day, accented by a quote from Murray Slaughter, MacLeod's alter ego on the series. "And that touched me deeply," he said. It was a line from the episode, "Murray Can't Lose" (November 26, 1976), in which Murray's victory as a news writer is all but assured – until the inevitable letdown when somebody else wins the local Teddy Awards that year. Murray's line from that episode was repeated at Mary Tyler Moore's service, as her casket was lowered into the ground:

"Mary, you achieve the impossible every day: you make people forget how beautiful you look, because they're too busy realizing how beautiful you are."

"Can you imagine?" MacLeod said, fighting back tears. "When I was told that line was used for her service, I just *lost* it. And I'm starting to lose it now, just thinking about it. Out of all those incredible lines from the show, they picked that to say at the service."

On Sunday, June 4, 2017, Mary's family, friends, and various V.I.P.s gathered at the home of James L. Brooks to pay their respects in an intimate memorial service. According to *People*, those in attendance included Oprah Winfrey, Dick Van Dyke, Valerie Harper, Bernadette Peters, Julia Louis-Dreyfus, director David O. Russell, Cloris Leachman, Wendie Malick, Jane Leeves, Valerie Bertinelli, Eric Laneuville, Ed Asner, and John Tinker, son of Grant Tinker.

Winfrey addressed Mary's legacy in the entertainment industry, mentioning how Mary's MTM Enterprises inspired her to invest in her own branding as a female media mogul.

Peters led the crowd in a rendition of Sonny Curtis' "Love Is All Around," after talking about how she and Mary collaborated on the founding of Broadway Barks which, after twenty years, continues to this day to promote shelter adoption and animal welfare.

At one point previously, Curtis had recalled how Mary once signed some sheet music for him. "She wrote something really sweet, like, 'Your poetry and lyrics are part of who I am. Thank you for the love.' Boy, do I keep that in a special place."

Meanwhile, Van Dyke, who referred to Mary as his "work wife," spoke in the present about his on-screen pairing with Mary in the past on *The Dick Van Dyke Show*. He told those gathered at the ceremony that she was his "Ginger Rogers," a twofold sentiment Mary would have embraced due to her early love and aspirations for big-screen musicals.

Only hours after first hearing of Mary's passing, Van Dyke had initially posted a few moving thoughts on social media platforms such as Instagram and Twitter. "There are no words," his Tweets read. "She was THE BEST! We always said that we changed each other's lives for the better." He added a link to a musical scene from *The Dick Van Dyke Show* episode, "*The Alan Brady Show* Goes to Jail," which originally aired November 11, 1964, in which he and Mary performed the song, "I've Got Your Number."

Shortly after, Van Dyke expanded his tribute in *The Hollywood Reporter*. In part he said, "I don't know what made her comic timing so great. On *Dick Van Dyke*, we had Morey Amsterdam and Rose Marie, both of whom were old hams and had razor-sharp timing, and mine wasn't bad either. But Mary just picked it up so fast. She had us all laughing after a couple of episodes. She just grabbed onto the character and literally turned us into an improv group, it was so well-oiled. That show was the best five years of my life."

The following morning he reminisced on the local Los Angeles TV talk show, *Good Day, L.A.* "It was not a shock, of course, but just something we were dreading and dreading, knowing it was coming."

Robert Levine was in a state of disbelief after losing his wife. "Mary was my life, my light, my love," he said in a statement to the press. The emptiness he felt was "without bottom." For him, "she was a force of nature who fiercely defended her autonomy even as her health was failing. Mary was fearless, determined and willful. If she felt strongly about something or there was a truth to be told she would do it, no matter the consequences. She was kind, genuine, approachable, honest and humble. And she had that smile. Oh to see her smile, that smile just once more; my sadness is only tempered by the remarkable outpouring of good wishes, tributes and personal 'Mary stories' told with heart touched by her grace. As long as we all remember her, talk about her, share our stories about her and what she meant to us, her light will never go out."

Sam Levine, a nephew to Robert who had become quite close to Mary, also shared his poignant thoughts. On Facebook, Sam stated: "Long before I knew who Mary Tyler Moore was, Mary was 'Auntie Mary' to me [*smiley face*]. I grew up visiting my Uncle Robert and her at their majestic country house. Mornings spent riding horses and smelling a fresh, divine air I didn't know existed; afternoons swimming in their pool and day-dreaming happy thoughts sprawled out on the grass; and nights watching some of the year's best movies in their intimate study…You'll be missed Auntie Mary. You were a gift to the world and a gift to me."

Valerie Harper offered a heartfelt Tweet: "To the world, I'll miss you, Mare. I will always be your co-pilot. I will always love you, darling Mary Tyler Moore."

Harper later said, "I cannot stop the emotions I'm experiencing. She was my colleague, my sister-soul-mate and, above all, one hell of a girlfriend."

Self-described "amateur" actor Tom Wyatt worked as an atmosphere player or "extra" in two of Mary's TV movies, *Finnegan Begin Again*, and *Lincoln*. Both were filmed in his hometown of Richmond, Virginia. In the Spring 2017 issue of *Films of the Golden Age* magazine, Wyatt recalled how Mary was "…a pleasure to be around" and "simply a delight [to work] with, even for a short time…[She] was such a bright star for so many years it somehow seemed not right that her personal life was so difficult. Through it all, she sure had a talent for brightening the lives of others."

Shortly after Mary's demise, Bob Newhart observed, "She never let [her pain] show. She had it tough, but boy, you'd never guess it. She was always happy and bubbly. You'd never know anything was going on."

"I never saw her when she wasn't up and smiling," he said.

In an interview with John Northcott and CBC News, Newhart mentioned that he and Mary "didn't see each other much" in her later years, though "talked to her on the phone a couple of times." He said that a report from years before that he and Betty White were going to do a show together for Nick at Nite or one of the retro channels was in error. "I was maybe going to do a show, and White was going to do a show, but not the two of us together."

"[But] Mary heard about it and she called up, and that's the last time I talked to her, maybe five-six years ago, and she said, 'I want in. I want to be part of it.' And I said, 'Well, Mary…those reports are in error, but you know, it would be great to work with you again.'"

With reference to a more contemporary show, HBO's *The Night Of*, Newhart likened Mary's voice to that of actress Jeannie Berlin, the daughter of Elaine May (born: Elaine Iva Berlin) and Marvin May, who played a female prosecuting attorney on the cable series. Upon hearing Jeannie Berlin, Newhart said, "I know that voice from somewhere…because she had the same delivery that Elaine did."

"And the same is true of Mary," he added. He watched her shows, and heard, "Oh, Rob!" or "Oh, Mr. Grant." "Her legacy lives on because she influenced so many young comedy actresses." Sure, the lines originated with the writers of *The Dick Van Dyke Show* and *The Mary Tyler Moore Show* – but Mary's delivery made the words distinctive and memorable. Through such memories, Newhart said, Mary "continues to live on in our lives."

"The diabetes and then the way she carried on through it was so symbolic of who she was," said Laure Redmond. "That is what separates her from most people. She would push through something but she would also know that, *I'm not going to do this.* She just had like…a will of steel."

"What the world lost when Mary Tyler Moore passed was that image of possibility," said Marc Shapiro, "…that image of *You can do whatever you want if you want it bad enough.* She inspired millions of women to *get out there* and deal with life in a way that was different from what it had been."

Said Treva Silverman, "She might wanna be remembered as the kind of woman who finally was able to love and be loved."

"Mary wanted everyone to be happy, and she made everyone happy," Ed Asner had said. "She was the most exquisite person in the world. I loved her and adored her. You couldn't have asked for a better star."

Another time, Asner added, "She was a meteor across the heavens…all too briefly."

But "like the phoenix…the mythical bird that rose from its own ashes," author Margaret L. Finn once noted, Mary granted "the world her sweetness," first as Mrs. Laura Petrie, then as Ms. Mary Richards. Despite one personal tragedy after another, Mary "…remade herself into the stately and sophisticated actress whose smile," as literary, television, film, and cultural critic John Leonard wrote, "…would have to be earned by the world."

Perhaps Mary's "perkiness," Leonard had also said, "…could save the world."

Paying homage to both Mary's life and career in the *Los Angeles Times*, movie critic Justin Chang named *Against the Current* as her finest film, which was also happened to her last. "The movie was a slog, but at least there was Moore, popping up in a typically and enchantingly random cameo. She was a scene-stealer to the end – spirited, glorious, and anything but ordinary." Her "famous grin," he added, "seemed one of TV's endless renewable resources, capable of buoying our spirits to the end."

In a statement to the press, shortly after Mary died, her publicist, Mara Buxbaum, then of PMK, now of ID-PR, said:

"A groundbreaking actress, producer, and passionate advocate…Mary will be remembered as a fearless visionary who turned the world on with her smile."

When once asked how she preferred to be remembered, Mary concluded, "[As] someone who made a difference in the lives of animals," and as someone "who always looked for the truth, even if it wasn't funny.

Epilogue

"Freedom, exuberance, spontaneity, joy – all in that one gesture."

That's what Mary Richards' hat-toss-in-the-air represented to Mary Tyler Moore. But could that description just have as easily defined the star's own essence? Would the actress have accomplished so much with her carefree-spirited bravado in public check, had she not so fiercely guarded her private life? Did the unhappy times and sorrow-inducing experiences contribute to the depth of her soul? Did solitary deprivation inspire her extensive and unending charity work?

The answers may rest somewhere amongst "maybe," "maybe not," and "no one will ever know." Ultimately, Mary was "a mystery, wrapped in a riddle," a famous quotation from *Seinfeld*, which was one of her favorite TV shows; a phrase originally immortalized by Winston Churchill, whose integrity, though lofty, matched Mary's more intimate nature.

Truth is, Mary always kept people guessing, and that was part of her charm. For her, life was about change; a change of residence, a change of face, a change of husbands, a change of friends; a change of jobs; changes even brought about by self-destructive, habitual behavior.

Mary once said, "There was a time in my life when I thought, 'You can do it all. You can have it all.'" She then later observed, "I know now that's not true."

Did she have it all? At what price? Is there another path for an individual's spiritual evolution besides pain and angst; without experiencing some dreadful form of abuse, or becoming addicted to any particular vice, as was Mary to alcohol?

In June of 2018, journalist Jo Ann Towle acknowledged her own struggles with drinking, and wrote a compelling essay for *The Miami Herald* that proposed an alternate view on the tragic demise of TV personality Anthony Bourdain. Bourdain combated his demons of choice and substance abuse. Both he and fashion icon Kate Spade committed suicide in 2018, seemingly at the top of their games.

While there was no evidence of substance abuse in Spade's life, her overwhelming fame apparently got the best of her. In discussing Bourdain's life and death in particular, Towle made no real distinction between alcohol or drug addictions. She was also frank in addressing how what many consider "the good life" is often quite the opposite.

"Alcohol is a drug," she wrote. "'Drugs' and 'alcohol' remain separate in conversations about addiction, like a 'bad sister' doing outrageous unthinkable things while the 'good sister' quietly nurses a prom hangover and shame from a blackout."

Towle described alcoholism as "a progressive, chronic, fatal disease with predictable stages. The brain science is in, and has been for years, yet it is ignored or given short shrift because drinking is such a huge part of our cultural fabric. We don't stop and think about it until we're forced to; until it's obvious, undeniable, that someone we care about is suffering.

"Alcoholics minimize, deny, believe their drinking is under control, and refuse to connect the dots – that drinking for escape, relief or to solve problems is creating more problems, and is taking a toll on self-worth and perhaps cognition. The substance they are drinking for 'a lift' is a depressant. The guilt, shame, powerlessness and depression can take them down."

Like many before or since, in public view or in secret solace, Mary suffered the costs of her own lapses of judgment with alcohol, cigarettes, food, or even excessive plastic surgery. She moved several times, traveled much, became bored easily, and was not one to sit still. Whether any of that was due to a compulsive need for stimulation, or a need for privacy, she kept her distance, retreating if she felt someone coming too close. The victim of sexual abuse at a very young age, Mary's childhood innocence was harshly wiped away. The experience may have ignited a measure of self-hatred, as it has been found to do. This may have been the root of her self-destructive behavior. It also began a lifetime of guardedness and a distant personality. Yet she gave the appearance of transparency and openness, which made her fans love her even more. True to form, Mary never played for pity. "I've had my share of my problems," she once said. But in 1995, she told Larry King, "I don't think there's a person on earth who hasn't had as much pain as I have."

In 1997, she shared a similar perspective. "I've known tremendous applause and happiness, but also tremendous pain. Other people get other things, other tragedies, but none of us get through this [life] unscathed. I would love to say I believe in the hereafter, where it all evens out, but I don't. This is just my deal; this is what I got."

Around the same time, she said, "I am a survivor. Some people do not survive tragedies. It doesn't lessen the pain. The pain is just as intense as it is for someone who gives up and gives in, but the change that has occurred in me is that I appreciate much more the *now*. I don't take tomorrow for granted, because it simply may not be there."

When a reporter wondered why she had changed, Mary once again credited Robert Levine. "Marrying Robert has certainly encouraged my outgoingness," she said, "if only because of who he is…I've been through some devastating moments in my life. I think that helps you put things in perspective. It makes me a little less afraid of life because I know I have withstood some pretty awful things. So I'm not fearful anymore. I've already seen the darkness."

But by fighting diabetes for more than half of her life, Mary became a symbol of hope and inspiration for others. Upon first learning of her diabetes, she thought she'd be "an invalid," which was one of the reasons she was happy to align herself with the Juvenile Diabetes Foundation, "to help others."

"I've had the fame and the joy of getting laughter," she said in *Parade Magazine*. "Now I want others to learn how I fell down and picked myself up."

Mary had one day envisioned herself in a "volunteer activity" that would make her "feel necessary, maybe working with old people, or kids. I've always had a soft spot for older people, for their uncertainty. I know what it must feel like to be old, when the confusion sets in. And children…that's obvious."

With the loss of her son ever on her mind, Mary added, "On some level, I'd like to go back and redo my relationship with my son…maybe through some other child."

Unfortunately, that never transpired. And in her later years, she many times lamented not having more children. "Because in losing my son," she once intoned in tears, "I lost all the future. There is no grandchild for me."

Mary was also periodically sad about the dwindling opportunities to practice her craft. "I'm happy with my life," she said in 1993. "But acting is so much a part of it that if I'm not careful, I get to feeling, sometimes, that I've failed because I'm not working all the time. Yet I know that's not true."

While that was indeed not true, Mary in her later years admitted to being more like her most famous TV persona when she debuted in the role. During another interview, she even went so far as to imply that the character was not as career-oriented as mostly everyone assumed. "When I was playing Mary Richards, I was wrapped up in my own career. Whereas, I don't think Mary Richards was. I think she was happy with her life. It's only now, after playing her that I've caught up to her. I like my work and still want to keep doing it, but if I don't work all the time now, it doesn't matter that much to me. I have Robert and the animals and the garden [in the Levine country estate], and I feel my life is well-rounded."

She recounted how many people would approach her and say, "Gosh, when I used to watch you, I wanted to be like you – like Mary Richards."

To which her response was always, "So did I."

She might have had more work had there not been "the strong image of Mary Richards," she observed in another moment. But she was content without the additional roles. She said the free time allowed her to "to have a life, a happy marriage, a country house, all sorts of things" she would not have experienced had she "gone from one movie to the next."

And there were times when she couldn't sleep at night, when she turned on the TV "and there we are," she said, a slight tremble in her voice, referring to catching a segment of *The Mary Tyler Moore Show*. "It's been so long, now, that I can't remember the episodes. So I watch the way everyone watches, wondering what's going to happen next. And I always feel at the end of those 30 minutes that the world is a little happier place and we're all the better off."

Clearly, Mary's emotional, psychological, and professional needs were at least partially met through her benchmark roles as Mary Richards, and Laura Petrie, combined with her personal victory over alcoholism. For an interview in 1986 with Canada's *Maclean's* magazine, she declared, "I am glad I was able to be a kind of role model for other women who identified with my ladylike qualities, who were then able to say, 'Well, if Mary can admit she had a problem with alcohol, then maybe I can, too.'"

Another time, she asserted, "It has been a wonderful life; absolutely terrific. There are few things I would go back and do differently if I had that control."

Truth is, most of us *do* have control over much of our lives, if we only choose to exert it. Intentionally or not, Mary directed most of her own life and career. She did what she wanted to do, when she wanted to do it, and was more than aware of the consequences each step of the way.

Comparisons to Lucille Ball, Carol Burnett, Doris Day, and Elizabeth Montgomery aside, Mary's experiences and influence were unmatchable. Whether her talent was considered marginal or exceptional; whether she was blessed or fortunate; whether she had bad timing or good luck; and despite some unproductive professional selections and a few unhealthy personal choices – Mary lived a rich and full life, and enjoyed a lengthy and prosperous career. And have we not become all the better for it, each of us a beneficiary of her talents and charity?

On film, videotape, celluloid, screen, DVD, Blu-ray, or somewhere online or anywhere amidst and between the varied worlds of real life and multimedia, the spirit of Mary, Laura, Mare, and others, continue to be transmitted into the hearts of millions.

Mary Richards' sentiment to her friends and co-workers in "The Last Show," the series finale of *The Mary Tyler Moore Show*, nicely summed up the connection, impact, and message Mary Tyler Moore left with her friends, co-workers, relatives, followers, fans, and admirers:

"What is a family anyway? They're just people who make you feel less alone and really loved. And that's what you've done for me. Thank you for being my family."

Timeline

Following is a list of the main benchmarks in Mary's life and career.

April 19, 1913	Father is born – George Tyler Moore
March 22, 1916	Mother is born – Marjorie Hackett
December 29, 1936	Mary is born in Brooklyn, New York
April 17, 1944	Brother is born – John Moore – the same year she begins ballet lessons
1946	Mary and family move to Los Angeles
1952-1956	Appears as Happy Hotpoint in TV commercials which air during *The Adventures of Ozzie and Harriet*
June 25, 1955	Weds Richard Carleton Meeker
March 20, 1956	Sister is born – Elizabeth Ann Moore
July 3, 1956	Mary gives birth to Richard Carleton Meeker, Jr.
1957	Dances on *Club Oasis* and *The Eddie Fisher Show*
1958	Makes uncredited appearance as a dance-hall girl in *Once Upon a Horse* TV show
1959	Debuts as Sam the secretary on *Richard Diamond, Private Detective* series, and guest-stars in *The George Burns Show*, *Schlitz Playhouse*, *Steve Canyon*, *Bronco*, and *Bourbon Street* TV shows
1959-1960	Guest-stars in two episodes of *Riverboat* TV series, three episodes of *77 Sunset Strip*
1960	Guest-stars on episodes of TV's *Overland Trail*, *The Millionaire*, *The Tab Hunter Show*, *Checkmate*, *Wanted: Dead or Alive*; *Johnny Staccato*, *Bachelor Father*, and *The Deputy*
November 29, 1960	Makes the first of two TV guest-appearances on the *Thriller* anthology series in an episode titled "The Fatal Impulse"
1960 to 1961	Appears in four episodes of *Hawaiian Eye* TV series
April 1961	Divorces Richard Carleton Meeker
October 3, 1961	TV debut of *The Dick Van Dyke Show* in which she plays Laura Petrie
November 21, 1961	Film premiere of *X-15* – Mary's first significant feature film debut

Also, in 1961	Guest-stars on TV's *The Garry Moore Show, Lock-Up, Stagecoach West, Surfside 6*, and *The Aquanauts*
1962	Guest stars on TV's *Straight Away, Here's Hollywood*, and *Stump the Stars*
1963	Emmy-nominated for Outstanding Lead Actress in a Comedy Series for *The Dick Van Dyke Show*
July 1, 1963	Marries Grant Almerin Tinker
1964	Wins Emmy for Outstanding Lead Actress in a Comedy Series for *The Dick Van Dyke Show*
1965	Wins Golden Globe for Outstanding Actress in a Television Series for *The Dick Van Dyke Show*
1966	Wins Emmy for Outstanding Lead Actress in a Comedy Series for *The Dick Van Dyke Show*
June 1, 1966	Final airdate of *The Dick Van Dyke Show*
March 22, 1967	Film premiere of *Thoroughly Modern Millie*, in which Mary plays Miss Dorothy Brown opposite Julie Andrews
July 5, 1968	Film of *Don't Just Stand There!* in which she plays Martine Randall opposite Robert Wagner
July 31, 1968	Film premiere *What's So Bad About Feeling Good?* in which she plays Liz opposite George Peppard
April 13, 1969	TV debut of *Dick Van Dyke and the Other Woman* special
November 10, 1969	Film premiere of *Change of Habit* in which Mary plays a nun opposite Elvis Presley as a doctor
November 18, 1969	TV-movie debut of *Run a Crooked Mile* in which she plays Elizabeth Sutton opposite Louis Jourdan as Richard Stewart
September 9, 1970	TV debut of *The Mary Tyler Moore Show*
1971	Wins Golden Globe for Outstanding Actress in a Television Series for *The Mary Tyler Moore Show*
	Emmy-nominated for Outstanding Lead Actress in a Comedy Series for *The Mary Tyler Moore Show*

1972	Emmy-nominated for Outstanding Lead Actress in a Comedy Series for *The Mary Tyler Moore Show* Golden Globe-nominated for Best Actress in a Television Series for *The Mary Tyler Moore Show*
1973	Wins Emmy for Outstanding Lead Actress in a Comedy Series for *The Mary Tyler Moore Show*
1974	Wins Emmy for Outstanding Lead Actress in a Comedy Series for *The Mary Tyler Moore Show*; Narrates "We the Women," an episode of *The American Parade* miniseries (March 17, 1994)
1974-1977	Plays Mary Richards in various episodes of *Rhoda* and *Phyllis*
1975	Emmy-nominated for Outstanding Lead Actress in a Comedy Series for *The Mary Tyler Moore Show*
January 22, 1976	Stars in first TV variety special, *Mary's Incredible Dream*
1976	Emmy Win for Outstanding Lead Actress in a Comedy Series for *The Mary Tyler Moore Show*
March 19, 1977	*The Mary Tyler Moore Show* ends its original run with the episode, "The Last Show"
1977	Emmy-nominated for Outstanding Lead Actress in a Comedy Series for *The Mary Tyler Moore Show*
February 15, 1978	Mary's sister Elizabeth passes away at age 21
September 24, 1978	TV debut of *Mary*, her first weekly variety show
October 8, 1978	Final airdate of *Mary*, her first weekly variety show
November 8, 1978	TV-movie debut of *First You Cry*, in which Mary plays journalist Betty Rollin
March 4, 1979	TV debut of *The Mary Tyler Moore Hour*, Mary's second weekly variety show
June 10, 1979	Final airdate of *The Mary Tyler Moore Hour*, Mary's second weekly variety show
1980	Wins Golden Globe for Best Actress in a Motion Picture Drama for *Ordinary People*; Wins Special Tony Award for *Whose Life Is It Anyway?*; nominated for Academy Award for Ordinary People; nominated for a Drama Desk Award for Outstanding Actress in a Play for *Whose Life Is It Anyway?*

September 19, 1980	Film premiere of *Ordinary People* which features her Oscar-nominated performance as Beth Jarrett
October 15, 1980	Mary's son Richie passes away at age 24
January 1981	Mary divorces Grant Tinker
December 17, 1982	Film premiere of *Six Weeks*, in which she plays Charlotte Davis opposite Dudley Moore
November 23, 1983	Mary weds Dr. Robert Saul Levine
September 30, 1984	TV-movie debut of *Heartsounds*, in which Mary plays the real-life Martha Weinman Lear opposite James Garner
1985	Wins Tony Award for Best Reproduction (play or musical) for *Joe Egg*; wins the Women in Film Crystal Award
February 24, 1985	TV-movie debut of *Finnegan Begin Again* in which Mary plays Liz DeHaan opposite Robert Preston
December 11, 1985	TV debut of new CBS new half-hour sitcom, *Mary*, co-starring James Farentino
March 21, 1986	Film premiere of Mary's return to the big screen with *Just Between Friends* co-starring Christine Lahti, Ted Danson, and Sam Waterson, and written and directed by Allan Burns (co-creator of *The Mary Tyler Moore Show*)
March 27, 1988	TV-mini-series debut of Gore Vidal's *Lincoln* TV miniseries in which Mary plays Mary Todd opposite Sam Waterson as Abraham Lincoln
October 26, 1988	Returns to weekly television in new half-hour dramedy *Annie McGuire*
November 4, 1990	TV-movie debut of *The Last Best Year*, in which she plays Wendy Haller.
November 19, 1990	TV-movie debut of *Thanksgiving Day*, in which she plays Paula Schloss (alongside co-star Tony Curtis)
December 26, 1991	Mary's brother John passes away at age 47
March 19, 1992	Mary's mother Marjorie dies three days before her 76th birthday

September 22, 1992	Mary receives her star on the Hollywood Walk of Fame; location: 7021 Hollywood Boulevard
March 25, 1993	TV-movie debut of *Stolen Babies* in which Mary plays real-life Georgia Tann, the corrupt head of an adoption agency in the 1940s
1993	Wins Emmy for Outstanding Supporting Actress in a Limited Series or Movie for *Stolen Babies*
Also in 1993	Makes the first of 12 appearances on the *Late Show with David Letterman* (with her final segment airing in 2009)
May 12, 1994	Lends voice to a character named Marjorie on the *Frasier* TV episode, "Frasier Crane's Day Off"
September 28, 1995	Returns to weekly television with one-hour drama *New York News* in which she plays tabloid magazine editor Louise Felcott
November 24, 1995	Publication of Mary's first memoir, *After All*
December 5, 1996	TV-movie debut of *How the Toys Saved Christmas* in which Mary serves as voiceover for a character named Granny Rose
April 12, 1996	Film premiere of *Flirting With Disaster* in which Mary plays Pearl Coplin
January 7, 1996	TV-movie debut of *Stolen Memories: Secrets from the Rose Garden,* in which Mary plays the mentally challenged Jessica
February 6, 1997	Makes the first of four appearances as Catherine Wilde in the TV series *The Naked Truth* starring Téa Leoni
February 10, 1997	Reunites with Ed Asner for the TV-movie *Payback* in which she plays Kathryn Stanfill
April 11, 1997	Film premiere of *Keys to Tulsa* in which Mary plays Cynthia Boudreau
1998	Makes the first of three appearances on Lifetime's *Intimate Portrait* TV series profiling herself, Betty White (2000), and Cloris Leachman (2003)
1999	Provides voiceover as Reverend Karen Stroup in *King of the Hill* TV episode "Revenge of the Lutefisk"
2000	TV-movie debut of *Good as Gold* co-starring Elliott Gould

February 7, 2000	Reunites with Valerie Harper for *Mary & Rhoda* TV-movie
November 7, 2000	Film premiere of *Labor Pains*, in which Mary plays Esther Raymond; also stars Rob Morrow and Kyra Sedgwick
May 20, 2001	TV-movie debut of *Like Mother Like Son: The Strange Story of Sante and Kenny Kimes* in which Mary portrays Sante Chambers Kimes/Eva Guerrero
December 17, 2001	Guest-stars on TV's *The Ellen Show* in "Ellen's First Christmess" episode
Also, in 2001	Makes the first of three guest appearances on *The View* TV talk show, the last of which occurs in 2009
May 8, 2002	MTM bronze statue is erected in Minneapolis, Minnesota
November 1, 2002	Film premiere of *Cheats*, in which she portrays Mrs. Stark
December 8, 2002	TV-movie debut of *Miss Lettie and Me* in which she plays Lettie Anderson
Also, in 2002	Makes the first of two TV guest appearances on *Larry King Live*, the last which is in 2005
October 5, 2003	TV-movie debut of *Blessings*, in which she plays Lydia Blessing
October 31, 2003	Mary's father George Tyler Moore passes away at age 90
May 4, 2003	Reunites with Dick Van Dyke for *The Gin Game* on PBS
Also, in 2003	Reunites with *The Dick Van Dyke Show* cast at the TV Land Awards, where she vows to not reprise Laura Petrie again
May 11, 2004	Reprises Laura Petrie in *The Dick Van Dyke Show Revisited*
Also, in 2004	Makes the first of two television appearances on the documentary, *TV Land Moguls* (her second segment airing in 2009)
November 20, 2005	TV-movie debut of *Snow Wonder*, in which she plays Aunt Luna
2006	Interviewed by filmmaker Carlos Ferrer for the video short, *An Intimate Talk with Mary Tyler Moore*
	Makes a guest appearance on the TV series, *In the Cutz*
January 26, 2006	Makes first of three TV appearances as Christine St. George on *That '70s Show* in episode "Sweet Lady"

May 29, 2008	Reunites with *The Mary Tyler Moore Show* cast on *The Oprah Winfrey Show*
Also, in 2008	Makes the first of three appearances on the PBS documentary TV series, *Pioneers of Television*, the last of which airs in 2014
September 24, 2008	Plays Joyce in "Chapter Eight: Pandora's Box" episode of TV's *Lipstick Jungle*
November 21, 2008	Appears in "Chapter Sixteen: Thanksgiving" episode of *Lipstick Jungle*
January 18, 2009	Film premiere of *Against the Current*, her final big-screen appearance, in which she plays Elizabeth Reaser's mother; and which she that year promotes on *The Bonnie Hunt Show* and *Good Morning, America*, among other outlets
January 26, 2009	Publication date of Mary's second memoir, *Growing Up Again*
2009 to 2011	Makes two TV appearances on *The Rachel Ray Show*, the second of which is a special reunion with Dick Van Dyke on a mock set of *The Dick Van Dyke Show*
January 19, 2011	Guest-stars on "Free Elka" episode of TV's *Hot in Cleveland*, in which she reunites with Mary Tyler Moore Show actress Betty White
October 30, 2011	Reunites with Dick Van Dyke for the TV documentary series *America in Primetime*, which pays tribute to *The Dick Van Dyke Show*
January 16, 2012	Makes special TV appearance at *Betty White's 90th Birthday: A Tribute to America's Golden Girl*, and says that White "will outlive us all"
July 8, 2013	Richard Carlton, Sr., Mary's first husband, passes away
September 4, 2013	Guest-stars on "Love Is All Around" episode of *Hot in Cleveland*, which she promotes with Valerie Harper and Betty White on the Katie (Couric) talk show
November 28, 2016	Grant Tinker passes away at age 90, the same age of Mary's father (who died in 2003)
January 25, 2017	Mary passes away

Sources/Notes/Permissions

Those who granted exclusive new interviews and commentary for **MARY: THE MARY TYLER MOORE STORY** include:

Ed Asner, Matthew Asner, Sam Bobrick, Joyce Bulifant, Carol Channing, Lydia Cornell, David Davis, Arnie Kogen, Karen (Sharpe) Kramer, Rita Lakin, Rick Lertzman, Stanley Livingston, Gavin MacLeod, Larry Mathews, Dr. William Narva, Bill Persky, James Pylant, Robert S. Ray, Betty Rollin, Sherry Diamant Schaffer, Treva Silverman, Randy Skretvedt, Michael Stern, Tom Wilson, David Van Deusen, and Daniel Wachtenheim. Said interviews were conducted from October 2018 through July 2018 in person or via telephone or email.

Additional quotes, commentary, and information otherwise noted, documented and/or referenced and/or paraphrased within the core contents and body of this book were either spoken at some point to the author (i.e. Harry Ackerman's commentary about *Bewitched* was stated in 1988); or were sourced from print material including Mary Tyler Moore's two memoirs *After All* (Putnam, 1995) and *Growing Up Again: Life, Loves, and Oh Yeah, Diabetes* (St. Martin's Press, 2009). Previous biographies about Mary were consulted, including (in chronological order) *The Real Mary Tyler Moore: A Strictly Unauthorized Biography* by Chris Bryars (Pinnacle Books, 1976); *Mary Tyler Moore: A Biography* by Jason Bonderoff (St. Martin's Press, 1986); *Mary Tyler Moore: Actress* by Margaret L. Finn (Chelsea House Publishers, 1997); *Mary Tyler Moore: The Woman Behind the Smile* by Rebecca Stefoff (Signet/New American Library, 1986); and *You're Gonna Make It After All: The Life, Times and Influence of Mary Tyler Moore* by Marc Shapiro (Riverdale Avenue Books, 2017).

The following videotaped or filmed interviews on TV talk shows, entertainment magazine shows, or documentaries with or featuring Moore and others also provided significant information and were culled from YouTube: *Remembering Television Trailblazer Mary Tyler Moore* conducted by David Susskind (March 1, 1966/Television Vanguard); *Interview of a Lifetime* conducted by Barbara Walters (originally broadcast on ABC, May 29, 1979); *Mary Tyler Moore in a Rare Interview* conducted by Eileen Prose (1987); *An Intimate Talk with Mary Tyler Moore* conducted by Carlos Ferrer (2006); *Archive of American Television* interviews with Grant Tinker (conducted by Morrie Gelman, April 8, 1998) and Nanette Fabray (conducted by Jennifer Howard, August 12, 2004).

Each of the previously published biographies of Moore, along with Carlos Ferrer's videotaped interview with the actress, proved particularly productive throughout the contents of this book, but especially helpful in researching the early years of her life.

The expertise and due diligence of genealogists James Pylant and Rhonda McClure provided and clarified Moore's cultural and historic lineage.

A main, all-encompassing resource for this book were issues of *Mary Magazine* (Volumes 1-15, Fall 1991-Spring 2008), which was founded and edited by the aforementioned David Davis, who is not to be confused with *The Mary Tyler Moore Show* producer of the same name. This book was significantly strengthened by Davis' extensive contributions, and the facts, event dates, and general data he provided from and with *Mary Magazine*.

Additional specific information was furnished by *MTM Show* producer David Davis, Allan Burns, Valerie Harper, Cloris Leachman, and Ethel Winant, some of whose commentary appears courtesy of Jim Romanovich, executive producer of TLC's 2002 TV special, *Behind the Fame: Mary Tyler Moore/Bob Newhart*.

Further supplemental insight from Marc Shapiro and Laure Redmond, along with pertinent remarks from Susan Kellerman, Dr. Linda Papadopoulos, and the key, extensive thoughts and statements from Dr. William Hunter appear courtesy of Steve Cheskin and Sarah Burney of the Reelz Channel and the 2018 TV documentary titled *Autopsy: Mary Tyler Moore*.

Other decisive data, commentary, and quotes for **MARY** were resourced from publications such as: *Lucy in the Afternoon: An Intimate Memoir of Lucille Ball* by Jim Brochu (William Morrow and Company, 1990); *The Complete Directory to Prime Time Network and Cable TV Shows* by Tim Brooks and Earle Marsh (Ballantine, various editions); *Total Television* by Alex McNeil (Penguin, 1991); *Sweethearts of '60s TV* by Ronald L. Smith (S.P.I. Books, 1981); *TV Guide*; *The Los Angeles Times*; *The Hollywood Reporter*; *Variety*; *Interview*; *Entertainment Weekly*; *People*; and *Closer* magazines; and websites like www.IMDB.com, www.IBDB.com, www.Wikipedia.org, and www.BrainyQuote.com.

Reporter Jack Major's interviews with Mary for the *Akron Beacon Journal* on September 30, 1962 and June 7, 1964, from the website https://major-smolinski.com, served as a key resource for Mary's commentary during *The Dick Van Dyke Show* years, as did Vince Waldron and his optimum publication, *The Official Dick Van Dyke Show Book* (Revised Edition, Chicago Review Press, 2011).

The websites www.Elvis-history-blog.com and www.neatorama.com served as rich resources for the events and experiences related to Mary Tyler Moore's involvement with the 1969 feature film *Change of Habit*, while www.PBS.org provided a similar service by providing access to extensive commentary from Mary Tyler Moore, Dick Van Dyke, and others associated with the televised 2003 PBS production of *The Gin Game*.

Laurie Jacobson generously granted permission to present portions of her article about and involving the *Mary Tyler Moore Show's 20th Anniversary* reunion TV special, originally published in the June 1992 issue of *Hollywood: Then & Now* magazine. It provided this book with much-needed elements of that benchmark television special.

Another article that proved particularly resourceful for this book was "How Nora Ephron Said Goodbye to *The Mary Tyler Moore Show*," which was originally published in the February 1977 issue of *Esquire* magazine, republished on January 25, 2017, and accessed on April 8, 2018. Those whose commentary was culled from this article, and mostly utilized in Chapter 13, include Ed Asner, Helen Gurley Brown, John Chancellor, Shirley Chisholm, Betty Ford, Lee Grant, Cloris Leachman, Carl Reiner, Norman Lear, Gloria Steinem, Barbara Walters, and Betty White.

The following three articles from *The New York Times* provided invaluable commentary from Moore, Grant Tinker, Allan Burns, Valerie Harper, and others that is presented throughout the entirety of the book: "What's a TV Star? Someone Who Is Beautiful and Sexy, But Not Threatening," by Tracy Johnson, April 7, 1974; "Rhoda's Wedding: It Looks Like the Social Event of the Year," *TV Times Magazine/The Los Angeles Times,* October 27, 1974; and "Mary Tyler Moore: I'm Not an Innately Funny Person," by Thomas O'Connor, December 8, 1985.

Several other newspaper and magazine articles from both the distant and recent past also served as germane source material for MARY, and were accumulated and/or downloaded between November 2017 and June 29, 2018, including (among many others): "Mary Tyler Moore: Using Her Voice and Her Smile to 'Turn The World On' to All Animals," written by Lori Golden, and published in *The Pet Press* in September 2002, and downloaded March 3, 2018. Much of Mary's comments and thoughts about pets and animals that appear throughout the pages of MARY were resourced from this article.

Various quotes also appear from the article, "Mary Tyler Moore: After All," written by Audrey T. Hingley, which was published in the November/December 1995 issue of *The Saturday Evening Post.* A few such references begin with, and/or includes the following words, terms, and/or phrases from the given individual so named here:

Chapter 11:   "Humor's important to me..." – Mary
Chapter 14:   "The hardest part about being a diabetic..." – Mary
Chapter 16:   "I like being me for the most part..." – Mary.
Chapter 21:   "When I turned 50..." – Mary
Chapter 23:   "Dancing established the habit of exercising for me...-"Mary
_____   "The hardest part of writing a book..." – Mary
Chapter 25:   "I like to go to work scared..." – Mary
Epilogue: "I am a survivor..." – Mary

Key commentary culled from *Closer* magazine that is otherwise not indicated in the narrative of this book begins with and/or includes the following words, terms, and/or phrases from the given individual so named here:

Chapter 3:   "We got to where we could..." – Dick Van Dyke, describing
               his close friendship and working relationship with Mary.
Chapter 16:   "The most that we ever exchanged..." – Timothy Hutton, in
               addressing his communication with Mary while working on
               Ordinary People.
_____   "She opened the envelope..." – Timothy Hutton
Chapter 35:   "Mary wanted everyone to be happy..." – Ed Asner

Key commentary culled from *People* magazine articles that are otherwise not indicated in the narrative of this book begin with and/or includes the following words, terms, and/or phrases from the given individual so named here:

Chapter 11:   "She bouncy, she's pretty…" - Valerie Harper describing Mary.

Chapter 18:   "not what you would call an alcoholic…" - Dr. Robert Levine describing Mary.

Chapter 35:   "was definitely peaceful…" - Mary's assistant Terry Sims describing Mary's passing

_____   "It was a beautiful marriage." - Bernadette Peters describing Mary's union with Dr. Robert Levine.

_____   "She never let [her pain] show." - Bob Newhart addressing Mary's courage with facing any of her life challenges.

Key commentary culled from *TV Guide* articles that are otherwise not directly indicated in the narrative of this book begin with and/or includes the following words, terms and/or phrases from the given individual so named here:

Chapter 1:   "angry…youngster…" - Mary

Chapter 3:   "I'm tired…" - Mary

Chapter 5:   "We all agreed it would…" – Mary

Chapter 12:   "Rhoda wishes she were Mary…" – Valerie Harper

Chapter 13:   "During the time of…" – Mary

Chapter 15:   "I hate my teeth…" – Mary

_____   "I only ever had confidence…" – Mary

Chapter 16:   "I think I understand…" – Mary

Chapter 17:   "experiment a bit…" – Mary

_____   "I began dating…" – Mary

Chapter 23:   "He was a human joke machine…" – Mary describing Morey Amsterdam.

_____   "The show was important because Mary…" – Joan Jett

Chapter 24:   "(But) we've been desperately…" – Gary David Goldberg

_____   "Sometimes I get cranky…" – Mary

Chapter 25:   "an answer to a dream…" – Mary

Chapter 26:   "No subject was taboo." – James Lipton

Chapter 28:   "It's not my nature…" – Mary

Chapter 32:   "It really is!…" – Mary

Epilogue: "I've known tremendous applause…" – Mary

_____   "volunteer activity…" – Mary.

_____   "feel necessary…" – Mary

_____   "because losing my son…" – Mary

_____   "When I was playing Mary Richards…" – Mary

Additional quotes and commentaries were resourced from supplementary publications and periodicals or television interviews and/or documentaries relating to or about Mary. TV and movie character quotes were culled from various shows and films associated with the roles performed by Mary and her co-stars in scripted performances.

The television program and film character quotes and actor commentaries from a variety of nonfiction and fiction TV shows or movies are reproduced within this book for educational purposes and/or in the spirit of publicity for those particular productions, be they scripted or unscripted by definition.

In each case, any commentary, fact, or piece of information or data that was acquired beyond the author's direct interview with the particular subject or party; any such third-party book, periodical, television program, motion picture, play, or website has been listed and documented in the Bibliography section of this book. Every effort was made to acknowledge specific credits whenever and wherever possible, and we apologize in advance for any omissions, and will undertake any and every additional effort to make any appropriate changes in future editions of **MARY: THE MARY TYLER MOORE STORY** if necessary.

Bibliography

**Previous Biographies, Books, and/or
Memoirs by or about Mary Tyler Moore**

Alley, Robert S. and Brown, Irby B., *Love Is All Around: The Making of The Mary Tyler Moore Show*. New York: Delta Books, 1989.

Armstrong, Jennifer Keishin, *Mary and Lou and Rhoda and Ted*. New York: Simon and Schuster, 2013.

Bonderoff, Jason, *Mary Tyler Moore*. New York: St. Martin's Press, 1986.

Bryars, Chris, *The Real Mary Tyler Moore*. New York: Pinnacle Books, 1977.

Editors, Charles Rivers, *American Legends: Mary Tyler Moore*. Cambridge, MA: Charles Rivers Editors, 2011.
Dick Van Dyke and Mary Tyler Moore: The Premiere Sitcom Stars of the '60s and '70s. Cambridge, MA: Charles Rivers Editors, 2017.

Finn, Margaret L., *Mary Tyler Moore: Actress*. Langhorne, PA: Chelsea House Publishers, 1996.

Moore, Mary Tyler, *After All*. New York: Putnam Adult, 1995.
Growing Up Again: Life, Loves, and Oh Yeah, Diabetes. New York: St. Martin's Press, 2009.

Shapiro, Marc, *You're Gonna Make It After All: The Life, Times and Influence of Mary Tyler Moore*. The Bronx, New York: Riverdale Avenue Books, 2017.

Stefoff, Rebecca, *Mary Tyler Moore: The Woman Behind the Smile – An Unauthorized Biography*: New York: Ultra Communications; New American Library, 1986.

General Books

Bloom, Ken, and Vlastnik, Frank, *Broadway Musicals: The 101 Greatest Shows of All Time*. New York: Black Dog & Leventhal Publishers, 2004.

Brooks, Tim, and March, Earl, *The Complete Directory to Prime-Time Network and Cable TV Shows, 1946-Present*. New York: Random House/Ballantine Books, Eighth Edition, 2003.

Brochu, Jim, *Lucy in the Afternoon: An Intimate Memoir of Lucille Ball*. New York: William Morrow and Company, 1990.

Cagle, Jeff, and Sutton, Larry, eds., *Mary Tyler Moore: 1936-2017: Celebrating the Life of a TV Pioneer*. New York: People Books, 2017.

Davidson, Telly, *Culture War: How the '90s Made Us Who We Are Today (Whether We Like It Or Not)*. New York: McFarland & Company, 2016.
TV's Grooviest Variety Shows of the '60s and '70s. Nashville, TN: Cumberland House, 2006.

Denkert, Darcie, *A Fine Romance: Hollywood/Broadway: The Mayhem. The Magic, The Musicals*. New York: Watson-Guptill Publications, 2005.

Greenfield, Jeff, *Television: The First 50 Years*. Wingdale, New York: Crescent Books, 1981.

Harper, Valerie, *I, Rhoda*. New York: Gallery Books, 2013.

Today I Am a Ma'am: And Other Musings on Life, Beauty, and Growing Older. New York: Harper Entertainment, 2001.

Hirschhorn, Clive, *The Hollywood Musical: Every Hollywood Musical From 1927 to the Present Day*. New York: Crown Publishers, 1981.

Hischak, Thomas, *The Oxford Companion to the American Musical: Theatre, Film, and Television*. Oxford, United Kingdom: Oxford University Press, 2008.

Jewell, Geri, *I'm Walking as Straight as I Can*. Toronto, Canada: ECW Press, 2011.

Kellow, Brian, *Ethel Merman: A Life*. New York: Viking Books, 2007.

Leachman, Cloris, with George Englund, *Cloris: My Biography*. New York: Kensington, 2009.

Mandelbaum, Ken, *Not Since Carrie: 40 Years of Broadway Musical Flops*. New York: St. Martin's Press, 1991.

Mordden, Ethan, *Open a New Window: The Broadway Musical in the 1960s*. New York: Palgrave, 2001.

Persky, Bill, *My Life Is A Situation Comedy*. Westport, Connecticut: Mandevilla Press, 2012.

Pilato, Herbie J, *Dashing, Daring and Debonair: TV's Top Male Icons From the '50s, '60s, and '70s*. Lanham, Maryland: Taylor Trade, 2016.

Glamour, Gidgets, and the Girl Next Door: Television Female Icons From the '50s, '60s, and '70s. Lanham, Maryland: Taylor Trade, 2014.

The Essential Elizabeth Montgomery: A Guide to Her Magical Performances. Lanham, Maryland: Taylor Trade, 2013.

Twitch Upon a Star: The Bewitched Life and Career of Elizabeth Montgomery. Lanham, Maryland: Taylor Trade, 2012.

Press, Joy, *Stealing the Show: How Women Are Revolutionizing Television*. New York: Atria, 2018.

Reiner, Carl, *Why & When The Dick Van Dyke Show Was Born*. Los Angeles: Random Content, 2015.

Sanders, Steven Coyne, and Weissman, Ginny, *The Dick Van Dyke Show*. New York: St. Martin's Press, 1993.

Smith, Ronald L., *Sweethearts of '60s TV*. New York: St. Martin's Press, 1989.

Suskin, Steven, *Show Tunes: The Songs, Shows, and Careers of Broadway's Major Composers (Revised and Expanded Third Edition)*. Oxford, United Kingdom: Oxford University Press, 2000.

Thompson, Robert J., *Television's Second Golden Age: From Hill Street Blues to ER*. Syracuse, New York: Syracuse University Press, 1997.

Tinker, Grant, *Tinker in Television*. New York: Simon and Schuster, 1994.

Van Deusen, David, *To Twilo and Beyond! My Walnut Adventures with The Dick Van Dyke Show Cast*. Bloomington, Indiana: iUniverse, 2005.

Van Dyke, Dick, *Keep Moving: And Other Tips and Truths About Living Well Longer*. New York: Hachette Books, 2016.

My Lucky Life In and Out of Show Business: A Memoir. New York: Three Rivers Press, 2012.

Waldron, Vince, *The Official Dick Van Dyke Show Book*. Chicago, Ill.: Chicago Review Press, 2011.

Andrews, Bart; Watson, Thomas J., *Loving Lucy: An Illustrated Tribute to Lucille Ball*. New York: St. Martin's Griffin, 1982.

White, Betty, *Betty White's Pet-Love: How Pets Take Care of Us*. New York: William Morrow & Co., 1987.

Winship, Michael, *Television*. New York: Random House, 1988. Wooley, Lynn, Malsbary, Robert W., and Strange, Jr., Robert J. *Warner Brothers Television: Major Stars of the Fifties and Sixties Episode-by-Episode.* Jefferson, North Carolina: McFarland & Company, 1985.

Periodicals

Adelson, Andrea, "Television South Purchases MTM," *New York Times*, July 7, 1988.

Alexander, Ron, "Mary Tyler Moore: A Late-Night Cult," *New York Times*, 1984.

Appleford, Steve, "Never Too Late to Get That Big Break," *Los Angeles Times*, July 7, 2017.

Aronson, Steven M.L., "Inside Mary Tyler Moore's Sunny New York Home," *Architectural Digest*, July 18, 2017.

Asner, Ed, "A Last Good-Bye from *The Mary Tyler Moore Show*," *Family Weekly*, March 13, 1977.

B., Kellie, "One Year Ago We Lost Comedy Star Mary Tyler Moore," *Tolucan Times and Canyon Crier* (via *ReMind Magazine*), January 31, 2018.

Balley, Diane, "Mary Richards Would Be Married Today," *TV Guide*, October 19, 1991.

Banta, Gloria, "Is Television a Man's World? Yes, Ma'am," *New York Times*, September 30, 1973.

Beck, Marilyn and Smith, Stacy Jenel, "Mary Tyler Moore Opens Up on Grief, Alcohol," *The National Ledger*, September 4, 2008.

Birmingham, Frederic A., "30 a Week and Lots of Credit Cards," *Saturday Evening Post*, October, 1974.

Blake, Meredith, "Pauley Still a Morning Glory," *Los Angeles Times*, May 27, 2018.

Boodro, M., "Finnegan, Begin Again," *Harpers Bazaar*, February, 1985.

Bosworth, Patricia, "Laugh, Cry, Be Thoroughly Entertained," *Working Woman*, October 1984.

Bowers, John, "From TV to Tiffany's in One Wild Leap," *The Saturday Evening Post*, November 1966.

Bradley, Laura, "How Mary Tyler Moore Inspired Michelle Obama to Dream Big," *Vanity Fair* (via *Variety*), January 26, 2017.

Brodesser-Akner, Taffy, "Moore: She Defined the Idea of Women in the Workplace – While Constantly in Search of Herself," *New York Times*, December 28, 2017.

Canby, Vincent, "Between Friends," *New York Times*, March 21, 1986.
"Screen: Salvation Through a Toucan; *What's So Bad About Feeling Good?* Opens Mary Tyler Moore and Peppard in Comedy," *New York Times*, May 25, 1968.

Calvillo, Frank, "Moore and Peters Enjoy 'The Last Best Year,'" *Cinepase.com*, June 2, 2017.

Cavett, Dick, "Eileen Heckart; A Phantom Tribute," *New York Times*, June 18, 2000.

Chang, Justin, "Review: Against the Current," *Variety*, January 23, 2009.
"Mary Tyler Moore on Film: In *Ordinary People*, an Extraordinary Transformation." *Los Angeles Times*, January 26, 2017.

Clehane, Diane, "Author Susan Silver Recalls Her Experiences with Mary Tyler Moore, Bill Cosby and Jim Morrison," *Adweek.com*, April, 26, 2017.

Connelly, Sherryl, "No Moore Heartache Far from Being Perfect, America's Sweetheart was a Lost and Lonely Alcoholic," *New York Daily News*, October 29, 1995.

Corinthios, Aurelie, "The Story Behind Mary Tyler Moore's Iconic Hat Toss," *Entertainment Weekly*, January 25, 2017.

Crean, Ellen. "Time to Toss Your Tam – Mary Tyler Moore's Minneapolis Statue," *Early Show/CBSNews.com*, May 8, 2002.

Dagan, Carmel, "Nanette Fabray, TV Star of the '50s and '60s, Dies at 97," *Variety*, February 23, 2018.

Davidson, Muriel, "Bright New World of Mary Tyler Moore," *Good Housekeeping*, January 1971.

Davis, David, *Mary Magazine*, Issues 1 – 15, Spring 1991 to Fall 2008.

Decaro, Frank, "Toss Your Hat: Mary and Rhoda Return," *New York Times*, December 7, 1997.

De Vries, Hilary, "Forever Mary," *TV Guide*, February 8, 1997.

Dugan, Christina, and Stone, Natalie, "Bob Newhart on How Mary Tyler Moore Hid Her Private Pain," *People Magazine*, January 25, 2017.

Donahue, Ann, "Blessings," *Variety*, October 1, 2003.

Ephron, Nora, "Saying Goodbye to *The Mary Tyler Moore Show*." Originally published in *Esquire Magazine*, February, 1977; republished online on January 25, 2017; accessed April 8, 2018.

Farber, Stephen, "Mary Tyler Moore to Get Another Chance on CBS," *New York Times*, May 27, 1986.

Farrell, William E., "Minneapolis Enjoying Heyday as an Upbeat Metropolis." *New York Times*, September 16, 1975.

Fierberg, Ruthie, "Why This Original Thoroughly Modern Millie Actor Says Mrs. Meers and Henchman Were 'Revolutionary,'" *Playbill*, February 13, 2018.

Fisher, Luchina, "Mary Tyler Moore, Star of *The Mary Tyler Moore Show*, Dies at 80," *ABC News*, January 25, 2017.

France, Lisa Respers, "Mary Tyler Moore, Beloved TV Actress, Dies at 80," *CNN*, January 26, 2017.

Francis, Paul; Gregor, Pat; and Tracy, Kathleen, "Mary Wants More Surgery to Look Young for Hubby," *The Globe*, February 26, 1991.

Fraser, C. Gerald, "Humanitas Prizes Go to 4 TV Writers; 'Green Eyes,' Episodes of *Roots* and *Mary Tyler Moore Show*, Earn Authors Awards," *New York Times*, July 9, 1977.

Freeman, Marc, "*The Bob Newhart Show*, 40 Years Later: An Oral History of TV's Game-Changing Comedy," *Hollywood Reporter*, April 18, 2018.

Fretts, Bruce, "A Life of Love and Laughter," *Closer Magazine*, February 13, 2017.

Fries, Laura, "*Miss Lettie and Me*," *Variety*, December 4, 2004.

Furse, Jane, "She's Mary Tyler Mercy – Aided Ill Kin's Suicide Try" *New York Daily News*, October 18, 1995.

Gannon, Michael, "Mary Tyler Moore Had Flushing Roots," *Queens Chronicle: Central/Med Queens News*, January 26, 2017.

Gates, Anita, "Television in Review; *Miss Lettie and Me*," *New York Times*, December 2, 2002.

Gent, George, "TV Will Drip Social Significance; New Season's Shows to be Relevant and Youthful," *New York Times*, September 7, 1970.

Gilatto, Tom (with reporting by Dugan, Christina; Jordan, Julie; McNeil, Liz; Strohm, Emily), "Mary Tyler Moore: 1936-2017," *People Magazine*, February 13, 2017.

Gittleson, Natalie, "Mary Tyler Moore Is in Good Shape," *McCall's*, January 1983.

Golden, Lori, "Mary Tyler Moore: Using Her Voice and Her Smile to 'Turn the World On' to All Animals," *Pet Press*, September, 2002.

Goodykoontz, Billy, "Next Time, Just Show Old 'Van Dyke' Clips," *Arizona Republic*, May 11, 2004.

Gordon, Meryl, "Mary Tyler Moore's Manhattan," *Architectural Digest*, December 1991.

Green, Michelle and Marx, Linda. "Twice-Divorced Mary Tyler Moore, 45, Heads for the Altar Again – And This Time, Her Heartthrob Is 30," *People Magazine*, December 5, 1983.

Gross, Ed, "From 'Mary Tyler Moore' to 'Up,' Ed Asner Reflects on His Career," *Closer Magazine*, June 1, 2018.

Gussow, Mel, "*Holly Go Quickly*," *Newsweek*, December 26, 1966.
"The Theatre: *Sweet Sue*, with Moore and Redgrave," *New York Times*, January 9, 1987.

Guthrey, Molly, "From the Archives: Mary Tyler Moore Tours Her Minneapolis 'Home,'" *TwinCities.com*, 1996; 2015.

Hajela, Deepti, "Sante Kimes, Convicted in NY Widow's Murder, Dies," *San Diego Tribune*, May 20, 2014.

Hammill, Geoff, "*The Mary Tyler Moore Show*; U.S. Situation Comedy," *Museum TV*, accessed March 10, 2018.

Harrison, Barbara Grizzuti, "I'm Not a Nice Girl Anymore," *McCall's*, January, 1986.

Helms, Marisa, "Mary Tyler Moore Statue Stirs Debate," *Minnesota Public Radio*, March 30, 2001.

Henderson, Kathy, "Mary Tyler Moore: I'm Alright Now," *Redbook*, May, 1988.

Hill, Doug, "Playing a Woman Who Stole and Sold Her Husband's State of the Union Address," *TV Guide*, March 26-Aril 1, 1988.

Hill, Michael E., "Mary Tyler Moore," *Washington Post*, December 8, 1985.
"*Thanksgiving Day* a Turkey In Spite of Its Stars," *Baltimore Sun*, November 19, 1990.

Hingley, Audrey T., "Mary Tyler Moore: After All," *Saturday Evening Post*, November/December 1995.

Holzer, Harold, "A Filtered Portrait of Lincoln Comes to the Small Screen," *New York Times*, March 20, 1988.

Honeycutt, Kirk, "Film Review: 'Against the Current,'" *Hollywood Reporter*, January 22, 2009.

Hopper, Hedda, "Mary Tyler Moore Has Many Talents," *Los Angeles Times*, April 21, 1964.

Horst, Carole, "*Stolen Memories: Secrets from the Rose Garden*," *Variety*, December 31, 1995.

Hughe, Clyde, "Mary Tyler Moore Nearly Blind from Losing Battle With Diabetes," *The Wire*, May 23, 2014.

Iaconangelo, David, "Mary Tyler Moore Expanded America's View of What a Woman Can Be," *The Christian Science Monitor*, January 26, 2017.

Isherwood, Charles, "Stage Review: *Thoroughly Modern Millie*," *Variety*, April 18, 2002.

Jacoby, Susan, "Helping Her Mother Die," *New York Times*, September 8, 1985.

Jarvis, Jeff, "The Couch Critic: New York News," *TV Guide*, November 25, 1995.

"Picks and Pans," *People Weekly*, December 16, 1985.

Johnson, Steve, "*The Mary Tyler Moore Show*: When In Doubt on the TV Beat...", *Chicago Tribune*, November 1, 1995.

Johnston, Tracy, "What's a TV Star? Someone Who Is Beautiful and Sexy, But Not Threatening?," *New York Times*, April 7, 1974.

Jordan, Julie, and Miller, Mike, "Mary Tyler Moore Honored at Intimate Memorial Attended by Oprah Winfrey, Dick Van Dyke and Valerie Harper," *People*, June 15, 2017; accessed July 25, 2018.

Justin, Neal, "Turning the Mall On With Her Smile; The Loving Crowd at the Dedication of the Mary Tyler Moore Statue Proved That Mary Richards' Experience Still Resonates," *The Minneapolis Star-Tribune*, May 9, 1992.

Kael, Pauline, "Just Between Friends," *New Yorker*, May 5, 1986.

Kelley, Seth, "Hollywood Reacts to Mary Tyler Moore's Death," *Variety*, January 25, 2017.

Ketcham, Diane, "Long Island Journal: Mother and Friend," *New York Times*, May 13, 1990.

Kennedy, Mark, "Breakfast at Tiffany's Aims for Broadway in 2013," *Yahoo News!*, October 10, 2012.

Keveney, Bill, "Love Is All Around for Moore on '70s,'" *USA Today*, January 23, 2006.

Kimble, Lindsay, "All About Mary Tyler Moore's Off-Screen Loves – and Finding Forever With Husband Robert Levine," *People Magazine*, January 25, 2017.

King, Susan, "Lessons from Troubled Dad: Richard Chamberlain Says Playing the Role of Dr. Austin Sloper in *The Heiress* Hits Close to Home" *Los Angeles Times*, April 18, 2012.

"Licensed to Steal: Adoption Scandal Is Subject of Lifetime's *Stolen Babies* With Mary Tyler Moore as Georgia Tann," *Los Angeles Times*, March 21, 1993.

Kirby, David, "Need a New Show? Just Dip Into Television's Past," *New York Times*, August 18, 2002.

Klemesrud, Judy, "Sunshine Girl Becomes Girl You'll Love to Hate," *New York Times*, September 24, 1980.

Knoedelseder, William K., "MTM Reported Sold to British Television Firm: Financial Times of London Says Price Is $325 Million," *Los Angeles Times*, July 2, 1988.

Kreizman, Maris, "Women Beat Odds to Alter Face of TV," *Los Angeles Times*, February 25, 2018.

Kroll, Jack, "Mary Tyler Moore," *Newsweek*, March 10, 1980.

Lague, Louise, "Addicted No *Moore*," *People*, October 1, 1984.

"Potentially Deadly Dependence on Alcohol Sends Mary Tyler Moore to the Betty Ford Center," *People*, October 1, 1984.

Laurent, Lawrence, "*First, You Cry* Stars Mary Tyler Moore," *Washington Post*, November 5, 1978.

Leonard, John, "The Subversive Mary Tyler Moore; Woman's Role on TV," *Life*, December, 1970.

Littleton, Cynthia, "Mary Tyler Moore on Grant Tinker: A 'Brilliant, Driven Executive.'" *Variety*, November 30, 2016.

Lloyd, Robert, "Remembering Mary Tyler Moore: Love Was All Around," *Los Angeles Times*, January 26, 2017.

Logan, Michael, "Back in the Game," *TV Guide*, May 3, 2003

Lowry, Brian, "TV Review: *Snow Wonder*," *Variety*, November 16, 2005.

MacPherson, Malcom, "Mary Tyler Moore and Her All-Star Team," *Newsweek*, January 29, 1973.

Major, Jack, "Mary Tyler Moore Interview," *Akron Beacon Journal*, September 30, 1962.

[The Second Mary Tyler Moore Interview] *The Akron Beacon Journal*, June 7, 1964.

Marks, Peter, "Like 'Mary Tyler Moore,' With Attitude and Accent," *New York Times*, March 30, 1997.

Martin, Judith, "Mary Tyler Moore: On the Hill..." *Washington Post*, November 18, 1975.

Maynard, Joyce, "Is Mary Tyler Moore Too Good To Be True?," *McCall's*, March 1974.

McBride, Jessica, "Robert Levine: 5 Fast Facts You Need to Know." *Heavy.com*, January 25, 2017.

McLellan, Dennis, "Actress Defined the Part of Modern Woman." *The Los Angeles Times*, January 26, 2017.

Menaker, Dan, "Don't Look Now, But TV Is Growing Up." *The New York Times*, May 20, 1973.

Min, Janice, "Strokes of Genius." *People Magazine* December 5, 1994.

Moore, Mary Tyler, "Living My Life My Way." *New Choices for the Best Years*, December 1988.

Murphy, Mary Joe, "Looking Back (and Learning From) *The Mary Tyler Moore Show*," *New York Times*, August 4, 2016.

Neumeyer, Kathleen, "From the Archives: The last Days of the Late, Great *Mary Tyler Moore Show*," *Los Angeles Magazine*, November 1976.

Nordyke, Kimberly, "*Mary Tyler Moore Show* Cast Reminisces at Lively Reunion," *Hollywood Reporter*, April 5, 2013.

O'Connor, John J., "TV: An Updated Mary Richards in *Murphy Brown*," *New York Times*, November 27, 1989.

"TV: CBS Presents *Lou Grant*; 'Comedic' Spin-Off Moves Asner From Electronic Newsman to City Editor of Major Paper," *New York Times*, September 20, 1977.

"TV: Mary Tyler Moore Does a Musical," *New York Times*, February 22, 1978.

"TV: The Kind of Show A Star Should Never Do; Miss Moore's Special Trite and Pretentious *Incredible Dream* on CBS Tonight at 10," *New York Times*, January 22, 1976.

O'Connor, Thomas, "Mary Tyler Moore: I'm Not An Innately Funny Person," *New York Times*, December 1985.

Parker, Ryan, "Ed Asner Remembers His "Tremendously Talented, Funny and Beautiful' Friend, Mary Tyler Moore," *Hollywood Reporter*, January 25, 2017.

Pearl, Diana, "How Mary Tyler Moore Helped Shape Modern Feminism," *People.com*, January 25, 2017.

Polskin, Howard, "Two Lighthearted Actresses Tackle a Heavyweight Drama," *TV Guide*, November 3-9, 1990.

Rafferty, Diane, "Mary, Queen of Sitcoms," *New York Times*, December 3, 1995.

Rakoff, David, "The Way We Live Now: 1-30-00: Questions for Mary Tyler Moore; Mary Richards," *New York Times Magazine*, January 30, 2000.

Rau, Nate, "That Time Mary Tyler Moore Had a Nashville Record Label Employing Trisha Yearwood and Scott Borchetta," *USA Today*, July 26, 2017.

Rauser, Chris, "Viewers Who Tune in *Kate & Allie* Monday Night…," *Chicago Tribune*, March 2, 1987.

Reed, James, "Mary Tyler Moore: TV Pioneer, Feminist Icon and…Album Cover Girl?," *Los Angeles Times*, January 26, 2017.

Romano, Lois, "Riding Accident Paralyzes Actor Christopher Reeve," *Washington Post*, June 1, 1995.

Rosenberg, Howard, "…and a Pink Slip in a Pear Tree: Mary Tyler Moore's *Annie McGuire* Merits 2nd Chance," *Los Angeles Times*, December 14, 1958.

"'The Last Beset Year' a Heartfelt Drama: Bernadette Peters, Mary Tyler Moore Play Two Women Brought Together By Cancer," *Los Angeles Times*, November 3, 1990.

Reeve, Christopher, and Moore, Mary Tyler, "Editorial: Seize the Promise Held By Stem Cells," *Los Angeles Times*, July 15, 2001; www.chrisreevehomepage.com; downloaded April 20, 2018.

Roush, Matt, "The Roush Review: Love Them, Not the Movie," *TV Guide*, February 5, 2000.

"Tribute: Mary Tyler Moore," *TV Guide* (Double Issue), February 13-26, 2017.

Rovin, Jeff, "The Special Strength of Mary Tyler Moore," *Ladies Home Journal*, April, 1985.

Rudolph, Ileane, "Mary Tyler Moore," *TV Guide*, March 13, 1993.

"No Moore Series For Mary?," *TV Guide*, December 30, 1995.

"The Petrie Dish," *TV Guide*, May 9, 2004.

Scott, Vernon, "Four Fascinating Women," *Ladies Home Journal*, September 1975.

Sessums, Kevin, "Laughter is a Gift," *Parade Magazine*, March 22, 2009.

Shales, Tom, "Mary Tyler Moore, Out on a Limb," *Washington Post*, March 3, 1979.

"Moore the Dearer," *Washington Post*, January 7, 1996.

Smith, Cecil, "*Mary Tyler Moore Show* and *The Waltons* Win Key Emmys," *Los Angeles Times* May 21, 1973.

"Mary Tyler Moore: Her Charisma Makes the Comedy Show Go," *Los Angeles Times*, December 13, 1970.

"Rhoda's Wedding: It Looks Like the Social Event of the Year," *TV Times Magazine/Los Angeles Times*, October 27, 1974.

Smith, Mary Lynn, "Artist Who Created Bronze Mary Tyler Moore Statue Dies Two Days After Star," *Star Tribune*, January 31, 2017.

Smith, Sally Bedell, "TV Notes: Mary Tyler Moore' May Play Another Encore," *New York Times*, January 19, 1985.

Stack, Tim, "What Julia Louis-Dreyfus Loves About Mary Tyler Moore." *Entertainment Weekly*, November 24, 2011.

Stang, Joanne, "Housewife Without Traumas," *New York Times*, May 9, 1965.

Stewart-Gordon, James, "Everyone's Mad About Mary," *Reader's Digest*, October, 1974.

Stone, Natalie, "Dick Van Dyke Mourns On-Screen Love Mary Tyler Moore: 'We Changed Each Other's Lives for the Better,'" *People.com*, January 25, 2017.

Strohm, Emily, "Joy Behar Recalls the Time Mary Tyler Moore Sent Her a Gas Mask," *People.com*, January 25, 2017.

Towle, Jo Ann, "Can We Talk About Alcoholism?," *Miami Herald*, June 18, 2018.

Unger, Arthur, "Mary Tyler Moore Calling, To Save a Failing Show, Star Believes in Her New TV Sitcom, Despite Low Ratings," *Christian Science Monitor*, November 23, 1968.

Upperco, Jackson, "Moore Tries Again – A Look at *Mary* (1985-1986, CBS)," *Jackson Upperco Blog*, 2013; accessed February 23, 2018.

Van Dyke, Dick (as told to Belloni, Matthew), "Dick Van Dyke's Tribute to Mary Tyler Moore: 'She Left an Imprint on Television Comedy,'" *Hollywood Reporter*, January 25, 2017; accessed January 25, 2018.

Warhol, Andy, "The New Mary Tyler Moore," *Interview Magazine*, February 23, 1981; accessed May 27, 2018.

Waters, H.F., "Mary," *Newsweek*, December 9, 1985.

Weingarten, Paul, "The Kitten That Roared: At MTM They Really Believe That Quality, Too, Can Win an Audience," *Chicago Tribune*, December 1, 1985.

Willistein, Paul, "*Just Between Friends* A Story by Adults for Adults Movie Reviews." *The Morning Call*, March 22, 1986.

Wilows, Mark Edward, "Mary Tyler Moore's Story," *Lake Country Star*, March 18, 1987.

Zad, Martie, "Mary Tyler Moore in Moving Role: *Stolen Memories: Secrets from the Rose Garden*," *Washington Post*, January 7, 1996.

Miscellaneous Periodicals

"About Mary and Flirting with Disaster," *Entertainment Weekly*, March 25, 1996.

"Actress' Son Dies; Mary Tyler Moore's Only Child, 24, Shoots Self," *Washington Post,* October 16, 1980.

"America's Sweetheart Plays Rough in *Ordinary People*," *Rolling Stone*, November 13, 1980.

"Mary Tyler Moore," *Los Angeles Times*, April 10, 2009.

"Asner, Walker Win Emmy Prizes; *Rich Man* father, Abigail Adams Roles Cited," *New York Times*, May 18, 1976.

"Behind Her Smile: TV Legend, Mary Tyler Moore, in an Exclusive Excerpt, Looks Back at a Marriage That Failed and a Son Who Died Too Soon," *People*, October 30, 1995.

"Cast of *The Mary Tyler Moore Show* to Reunite," *SOP Newswire*, January 25, 2007.

"CBS Cancels 'Mary,' But Not Mary Tyler Moore," *Los Angeles Times*, October 14, 1978.

"'CBS This Morning' Co-Host Gayle King to Anchor 'Mary Tyler Moore: Love Is All Around,'" CBS Press Release, January 26, 2017.

"Chronic Drinking Rewires Brain and Increases Anxiety Problems," *Amen Clinics*, September 11, 2012.

"Dick Van Dyke and Mary Tyler Moore Set to Star in *The Gin Game* For KCET/Hollywood's PBS Hollywood Presents," PBS Press Release, 2003.

"Gold Derby: Are Amy Poehler and Tina Fey Secretly Channeling Valerie Harper and Mary Tyler Moore?," *Los Angeles Times*, April 10, 2009.

"Gossip Home: Mary Tyler Mo' Money," *New York Post*, August 3, 2006.

"Here's Mud in Her Eye," *TV Guide*, December 29, 1984.

"How to Succeed Though Married," *Time*, April 9, 1965.

"Mary at 60: A Look at Mary's Happy Life Today," *Mary Magazine/The Star*, January, 1997.

"Mary, Mary Quite Contrary," *New York Times Magazine*, December 17, 1995.

"Mary Plays Sante Kimes," *Philadelphia Enquirer*, May 13, 2001.

"Mary Returns to the Big Screen in Flirting With Disaster," *Venice Magazine*, April, 1996.

"Mary Richards Statue," TVAcres.com, May, 2002.

"Mary Tyler Moore: Adorable, Funny, Hugely Talented – with the Force of a Magnet She Attracted Millions of Viewers to a New Kind of TV Woman," *People*, May 4, 1989.

"*Mary Tyler Moore*, at Series' End, Can Now Savor Its Innovations," *New York Times*, May 18, 1976.

"Mary Tyler Moore: Elvis Presley's Leading Lady," *Elvis History Blog*, accessed March 14, 2018.

"Mary Tyler Moore, Husband Separate," *Los Angeles Times*, December 29, 1979.

Mary Tyler Moore Interview with *Biography Magazine*.

Mary Tyler Moore Interview with Timothy White of *TV Guide*, March, 1993.

Mary Tyler Moore and Valerie Harper Interview with Lisa Kogen, February, 2000.

Mary Tyler Moore Interview with Ramin Setoodeh of *Newsweek*, January, 2006.

"Mary Tyler Moore Is Wed," *New York Times*, November 24, 1983.

"Mary Tyler Moore Leaves Alcohol Treatment Clinic," *Los Angeles Times*, October 6, 1984.

"Mary Tyler Moore's Mission to Moscow," *TV Guide*, June 26, 1976.

"Mary Tyler Moore: Reason to Smile," *Washington Post Herald/Times Herald*, February 21, 1971.

"Mary Tyler Moore Researches a Role," *Washington Post/Times Herald*, August 16, 1970.

"Mary Tyler Moore Reveals Role in Attempted Suicide," *Chicago Tribune*, October 18, 1995.

"Mary Tyler Moore Signs CBS Pact," *Los Angeles Times*, September 18, 1969.

"Mary Tyler Moore: The Divine Miss M," *Screen Actor Magazine*, Fall 2011.

"Mary Tyler Moore: The Shocking Story Behind the Smile – Her Alcoholic Mother, Her Painful Divorce and Her Son's Death," *People Magazine*, January 25, 2017.

"Mary's Co-Star Dies at 91," *CBS News*, December 1, 1999.

"Mary's 5 Best Interviews," *Variety*, January 25, 2017.

"Neighborhood Report: Brooklyn Up Close; Mary Tyler Moore, Brooklyn's Girl Next Door? Yes, I Am!," *New York Times*, April 21, 1996.

"News: Mariette Hartley Is a Buffalo Gal at Williamstown, June 12-24," *Playbill*, June 13, 2001.

PBS Hollywood Presents, PBS Press Release, 2003.

"Primetime: A Mary for the '80s?," *TV Guide*, December 29, 1984.

"Recreating History," *Oprah.com*, May 29, 2008.

"Remember Mary Tyler Moore; Don't Grieve Her Death," *Federalist*, January 27, 2017.

Review: "Miss Lettie and Me," *Star*, December 10, 2002.

Review: "Thoroughly Modern Millie," www.tvropes.com, accessed March 15, 2018.

Review: "What's So Bad About Feeling Good?" www.thevideobeat.com, accessed March 30, 2018.

Review: "What's So Bad About Feeling Good?," www.thevideobeat.com.

"Shepherd Mourns the Death of Mary Tyler Moore," Shepherd University, 2017.

"Talking with…Mary Tyler Moore," Nancy Matsumoto, June 1998.

"Talking with…Mary Tyler Moore, Ericka Sóuter, May, 2001.

"They May Look Perfect on the Big Screen, But Even the Biggest Stars Have Hit Some Bumps on Their Paths to Perfection," *Celebrity Focus* magazine. [Date Unknown.]

Fall Preview Reviews of *Annie McGuire* and *The Van Dyke Show*, *TV Guide*, October 1, 1988.

"TV's Funny Girls," *Time Magazine*, October 28, 1974.

"Under (Wear) Achievers, Style," *Entertainment Weekly*, April 19, 1996.

Valerie Harper Interview with David Martindale.

Video Interviews

Remembering Television Trailblazer Mary Tyler Moore; interview conducted by David Susskind (March 1, 1966) https://www.youtube.com/watch?v=izsmIc_XzuU

Mary Tyler Moore / Barbara Walters – *Interviews of a Lifetime* (ABC, 1979) https://www.youtube.com/watch?v=N9Y3DP-wiDA

Bobbie Wygant Interviews Mary Tyler Moore for *6 Weeks* (12/7/82) https://vimeo.com/25936640

Mary Tyler Moore interview conducted by Eileen Prose [in 1987; uploaded by Prose on YouTube May 1, 2017] https://www.youtube.com/watch?v=Pbjyfm3qoTo

Bernadette Peters / Mary Tyler Moore Interview on *Good Morning, America* (1991) https://www.youtube.com/watch?v=_M2PvVISfxk

Grant Tinker on Meeting Mary Tyler Moore – EmmyTVLegends.org; conducted by Morrie Gelman (April 8, 1998 in Bel Air, CA). https://www.youtube.com/watch?v=g0I4cu4ngCk

Mary Tyler Moore, Dick Van Dyke full interview on Larry King (December 29, 1999). https://www.youtube.com/watch?v=_H1ax3puBMs&t=3s

Nanette Fabray discusses working on "The Mary Tyler Moore Show" – EMMYTVLEGENDS.ORG. Interview conducted by Jennifer Howard on August 12, 2004 in Pacific Palisades, CA.) https://www.youtube.com/watch?v=Mo2wrRKwYVY

An Intimate Talk with Mary Tyler Moore conducted by Carlos Ferrer (2006) https://www.youtube.com/watch?v=aTJM_L5tlaE&t=8s CBC/John Northcott phone interview with Bob Newhart (1-25-17) https://www.youtube.com/watch?v=OMI8VhWIblo

Genealogy

The following information, which served as basis for Mary Tyler Moore's genealogy in Chapter One was researched and provided by James Pylant:

Photo Record: Col. Lewis T. Moore, "Stewart Bell Jr. Archives Handley Regional Library," online http://handley.pastperfectonline.com/photo/DEF0F387-5F05-48D8--700569942215: accessed June 7, 2018).

Thomas J. Ryan, *Spies, Scouts, and Secrets in the Gettysburg Campaign: How the Critical Role of Intelligence Impacted the Outcome of Lee's Invasion of the North, June-July 1863* (El Dorado Hills, Calif.: Savas Beatie LLC, 2015), p. 92.

Mary Franny Bragonier Moore memorial, no. 142,939,687, *FindAGrave*, online database with images (www.findagrave.com : accessed June 7, 2018.

Danl. G. Bragonier household, 1860 U.S. census, Berkeley Co., Va., Martinsburg, population schedule, p. 87B, dwelling 902, family 903, National Archives microfilm M653-1335, listed Daniel G. Bragonier, "German R. Preacher," and Mary E. Bragonier, with four others, including Mary F. Bragonier, age 15;

Rev. D. G. Bragonier obituary, *The Daily Dispatch* (Richmond, Va.), November 3, 1868, p. 3;

Mary E. Bragonier's last will and testament, Jefferson Co., W. Va., 19 August 1892, "West Virginia, Wills and Probate Records, 1724 – 1985," online database with images (www.ancestry.com; accessed 7 June 2018), identified Mary Moore as a daughter.

George Moore household, 1920 U.S. census, Kings County, N. Y., Brooklyn, population schedule, ED 1359, SD 3, p. 10A, dwelling 119; National Archives microfilm T625-1178, listed George Moore (48; born in Va.), secretary at "electrical house," with wife Anna (37; born in NY), and three children – the youngest being Tyler (six; born in NY).

George Moore household, 1930 U.S. census, Kings Co., N.Y., Brooklyn, population schedule, ED 24-883, SD 30, dwelling 27; National Archives microfilm T626-1538, listed George Moore (57; born in Va.), wife Anna (43; born in N.Y.), and son Tyler (16, born in N.Y.), a pupil at "private school."

Anna Veronica Tyler Moore memorial, no. 134,837,298, *FindAGrave,* online database with images (www.findagrave.com: accessed June 7, 2018).

George T Moore/Marjorie Hackett record, "New York, New York, Marriage License Indexes, 1907 – 1995," online database (www.ancestry.com: accessed June 7, 2018).

D. Kenamond, *Prominent Men of Shenandoah During Its First 200 Years* (Shepherdstown, WV: Jefferson County Historical Society, 1963), p. 107.

Acknowledgments

In addition to all of those individuals, groups, companies – and more – that have been acknowledged in the Sources/Notes/Permissions, and Bibliography sections of this book, the individuals subsequently mentioned herewith worked unfailingly to insure the publication of **MARY.**

To my publisher, including Director of Operations Steven Kates, Project Coordinator Sondra Burrows, Editor Mark Alfred, and all the great and talented people at Jacobs/Brown Media Group. Thank you for believing in **MARY**, and everything its creation, formation, development, publication, and release entailed.

Thank you also to my research team including: Ken Gehrig and Dawn McElligott; to the editorial counsel of Lynne Bateson, Bill Kay, Jim Knuttel, and Matthew Polly, and again to David Davis for his unending dedication to **MARY.**

For assistance and support in a variety of ways, appreciation is extended to: Keith Anderson, Rudi Rudenski, Liza Asner, Matthew Asner, Bob Barnett, Dr. William Birnes, Harlan Boll, Edgar Bullington, Marie Burgos, Melissa Byers, Marc Cushman, Joel Eisenberg, Lorie Girsh Eisenberg, Katharine Kramer, David Leaf, Kristen Marino, Pamela R. Mastrosimone, Rose Narva, Terri Meyer, Caryn Richman, Helen Richman, Howard Richman, Peter Mark Richman, Nevine Salvade, Lloyd J. Schwartz, Douglas Snauffer, Vince Staskel, Vince Waldron, Tripp Whetsell, Greg Williams, and Mark Edward Wilows.

My deepest gratitude is saved for my parents, Herbert Pompeii Pilato and Frances Turri Pilato, now in Heaven, along with my cousin Eva Easton Leaf, and so many more dear loved ones, friends, and colleagues, in this world (including my dear sister Pamela R. Mastrosimone) and the next, all of whom helped to bring me exactly to this moment, one way or another. And most of all, thank you, God.

About the Author

Dan Holm Photography

Herbie J Pilato is a television writer, producer, and personality whose credits include CNN's eight-part series, History of the Sitcom, the Reelz Channel's Autopsy on Elizabeth Montgomery, Bravo's five-part series, The 100 Greatest TV Characters, Bewitched: The E! True Hollywood Story (the seventh-highest-rated True Hollywood Story in E!'s history), and TLC's Behind the Fame specials on The Mary Tyler Moore Show and The Bob Newhart Show, among others. Pilato has also served as a consulting producer and on-screen cultural commentator for various classic TV-DVD documentaries for Sony, NBCUniversal, and Warner Bros., including box sets for The Six Million Dollar Man, Kung Fu, and CHiPs.

Pilato has also worked behind-the-scenes on shows like The Tonight Show starring Johnny Carson and Family Ties, while as an actor, he's appeared on other shows such as Highway to Heaven, The Golden Girls, General Hospital, and The Bold and the Beautiful. His top-selling, critically-acclaimed pop-culture/media tie-in books include Dashing, Daring and Debonair, Glamour, Gidgets, and the Girl Next Door, The Essential Elizabeth Montgomery, Twitch Upon a Star, Bewitched Forever, The Bionic Book, The Kung Fu Book of Wisdom, The Kung Fu Book of Caine, and NBC & ME: My Life as a Page in a Book, among others.

Today, Pilato is a Features Writer for the Television Academy and Emmys.com; serves as a Contributing Editor Emeritus for Larry Brody's TVWriter.com, and is the host and an executive producer of Then Again with Herbie J Pilato, a classic TV talk show now streaming on Amazon Prime and Amazon Prime UK. His upcoming new books include biographies of Sean Connery (for the University Press of Kentucky, 2022), Diana Rigg (University Press of Mississippi, 2023), and a combined book about George Lucas and Steven Spielberg and their classic films (University Press of Kentucky, 2024).

For more information, visit www.HerbieJPilato.com.

You may also enjoy these other books published by Jacobs/Brown Press

These Are the Voyages: Star Trek the Original Series [TOS]
by Marc Cushman
Season One, ISBN 978-0-9892381-0-6
Season Two, ISBN 978-0-9892381-4-4
Season Three, ISBN 978-0-9892381-7-5

Irwin Allen's Lost in Space,
The Authorized Biography of a Classic Sci-Fi Series
by Marc Cushman
Volume One, ISBN 978-0-692-75018-6
Volume Two, ISBN 978-0-692-74756-8
Volume Three, ISBN 978-0-692-81426-0

The Show Runner – An Insider's Guide to Successful TV Production
by Cy Chermak
ISBN 978-0-9988663-1-4

Previously on X-Men – The Making of An Animated Series
by Eric Lewald
ISBN 978-0-9988663-2-1

Long Distance Voyagers: The Story of The Moody Blues, Volume 1
by Marc Cushman
ISBN 978-0-9988663-9-0

Irwin Allen's Voyage to the Bottom of the Sea
The Authorized Biography of a Classic Sci-Fi Series, Volume One
by Marc Cushman and Mark Alfred
ISBN 978-0-9995078-2-7

Jacobs/Brown Media Group, LLC
Jacobs/Brown Press

"Where truth is better than fiction"

jacobsbrownmediagroup.com